The Political Transformation of David Tod

The Political Transformation of David Tod

Governing Ohio during the Height of the Civil War

Joseph Lambert Jr.

THE KENT STATE UNIVERSITY PRESS
Kent, Ohio

© 2023 by The Kent State University Press, Kent, Ohio 44242
All rights reserved
ISBN 978-1-60635-466-7
Published in the United States of America

No part of this book may be used or reproduced, in any manner whatsoever, without written permission from the Publisher, except in the case of short quotations in critical reviews or articles.

Cataloging information for this title is available at the Library of Congress.

27 26 25 24 23   5 4 3 2 1

This book is dedicated to the memory of my parents, Joe and Sophie.

Contents

Preface ix
Acknowledgments xxi
1 A Democrat in the Making, 1800–1838 1
2 The Coolest, Most Collected Gentleman, 1838–1840 17
3 A Hard Money Man, 1840–1844 29
4 Not an Office Seeker, 1844–1846 44
5 It Becomes Us to Act, 1847–1851 52
6 Party Patriarch, 1851–1856 64
7 A Private in the Ranks, 1857–1859 76
8 A Conflict Cometh, 1859–1860 88
9 I Am for My Country, 1861 99
10 Taking Hold, January–June 1862 113
11 Partisans and the Patriot, July 1862–September 1862 128
12 Democratic Thunder, October 1862–May 1863 143
13 Rising above the Political Muck, May 1863–July 1863 160
14 A Crumb of Comfort, August 1863–December 1863 175
15 Shin Plaster and Pot Metal, January 1864–June 1864 191
16 The Condition of My Crops, July 1864–December 1865 205
17 Duties Discharged, 1866–1868 216
Epilogue 232
Notes 236
Bibliography 272
Index 288

Preface

WHEN DAVID TOD was sworn in as Ohio's twenty-fifth governor on January 13, 1862, the United States was 10 months into a civil war. The future of the nation and the state of Ohio hinged upon the outcome of that war.

Tod was the second of three men to serve as Ohio's governor during the conflict. He was preceded by William Dennison (1860–1861) and succeeded by John Brough (1864–1865). Dennison's tenure saw the outbreak of hostilities while Brough's administration saw the victorious conclusion of the war. All three men served admirably but only Tod's term began and ended with the conflict raging, 1862–1863, two of the most tumultuous and uncertain years of the entire struggle. Of the three governors who served Ohio during the Civil War, Tod's term was exposed to nothing but war and was the longest under wartime conditions. Each of Ohio's wartime governors served just one term and none was renominated. Collectively, their tenures have been described as "efficient and competent. Each was diligent, patriotic, devoted, and hardworking." Their service together and individually was "of tremendous importance to the nation."[1] Not one of them was very popular when his administration ended as evidenced by their single terms of office. However, without Ohio the war would have been lost. This biography will introduce David Tod with an in-depth review of his political life; his service as governor; and his political transformation during the antebellum, Civil War, and Reconstruction eras.

During the antebellum period and Civil War, Ohio was an extremely important state. In many ways, argues the historian Adam Goodheart, Ohio represented the nation in microcosm. Its Middle West location was geographically situated among the population centers of the nation. With its great resources of men, it was expected to furnish volunteer soldiers to help fill the ranks and it produced a vast array of political and military leaders. It was a key manufacturing and agricultural center, and its internal transportation system could deliver men and materiel quickly and efficiently. Its position north of the Ohio River was strategic and would need to be defended. Within its border, the cultural and political values of its northern and southern sections eerily resembled the nation's North-South sectional divide.[2] This characteristic was also the case in Indiana, Illinois, and Michigan.[3] Whoever occupied the governor's chairs in these midwestern states had to understand the entanglements of their political diversity and work hard to suppress dissent that threatened to undermine the efforts to support the federal government.[4] It was a complex set of circumstances that the governors would have to manage.

David Tod was an ambitious young man before he occupied the Ohio governor's chair. He first studied law and passed the bar in Trumbull County. It was during this time that he fell under the spell of Andrew Jackson and joined the Democratic Party. There, Tod mixed with individuals who shared a "similar set of values, beliefs, and interests" that would advance his political career. The historian Joel H. Silbey explains that political parties of the time helped to give a man standing in the minds of voters where "general positions about the nature of society, its direction, and what government should and should not do" could be taken in. Silbey writes that individuals grew so loyal to parties that they withstood immense "pressures [even from family] to change."[5]

Tod became a Democratic Party devotee and resisted the political pressure of his well-known father George Tod while residing in the section of Ohio known as the Western Reserve, a highly antislavery, abolitionist stronghold. Membership in the Democratic Party helped to "shape the way [Tod] view[ed] each new situation that [came] up in a political campaign." So, his break from the Democratic Party at the onset of hostilities that became the Civil War was no small undertaking. His lifelong ties to the party were strong but he broke those bonds once he recognized that the life of the nation was in peril.[6]

Tod brought minimal public administrative experience to the governor's office. His training consisted of one term as the mayor of Warren. His other political experience was a short, albeit impressive, stint in the Ohio senate in the 1830s, when his political career seemed to be on a high trajectory. His star, however, flamed out after he lost consecutive campaigns for the governor's seat in the 1840s. But he continued to demonstrate loyalty to his party by stumping for Democratic candidates across Ohio. His speaking skills and his power of persuasion, skills he sharpened as a successful lawyer, brought him fame and notoriety among Ohio Democrats. He gained the title of "giant of Democracy," and became known as a Whig "coonskinner."[7] President James Polk was sufficiently impressed with Tod that he selected him to serve as minister to Brazil.

Upon his return from South America to the United States Tod plunged back into the political fray of the 1850s as the great question of the day, the extension of slavery, was at a boiling point. Tod eagerly latched onto the platform of Illinois senator Stephen Douglas, who took on the issue of expansion of slavery in the United States. Tod supported Douglas's call for popular sovereignty to determine the future course of slavery in the territories. But this path ultimately led to Douglas's political downfall after he introduced the Kansas-Nebraska Act into the US Senate as a way out of the crisis. In fact, the measure did more to lead the country down a self-destructive path rather than to salvation.

In 1860, as a supporter of Douglas's candidacy for president, Tod was on hand as his beloved Democratic Party was torn apart by the slavery issue at the disastrous presidential conventions in Charleston and Baltimore. Tod worked hard trying to get Douglas elected the sixteenth president of the United States, but the Democratic candidate would lose to the Republican Abraham Lincoln and die shortly afterward. Tod would continue to carry with him Douglas's popular sovereignty ideology. Like Douglas, Tod looked at enslavement as "an institution of local significance only, one that must, therefore, be decided on the local level" with the use of the ballot box.[8] Tod had always been an advocate of popular sovereignty and a strict interpreter of the US Constitution. Democrats like Tod were strong proponents of states' rights and the rights of the voters and placed such questions like institutionalized enslavement with the "final authority in the people."[9] Tod had adhered to the principle that enslavement was legal because he believed the Constitution said it was.

As the crisis of the 1850s threatened to split the country apart, political saviors like Douglas tried to find a peaceful solution. But there was none.

During the early days of secession, Tod's leadership and desire to hold the Union together were inspirational, so much so that Ohio's citizens of all stripes thought he as governor could unify the political factions within the state and assist the national government's effort to reunite the country. The electorate of Ohio rallied behind Tod's candidacy and elected him the state's twenty-fifth governor. His marching orders were clear: Put the Union above the state even if that meant yielding to a growing national authority to help the president of the United States quash the rebellion, restore order under the Constitution, and reunite the nation. Tod willingly and knowingly accepted and wholeheartedly agreed with the assignment.

Throwing partisan identity aside, or as he said, "away with everything partisan," the patriotic Tod accepted his responsibilities as a wartime governor and put all his efforts into helping to save his beloved Union.[10] By doing so, he wrote his political obituary. Surely, he must have realized that he would never be accepted as a true Republican and his once-Democratic brethren could never welcome him back into their camp. Nonetheless, the alliance between the governors and Lincoln that the historian Stephen Engle speaks of was a compact already established and it coalesced through the alliance that formed between Lincoln, Tod, and the other loyal war governors.[11]

The Confederate bombardment of Fort Sumter was a defining moment for the nation and for David Tod. He viewed the shelling as an attack on his country, the Union, and the Constitution and in that instant, he became a staunch, conservative Unionist. Once the war started, his energies were devoted to nothing but saving the Union and he believed that his state should do everything in its power to help in that glorious endeavor. By nature, he was not a man of violence but he seethed with revenge and advocated no mercy to any traitor who took up arms against the flag.

During the war, each of the governors of the loyal states became "war ministers." Their role, according to the historian William C. Harris in his important 2013 volume on the relationship between the loyal governors and President Abraham Lincoln, was a constant work in progress. This was evident with Tod. The federal government, with Lincoln at its head, shared the same goal as each of the loyal states: Defeat the South in this war of secession and reunite the country. The governors of the Northern states that remained in the Union struggled in the early months and years of the war to understand their role while the federal government learned to understand its limits and rationalize its growing authority while respecting states' rights within the framework of the Constitution. Interpretations are still debated. As much as Lincoln was the commander in chief of the armed forces, the state governors, according to Harris, became the president's war ministers, none of whom, including Lincoln, brought any real or practical experience to bear upon the unprecedented situation that befell the nation. But in many instances, Harris contends, Tod and his fellow "governors were often ahead of Lincoln in raising troops, providing for their needs and those of their families, and suppressing 'traitors' at home."[12] Lincoln realized from the beginning that he needed the support and cooperation of the governors if the Union stood any chance of reunification, this even though some governors could be "wrongheaded and obstreperous."[13] Yet Lincoln supported each of them as they faced their own monumental challenges. He recognized their authority, respected their political intuition, and knew that he must rely on their political influence within their home states. Just as important, he understood but wrestled with his own limits of constitutional authority.[14]

Gary W. Gallagher's *The Union War* reminds us that the Civil War generation of the loyal states went to war to save the Union. Citizen soldiers and politicians like David Tod "opposed secession and supported a war to restore the Union. This group encompassed Republicans as well as the portion of the Democratic Party that stridently opposed emancipation and other policies of the Lincoln administration but remained committed to" the goal of saving the Union. They approved new war measures as necessary for the sake of the Union cause.[15] This was a war to save the Union, a conviction that served as the foundation of Tod's new political outlook once the nation came under attack. As governor, he consistently advocated "the great and holy purpose of maintaining our National Union."[16] This will help explain his cooperation with and unwavering support of the administration of Abraham Lincoln even if it meant approving new strategies like emancipation.

Despite his best efforts, Tod's service was limited to one term due mainly to partisan hostilities. As if he hadn't had his hands full with the responsibilities of governor, Tod not only had to stave off political subterfuge from elements of the Northern Peace Democrats who opposed the war; he also faced opposition from factions within the new Union Party that helped him get elected in the first place. The former compelled Tod to take actions inconsistent with his veneration of the Constitution; the latter warily doubted Tod's commitment to emancipation even though he was one of the first governors to support the government's official position.

Although his tenure was generally met with mixed political reviews by his contemporaries: condemnation from Conservative Democrats, suspicion from Radical Republicans and abolitionists, and gratitude from soldiers and Lincoln, Tod had nonetheless earned a reputation of unwavering dependability in aiding the Union war effort. Lincoln reportedly once said, "Governor Tod aids me more and troubles me less than any other governor."[17] Even after failing to secure the Union Party ticket for a second term as governor, Tod put forth a tireless effort working to support the election of the Union Party's chosen candidate to succeed him, John Brough, in one of the most important state elections for Lincoln and the Union cause.

Compared to Dennison's and Brough's terms, David Tod's had been the most politically charged because it came at a time when the outcome of the war was at its most uncertain. Military victories eluded the federal army, which put the outcome of the war in doubt. As fear and frustrations over the war's outcome mounted, political opportunists from all sides emerged and took aim at the war efforts and at those who were managing it. In Ohio, the biggest target was Abraham Lincoln and by default, Governor David Tod because of his unyielding, almost blind, support of the president from the start.

Appreciating his devoted service as governor the president offered the treasury post to Tod, even though some believed the former governor was either unqualified for the job or that his stance on money matters differed entirely from Lincoln's.[18] US Senator John Sherman of Ohio and future secretary of the treasury himself, said of Tod, "If the Members had known Tod as well as I did, they would have known that he was . . . a sound, able, conservative business man, fully competent to deal with the great office."[19] Even if he was short on government finances as other critics suggested he was a successful and wealthy businessman all the same. In such an important political state as Ohio it is fair to suggest that the politically astute Lincoln looked for all the favor that he could muster to help secure his own reelection bid in November 1864. Without Ohio's electoral votes Lincoln would not only lose the chance of a second term but surely the

Union itself. Perhaps putting Tod in his cabinet in place of Ohio's Salmon P. Chase, replacing one Ohioan for another, would curry favor in his own reelection effort, which looked at the time to be very much in doubt.

But Tod's political life was at an end when Lincoln reached out to resurrect it. His physical health was likewise in jeopardy. Respectfully and without hesitation, Tod sent word to Lincoln declining the president's offer due to poor health. (In less than five years from the time of Lincoln's invitation Tod was dead.)

Historians have generally been kind toward David Tod. One wrote that Tod's efforts "gave the State an efficient administration, which made it one of the strong forces in the prosecution of the war."[20] Another concluded, "Again and again the President spoke of Tod as one of the few governors . . . in whom absolute dependence" was placed.[21]

In 1974, the historian James A. Rawley reminded us that Lincoln inherited not only a divided nation but also a weak and ineffective executive branch thanks to the wanting administrations of Franklin Pierce and James Buchanan, Lincoln's immediate predecessors. Fearful of losing the South the fourteenth and fifteenth presidents practiced a policy of "deference." Lincoln's cupboards were empty when he moved into the Executive Mansion, and he had no choice but to regain lost influence and power. The trouble was, he may have overreached in his zeal to save the nation. To conclude that the presidency "metamorphosed into a quasi-presidential dictatorship" under Lincoln's command is a jarring description but Rawley assures us that it was not by design. Writes Rawley, "Whatever may be said about Lincoln as nationalist and even dictator, he never intended in his war against secession to annihilate states['] rights. He did not believe in state suicide."[22] If Lincoln never intended to seize power, it is reasonable to suggest, therefore, that the governors willingly gave it up. If so, then nationalism was a direct outcome due to the life-or-death struggle facing the country. Nationalism was the result of self-preservation; the alternative was self-destruction.

The most recent study on the relationship between Lincoln and the war governors is by the historian Stephen D. Engle. In Engle's impressive and thoroughly researched *Gathering to Save a Nation: Lincoln and the Union's War Governors* (2016), he argues that the relationship "was as much a story of cooperation as it was of conflict." Lincoln is revealed as a willing partner who worked hand in hand with the multitude of loyal governors. Governors like Tod willingly offered their support to save the Union, even if their actions chipped away at the sovereignty of their own states. This is not to suggest that the relationships were always smooth and continuous; they were not. The cooperation that eventually won out was a constant work in progress. Conflicts and concessions ebbed and flowed between the federal government and the state executives, especially during the early months and years of the war. It remained a delicate balancing act heightened at times by political exigencies during important elections. Inevitably, before the war ended, the dominance of the national government was established but it was not because Lincoln made a grab for power by outsmarting the loyal and hardworking governors. Rather it was an organic progression. The single goal of all was to save the Union and as a result, it "gave the appearance of nationalism [because] it required governors to play a crucial role in the war effort." However, it was a role, sometimes subservient, they each accepted. They were not outsmarted or outwitted by Lincoln. Without their cooperation there would be no United States of America. Writes Engle, "they placed nation above state and relied on the union's strengths to support a national authority. That strength sprang from the alliance between Lincoln and the governors"[23] and coalesced into a new national identity. Engle's interpretation of governors like Tod and Gary Gallagher's explanation of their motivation together help to explain the actions of David Tod. All these studies helped to shape an understanding of the challenges thrust upon Tod and the Union governors and how historians have judged their response.

While Governor Tod's admirers praised him for supporting Lincoln, his critics saw him as a political chameleon who thought nothing of shedding his lifelong Democratic affiliation to gain the governorship and, once there, conceded the rights of his state, all the while augmenting the power of the national government. But this development was a natural if not inevitable evolution. Once he abandoned his states' rights doctrine he then clung to his newfound nationalist ideology. This new tenet came to define his brief but critical two-year term.

After he left office and the war was over, Tod remained an active member of the Republican Party because he was disgusted by what he believed the Democratic Party had done to the country and what it had become. He had no desire to return to the party that had been his political family throughout his career and its members had no desire to welcome him back. Tod had been with the Union-Republican Party during the last seven years of his life. Joining the Republican Party was the only logical option available. Brough, Lincoln, Grant, and the Republican Party all called on him to serve their needs and he did so within two months of his sudden and unexpected death. Critics of Tod said and say that he was a political opportunist and willing turncoat to advance his personal agenda. I respectfully disagree with this charge. By the time Tod completed his political conversion, his health was suffering, and more important, his political career was at an end. He longed for nothing more politically; his dream of serving in the US Senate was put to rest long before. The five remaining years of his life after he left office were mostly spent as an active member of the Republican Party working against the Democratic Party that had once championed his political career.

Throughout all of this, first and foremost, David Tod was a strict constitutionalist, and this helps to understand his evolution on moral and legal matters such as abolition, citizenship, and suffrage for African Americans. Before the war, according to the US Constitution, slavery had been legal. Once the Thirteenth Amendment forever abolished slavery, followed by the Fourteenth and Fifteenth Amendments that bestowed citizenship and suffrage, Tod had legal grounds to support these changes. As the Constitution evolved, David Tod evolved, and so, too, did the Union.

David Tod spent his entire life (1805–1868) in Ohio's Mahoning valley and during that span he was regarded as the most revered and beloved of its citizens. Yet today there is little to note or recognize his service. In both Warren and Youngstown, there are streets named after him. In Girard, the city he helped to found, there are a street and a city park named for him. On Youngstown's north side, the Tod Homestead Cemetery forever occupies the location where his estate once stood. That land was donated to the city in 1908 by Tod's son. There is no statue of David Tod—anywhere. In Niles, Ohio, there is a beautiful bronze bust of David Tod that sits in the Court of Honor at the Birthplace Memorial of Niles native President William McKinley. Tod's bust is one of 10 by the noted sculptor J. Massey Rhind. Most of the busts depict members of McKinley's cabinet but include such figures as Presidents Theodore Roosevelt, William Howard Taft, and Warren Harding. Inside the adjacent library are busts of industrialists Henry Clay Frick and Joseph G. Butler Jr. Tod's bust occupies a place outside in the Court of Honor. Inscribed below Tod's likeness is a list of his lifetime of service: minister to Brazil; war governor of Ohio; Mahoning valley pioneer in coal, iron, and transportation; and beloved citizen. The McKinley Birthplace Memorial was dedicated in 1917.

Tod's bust seems oddly out of place. Why? The simple answer is that the man who conceived the idea of a memorial to McKinley, Joseph G. Butler Jr., was a childhood friend of the martyred president and in his later years, a young business partner of Tod's. Butler's autobiography, published in 1925, warmly recalls "the famous War Governor of Ohio." With heavy personal bias and admiration Butler describes Tod as "one of the greatest men Northeastern Ohio has produced" who "rose to a position of eminence in the history of his country during its most troublesome times." The trouble today, if we are to accept Butler's opinion, is that history seems to have forgotten Tod. It was Butler's own ideas, energy, and personal largesse that got the McKinley Memorial erected. He hoped that citizens would be so inspired one day to erect a "public memorial" to honor David Tod's service. Wrote Butler, Tod "needs no monument among those who knew him and his works, but coming generations might be benefitted greatly by a reminder."[24] I could not agree more.

Unfortunately, on a much larger stage, David Tod's collective contribution to American history and to the Civil War is largely unknown. Excluding students of Ohio history, few in the Buckeye State even recognize his name and fewer are aware of his role in the state's history. Local historians are more familiar with his name but not to any great degree. Serious scholars and historians of the Civil War have likely read about him in some larger study or in someone else's biography. Stephen Engle's groundbreaking study on the collective efforts between the Union's war governors and President Lincoln is an outstanding contribution that highlights the important role this loyal group played to successfully execute the war. The work is unparalleled. But even in this, important figures like Gov. David Tod have been understudied and underappreciated.

In 1974, James Rawley also wrote, "every Civil War politician seems to have found at least one biographer."[25] In fact, one is hard-pressed to find contemporary biographies of Union Civil War governors aside from A. James Fuller's excellent study of Indiana's forceful Civil War governor Oliver P. Morton, (2017).[26]

This book is the very first full-length biography of David Tod. There are few studies devoted to any aspect or interpretation of his life. Delmer

Trester's master's thesis, completed at the Ohio State University, focused on Tod's political career but was never developed into a full-scale biography. Nevertheless, it was extremely helpful with this project. The rest of my interpretation of Tod's life is based on several manuscript and correspondence collections located at the Ohio History Connection that include Ohio Governors Papers (David Tod, January 13, 1862 to January 11, 1864); *Message and Reports to the General Assembly and Governor of the State of Ohio for the Years 1862, 1863, and 1864;* the Correspondence to the Governor and Adjutant General of Ohio (OHC SA 147); the David Tod Papers (OHC MSS 306 David Tod); and the Ohio History Connection Notes (MSS 8277). In addition to the monumental war tasks that weighed him down, these collections reveal the mundane and sometimes trivial responsibilities Tod had to endure. Letters to and from Tod were also found in the Official Records of the War of the Rebellion, the published correspondences of Presidents Lincoln, James Polk, and Salmon P. Chase. Personal correspondence was also found in local historical societies. It also relies heavily on a rich trove of contemporary newspapers. Although highly partisan in their reporting, they nonetheless offer a collection of political opinions. These accounts, particularly those serving local communities, help to frame the mind-set of ordinary citizens in their views on people and events shaping their times and lives. The same newspapers, especially those during the Civil War period, printed entire speeches and unaltered official announcements by the government. There are numerous secondary sources relevant to this study, many of which note Tod's role in some way. The endnotes in these secondary sources led to other primary sources. All these pieces have been pulled together to help tell this story. I hope this study of Tod will add to the recent contributions of Engle, Harris, and Fuller.

David Tod's name and his efforts have been subjected to a passing reference or placed among the endnotes for far too long. I believe his name deserves its own title page. A thorough examination of Tod's political career, highlighted by his role as a Civil War governor, is long overdue. The same may be said for a host of other Civil War governors whose lives and services merit further attention. I hope this biography sheds light on the important role David Tod played to help save the Union.

Acknowledgments

THE ASSISTANCE OF so many has made the completion of this work possible.

I am forever grateful to the late distinguished historian Professor Frederick J. Blue whose encouragement at the very beginning of this project convinced me to take it on. When I was an undergraduate and a graduate student at Youngstown State University, he was always supportive. It was an honor to be a grad assistant for Professor Blue.

My lifelong and talented friend, James A. Marling, committed an indeterminable amount of time and energy to reading the early drafts, which must have been, although he would never admit to it, a grueling experience. Yet he persevered without fail. I am eternally grateful for his generous time, effort, continued encouragement, and most of all for his enduring friendship.

I would like to thank the archivists and their staff at the Ohio History Connection; the Mahoning Valley Historical Society, especially Pam Speis and Chelsea Hess; the library staff at Youngstown State University and the Kent State University; the Public Library of Youngstown and Mahoning County; the Local History and Genealogy Center at the Warren-Trumbull County Public Library; and the staff at the Tod Homestead Cemetery.

I am grateful to the following for allowing me the usage of the images in this book: the Mahoning Valley Historical Society, the Library of

Congress, Ohio History Connection, Capitol Square Review and Advisory Board at the Ohio Statehouse, HarpWeek/ProQuest LLC, and the Office of Art and Archives at the United States House of Representatives.

A special thanks is extended to Dr. Frank Veres, DO, who was kind enough to share with me his knowledge of nineteenth-century health practices, diagnoses, and treatments related to malaria and heart disease.

The editorial staff and the readers at the Kent State University Press, who helped to clean up a rambling repetitive manuscript, are owed a big debt of gratitude. Their detailed, critical advice and important suggestions improved this work immeasurably. Thank you all for sticking with it.

Of course, my family has been there for me every step of the way. They have been my biggest support system. My wife Tracy was always understanding and supportive during the many years required to research and write this project. I am grateful for her companionship and devotion to my interests as well as for her constructive advice, which helped develop the text into a more readable product. My daughter Sidney, while engrossed in her studies at the Ohio State University, made time to critically read parts of the manuscript. Likewise, my daughter Alexandra, a Kent State grad, was always there to provide much needed encouragement and support. My son Matthew was my loyal and diligent photographer, capturing many images of places relevant to Tod. Again and again, this generation continues to provide me with information technology training and advice. All have also been faithful travel companions to points of historical interest and attentive listeners to my stories. A heartfelt thank you to each of you.

I would also like to extend my appreciation to descendants of the David Tod family, particularly David Tod II and Bruce Tod, for their interest in and excitement about the project. Rick Rowlands also deserves a special thanks for his time.

Finally, I would like to recognize my late parents Joe and Sophie, whose unconditional love, devotion, and support of their children Tom, Mary Frances, and me, knew no limits. Long after their passing their values, work ethic, determination, and ability to push through adversity continue to inspire their children and five grandchildren, who include Emily and Michael Wolfgang.

1

A Democrat in the Making, 1800–1838

ON A SPRING DAY in 1823, Rufus Spalding, a Yale graduate, Martha's Vineyard native, and practicing attorney from Warren, Ohio, knocked on the door of Judge George Tod's home at his Brier Hill farm in nearby Youngstown. Spalding had appeared in the judge's courtroom in Cleveland that March. The Tod children had grown used to friends and strangers calling on their well-known father and had grown accustomed to performing parlor music for guests at his request.

After dinner this evening, the judge summoned his fourth-born child David to sing solo for Spalding. The tall and husky teenager was 18 years old and had recently completed his studies at the Burton Academy. When the young man appeared in the doorway, Spalding remembered, "a greener looking lad I never saw, a great awkward lout, dressed in jeans and homespun, with rough, stolid countenance." The young soloist composed himself and, "without expression, without moving a muscle of his face, he started: 'Old Grimes is dead. That good old man,' and carried the air through." After he had finished the well-pleased father said to his visitor, "Mr. Spalding, there is more in that boy than comes to the surface. Oh, if it could only be developed." "Why not send him on to college?" asked Spalding. "Because," said the judge, "I am so poor I cannot afford to do it. My farm is mortgaged and I can't afford to give him an education."[1] Spalding's unplanned visit, however, proved fortuitous for young David Tod.

As the two men talked on that fateful spring evening and discussed the boy's potential, Spalding invited the judge to send David to Warren to live with him. There, as custom would have it, David could study the practice of law with a local attorney and in time become a lawyer himself. Spalding would make all the arrangements. The judge eagerly and graciously accepted the generous, albeit unexpected, proposition on the spot. "In this manner," recited Spalding, "David Tod left his father's log-cabin at Brier Hill, and entered upon [his] course of study.[2]" Soon after, "the boy came to Warren with me and went through his school days, studied law, began his practice, and at length became Governor David Tod."[3] Little did Judge Tod know that he forfeited his son to a Democratic apprenticeship. After two years of study under Spalding's roof not only had David Tod become a lawyer, but he also became a Democrat. This was a shock to his father, a distinguished political figure who by this time had grown disillusioned with the Democratic-Republicans over the process of Ohio statehood and had turned to the Federalist persuasion of territorial governor, Arthur St. Clair.[4]

David's political attraction to Andrew Jackson and the Democratic Party has long been contemplated. One report describing David's political identification years after his death offered that, "an old friend," said that it "was due to the influence of an old Southern Judge who had settled in Northern Ohio, and into whose society young Tod was frequently thrown."[5] Roswell Stone, who was David Tod's law mentor and friend, closely fits that description. Stone was originally from Connecticut like the Tods, and he once spent time teaching in Maryland before moving to Warren. It is conceivable that Stone helped to shape the political identity of young Tod. The more logical influence of David's turn to the Democratic Party, however, was Rufus Spalding, who also spent a year in the south, in Little Rock, Arkansas, early in his career.[6] Under Spalding's roof and by his fireside, David had his meals, rested his head, and studied his Blackstone's law book by the glow of candlelight. In Spalding's company, David listened to his benefactor expound on the doctrine of the Democratic ideology and learned of the injustice served Andrew Jackson in the presidential contest of 1824.

Rufus Spalding had been an enthusiastic supporter of Andrew Jackson and the Democratic Party. Spalding favored universal suffrage for white males, believed in a limited federal government, and was a strict constructionist of the US Constitution. He also believed in western expansion and with it, free soil for the poor western settler trekking across the Appalachian Mountains. "During the greater portion of his life," remembered one former bar associate, Spalding "identified with the Democratic party" and had "intense anti-slavery sentiments."[7] Although Spalding's political fervor had a powerful effect on the ideology of the impressionable David Tod, the fiery antislavery sentiment was one David's political opponents would never accuse him of possessing. But it was under Spalding's roof where David most certainly learned the tenets of the Democratic Party. This transformation was a blow to his father.

George Tod was already an experienced lawyer when he migrated to the West. He came not for land but for greater opportunities that the law profession could offer. He hoped to advance his standing in the West through the political connections within the Federalist Party that he established back east.

George Tod was born in 1773, graduated from Yale, studied law at the Litchfield Law School, and began his legal career in partnership with his brother John in Suffield. Business was slow and this prompted George and his wife Sallie Isaacs to uproot and depart from under the shadow of his father's very elegant house for a new start in the far-off, underdeveloped Ohio territory.[8] They were among the first "people of Connecticut [to] tear up their established homes, load a selection of their goods on wagons, and make the two or three months' journey of anguish through the wilderness of Upper New York and Pennsylvania into the Ohio country."[9]

The Tods were part of a new band of settlers from New England who excitedly set out for the West in hopes of making a fresh start for themselves. Glowing reports from returning surveyors and land speculators called out to the restless land-hungry Yankees from New York and Connecticut. In 1800, the Tods, who included infants Charlotte and Jonathan, trekked across the Allegheny Mountains to Pittsburgh, then marched along the northwest trails to the Mahoning River valley and into the Western Reserve. There they found themselves in an untamed and sparsely populated wilderness. These travels were "stern and rugged adventure[s]," notes one historian but they were "coming into a potentially rich land."[10]

The reserve was just one section of Ohio that attracted newcomers. Migrants from Virginia, Maryland, and Delaware also streamed into the Ohio valley. All these various groups brought with them their own set of values, religion, prejudices, speech, architectural styles, and societal norms, which they lent to the diversity of the population. As the population increased sections of Ohio began to take on distinct characteristics. Virginia veterans of the Revolutionary War settled Ohio's Military Tract. The Yankees who settled the Western Reserve advanced its distinctive antislavery and abolitionist sentiments. A splinter group of Quakers also settled just south of the reserve. Although the Northwest Ordinance, followed by Ohio's constitution, prohibited enslavement, "Black Laws" severely restricted the rights of free Blacks residing in the state. The Western Reserve that the Tods helped to settle, however, proved to be more "tolerant" of diversity. In no time, antislavery sentiment turned to outspoken abolitionism in words and deeds and the reserve became known for its role in the Underground Railroad. One historian described it as "the West's most reliable antislavery area"[11] and David Tod would forge friendships and business associations with those who gave assistance to freedom seekers.

Youngstown was just a tiny village with a handful of residents in what was then Trumbull County when the Tods arrived. Landowners, the educated, and the politically connected came to the forefront to claim positions of leadership; George Tod possessed all three. His friendship with the governor of the Northwest Territory, Arthur St. Clair, along with his legal training certainly presented George with political opportunities and he rose from prosecuting attorney, township clerk, and state senator to Ohio Supreme Court justice. Regardless of rank or aspiring career goals however, subsistence farming was an absolute necessity for survival.

Life for the Tod clan centered around Brier Hill, the name given the farm that George purchased in 1805.[12] Brier Hill was located about two miles north of the village where thickets of briars covered the western hillside. The surrounding land would provide ample space for the active Tod children. Standing atop the forested hill, a scenic vista of the Mahoning River valley below and the setting sun off to the west, Brier Hill offered a view no visitor would soon forget. Referring to the picturesque piece of six hundred acres as a farm was always a stretch. One local historian of the reserve drily opined that the "Tod farm was inclined to be barren and unproductive, and the Judge was a better lawyer than farmer, with the result that his latter days were involved in undeserved financial difficulties."[13] The times proved to be a boon to his legal and political endeavors but, they lacked financial rewards due in large measure to George's integrity and honest character.

David Tod was born inside his parents' simple one-room log cabin on February 21, 1805. A sister Mary was the first Tod born in Youngstown in 1802. Julia came along in 1807, followed by Grace in 1811, and finally George Jr. in 1816. At the time of David's birth, Ohio had been a state less than two years. Thomas Jefferson, the nation's third president, would be sworn in for his second term in less than two weeks. In November of that year the famed Lewis and Clark expedition, sent out by Jefferson in 1803 to explore the Louisiana Purchase, would reach the Pacific Ocean.

David was named after his paternal grandfather, who had left his native Scotland for America in 1761. This David Tod had been a merchant in Suffield, Connecticut, and "a zealous American Patriot" at the outbreak of the American Revolution.[14] This was not so of David's maternal grandfather, Ralph Isaacs Jr. Making a comfortable living in the shipping business Isaacs remained loyal to the British crown during the early days of the American Revolution. In 1778, his sentiments changed, and he signed on with the American cause. That same year, Isaacs's wife, Mary Peyret Isaacs, gave birth to David's mother Sallie. Both grandfathers foretold David's business acumen, which would bring him great wealth in between his political forays.

Sallie was the main influence in the lives of her children. A demanding work schedule took George away from home for stretches and he relied on the older children, Jonathan and David, to help keep the farm going. The judge once wrote to the boys promising "a present . . . provided they prove to me that they have been good boys & take good care of the sheep & lambs."[15] Clearly, George Tod was not an overbearing or boorish father figure, but he and his wife were able to instill the value of hard work and responsibility in their children.

One incident that occurred shortly after the family's arrival in the reserve, and before David's birth, gave Sallie the scare of a lifetime. As the family account goes, George was at the home of a neighbor some ways off from Brier Hill, leaving Sallie behind with Charlotte and Jonathan. All alone, Sallie was visited by one of the local Native Americans who was in search of flour. Frustrated that Sallie had none to share, the local native "took baby [Jonathan] from his cradle and made off with him" into the woods. When George returned to find Sallie frantic, he did his best to assuage her worst fears, hoping that in the end the mischief was nothing more than a dirty trick and that the baby would be safely returned. George's hunch proved correct as baby Jonathan was placed unharmed outside of the cabin that same night.[16]

George Tod was known as "a man of marked ability and character, [but he] did not possess the faculty of accumulating wealth."[17] David once talked about his upbringing to an English professor who was traveling through the Mahoning valley years later. "He told his history," said the professor, "which comprised hardships and struggles, surmounted by industry and perseverance."[18] The family may have wanted for possessions, but they were steeped in traditional family values: virtue, purity, integrity, propriety, and religion.

Sallie Tod provided her children with religion, education, and exercise, in that order. One incident retold by an old family friend occurred at a camp meeting and alludes to Sallie's penchant for religion as well as David's emerging wit. "During the height of the religious excitement," as the story goes, "an old lady jumped to her feet, and, striking herself over the head with her hymn book, cried out, 'I'm the bride of the Lord!' This was too much for young [David] Tod, and he called out to her: 'You have married into a mighty good family.'" The wisecracking youngster was soon grabbed by his collar by "a brawny church elder" and promptly removed from the services.[19]

Affectionately referred to by both husband and children as "mama," Sallie was resourceful considering the hardships and struggles of pioneer life. Where luxuries were few and simple, she had acquired a small collection of books for the children, one of which surely was the Bible.[20] It was true that the children wore homespun clothing, but David remembered his mother's systematic approach to equitably distributing new garments to her children. She "tried very hard to keep all her boys clothed," he said. "The new hat had to be given to one, and the new pantaloons to another. We could never each get a full new suit at once. Many a time when I got the new hat I had to dispense with the new coat."[21]

The Tods endured their hardships yet somehow managed to lend their support to others. Jesse Grant, whose son Ulysses would one day become the nation's eighteenth president, fondly remembered the Tods' support. In 1805, Jesse's mother died and for the next two years his father struggled to care for his seven children. The two oldest, Jesse and his sister, were placed with George and Sallie Tod at Brier Hill in the fall of 1807. Jesse remembered that the Tod family "was extremely poor." The staple of the children's diet was mush and milk, a rare treat for the Grant siblings. Jesse Grant also remembered young David as "one of the best and most amiable little fellows I ever saw."[22]

David claims to have remembered his parents showering the Grant children with equal love and affection as if they were their own. President Ulysses Grant would one day write that his father "looked upon Judge Tod and his wife with all the reverence he could have felt if they had been parents instead of benefactors. I have often heard him speak of Mrs. Tod as the most admirable woman he had ever known."[23]

Though the farm demanded much of the children's time, David and his siblings were the offspring of parents who placed a high value on education. David Tod's future successes aside, one could certainly look to the vocations attained in adulthood of his brothers as evidence of this sentiment. Older brother Jonathan was remembered as a "great student" and went on to become a physician and Ohio senator. George Jr. returned to farming after serving as a justice of the peace in Ottawa, Wisconsin.[24] Even older sister Charlotte studied music in Philadelphia.

Charlotte's fate was a tragic one. The oldest of the Tod children, Charlotte was known as "quite a young lady and a great assistance [with her mother's] domestic concerns, as well as a companion, at all times."[25] Sadly, while visiting family in Philadelphia, she died at the age of 16 from hydrocephalus, commonly referred to then as water on the brain. Although childhood mortality was all too common, the family was heartbroken, all the same.

One important friendship David's father had was with John Ford, a noted attorney in Burton. Ford, like George Tod, was a transplant from Connecticut. George arranged for David and Jonathan to board with the Fords and attend the Burton Academy. Burton Academy, which opened in 1806, was much like modern day high school. Its curriculum focused on preparing students for college and had an excellent reputation. "The Brahman families of Northeastern Ohio towns," said one historian, with the many Connecticut transplants now living in the reserve, "sent their sons to Burton Academy to be fitted for Yale College."[26] For 47 weeks between 1821 and 1822, George paid Ford a total of $80.95 for room and board to house his sons plus $3 for two cords of firewood.[27]

At Burton, David, Jonathan, and their fellow classmates benefited from a new building and a "thorough" academic curriculum. Fellow Youngstowners Henry and Samuel Wick, and the Perkins brothers from Warren, Joseph, Jacob, and Charles, joined the Tod brothers at Burton. The students were under the tutelage of Rev. David L. Coe, a graduate of Williams College in Massachusetts.

Although David took to his studies with zeal and "got on well in his classes [he] always had time for fun," classmates remembered. One such incident at the academy occurred in the winter of 1821 when David dared a boy to shed his shoes and stockings and climb the town's liberty pole. As the unsuspecting lad climbed toward the formidable height of 20 feet, David made off with the discarded foot coverings, leaving his victim to traipse home barefoot through the cold, wet snow.

Even his host John Ford once found himself the victim of another one of David's adolescent pranks. Leaning over the top rail of his hog pen to "pour the swill to his pigs" Ford found himself crashing headfirst into the slop and scraps below. David had scoped out his victim beforehand and secretly sawed through the fence rail, which gave way under Ford's weight.

Signs of David's coming-of-age in the small town of Burton also emerged when a young girl named Arvilla Cook caught his fancy. To capture her attention one day, David needed to overcome his fear of a local gaggle of geese that "were always hissing at him" on his way to class. He hoped to fend off his honking tormentors by arming himself with a branch. But his plan backfired for while he successfully defended himself from attack, he unintentionally forced the flock upon the object of his affections, the innocent Arvilla.[28]

David's time at Burton Academy impressed upon the young man that this was but one major step along the path of his educational development. Of his mother's role during this phase David remembered that she wanted him to become a blacksmith, "but unfortunately I turned my attention to the law."[29] David Tod truly revered his mother and time would only strengthen his deep and affectionate love for her. Repeatedly he would speak lovingly of her. "No kinder mothers lived than we had," he reminisced years later.[30]

As a lifelong public servant, David's father had earned a modest income of about $1,100 dollars annually. It is also true that he had to mortgage Brier Hill the year David was born and never did pay it off. Yet David and his siblings fared no worse than others of the time and certainly enjoyed more educational opportunities and parental support than most. The fact of the matter is that David and his brothers went on to distinguish themselves in their chosen careers aided in no small part by their hardworking father and his disdain for the farming life. George Tod could neither offer any of his children financial support for higher learning nor any semblance of an inheritance. What financial means the judge may have lacked he substituted with his love, support, and encouragement.

Of his father's influence on his upbringing David took to telling folks, "I was born with a pewter spoon in my mouth. My honored father could do but little more for me than to teach me integrity of purpose and industry."[31] This was not so much a critical slight of his father's lack of financial means but a salute to the judge's integrity. It is also a testament to David's truly modest upbringing before he moved to Warren to pursue a career in law.

When he finally arrived at Spalding's home in Warren, he found a bustling town full of people. His father had spent time there over the years as the county prosecutor and had friends in the city. David's sister Mary now lived in Warren after marrying local businessman John McCurdy in 1822. So there were familial comforts for David to turn to and the Tod name was well established.

Rufus Spalding had kept his promise to George Tod and arranged for David to study in the office and under the watchful eye of Attorney Roswell Stone. Stone possessed "a fine physical form and constitution"[32] and had no tolerance for mischievous behavior.

David studied the fundamentals of law with Stone: reading, researching, learning to write briefs, filing, and running a law office along with the mundane tasks associated with operating a practice. Tod served as Stone's apprentice, plugging away in his mentor's office. The student followed his teacher back and forth to the Court of Common Pleas where he observed the coming and going of prominent lawyers like Ben Wade, Joshua Giddings, Edwin Stanton, and Elisha Whittlesey, all members of the Trumbull County Bar long before they gained fame later in life.

During his two years of study, David's five-foot ten-inch frame was a familiar sight around town and at the courthouse.[33] One issue he wished he could escape from was the legal status of his father's farm. Judge Tod was in debt and his homestead was about to be foreclosed upon. Looking to resolve the matter respectably considering George Tod's honorable reputation, the court deeded Brier Hill to one Calvin Cone.[34] The parties agreed that Cone would continue with a lower payment schedule with Judge Tod. Surely the whole matter was an uncomfortable one for David as it played out in the courts in a most public way. Although he enjoyed his father's fame, he could not escape the trials of the judge's financial struggles. The situation surely fueled David's drive for financial security. In 1827, Tod completed his internship, studied, passed the bar, and thus became the first lawyer born in Youngstown.[35] He took as a partner an equally promising new attorney, Matthew Birchard.

The new partners enjoyed similar interests and spent time in the same social circles while finding time for rest and recreation. One excursion on the Mahoning River almost did the partnership in before it even had a chance to start. The river was the scene for recreational activity in all seasons including swimming and fishing in the warmer months and ice skating and sledding when frozen over. Birchard was not a strong swimmer, yet he found himself in a boat as it drifted uncontrollably toward the dam above Warren. Friends ashore, aware of the rocks below, feared for the safety of their friend and yelled out to Birchard to jump ship and make for land. The more they yelled out to the inexperienced swimmer the tighter Birchard clung to his boat as the current swept him closer to the dam. Tod, observing the predicament and having learned his partner's idiosyncrasies from their time studying together, used a bit of reverse psychology and hollered out, "Stick to the boat, Birchard, stick to the boat, don't jump out!" At that, the wayward boater released his grip, jumped ship, and made for shore, where his anxious friends pulled him to safety.[36] Birchard and the partnership were both saved.

When the partners hung their shingle outside their office David Tod was in financial debt. Room and board may have been on Spalding as he had promised the judge, but Stone's tuition came with a price. Spalding had loaned young Tod about $1,000 accompanied by a payback plan to settle in full.[37] Spalding would accept payments from David Tod as the debt was eventually whittled down and satisfactorily resolved in the ensuing years. Until that time the encumbrance weighed heavily on Tod's mind. Settling this obligation was extremely important to Tod and he would experience an enormous sense of pride and relief when it was paid off. In the meantime, the two new partners prepared to make a go of it in Warren and looked forward to a promising future.

David Tod's active legal career was short. The 16 years he spent at the bar were based out of his Warren office. He had been right to estimate that a law career could be advantageous in affording him other career advantages. The exposure, connections, and friendships that he made, coupled with being the scion of one of the most prominent jurists of the Western Reserve, certainly created favorable circumstances for prospects to come his way. One such opportunity was of a military nature.

In 1827, the same year Tod was admitted to the bar, Governor Allen Trimble appointed Tod a militia officer, inspector of the first brigade of the Fourth Division.[38] It was a peculiar appointment because Tod had no previous military experience or motivation for such affairs and was hardly a man of accomplished means. In fact, he had acquired nothing on his own other than the debt he owed to Spalding. Plus, whereas Tod by now was an avowed Jackson Democrat, there was no bigger opponent to Jackson in Ohio than Allen Trimble. Perhaps Trimble remembered Tod's father as a fellow veteran of the War of 1812 and believed he owed him a debt of gratitude for his service and therefore, offered the appointment to his son. Or Trimble was trying to lure the wayward young attorney away from the influence of Jackson. Periodic inspecting and drilling were the extent of Tod's miliary experience with the First Brigade of the Fourth Division but the exposure to the life and discipline of the common citizen soldier would be enlightening when he later assumed his responsibilities as a war governor.

The early years of Birchard and Tod were unremarkable although the duo courted and retained a base of clients that earned them a modest income. Tod was said to have possessed a "rare combination of talent and tact" where his approach to things was more "Practical than Philosophical."[39] Attorney Tod learned to talk directly to the jury where his style appealed to the jurors as he worked to gain their trust. One observer attributed Tod's "success" as a trial lawyer to his "unsurpassed ability in the examination of witnesses and to his power in gaining and holding the confidence of the jury, which he did by a manifest frankness, fairness and earnestness, together with his clear statement of argument."[40]

Modest success and the flow of income allowed David to address his father's debt. The possibility of his father's creditors moving in to "sell the old family mansion" and evict his parents worried him immeasurably. He had to act and reached out to the affluent General Simon Perkins of

Warren for help. George Tod and Simon Perkins had been old friends; their relationship dated back to their service together during the War of 1812. If Perkins would buy out the Brier Hill deed from Calvin Cone, David would make payments to Perkins. So, in February 1828, a deal was reached. Perkins bought out Cone and David Tod took financial responsibility for his father's farm by making payments to the former general.[41] David desired nothing more than to give his parents security in their old age. A close friend recounted much later that the very idea of "his aged father and good old mother, tottering with the infirmities of age, should become homeless wanderers, stirred his soul to its utmost depths, and inspired him with the resolve that such a calamity must not and should not occur."[42]

As clients and success grew, for the first time David Tod sensed his own reputation in the making. How much of it was due to his father's professional achievements is debatable but David worked diligently to make his own name and it was important that he achieve success unaided by his father's influence. He clearly used his time in front of jury and judge to find his own identity. Only later would David come to fully appreciate the esteemed name and reputation that his father had passed on.

With his commanding height and a "deep toned, musical voice" David presented a striking appearance in the courtroom or wherever he went. A friend once described him as "magnanimous and genial, of commanding appearance, great sociability, and was always listened to with delight, and was the life and charm of society."[43] And he used his attractive traits to help find a bride.

Justus and Charlotte Smith arrived in Warren from New York in the spring of 1813 with plans to build one of the area's first grist mills. Soon after arriving, however, with the project hardly under way, Justus died. His widowed wife was pregnant with the couple's fifth child, Maria. She was born on July 25, three months after her father's death. The young widow Charlotte was a hardy soul, picked up the plans for the mill, and got the project going.[44]

The widow Charlotte nurtured her children and her business on the banks of the river. Maria was quite lovely, and the young woman drew the attention of the young men about town. Her beauty caught the eye of the rising attorney David Tod. After Maria and David met, they fell in love. Maria accepted David's proposal of marriage and they wedded one day shy of the bride's twentieth birthday, July 24, 1832.[45]

The newlyweds purchased a house on the west side of Main Street and would make Warren their home for the next 12 years.[46] The new Mr. and Mrs. Tod wasted no time starting their own family as the focus of David's social life shifted to the house on Main Street. They celebrated the birth of their first child Charlotte, named after David's late sister, on October 28, 1833. A second child, a son John, arrived in November 1834.[47] This latter event was the same year in which Tod mourned the passing of his friend and mentor, Roswell Stone.[48]

Overall, the 1830s was an exciting time for Tod as he experienced great personal and professional satisfaction. In 1832, President Andrew Jackson appointed Tod postmaster at Warren. Postmaster appointments were strictly political plums that were handed out for partisan loyalty or reward in exchange for hard work in a successful campaign. Prior experience was not required. Tod was able to maintain his law practice while taking on postmaster tasks. The postmaster was expected to keep business hours Monday through Saturday where he would sort and prepare outgoing mail and affix proper fees for arriving mail since postage was due upon receipt. Reports were submitted quarterly to the postmaster general in Washington where a percentage of all quarterly sales determined a postmaster's pay.[49] Postmaster Tod earned $384.91 in 1835.[50] Coupled with the income from his law practice his steady and increasing earnings helped Tod to pay off his debt to Spalding while improving his personal financial condition overall.

For enterprising men about town anything that affected commerce was front and center. The main topic of the period was the crosscut canal that would connect Pennsylvania via Warren to Akron. At Akron the crosscut would meet up with the Ohio Canal that ran from Lake Erie to the Ohio River. David supported the plan from the onset. He was present at one of the first meetings concerning the project held in Warren on November 13, 1833. At such an early age he made a good showing for himself and was able to keep company with the most politically and financially influential characters of Trumbull County. Infrastructure improvement was a hallmark of Whig ideology, but it was easy for local Democrats like Tod to get behind the project because it was financed with private funds.

In 1837, Tod was elected a trustee to Warren's municipal council and was also a stockholder in the Pennsylvania & Ohio Canal Company. That same year he took Birchard, John Collins, and John Seeley for business partners.

The forward-looking foursome invested in property along the banks of the Mahoning River in Liberty township as the canal work progressed. With the promise that the canal would serve as a public highway for the coming decades local entrepreneurs were "induced to build furnaces and manufactories on said canal on account of its advantages in shipping materials and getting their manufactures to market."[51] Major economic growth was promised by canal supporters like Tod but one of the worst recessions to ever impact the United States began in the spring of 1837.

The cause of the economic downturn began when Andrew Jackson struck down the charter of the Bank of the United States in 1832. "Having destroyed the national bank and, with it, the paper currency in which people had the most confidence," writes Daniel Walker Howe, "Jackson then planted, through his Specie Circular, the seed of fear in the public mind that state bank paper was not safe either. Bank note holders therefore quickly became frightened by the string of failures."[52]

The act further directed the sale of federal lands in exchange for cash backed by gold or silver. This sent investors into a panic. "Everybody was trying to hoard gold and silver," Howe explains, "the banks, the states, the public, even the federal government, through the Specie Circular." The unsupported paper currency already in circulation led to inflation and panic by domestic and foreign investors. The country's financial world was turned on its head. Banks everywhere stopped specie payments; others closed. "Repercussions of the panic extended throughout the economy."[53] Businesses went bankrupt, laborers lost their jobs, wages were cut, and food riots ensued in major cities. Ohio would not escape the ruinous effects of the Panic of 1837. The causes of the disaster would forever influence Tod's financial outlook. This marked the unfolding of Tod's hard money philosophy, Jacksonian enthusiast that he was.

Tod had become so popular among the locals that Warren's citizens elected him their mayor in April 1838.[54] Democrats hailed the victory in the Whig-dominated town. Positive developments continued for Tod. Earlier in the year he enjoyed the greatest satisfaction of finally paying off the mortgage owed to General Perkins for his father's Brier Hill farm. It was a hard, 10-year endeavor but he had achieved his goal. With the deed secured and titled in his name David then leased the property to his parents "for the term of their natural lives," all for the generous onetime fee of $5. Finally, peace and security were attained for his parents and David's fears were alleviated. And an embarrassing financial situation was ameliorated. The elimination of the Perkins debt freed up capital for other investments. In June, Maria gave birth to the couple's third child, a son, Henry.[55]

Meanwhile, politics and public office beckoned to Tod. In 1838, Trumbull County Democrats persuaded Tod to run for the state senate. He must have been delighted with the marked confidence that the more senior party enthusiasts showed him especially since he was not born a Democrat. No one "was ever born a Democrat," the historian Jean H. Baker writes, rather "they had learned to be Democrats." In Tod's case he was "influenced . . . by friends and community," namely Rufus Spalding and Roswell Stone. "Every generation," according to Baker, "makes fresh contact with a different world, and [David Tod's generation] moved from political adolescence to maturity during the years when Jackson was the epicenter of American life."[56] Tod's move to Warren was his first exposure to a world different from what he had known at Brier Hill. He grew from adolescence to political independence under the influence of Andrew Jackson, guided by Rufus Spalding. George Washington was "a man called to power not only because of his views but also for his reassuring bearing," and inspired George Tod's generation. The David Tod generation was similarly inspired by Andrew Jackson, whose "appeal came out of the same tradition," the historian Jon Meacham explains. That tradition rested on "a covenant of mutual confidence between himself and the broader public."[57] For David Tod's generation, George Washington had already attained his apotheosis whereas Andrew Jackson, a man of the people, inspired as he walked among them.

To conclude that Judge Tod, who became an admirer of William Henry Harrison and would go onto to become a member of the Whig Party, was chagrined by his son's infatuation with Andrew Jackson and his attraction to the Democratic Party puts it mildly. Jackson's message of self-sustaining individualism and limited government strongly appealed to David Tod, and he was convinced that he found a home within the Democratic ranks. The father must have wrestled with his son's waywardness. Baker reminds us that "there have always been differences between fathers and sons on public policy" but sons usually found a way to adhere to their father's party even if they rejected "some of its political programs." This was not so for David and George Tod. Baker explains that "the conflicts of each generation have been different," and that one's "family attachments" were usually strong enough to overcome outside influences.[58] The Jacksonian allure was too strong to combat George's patriarchal influence and he let his guard down when he shipped his son off to Warren to study law where partisan recruiters swooped in and led him astray. Despite his son's growing political prominence, George would never accept his son's newfound political philosophy. "While father and son remained united in the bands of paternal and filial affection," writes one historian of the Tods, "the older man never became reconciled to his son's departure from what seemed to him the true party of patriotism."[59]

2

The Coolest, Most Collected Gentleman, 1838–1840

THOUGH HE HAD proven himself to be a fine lawyer we cannot know David Tod without understanding that he was, more than anything else, a politician. He had already served the city of Warren as a councilman and mayor. Known for his splendid public speaking abilities his speeches were characterized as "direct, clear, and interesting [and] generally described by the word 'clever.'"[1] He would need to use his communication skills effectively to defeat his senate opponent, John Crowell. Crowell and his newspaper allies would force Tod to take positions on the controversial issues of the day: the role of banks and slavery. Although the candidates followed their party's lead on banks, the issue of slavery posed a more precarious path for Tod and his handling of the sensitive topic revealed more than anything his ambivalence on the matter. Democrats were minorities in Trumbull County and Tod's previous political success and personal popularity aside, the politician knew he had to be careful explaining his political opinion on slavery. Antislavery agitation and abolition sentiment were growing political movements in Trumbull County and the coming campaign would reveal Tod's indifference toward the institution. Tod chose a practical approach to explain his stance. It was not a question of morality but a legal matter. He revered the US Constitution as the law of the land, and it was the Constitution that protected the practice of enslavement. Unless the Constitution was amended or each individual sovereign state chose to ban it, the institution had a legal pathway to exist. Therefore, neither morality nor his opinion mattered. That was all the lawyer in Tod needed to explain his position. Beyond the challenge of the election, Tod hoped to land in a Democratic-controlled senate with a Democratic governor where Ohio's banking policy and not the virtues of the state could be addressed.

Tod's rival in the senate race, John Crowell, was a Whig newspaperman and Warren councilman. Crowell was born in Connecticut and moved to the Western Reserve with his family as a child. Like Tod, Crowell studied law in Warren and was admitted to the bar in 1827. He was also part owner, writer, and editor of the *Western Reserve Chronicle* and he used it as an organ of the Whig Party.[2] Crowell would prove to be a tough political opponent and he used his newspaper to bash Tod and the Democrats. Without a partisan newspaper of their own Democrats like Tod were defenseless against political attacks. It became custom for Whigs to habitually refer to Democrats as *Loco Focos,* a faction within the Democratic Party made up of hard-working laborers who took pride in their stance for hard money, limited government, free trade, opposition to state banks, and the overreach of government influence.[3] Time and again, Crowell and his newspaper, like countless Whig party editors throughout the country, used the term derisively.

The banking campaign of 1838 in Ohio was born two decades before when "passions were swallowed up in a sensational campaign against the national bank." For varied reasons, unlikely allies of farmers and entrepreneurs drove from office pro-banking legislators. Farmers grew to despise the banks while businessmen and investors saw the national bank as competition to their shareholdings in state banks. The antecedents of the bank wars arose over what historian Charles Sellers described as a struggle between agrarian America and its emerging capitalistic class. Leading the charge for American farmers was Andrew Jackson who, simply put, slew the national bank on behalf of the average person. The war on banks, Sellers writes, "was the acid test of American democracy. Never has the farmer/worker majority given a more radical mandate to a more indomitable President." Jackson's assault effectively "mobilized a seemingly invincible army of disciplined Democratic voters"[4] and every Democratic candidate for office from Congress to city councils needed to pay attention including Tod running for his state's senate. The historian Donald

J. Ratcliffe further develops Sellers's argument relative to Ohio's farming community. The market revolution in Ohio was fueled by a transportation revolution in the form of infrastructure improvements, for example new and better roads and, most especially canals. These new arteries excited subsistence farmers who envisioned a future in commercial farming. The privately financed Pennsylvania & Ohio Canal aroused these sentiments in Trumbull County. Increased wages to farmers and manual laborers, the latter attracted to canal and road construction, helped stimulate the local economy. The canals not only exported local crops and wares, but they also imported cheaper household goods from outside markets. The consequence of the new commercial system, Ratcliffe explains, was that a "sufficient and reliable currency and [an] effective banking system capable of servicing" these new demands was needed. The "speculative boom" however, collapsed with the Panic of 1837. The bank failures that followed sunk produce prices and consumer confidence simultaneously. Democrats, writes Ratcliffe, "were blamed for upsetting the new world of commercial transactions that many Ohioans had begun to enjoy."[5]

By 1838 the bank war came to illustrate the financial dissimilarities between the Democrats and the Whigs. The antislavery Whigs of the era supported a national bank, in addition to favoring protective tariffs, and welcomed government-funded internal improvements like roads and canals. The Whig philosophy sharply opposed that held by the Jacksonian Democrats like David Tod who saw a limited role for state banks: those under strict oversight and control. In lockstep Tod proudly proclaimed that he "opposed, tooth and nail, heart and head ... a United States bank." Nor did he believe in the necessity for "a United States Bank to control our state banks." He believed that state banks should be controlled by the populace. He told voters of Trumbull County that bank reform measures were needed but above all, "we want ... to control them ourselves." Tod's suggestion to make state banks more acceptable was to make "the private property of the stockholders [and not public funds] liable for the debts of the bank."[6] Too many local banks, without security for local investments, had failed. State-chartered banks, he believed, could safeguard funds if they were under closer control of the people through their locally elected officials serving in the general assembly. But the cry of bank reform was nothing new for Democrats. It was nothing but used-up, old party drivel, charged Whigs. Democrats had had their chance to reform banks. "They have chartered an hundred or more banks, and why have they not chartered them according to the reform mode?" asked the *Cleveland Herald*. And, most importantly, "Why have they not made the stockholders responsible?" Because they had no intention to do so. Their words were "mere folly" to stir up their base, concluded the *Herald*.[7]

These philosophical differences, Ratcliffe suggests, were the result of the "marked cleavage" emanating from the view of banks and in Ohio, party loyalists followed suit. In Ohio, and certainly in Trumbull County, where population growth was spurred by Eastern newcomers as well as Irish immigrants who followed canal work, voters "responded to the considerable economic, social, and ethnocultural changes" taking place.[8] This may explain why the "market revolution" that Sellers and Ratcliffe speak of affected voter reaction at the polls more than other social issues of the day like abolition.

The other issue of the day was indeed the antislavery movement. Even though its impact at this time on local elections was insignificant, it was an emerging issue nonetheless and one that was not to be ignored, especially in Ohio's Western Reserve where candidates like Tod were forced to confront it. Most descendants of Connecticut Yankee stock found the practice incompatible with the founding principles and their efforts to mount social and political resistance to it were under way.[9] The majority was just not enthusiastic enough to do much about it. One historian best describes the position of northern Democrats of the period writing, "It was not that many of them liked slavery. They did not. But they argued that it was a local matter, not their business, whatever their personal views about it were. It was constitutional, a fact of life in the southern states, and would continue there as long as southerners wished it to. There was no issue to be made about it."[10] This is a fair description of Tod's position on the matter. However, the slavery issue would chase after Tod throughout his career much as it did the nation itself. According to historian Vernon L. Volpe it was not an issue in the Tod-Crowell contest of 1838 nor any other contested election across the state.[11] But the Whigs would try all the same to make it one.

The abolitionist movement in the north had a strong foothold in certain segments of Ohio. The small community of Oberlin for one, with its new college serving as its moral beacon, was more organized than reformers in the vast Trumbull County where pockets of abolitionists were scattered. But strangers still needed to think twice before taking to the stump to offer inflammatory rhetoric because, "social violence was not uncommon," notes one historian.[12] For example, in June 1837 Marius Robinson, a traveling abolitionist preacher, was to find this out in the cruelest of ways. Robinson stopped at the village of Berlin to share his message on the evils of slavery but, before he could deliver his sermon, a mob of 12 men dragged him from the house of his Quaker host and severely assaulted him. Beaten and tarred, the mob tossed Robinson into the back of a wagon and paraded him around town as a warning to other like-minded activists. Bruised but not cowed, Robinson reappeared the next day to deliver his antislavery message unmolested.[13] The incident shows the divisiveness and extreme passions on both sides of the slavery issue that existed in Trumbull County at the time. It was also emblematic of the rise of mob violence during the Jacksonian era that saw, suggests the eminent historian Daniel Walker Howe, "a transition in the composition of mobs from elite-led, politically motivated, and relatively restrained collective actions to impromptu violence."[14]

Antislavery sentiment, membership in active societies, and an active Underground Railroad shepherding Freedom Seekers northward, prevailed in Trumbull County but their political influence in this decade does not appear to be consequential, at least not in the Tod-Crowell campaign despite attempts to make it so. As antebellum historian Stephen E. Maizlish points out, Democrats were not "greatly exercised over the moral issues involved in African-American bondage."[15] And for Tod, its ineffectiveness was a good thing for he was ill prepared to explain his stance.

The Youngstown Anti-Slavery Society, however, forced the issue into the Tod-Crowell campaign by publicly soliciting the opinions of the candidates through "interrogatories" conveniently carried in Crowell's *Western Reserve Chronicle*. Eight queries pressed both candidates to state their positions on the role of Congress relative to the existence of slavery, the expansion of slavery, the trade in enslaved persons, and whether various constitutional rights applied to persons of color.

It could have been the best opportunity for candidate Tod to articulate his opinion on slavery and its future, but the natural politician inside Tod was unwilling to clearly state his position. In one response Tod explained that a Freedom Seeker who had found freedom in the North had the right of a jury trial, yet he opposed any person of color serving as witnesses.[16]

In another, Tod said that Congress had the right to abolish slavery in the District of Columbia and he believed that Congress had the authority to regulate and even abolish the slave trade between and among the states and territories. However, he said, "I should oppose the exercise of it, unless by the consent of the slaveholding states." That Tod believed Congress had the constitutional authority he made clear but why did he want consent from the southern states? Because if most of the Congress should take such drastic action, it would invariably be through force. If the states should consent to such action, it would be viewed as a choice, a peaceful solution through the exercise of popular sovereignty. As fantastic as that scenario sounds, Tod would have been delusional if he really believed it was viable. And if either of these scenarios should bring an end to slavery Tod would have wanted the rights of both enslavers and newly Freed Blacks protected. "Pay the master for his property," he said and give "justice to the . . . slave."[17]

During the campaign, Tod also publicly stated, on the one hand he "would give all he is worth or ever expected to be, to get rid of slavery" yet on the other hand he was "opposed to free negroes too."[18] Tod's response reflected the larger party view that free Blacks were a threat to free white laborers and therefore not welcomed. It also reflects the sentiment that "racism [was] a very real and powerful force in early Ohio." And, as historian John Craig Hammond points out in his study on politics, slavery, and race in early Ohio, not just escaped enslaved persons but also free Blacks "found that many whites proved willing to recognize and protect blacks' claims to freedom, [but] steadfastly opposed blacks' desires for equality and citizenship."[19] And Crowell's newspaper pounced on Tod's doublespeak, "It is certainly an unfortunate situation, for a candidate for office to be under the necessity of imbibing his principles from the people, for as in this case he will often make but an awkward attempt at fitting them on."[20] In fact, during the length of his political career, up until Fort Sumter, Tod positioned himself squarely behind the states' rights argument. He and his fellow Democrats would ignore the moral questions and evils of slavery. In short, when it came to the slavery issue, Tod's position would always be based on the US Constitution.

As much as the Whigs or the Youngstown Anti-Slavery Society attempted to make it an issue, most concerning to Ohio voters was the economic depression gripping their state and the country at large.[21] Ohioans went to the polls on October 9 and Democrats rejoiced over word of Tod's victory. The voters of Trumbull County put more weight on the state of the economy than the state of slavery. The *Western Reserve Chronicle* conceded the outcome with a subdued statement, "We ... are disappointed in the result."[22] The results were the same throughout the state.

It was only after his sustained, firsthand observations of the cruel reality of slavery in Brazil do we see any acknowledgment by Tod of its inhumanity. Otherwise, he remained silent and in lockstep with his party until the opening shot of the Civil War. He would much rather discuss banking or finances than the morality of slavery.

In Columbus, the new Senator Tod quickly established himself as a no-nonsense legislator. Soon after taking his seat among most likeminded Democrats a correspondent from the *Cincinnati Gazette* commented, "The young Senator Tod, from the Yankee county has much of the tact of older heads, and promises well." What prompted this observation was Tod's response to William C. Walton, a Democratic senator from Monroe County who was electioneering for the senate's speaker's chair. Tod was sincere when he thought the move of his veteran colleague ill timed and in response effectively countermanded his notion when he "expressed his desire to serve him, but added, how can we spare you from the floor? Without you there to do battle with the Whigs, how shall we be able to sustain ourselves? We can't spare you, my dear sir," he said. In the end, "The aspirant was satisfied to postpone his pretensions."[23] What was apparent in this early display of influence was Tod's confidence and command. The senior members of the senate would not control the new member and with ease Tod quickly took on a leadership role.

The new governor, the Democrat Wilson Shannon asked the Democratic-controlled legislature for more control of banking and paper currency. Without a national bank or uniform national currency, state governments had to tread lightly due to the struggling economy. Shannon knew that he could not do away with soft money, or paper currency. He called for "a sound and healthy currency adapted to the wants and interest of the people." State chartered banks, he warned, "should never be created unless for the public good." State chartered banks were needed to faithfully serve the public but if they "violate their obligations, they should be held amenable at the bar of public justice." Tod could not have agreed more. Shannon further appealed to the legislature to hang onto "the power of altering, amending, or repealing bank charters at pleasure" to keep stockholders of the banks accountable to the people. Adhering to Jacksonian principles he resisted any effort to resurrect another Bank of the United States.[24] But many in the party believed Shannon did not go hard enough against state banks.

As a western state Ohio was inundated with new settlers and farmers. Their success was vital to the state's economy. Sometimes these groups needed creditors and their needs helped to drive the demand for more state bank charters. New banks meant more notes and their value was viewed with suspicion. Existing banks feared new competition while corruption was feared by all.[25] Instituting regulation, therefore, was essential for the Ohio General Assembly. The main issue for the Democratic-controlled legislature was to correct the ills of the economy through banking and currency reform.[26]

But Tod and fellow incoming freshmen quickly learned of Benjamin Franklin Wade; the fiery abolitionist Whig from Ashtabula wasted no time in starting the drumbeat of his antislavery and anti–Black Codes agenda. His biographer writes that in this legislative session Wade "repeatedly offended his pro-slavery colleagues with the introduction of petitions for the repeal of the state's discriminatory Black Codes." On January 19, 1839, "he had the temerity to present a petition from a group of Negroes seeking to incorporate for school purposes."[27] In response, Democratic senator George Holmes of Hamilton County, who sat on the judiciary committee with Tod, quickly "moved to reject the petition." On January 23, Wade stood again to offer a petition from the citizens of Trumbull County asking Congress "to abolish slavery and the slave-trade in the District of Columbia, etc."[28] Ironically, Tod had publicly agreed with this very position during the previous election campaign, pending "the consent of the slaveholding states" of course.[29]

As much as Wade represented the antislavery sentiment in the Western Reserve passions swung the other way in the opposite part of the state, a region heavily settled by migrants from Maryland, North Carolina, Virginia, Tennessee, and Kentucky. They and their descendants clung to Southern values. Fearful that the state would attract a sizable free Black population, Ohio enacted a series of Black Codes meant to discourage such growth. These codes severely restricted movement and personal freedoms of free Black people otherwise enjoyed by white citizens. Although the state would repeal the codes in 1849, as historian Nat Brandt points out, "the relationship between the races throughout most of Ohio was precarious, and blacks never achieved full equality in the antebellum period."[30]

The case of John Mahan was the most famous incident that highlighted the tension brewing in southern Ohio at the border with Kentucky. Mahan, a tavern operator in Sardinia, Ohio, was rumored to be a conductor on the Underground Railroad. William Greathouse lived across the river in Kentucky and charged Mahan with luring his enslaved persons to freedom in Ohio. Once there, Mahan allegedly gave aid and comfort before moving the Freedom Seeker northward. Kentucky officials reached out to Ohio governor Joseph Vance for help. Vance, an antislavery Whig, surprisingly had Mahan arrested and extradited to Kentucky for trial. The November 1838 trial, however, found Mahan not guilty.[31]

After the jury acquitted Mahan, he sought financial compensation from the state of Ohio for his legal troubles. Tod's judiciary committee determined "that the prayer of the petitioner[Mahan] ought not to be granted." The vote of the senate concurred by a 31-to-1 vote, with Wade the only nay.[32]

After continued pressure from the state of Kentucky, however, Governor Shannon asked for legislation that would alleviate the growing tension caused by the Mahan affair. What he got was a new law crafted to "both deter inducers of slave escapes and facilitate recovery of those enticed to flee" to Ohio.[33]

Tod voted in favor of the bill. Once again, he cleverly sidestepped the ethical issue of slavery and invoked the argument of maintaining law and order under the state constitution. "Our actions," Tod said, "must be to prevent crime" by enforcing the law as written even if that law protected the property rights of enslavers.[34] Tod's vote in favor of the new law helped to give Shannon what one historian describes as "perhaps [Ohio's] most infamous Black Law."[35] Critics would point to Tod's support of the measure in future political campaigns.

The state senate would also be selecting Ohio's next US senator. The candidates were Benjamin Tappan and Thomas Ewing. The winner would serve a six-year term beginning March 1839. Ewing, a Whig, had previously served one term in the US Senate but the state senate declined to send him back. Now, he appeared again as his party's nominee.[36] Ohio's leading radical Democrat of the day, Benjamin Tappan, abhorred slavery but supported Andrew Jackson's anti-bank sentiments. There was uncertainty of what Tappan would do with slavery if he were sent to the US Senate. Although the Missouri Compromise of 1820 determined the course for the future of slavery, debate over the issue never ceased. The slavery question went unanswered, solutions were always temporary and debate in the US Senate never went away. State legislatures determined the existence of slavery in the territories. The Missouri Compromise of 1820 allowed the state of Missouri to enter the Union as a slavery state while Maine entered as a free state. The addition of Missouri, coupled with the entrance of Maine as a free state, brought the total number of states to 22: 11 free states and 11 slavery states. Maintaining the balance of power was essential. The compromise also prohibited slavery above 36°30.' Tappan once said that it was wrong to equate his support for Jackson with support of slavery but, on the contrary, his "public posture was one of strong, and even extreme, antislavery."[37] More importantly, like all good Jacksonian Democrats he viewed the Second Bank of the United States as the greatest source of abuse.

When the votes were counted in the senate Tappan bested Ewing with Tod casting a vote in favor of Tappan. It would not be a mistake to conclude that Tod put more value on Tappan's anti-bank posture than his stance on slavery. Either way critics within his own party would always remember that Tod helped to send an antislavery senator to the United States Senate.

In the meantime, Governor Shannon waited on comprehensive bank reform. One of Tod's early efforts on this subject came in January when he reacted to a proposed bill that attempted to limit the issuance of small notes. He argued for the measure because he believed in the importance of making capital available for borrowers but with limits to protect the vulnerable and unsuspecting common farmer. And forceful punitive measures were added to keep banking institutions in check. His speech was picked up by the *Ohio Statesman* and praised as "the coolest, most collected ... and powerful argument we ever listened to in the Ohio Legislature." The compliment seems a bit much even for the Democratic paper. Yet, the coronation continued. Tod was now worthy of an "elevated position as a logical and sound lawyer and able politican [sic]." The bill passed by a hard party line vote.[38]

In response to Shannon's call for bank reform, Tod delivered a bill from the standing committee on the currency. Tod, recorded the *Journal of the Senate*, "to which so much of the Governor's message . . . was referred," reported to the whole body what in large part would be presented to Governor Shannon.[39] In its final form, Shannon accepted and signed a bill that attempted to introduce trust in the banking industry with the creation of a bank commission. The Democratic majority was pleased.

The distinguished historian Eric Foner explains that Jacksonian Democrats "believed that the social opportunity inherent in northern society would enable most laborers to achieve ownership of capital." An economy working for all classes would help to spread the wealth, "rather than merely adding to the holdings of the rich." That wealth was earned honestly by the industrious hand of labor.[40] And the Bank Commission would keep speculative financiers in check and ensure protection for the aspiring landowner or small farmer who needed the credit to make small but necessary improvements to his business. The Bank Commissioner Act also took aim at the liability of Ohio banks by placing limits on bills in circulation. That amount was dependent upon the specie, excluding deposits, owned by the bank outright. Additional assets were the personal responsibility of directors and stockholders. This was a measure that Tod heartily endorsed. The final decisive factor was that if a bank could not pay its notes with gold or silver, it would be shuttered in 30 days.[41]

Tod was the main cog of the senate during this session as he sat on the two most influential committees: the Judiciary Committee and the Currency Committee. The latter, through the bank reform measures, helped to shape the financial future for the state's commercial development, which would go on to affect both lenders and borrowers. After the first year of the session's two-year stint, Tod was considered among the leadership. His immersion, assimilation, and natural leadership in the first year said much about his instincts and intuition. The second year of the session was more of the same.

At last, March 23, 1840, the final day of the thirty-eighth session had arrived. Members were at their seats at 2:00 A.M. and pushed through a mountain of work to adjourn at 6:00 A.M. No less than 112 acts, 84 resolutions, and 8 reports were reviewed and acted upon. As he packed up his belongings and made ready for the return journey home only Tod knew for sure just what his future plans were. Should he so choose to seek reelection it was clear the path would not be without its obstacles. There stood the ever-nagging figure of his political nemesis John Crowell, who patiently waited for a rematch. But David Tod chose not to seek another term, virtually forfeiting the seat to Crowell and the Whigs.

Tod's decision to leave the senate so abruptly after just one extremely productive two-year term was puzzling. Though there are no notes to record his thoughts on this critical decision it leaves one to speculate on the reasons for his departure. He either tired of the pace, the distance from home and family, or the politics of it all. The last is highly unlikely. However he felt entirely confident of the opportunity for higher political office, namely the governorship itself, after seeing it up close and personal. As effective as Tod was on financial policy, he clearly was not interested in social reforms. What he had been interested in was providing banking reforms and he felt he helped to accomplish that goal after the adoption of the Bank Reform Bill and the Bank Commissioner Act. And the Democrat Tod was not interested in the slavery issue to be sure. But as much as he or any other Democrat would find, trying to evade the issue would be impossible. Up until the Civil War, conflicts over race and slavery "would continue to shape politics, public life, and the meanings and practices of race, slavery, and freedom in Ohio."[42]

Tod's senate term in the state capital exposed him to party leaders who would play an instrumental role in shaping his political future. Regardless of his stance on any topic Senator Tod could not be overlooked as a candidate for higher office. A run at the governorship or Congress was not out of the question. He was a rising political personality within the Democratic Party, and he was "ambitious for political power." In fact, he was so driven, one historian asserts that he would do anything "to suit whatever faction controlled the [Democratic] party."[43] This tendency would prove problematic for Tod's future political endeavors.

3

A Hard Money Man, 1840–1844

JUST WHAT POLITICAL plans David Tod had in mind after his senate term ended was unclear. He was still an intensely ambitious man yet choosing not to seek office was political suicide. Although he was now out of office, for the rest of his life he was never out of politics. That he had an inclination for politics there was no doubt, but this did not mean he was a good politician. During the 1840s, although he continued to practice law, he started several business ventures that would eventually yield him a fortune. Stepping toward these new economic opportunities Tod eventually walked away from the bar. However, with the newfound income that these new projects provided he would find the freedom to stay active in politics and within the Democratic Party, where his true passions remained. And impending party failures would give him the time to reflect on his law career, political future, and new businesses. With no responsibilities of office to weigh him down he used the freedom to help fellow Democrats gain office.

Upon Tod's return from the Senate the *Western Reserve Chronicle* welcomed the one-term senator home with a negative critique of his performance. Characterizing his time in the Senate as a letdown to duty and to his party, the newspaper reported that Tod "was a miserable failure in the eyes of his friends."[1] Tod, however, had found more waiting to welcome him home. The *Trumbull County Democrat* began publishing in 1839 as a Democratic Party newspaper. It had its origins several years before as a supporter of Jackson and now provided a worthy counterbalance to the Whig's *Western Reserve Chronicle*.[2] The owner-editors of the *Trumbull County Democrat*, Christopher Columbus Seeley and William Baldwin, did not shy from countering or attacking the *Chronicle*'s owner John Crowell, referring to Tod's rival as a "self-appearing Demi-God."[3] Both newspapers continued on to fulfill their partisan duties blindly, faithfully, and enthusiastically. Finally, Tod and local Democrats had political coverage and cover to combat the partisan vitriol spewed from the pages of the *Chronicle*.

David Tod returned home to his wife and children where Maria was pregnant with the couple's fourth child. Back at his law office in Warren he brought on a new partner, a former law student, John Hutchins. When Hutchins, the secretary of the local Anti-Slavery Society, joined Tod his neighbors recognized him as one of the county's most enthusiastic abolitionists and activists for the Underground Railroad. Tod was unaffected by his partner's social and political activities. His law firm was a business and he kept politics out of his business. He represented Jean Baker's assertion that "not all Northern Democrats took race as the foundation of their political thinking."[4] Tod based his political philosophy not on race but banking and business. His first summer home he spent working for the Democratic Party by campaigning for the reelections of Pres. Martin Van Buren and Gov. Wilson Shannon. Tod's name became more popular outside of Trumbull County because of his campaign work that summer. If he cared not about his own political career his actions that season suggested otherwise. He continued to believe that the Democratic leadership would lead the country to economic salvation; so for this reason he went back to work for his party that season.

The presidential contest of 1840 pitted the incumbent Van Buren against William Henry Harrison, the hero of the War of 1812. In those days, political campaigns, as Baker reminds us, "were noisy affairs filled with incessant staccato of friendships, guns, cries, and yells."[5] These raucous scenes were common throughout the Western Reserve and indeed throughout Ohio. The stakes were high as the country tried to free itself from the ongoing effects of the Panic of 1837. Of course, the "prevailing distress obviously called for a scapegoat upon which public passion might vent itself, and [Van Buren's] Democratic administration" took the blame.⁶ But Tod was attached to Van Buren, who maintained that his party "protected the people by diffusing power and preventing its centralization, whether in the form of high tariffs, a public debt, or a United States bank."⁷ For Tod, Van Buren had taken the mantel from Jackson as the "hard money anti-bank" leader of the Democratic Party.⁸ The growing Whig sentiment to throw the Democrat Van Buren out of office spilled down to the state level.

In Ohio, the gubernatorial campaign saw Shannon challenged by a popular Whig, the five-term congressman Thomas Corwin. The campaigns of both men would see them visit nearly every county in the state. Corwin blamed Shannon and President Van Buren for the struggling economy. Ohio Democrats, however, played the race card and labeled Corwin a supporter of abolition calling him "black Tom" and a "great gun of abolition Whiggery."⁹

Trumbull County Democrats rallied for their candidates led by Tod, who robustly attacked the Whigs while praising Van Buren and Shannon. Tod's easy speaking style and party message appealed to many as he espoused the abilities and accomplishments of both. The *Trumbull County Democrat* praised Tod for his efforts. After one three-hour speech Tod was lauded for exposing "the frauds and machinations of the [Whigs] . . . at the same time, he portrayed in all their original simplicity, the principles of the Democratic faith, which . . . shone forth in ten-fold brightness." Like the religious revivals taking place in the country the *Democrat* conjured an image of Tod leading the faithful from the oppressive darkness of Whig ideology into the enlightenment of the Democratic Party. Politics of the period was regarded as "the nation's secular religion" and was "at the center of many a white male's universe."¹⁰ Interestingly, Tod joined his abolitionist law partner, John Hutchins, at one rally where Tod "eloquently addressed" the faithful.¹¹

It is not far fetched to speculate that Hutchins made antislavery remarks. That movement was at the political heart of Hutchins and strengthening in the Western Reserve. In fact, according to historian Christopher Phillips, Ohio's Western Reserve contained "the largest number of activists" in the nation at the time.¹² The crowd welcomed the speakers and there was no evidence that Tod tried to distance himself from or object to any of the points made. "The several addresses were listened to with the utmost attention, interest, and approbation," reported the *Democrat*. Though the report left out the details of the speeches it nonetheless praised Tod's efforts as "the most able and eloquent speeches to which we ever listened. With that comprehensiveness of thought, that earnestness of manner, and that depth of feeling, for which he is so eminently distinguished he surveyed the prominent features of the campaign and in a powerful & unbelievable exhortation, indicated the policy of the State and General Governments, from the violent and unprincipled attacks of the opposition,"[13] overstated the *Trumbull County Democrat*.

In September, in response to Tod's invitation, the state caravan finally made its way to Warren and spawned the largest political gathering ever seen in the city. The banking issue remained a topic of division between the parties even though Tod, Shannon, and the Democrats addressed banking reform during the last legislative session. Because of Tod's history on finance reform, supporters referred him to Ohio Senator Benjamin Tappan as a dependable ally against the banks and against paper currency. The Steubenville attorney Edwin Stanton, an emerging party leader, wrote Tappan that on these matters, "Tod is true as steel."[14]

On the same day as the Warren rally a letter from Tod appeared in the *Trumbull County Democrat*. Tod put pen to paper and attacked the district's first-term congressman from Ashtabula, Joshua Giddings, who was also up for reelection. Tod thought he had discovered serious discrepancies with Giddings's travel reimbursement requests. He also believed that Giddings falsified his worked days. Congressmen were allocated 40¢ per mile for official travel and paid $8 per worked day. These standards had been set up long ago. Tod found Giddings's requests problematic for they "appeared" to exaggerate distance traveled and days worked all to the congressman's financial advantage and to the detriment of the US Treasury. Tod concluded that Giddings overcharged his travel claim by $153.00 and days worked by $80.00, and he attempted to publicly take the congressman to task in the pages of the *Trumbull County Democrat*. Giddings authored a detailed "answer" to Tod's charges. Not surprisingly, the *Democrat* refused to publish the rebuttal, so the *Western Reserve Chronicle* published both Tod's original attack and the congressman's lengthy yet polished and legitimate defense. Giddings first expressed his thanks for "Mr. Tod's regard to our public expenditures." Like the skilled and experienced attorney that he was Giddings then proceeded to destroy Tod's weak and unprepared charges by explaining the congressional rules for reimbursement, his proof of travels and days worked, all accurately justified, along with official approval of his expenses. Giddings even managed to incriminate President Van Buren for his own misappropriation in the highly charged political give and take. Giddings's legitimate defense of the implication put an abrupt end to the matter.[15]

Although Tod's speeches were unrecorded the rival *Chronicle* can at least be relied upon to deliver critiques of what he said. Knowing their editors leveled strictly partisan attacks against Tod credence can still be attached to their reports. For instance, Tod on more than one occasion criticized William Henry Harrison's oversight when the general served as governor of the Indiana Territory in the days before Hoosier statehood. "We are informed that in most public speeches," read the *Chronicle*, Tod "charges General Harrison with having 'approved,' as governor of Indiana Territory, a law requiring an elector to hold fifty acres of land as a qualification." The allusion that Tod was trying to make on this point was that Harrison was responsible for the decision to deny suffrage to the common white man who could ill afford such a sizable lot while rewarding well-to-do landowners the right to vote. Tod was clearly promulgating the Democratic Party's message that it was Van Buren who truly had the best interests of the average person at heart and not aristocratic Whigs like Harrison. In response, the *Western Reserve Chronicle* advised Tod to read the Ordinance of 1787, which addressed the governance of the Northwest Territory. There, Tod should come to "understand that congress had fixed the qualifications of an elector, under the territorial government of the northwestern territory and that had Gen. Harrison interposed his *veto*, he would not only have overruled the expression of the public voice, but would also have violated the ordinance of congress, and his oath of office." In any case, Tod was establishing a reputation as a pugnacious party loyalist bold enough to attack the likes of Harrison and Giddings.[16]

Tod's political support for Van Buren and continued criticism against Harrison, however, had unintended consequences when again he touched upon his father's ire. The father and son remained firmly entrenched at opposite ends of the political spectrum, but this time Tod's target was someone whom his father held in high regard. The elder Tod was chairman of the local convention at Warren that championed Harrison's candidacy.[17] Not only that, the two old soldiers, Harrison, and George Tod, were both veterans of the War of 1812, and had much in common. Despite his father's feelings David Tod remained unmoved against his political alliances as his popularity among Democrats grew.

In the closing days of the campaign Tod had to briefly step aside for a more urgent personal matter. On October 8, Maria gave birth to the couple's fourth child, a son whom they named George in honor of his father.[18] Naming the newborn after the judge was a sign of the respect David had for his aging father despite their continued political disconnect. The tribute was an indication that political differences could not sever family bonds, at least not among the Tods. Soon afterward the proud Democrat was back on the campaign trail for a final push.

In the end, the efforts by Tappan, Tod, and others were not enough to overcome the negativity surrounding Van Buren in Ohio. Nor were they enough to fend off Thomas Corwin, who defeated Shannon. An even harsher rebuke was the fact that Democrats surrendered control of the Ohio House of Representatives though they managed to maintain their power in the senate. The Democrat hold on the senate would prevent the Whigs from taking total control of the general assembly and enacting partisan legislative reform. Given the circumstances the Democrats suffered a real thrashing and could not shake off the cynicism associated with Van Buren and the sad state of the economy.[19]

Despite the outcome Tod's effort during the historic campaign of 1840 earned for him a reputation as a top-rated speaker and an aggressive party campaigner, which gave rise to all sorts of political possibilities for the one-term senator. Whatever his intentions were that campaign summer of 1840 Tod's performance enhanced his image in the eyes of party loyalists. The famed author and historian Whitelaw Reid, in his history of Ohio, reflected years later that Tod "won a reputation as a speaker which at once gave him prominence among the orators of the State."[20] What became abundantly clear was that David Tod had a voice. A sharp-witted, yet rich, eloquent-sounding voice that had a command of the English language whose possessor was not the least bit afraid to use it, especially against his political adversaries. Among Democrats Tod gained the title of "giant of Democracy."[21]

Although admirers heaped praise upon Tod for his campaign efforts the fact is that he failed to deliver the voters of Trumbull County for Shannon or Van Buren. Corwin defeated Shannon in Trumbull County by a vote of 4,031 to 3,420. Yet in fairness, Trumbull County had not supported Shannon in his victorious 1838 contest when he lost the county by 87 votes. More noteworthy, the Whig candidates in Trumbull County made a clean sweep, carrying the ticket from top to bottom. Voters also reelected Giddings to Congress and elected John Crowell to the state senate, and fellow Whigs Peter Allen and Josiah Robbins Jr. to the state house of representatives.[22] These results beg the question of what political influence did Tod have over elections if he could not deliver local votes? The answer is extraordinarily little. If Tod could not influence voters in his own backyard, it is reasonable to surmise that he could not have been a viable candidate in future contests. The election of Crowell to the Senate seat that Tod had just vacated must have been a stinging rebuke. However, the Whig victory may indicate just how much of an anomaly Tod's 1838 election was in Trumbull County, the emerging hotbed of the antislavery movement that it was. Holding no office and no patronage positions available to him Tod's political options were naught despite his new popularity within the ranks. Democrats were on the outside looking in and Tod had to refocus on business endeavors especially with a growing family to support. For Tod, the political disappointment of 1840 was nothing more than an economic opportunity in disguise.

In the months after the election Tod worked diligently at his law firm to reenergize the business that undoubtedly suffered because of his absence. He and his partners aggressively took on cases representing both plaintiffs and defendants, concerning real estate matters, settling contested wills including debts of the deceased and the division of assets among survivors, and other contractual disputes. Short on excitement these cases generated income and the partners took in whatever work came their way. In one instance, for example, on April 6, 1841, Tod oversaw the auction of a "Brick house . . . in the village of Youngstown."[23]

Five days after the auction, on April 11, the Tod family received the most sorrowful news that George Tod the family patriarch had died. By the "comfort of his frugal but happy fireside" at his beloved Brier Hill farm George Tod, suffering from "advanced age and impaired health," quietly passed at the age of 67. Out of respect for David Tod, the *Trumbull County Democrat* set partisan politics aside and praised the judge for the "good qualities of his heart, and to the real virtues of an honest and benevolent man."[24]

George Tod, despite being "one of the most accomplished men of his times," left behind no financial assets for his heirs, no money, no property, no business concerns, and no investments. Instead, he left a character legacy that few of his children could match.[25] He was remembered as a loving husband and father who ensured that his children, if nothing else, received an education. He was a benefactor of the early public schools and he helped to ensure that every child of the community who sought a basic education had the opportunity to receive one. He and his benevolent wife took in and provided for orphaned children. He was a leading pioneer of the Old Northwest Territory, a political leader at the state and local levels, a state senator, a veteran officer of the War of 1812, a prosecutor, a presiding judge, and an excellent lawyer. Years later Henry Tod acknowledged his grandfather's inability "to lay up property for his family" but he was proud of his "reputation of being a kind, generous citizen, beloved by all his neighbors."[26] David, long after his father's death, took occasion to laud his father's memory stating he lived a life "full of years, and full of honors, both civil and military."[27]

The only tangible asset that George Tod passed on was the Brier Hill farm and even that, legally, had already belonged to David. But only now did David take physical possession of it. During the early 1820s the judge had replaced the old log cabin with a new farmhouse and was given financial assistance from David, who paid for its ongoing renovations. The Federal style clapboard-sided house was "sited at the crest of the river bank" where shards of coal broke through the surface.[28] The loyal son that he was, he devotedly looked after his now widowed mother Sallie until her death. Little could he have known that his noble actions to secure the estate for his parents back in 1838 would someday bestow financial rewards upon him. Some said "that the old farm in its early days was picturesque. It was not then known that it contained valuable mineral products in the shape of coal . . . and for many years nothing . . . was done to [Brier Hill] to destroy its natural wildness."[29] How much coal was underground was anyone's guess. And no one at the time could have predicted its large yield or its financial reward. David Tod was one of the first to experiment with this coal. As he discovered its various uses as a fuel source he began to harvest the supply and sell it to his neighbors who cooked their food and heated their homes with it.

With the Pennsylvania & Ohio Canal now fully operational, every conceivable manufactured or farmed produce from the Mahoning valley was connected to Pittsburgh and Cleveland, growing cities that offered new markets for local goods. Tod set his sights on Cleveland, by now a busy port city on Lake Erie and a base of operation for a small fleet of steamships. Steamship operators by this time had changed over to burning coal in place of wood to generate the steam to power their ships. Tod soon tapped into this market and as a result the move quickly demanded large supplies of Brier Hill coal. This appeal sparked a mining boom in the Mahoning valley. Tod and other mine operators had to produce at a furious pace to keep up. Tod's gamble was soon paying dividends for himself and for the local economy. No one could have predicted the economic fortunes of the Mahoning valley and the industrial developments that Tod's hunch on coal touched off. It was his confidence and his determination alone that persuaded Cleveland operators to try his coal while at the same time demonstrated the value of the canal. Deservedly, local historians have dubbed Tod "the pioneer miner of the Mahoning valley."[30] If any one person should receive credit for giving birth to the coal mining industry on a large scale in the valley, it is David Tod. At Brier Hill he "saw the possibilities in the valley's coal supply" and set about to exploit them.[31] So, as the fortunes of the valley's future lay in industrialization so, too, was it true for David Tod. The financial fortunes of the lawyer-politician had its genesis in his early experiments with his Brier Hill coal as a fuel.

Tod's enterprising spirit soon rose above his old lawyer's ambition, and he gave up practicing law altogether. Without the law practice in Warren to look after Tod moved his family to Brier Hill to live with his widowed mother, Sallie.[32] Retiring from an active law practice and moving to Brier Hill placed Tod in closer proximity to his growing coal operations. In Girard, within sight of Brier Hill and the tiny mining village of Mineral Ridge, Tod built a loading dock on the canal to ship his coal. Tod's newfound financial security provided him the freedom to engage in politics, where his true passion remained. And, in July, Maria delivered another son, William, to the family.

While Tod was developing his coal empire lawmakers in Washington and Columbus fretted over the state of the economy. Ohioans blamed the collapse of the once-prosperous new market economy on government's meddling. There was "no force," writes Stephen Maizlish, that "seemed more responsible for the destruction of their former security than government."[33] Between 1837 and 1843, Americans passed through "the deep hollow of a great economic cycle [where] the air became heavy with doubt and distress." Billions of dollars had been lost, bringing ruin to both private and public finances. When the 1840 election brought much of the same, "when prosperity did not come promptly, at the mere bidding of the Whigs, they were exposed in their turn," writes historian Samuel Rezneck.[34] Relief remained elusive as the depression maintained its grip. All that both parties managed to do in Columbus was to do battle over what type of banking system should be in place, all the while losing the trust of its citizens.

Governor Corwin had called for "a permanent system of banking" where a state bank would operate branches in major cities and the state would own a part of the stock; the second feature of his plan would recharter existing banks with limits placed upon the dividends that stockholders could keep. But Democrats in control of the Senate blocked it. Neither party showed any spirit of compromise. When Corwin's two-year term as governor ended Ohioans went back to an old Democrat, Wilson Shannon, in 1842. Blaming the Whigs was part of a "nationwide reaction" since they had failed to correct the nation's economic woes.[35]

When Governor Shannon delivered his annual address in 1843, he shocked Radical Democrats when he promoted the Whig position that a government-regulated system of local banks could help to resurrect the stagnant economy. A conservative faction of the party helped to modify the Latham Law, which had provided protection to stockholders. Even Tod's old Democratic guru Rufus Spalding supported the governor's new position. The divisions that began to emerge tested party unity. The radical, anti-bank faction of the party held firm to its principles, which led to a movement to make Tod the party's nominee for governor. Tod's well-known anti-bank position and his work for Van Buren along with his newfound popularity during the election of 1840 were not forgotten. He had been active for the party as much as possible since then. In fact, because of his aggressive attacks on the opposition he had become known as an "expert Whig coonskinner."[36] Tod appeared to be a strong candidate but looks can be deceiving.

A man with a long memory who wielded a tremendous amount of political influence behind the scenes in Columbus was Samuel Medary, the editor of the *Ohio Statesman*. Medary, a devoted Democrat and newspaperman, had already served one term in the Ohio house and one in the Ohio senate, had been impressed with Tod since his term in the senate, and was delighted with his hard money position. Medary tried to convince Shannon to take the same position. But when the governor rebuffed the newspaper editor's cautionary advice "Medary sentenced him to political death." Shortly thereafter, Tod was in Columbus where party leaders sought his position on such issues as the Latham Act. The Latham Act attempted to introduce uniformity to bank charters by enforcing "specie payments by banks" and most importantly it endorsed the Bartley Act that called for personal liability of bank officials and their stockholders if a bank failed. Though Tod's candidacy passed the litmus test with this small group of Democrats other members remained divided. Tod faced a difficult challenge. Could he unify the party made up of anti-national bank advocates (like himself) and more importantly, those willing to modify their stance to lead them on to victory over the Whigs?[37] While Tod set out to prove the viability of his candidacy, Medary would pave the way for the candidate with his influence over newspaper editors across the state. With Medary's oversight Tod secured the party's candidacy for governor.

Tod's acceptance speech on January 8, 1844, hit on all the right chords reaffirming his pledge to Medary. Democrats, he declared, insisted "that the banker should not be exempt from the payment of his debts, while the farmer is compelled to pay his" as he called for the liability of individual bank officers. Opposition to a national bank must be firm and inflexible for likewise, it gives "to a few the control of the currency of the country, and the custody of the funds of the nation, and induces them to urge the re-establishment of the Independent Treasury law." Tod said he would also make the upcoming contest one of class struggle hearkening back to the Harrison–Van Buren campaign. The Whigs, he declared, were all about consolidating power among the wealthy by exploiting the poor. But Tod would hardly mention this theme again during the campaign.[38] The Democratic Party's platform demanded "the enforcement of the laws upon the subject of Banking now in force,"[39] namely the Latham Law. Behind Tod Democrats pledged unity so that "nothing will or can prevent the Democracy of Ohio from achieving a complete victory."[40] The contest was to be no ordinary campaign. The *Western Reserve Chronical* called his speech, the "lowest trash" that originated from "the cranium of a small beer politician." Tod's Whig opponent was former state senator Mordecai Bartley.[41]

The state campaign ran concurrently with the presidential campaign between the Whig Henry Clay and James K. Polk. Polk had wrestled the

Democratic nomination from Martin Van Buren. The issue that elevated Polk to unseat Van Buren was the annexation of Texas. Polk was a proslavery Democrat and advocated its expansion in the newly acquired southwest territories whereas Van Buren opposed its spread and lost the support of the Southern delegates at the party's convention.[42]

Tod should have been his own best asset during the campaign against Mordecai Bartley. Wherever Tod went his now famous charisma made him a crowd favorite. With his colorful attacks and long anecdotes, he held the attention of spectators for great lengths of time before they would burst into an approving cheer. One three-hour candlelit speech, with Old Glory unfurled beside him, Tod shone as "a man of, with, and for the people. His very appearance shows it," glowed the *Ohio Democrat*. "No one that sees that honest eye, observes that frankness of manner, or hears that plain blunt language of his, but admit that he is a whole souled freeman, laboring with all his heart for the good of his country, and welfare of the people."[43] Medary was excited by Tod's "straight forward, open-hearted, [and] fearless manner of expressing himself."[44] One speech occurred in front of more than 1,500 Democrats in Montgomery County. "If there is a man on earth that has been misrepresented, wilfully [*sic*] and maliciously slandered, it is David Tod. We are rejoiced," said a party loyalist, "that he is giving so many of the freemen of Ohio an opportunity to become acquainted with him personally. He makes friends wherever he goes, for the very impress of an open hearted, honest and honorable man, are stamped upon every feature and expression of his countenance, by the finger of the Creator."[45] This saintly comparison was commonplace for nineteenth-century election rallies.[46]

Indeed, the campaign rhetoric that season was as religious and rough as any. Tod's patriotism and religious beliefs came under attack by critics who labeled him an "infidel of the worst and most desperate caste ... an open scoffer and reviler of every thing like religion." "The sneer, vulgar joke, and coarse ribaldry, were his common aliment, until he came before the people as a candidate for [this] office."[47] His Methodist friends in Warren, where he worshipped, came to a spirited defense.[48] But Tod himself was not above leveling harsh personal attacks against Bartley. During the campaign battle he once referred to his 61-year-old opponent as "an imbecile old man" who could not make a coherent speech if his life depended on it. Bartley's friends, said Tod, once had to "haul" the tired old man to Cleveland where they "propped him up on the stand, while he spoke about a minute and half [then] fizzled out."⁴⁹ Notwithstanding, the use of personal attacks was not new to American party politics of the nineteenth century. But Bartley needed to exert little effort because Tod's own feeble campaign performance would prove self-destructive.

Rhetoric aside, the substantive issues of the contest remained banking and currency reform. Early on, Tod proclaimed his advocacy of the Bartley Amendment, which provided banks more freedom than the stricter Latham Law. What may have been a move to build unity between the two factions within his party caused consternation among the Radicals. Out on the trail, Tod's speeches denounced the Whigs for their support of soft paper currency as he reiterated his stance for sound, hard-backed money. If not gold or silver, said Tod, he would "prefer pot metal money to shin-plasters." Thus, the Whigs coined the nickname "Pot Metal Tod." One of Tod's friends recalled the sight during a Whig rally of "a large wagon, drawn by eight horses . . . laden with a cupola in full blast molding 'Tod Dollars,' which were about two and one-half inches in diameter and half an inch thick; on one side were the words 'Tod Dollar.'" The Whig activists threw them into the street as fast as they could, where parade watchers quickly gathered them up.⁵⁰

The Radical and Conservative factions within the Democratic Party continued to fight for control of the candidate. Conservative members claimed they had convinced "Tod to modify his views on monetary matters" because it broadened his support among all the members. But his new modified stance had the opposite effect and sowed further dissension. These self-inflicted wounds weakened the party's cohesiveness and enthusiasm for Tod's candidacy.⁵¹ His prospect for victory deteriorated. In his efforts to placate both sides he failed to present a strong advocacy for his modified position. He began to look confused. As gifted a speaker as he was, he failed to clearly lay out his vision. Party leaders in Cleveland voiced concern with Tod's muddled position on banking and they asked him for a clearer explanation. This should come as no surprise. On controversial issues, such as his explanations about slavery during his Senate campaign, Tod attempted to satisfy all. This troublesome flaw did not serve him well. He could get away with this in local elections, but these party leaders were more sophisticated and not easily manipulated. He had to answer the Cleveland committeemen without appearing to contradict himself. Therefore, he carefully prepared a detailed response.

The hard money man that he was, Tod explained that he subscribed to "the old system of banking" before the passage of Latham and the Bartley initiative but only if specie was backed by gold or silver. He believed stockholders must be personally liable, loan amounts limited to one half of a bank's stock, bank issues curtailed to three times the amount of specie, and severe penalties levied against bank officers in the case of fraud. "With these provisions," Tod wrote, "the bill holder will be safe at all times. This object accomplished, banks would in my opinion conduce to the interests of the people; but without it all must certainly agree that they are a great curse." Tod's preference for the way things were before Latham and Bartley was a slick attempt to pacify the conservative faction where, writes historian Delmer Trester, banks could "obtain their charters individually from the legislature." Though Tod presented the five provisions as a novel idea they "were the same as those of the current law!" and, according to Trester, nothing more than an attempt by the candidate to appease the radical faction of the party.[52] Democratic voters became disillusioned, writes another historian. In the hour of need, they "became confused when Tod receded from his former Radical position . . . in which he admitted the necessity of a banking system."[53] The consequences would prove disastrous as the emerging charge against Tod, that he would do or say whatever he needed depending upon the audience he was addressing, was growing harder to ignore.

Back and forth Tod appeared to move reiterating support for Bartley then walking it back. These incidents provided Whig editors with great fodder to attack the candidate relentlessly. The *Carroll Free Press* called Tod out, claiming that he had "in two short months taken *two* positions *wide apart as the poles,* on the great questions before the people . . . only to obtain their votes and confidence that he may *betray* them!! . . . Poor, weak man; ingloriously did he open the campaign; but more ingloriously for him will it close!"[54] The prediction could not have been more accurate.

It was not long before Tod realized the error of his ways, but it was too late. The anti-bank radicals and the conservatives were at opposite ends of the banking issue and there was no way Tod could bring them closer together. His attempts to appease both sides not only hurt his electoral chances, they also damaged his reputation. For the remainder of the campaign the Whigs charged Tod as two-faced.

Tod's inability to stand firm no doubt hurt his chances within his party even though appeasing either one of the factions looked impossible. His wavering clearly did not help matters. Jumping from one side of the fence to the other to unite both factions of the party was disastrous. He would have been better off, writes Trester, to have taken a firm stance. "Had he kept his original position, and then made an attempt to go slow on banking while he emphasized other issues, particularly his 'rich against the poor' argument, it is possible he could have won."[55] Clearly, Tod's political instincts failed him, and they needed to be honed if he were to survive in this arena. His tendency to attempt to satisfy all rather than take a position and stick to it was going to be problematic to his political future.

Before election day arrived, Tod "realized that the Cleveland letter had cost him" dearly and that his perceived break from the platform weakened party enthusiasm for his candidacy.[56] Not only had he "found that he was too radical for the conservative Democrats [he was also] too moderate for the extreme." His miscalculation "brought down on him the denunciations of some of his highly esteemed friends" including Senator Benjamin Tappan, who had stumped hard for the candidate.[57]

One historian even credited Tod's defeat to the moniker Pot Metal Tod. The "cry doubtless had much to do in bringing about his defeat by a slender margin, showing that small things are often effective in [close] political campaigns."[58] The Whig newspaper, *Ohio State Journal*, read that Tod was sent home where he was "much better suited for private than public life" and was "restored safely to the arms of his anxious mother."[59] The Whigs now controlled both legislative bodies as well as the executive branch and they wasted little time in pursuing their bank reform measures.

4

Not an Office Seeker, 1844–1846

BETTER SUITED FOR private life or not, David Tod found himself once again devoid of public office. If he had not realized it before, Tod had learned firsthand that political campaigns could be rough-and-tumble affairs. Being the party standard-bearer was altogether different. Every opposition newspaper and party tool in Ohio assailed his character, religion, patriotism, name, and more, let alone his actual position on issues. Not 40 years of age, Tod was hearty enough to endure these mean-spirited contests, but did he want to?

The Democratic failure of 1844 left the Whigs solely in command of the political affairs of Ohio. A disappointed Democratic Party chairman Samuel Medary had anticipated a victorious outcome and with it he expected a Democratic majority to select him to be Ohio's next US senator. But defeat dashed Medary's dream. Tod undoubtedly felt badly about Medary's letdown. To make amends, Tod wrote to President-Elect James Polk to request the appointment of Medary to the postmaster general's spot in the new cabinet. It was a bold request considering Tod had no previous relationship with Polk. "Your name had been so intimately associated with mine in the past political struggle in Ohio that although I cannot claim a personal acquaintance with you," Tod wrote Polk, "I feel at liberty to introduce myself to you in this abrupt manner." Tod praised Medary as "honest and capable," assuring Polk "that no man in the Union is more worthy of your confidence." Although the president-elect did not select Medary he would remember Tod in the future.[1]

Meanwhile, the Whigs in Columbus were in control and wasted little time getting busy, for "the way was open for [them] to exercise their ingenuity on the problems of banking and currency."[2] They passed the Kelley Bank Bill. The measure created two different charters, one for the State Bank of Ohio and the other for the operation of private banks. A dozen districts were set up under the auspices of a board of control. The board's oversight prevented the centralization of power. But the law came up short as far as Tod and the Democrats were concerned because stockholders in the banks remained free from personal or financial liability for failures. Such an act, Whigs insisted, would discourage the influx of private investments. Whigs wanted Ohioans to have access to private loans. Although Democrats also wished to bring relief to the citizenry they believed that the law put residents at risk of personal destruction due to the frequent failures of banks. The Kelley Bank Bill required banks to keep 30 percent of their total funds in gold or silver in reserve as a surety deposit. Whigs had hoped that the measure would bring about a "revival of business, the increase of the wages of labor, and the rising prosperity of the State." Democrats insisted that the 30 percent specie requirement opened the market to a flood of vulnerable paper currency.[3]

The season of discontent continued for the Democrats as Whigs also introduced legislation for new taxes. Democrats cried foul when Whigs limited the tax rate on banks based upon their net dividends. It was another case of special treatment, cried Democrats, who believed tax rates should be the same for all. But the success of "modern civilization," argued Hamilton County Whigs, depended upon a vibrant banking system.[4] The difference in treatment, argued Democrats, highlighted the Whigs' favoritism of bankers and the moneyed class and their disregard of the common hardworking yeomanry of society.

Toward the end of 1845, Governor Mordecai Bartley was tired of Ohio politics and opted not to seek another term. His pending retirement hastened the political debut in 1846 of a new Whig, William Bebb.[5] Bebb, a lawyer by trade, was otherwise short on political experience but was considered "a man of uncommon ability, a powerful debater, and a man of unsullied purity of [a] person's character." He was a proponent of the Kelley Laws and viewed as a safe bet for the party. The Democrats once again pondered a Tod candidacy. The Whigs were excited about the prospect of facing Tod once again, believing that Bebb would give the Democrat "a dreadful time of it in canvassing the State."[6] They could not have been more right.

After the election of 1845, the Democratic Party of Ohio was disjointed, its message divided, the electorate afforded it no confidence, and it proved ineffective against the Whig message and campaign attacks. Radical Democrats blamed the conservative faction of their own party and vowed to retake control at the upcoming state convention in January. They wagered that Tod could heal the schisms, unite the party, and take back control of the state in a grand and sweeping victory in 1846. Eager to get a jump on the matter they began their work in earnest that December. The resurrection of David Tod's candidacy was once again rooted in this internal strife.

Tod's voter support in the 1844 contest was not forgotten but neither was his failed attempt to appease both radicals and conservatives. Both factions gave his candidacy consideration to head the ticket in 1846 but this time each wanted his assurance that he would solely represent their ideals. He would either lead the radicals or he would lead the conservatives. He could not represent both. Radicals gave him the opportunity to come out publicly as a hard-money man. If he did not, they would look for another hard-money candidate, Edwin Stanton perhaps. There was work to be done on both sides to get Tod off the fence for the last time. At present, he still aroused suspicion among the Radicals, who wanted him to come "out straight for the Hards," and away from the "d—d corrupt rascal[s] in the Conservative Ranks."[7]

The main reason that cemented Tod's selection at the January convention was the efforts of the radicals that December. They had gotten out in front of the conservatives to ensure the selection of hard-moneyed delegates for the state convention. The first move was the selection of Medary as president of the convention. Medary did his job ably when he shared a letter from Tod, who confessed his onetime dalliance with banks but now was convinced of their evil. Moreover, the Whigs had proven themselves too dangerous; their continued control of the general assembly could not be "guarded and restricted by legislative provisions" alone.[8] The inequities of the Kelley Banking Law for one had been the tipping point for Tod as his evolving position on banks moved his nomination back into Medary's embrace. Tod's views now resounded with the party's adopted platform: support for hard money backed by gold or silver and opposition to protective tariffs.⁹

Radicals now united behind Tod "with renewed vigor" vowing "never [to] surrender their principles." The editor of the *Portage Sentinel* asked conservatives to "take a retrospect[ive] of the past and then tell us what, if anything, has been gained" by the bank reform measures of the Whigs. Real change needed to follow Tod's proclamation to "shut out forever all possible conexion between Democracy and paper money, and purged the party from the frauds and corruptions of banking." It was the Whigs who were responsible for the "crimes of banking," and it is they who "must bear . . . the scorn of honest men for the crimes of bloated paper issues."¹⁰ But if the Democrats were to prevail against William Bebb Radicals and Conservatives needed to unite.¹¹

In February 1846 political observers spotted Tod in Washington, where President Polk cordially received him. The two men discussed Tod's recent nomination as well as national issues of the day including the acquisition of the Oregon Territory. Since the end of the War of 1812, the United States and Great Britain had jointly occupied the Oregon Territory. But the time had come for America to assert its authority over the territory. The British were ready to acquiesce. The most aggressive members of Congress wanted the Oregon border with Canada set at 54 degrees 40 minutes and pressed Polk on this. Tod advised Polk not to yield below the forty-ninth parallel; otherwise he would lose the support of Ohio's Democrats. This, Tod oddly opined, "was all he feared in the coming political contest in Ohio." Polk was noncommittal. If the Oregon issue should lead to war, Tod assured the president that Ohio could be counted on for support, presuming Tod won the election.¹² It may seem peculiar that Tod was interested in the Oregon issue but, suffice it to say he fell into the category of "Ohio expansionists [and] demanded that American sovereignty be extended over the territory."¹³ The president settled on the forty-ninth parallel, an acceptable resolution to both nations. If Tod had visited the capital to lobby for an appointment for Medary or for himself, Polk did not record it. Tod's trip and his comments to the president do not reflect the views and opinions of a disinterested or an ambivalent candidate though he would be suspiciously absent from the campaign trail and out of the public view.

In April, a US war of expansion with Mexico was commenced, drawing further political divisions among and within the parties. On the heels of acquiring additional territory, whether through a war with Mexico or by acquiring the Oregon territory, was the nagging issue of slavery expansion. Territorial expansion and the introduction of slavery therein, writes historian Michael A. Morrison, "together constituted the dividing line between parties much as the bank and tariff had done . . . among the rank and file and between sections."[14] Antislavery advocates believed that the growing slave power in the South with the acquisition of more territory, "were conspiring to dominate the national government, reverse the policy of the founding fathers, and make slavery the ruling interest of the republic."[15] Democrats, and the Southern slaveocracy, Northern critics claimed, were zealous in their designs for expansion.

In February conservative Democrats came out against Tod. The *Cadiz Sentinel* warned that "no good can possibly grow out of" a Tod candidacy "and it will only produce further dissensions in our ranks." But the *Sentinel* conceded that all must line up behind Tod even though "he may not count very confidently upon his own election."[16] This last comment is very suggestive, indicating that Tod lacked confidence in the prospect of his own victory.

There may have been something to this given that Tod had not actively sought the nomination. Early on his commitment to another rigorous campaign came under scrutiny. Was his heart or desire not up to the task? He was slow to get out of the starting gate and in fact he made few public appearances during the entire campaign. One article from early April said he had been out of the state on business but had since returned home; "We may soon expect to hear from him" to address "the oppressive laws of [W]higgery."[17] Rumors of business matters drawing him out of town or pulling him away proved accurate. His Brier Hill coal was becoming equally well known. One sharp-witted partisan penman cleverly connected Tod's coal interests with the political issue of the day. "Tod owns one of the best Banks in the State," wrote the *Holmes County Farmer*, "but it is a *coal bank!* This is the nearest advance that can be made towards a proof of *coal*-ition between honest Dave and the swindling bankers."[18]

Gradually, there appeared to be signs of unity among Ohio Democrats. One Philip Lawrence, of Sandusky, came back into the fold after first denouncing Tod's nomination. Believing he "was deceived by interested bankers" Philips aligned with the Whigs. However, he reconsidered his earlier anti-Tod position and later proclaimed, "You may set me down for David Tod and a Constitutional Currency."[19] Farmer William Auble, of Seneca County, a longtime Whig supporter, would have no more Whiggery as well. "But in view of the present issue between Tod and Bebb, believing, as I do, that the latter is in favor of the present unequal tax law, and unrestricted banking, thus taxing the great mass of the people for the benefit of a few rich speculators, I have come to the firm conclusion to vote for David Tod and the people's cause, and against Bebb and Banks."[20] With these sentiments on the rise one Democratic newspaper was optimistic that "the luke warm, are becoming ardent—the doubtful are perpetually wheeling into line—the wavering are gaining courage, and many of our old enemies are gathering under the broad and tolerant banner of democratic law."[21]

In the meantime, Bebb's supporters were well pleased with their candidate and hailed him as "a fine speaker, pertinent in his illustrations, and eminently qualified to win the affections of the People." Short on political experience, Bebb, while touring southern Ohio in June, introduced the issue of race and Ohio's Black Codes into his campaign. Citizens of southern Ohio used the codes to deter free Black migration into the state. Northern Ohio favored abolition and repeal of the Black Codes.[22] Each candidate needed support of both sections if he were to win the election. However, it was feared that a declaration on either side of the matter would gain support of one side and all but lose the support of the other. Making matters worse for Tod in southern Ohio was the fact that he had once previously supported the right to an education for all citizens, including free Blacks during his senate campaign in 1838.

The race issue had reemerged during the campaign under the influence of Salmon P. Chase and his third party,the Liberty Party. Founded on antislavery principles, the party tried to make race the major campaign issue.[23] When Bebb obliged, it was enough to further scuttle Tod's campaign.

Bebb first employed his strategy in the north. Recognizing the solid antislavery sentiment in the Western Reserve, he hoped to corner Tod by forcing him to state his position publicly. Bebb knew Tod's history and was aware of Tod's vote in the senate that supported the Fugitive Slave Act. Now he hoped to remind antislavery followers and abolitionists of the reserve of that fact. Bebb claimed that he would fight hard to oppose slavery, but he would not break the law. He would only "go as far as the Constitution would allow . . . for the destruction of Slavery, and the amelioration of the condition of that portion of the human race." While Bebb criticized the Black Codes of Ohio as oppressive[24] critics labeled Tod "an obsequious instrument of pro-slavery men!!!"[25]

Pressed once again by factions within his own party, this time emanating from the South, Tod was forced to publicly come out against the repeal of the Black Codes.[26] Soon afterward Bebb was in southern Ohio espousing enforcement of the codes after taking the opposite position while in the northern part of the state.[27] Critics recognized that Bebb was "most materially changing his ground"[28] and his position, depending on his geographic location. Now it was the Whig candidate's turn to be labeled deceitful because there was "little question that Bebb was guilty of duplicity in these maneuvers." But it was too late for opposing newspapers to take note.[29] Instead, Democrats were concerned with a new Tod slogan that surfaced, tying the candidate to his support of the Black Codes. "Who would have thought," wrote Edwin Stanton to Salmon P. Chase, that the contest would evolve from the issue of hard versus soft currency to cries of "Tod & the Black Laws?"[30]

Finally, under immense pressure in late summer, Tod confided to a reporter that his reluctance to venture from home was not due to harvesting season after all but rather due to his ailing wife.[31] For some time, Maria had been suffering from "consumption, cancers, bleeding of the lungs, palpitation of the heart, affection of the spine or liver" and other afflictions.[32] With such serious symptoms it was no wonder Tod remained at his wife's side and out of the fray.

Coincidentally, at the same time, it appeared that businessman Tod had a particularly good and profitable excuse for staying close to his coal banks. A letter to the *Pittsburgh Gazette* in August announced that an iron furnace in Poland, Ohio, was blown in using raw bituminous coal for fuel. When it was tapped the next day, it "let out 100 pigs of No. 1 gray foundry pig. Thus, for the first time on this side of the Atlantic has a blast furnace been blown in on raw coal." The *New York Herald* ran the story later that month, indicating the significance of the feat.[33] This was another fortuitous business development for David Tod. He had already demonstrated the efficiency of his coal for home heating, and for powering steamships. Once extracted from the ground in its natural form, the dense material provided a slow, steady burn for heating, cooking, power, and now the production of molten iron. Later in the year, iron men constructed a new blast furnace designed specifically to use Brier Hill coal. In time, ironmen regarded Tod's Brier Hill coal as "one of the best furnace fuels known, half the iron produced in the state being made with it."[34]

On the eve of the election the political attacks heated up. The *Carroll Free Press* called Tod a "mousing trickster" who was not trustworthy "to take charge of the helm of the good ship of State."[35] In the end, once again, a slim majority agreed. William Bebb was elected governor with 118,869 votes; David Tod received 116,484.

Just one month after the voters denied him the governorship for a second time, Tod wrote Samuel Medary informing the party leader not to bother him in 1848. Medary should consider this "full and ample [notice] to make a selection of a[nother] standard bearer for the next contest." Grateful for the past honors to represent the party, Tod claimed to harbor no ill will and wanted nothing more than "an opportunity of walking through this State, from stump to stump—entirely untrammeled—having no other or further interest in the result than the most humble hearer who may honor me with his presence."[36]

5

It Becomes Us to Act, 1847–1851

UNBURDENED BY THE troubled affairs of his state and the rift within his fractured Democratic Party, David Tod looked forward to better times. Whatever thought he had of settling in at Brier Hill as a private businessman or of even walking the state untrammeled he quickly learned that others still had designs for him. Shortly after his latest political defeat, Tod was called to his future mission. But this time, it was not the leader of his political party calling him but rather the president of the United States, James K. Polk.

After Polk won the Democratic nomination from Martin Van Buren, he defeated his Whig opponent, Henry Clay. Polk was a proslavery president with manifest destiny on his mind when he came into office. In 1846, he went to war with Mexico over a dispute with Texas. Achieving victory over Mexican forces in 1848, Polk acquired the territory of Texas, New Mexico, and California. The expansionist that he was, he then peacefully acquired the Oregon Territory.[1]

As early as November 1846 Tod was under consideration by the Polk administration as an appointee to the Brazilian foreign missionary position. In fact, a sleuth for the *New York Herald* predicted that Tod "will be the man"[2] chosen by Polk. Despite losses in his last two high-profile contests, Tod remained a popular Democrat. "Although young in years, he enjoys an enviable reputation among the distinguished men of the country; and the manner in which he has been sustained at the late election, under all the adverse circumstances," concluded the *Daily Union*, "gives ample evidence of his great popularity at home."[3] Over the past two years, Tod and Polk maintained a relationship mostly through Tod's written correspondence going back to his introductory letter on behalf of Medary in 1844. Tod's trip to Washington in 1846 was the start of their personal acquaintance.

Polk was obviously impressed with Tod when he first welcomed the Ohio Democrat to the Executive Mansion. Just what the president saw in the inexperienced and untested Tod that qualified the one-term state senator and two-time unsuccessful gubernatorial candidate to serve as a foreign emissary is unknown. Tod's travel experience was extremely limited, he had hardly set foot outside of Ohio, and he was unschooled in foreign affairs let alone the current precarious entanglements between the United States and Brazil. Even a family historian recognized "the total lack of experience on the part of David Tod in diplomacy and court etiquette."[4] Yet, despite these shortcomings, Polk offered Tod the diplomatic post.

Tod initially was hesitant to accept the offer because of his wife's delicate state of health. The cause for the couple's concern was the fact that Maria, afflicted with her ailments as she was, had recently revealed that she was carrying the couple's sixth child and was expecting in December. Once satisfied that his wife could make the long and treacherous journey to Brazil, Tod "concluded to accept the Mission."[5]

When word of Tod's appointment and confirmation as envoy extraordinary and minister plenipotentiary became public, supporters and critics alike reacted. "Mr. Tod," submitted the *Richmond Enquirer*, "is one of the most eminent statesmen in Ohio—singularly popular in his manners, and amply qualified to discharge the duties of office."[6] Referring to Tod's retirement letter and his intentions to walk the state of Ohio, the *National Whig* however wondered if "he intends to make the journey [to Brazil] on foot?"[7] Ohio Whigs were even more disparaging of Tod's appointment. The *Carroll Free Press* crowed Tod was fortunate that Ohioans "were not called upon to ratify his nomination" because he would suffer the same fate as his two failed gubernatorial bids.[8] Not long after a local passerby called on Tod to pay his respects to the new minister. "Well Dave," said the head-scratching neighbor, "I always knew you were pretty smart, but I'll be damned if I ever thought you would turn preacher."[9]

Samuel Medary had also worked tirelessly for Polk during the presidential campaign, and he, too, expected a political plum in return, even a coveted cabinet position. Polk did not overlook Medary and offered the political operative the postmastership of Columbus. An infuriated Medary considered the gesture an insult and accused Tod of double-crossing him. Tod, claimed Medary, "had promised to aid him in securing" the coveted consular appointment and when Polk selected Tod, Medary believed that he was "tricked." This development forever strained relations between the two Ohio Democratic heavyweights.[10]

The value and service of the current minister to Brazil, Henry Wise, an appointee of President John Tyler, had run its course. Tyler was a member of the slaveocracy and as a Southern congressman fought attempts to ban slavery in the District of Columbia. Known for his independent spirit Wise began his political career, like Tod, as a Democrat. But, after Andrew Jackson killed the Second National Bank Wise abandoned the party in protest and joined the Whigs. President Tyler once called Wise "the most incorrigible" person he knew but in 1843 appointed him minister to Brazil anyway.[11]

Even though Wise was himself an enslaver, he took great umbrage at Brazil's continued participation in the international trade of enslaved persons and he made his displeasure known. The sight of American merchant ships transporting imprisoned Africans bound for a life of forced labor under cover of the flag of the United States was particularly upsetting to him. His position along with his intractable quality did not sit well with Emperor Dom Pedro II, who took offense at the American ambassador's criticism of his country's business. This led to strained relations between the two countries. Describing Wise's time in Brazil as "a good long sojourn at Rio" the *New York Herald* wondered if the emperor wished to bid Wise a long good riddance.[12]

Wise's troubles with Emperor Pedro II began one year previous under auspicious circumstances that became known as the Davis Affair. Reportedly three of Lieutenant Alonzo B. Davis's crew were publicly intoxicated as they stumbled their way back to their US ship docked in the harbor at Rio. Local authorities arrested the three American sailors and charged them with disorderly conduct and public inebriation. When Davis physically interceded on behalf of the sailors, he was likewise arrested. Wise furiously demanded the release of his compatriots. Making matters worse, Wise protested by declining to attend the christening of the emperor's daughter. After this latest affront, "the indignation of the Brazilian authorities appeared to have reached a climax."[13]

The Davis Affair, Wise believed, was an insult to the United States and a dishonor to the American flag. He expected no less than a full apology from the host country. His demands and his ongoing attempts to "suppress the African trade of enslaved persons, so extensively carried on by Brazil," however, so offended the emperor that Wise's continued presence was considered intolerable and necessitated a change.[14] Enter minister-designee David Tod.

Meanwhile the Davis Affair simmered unresolved. Although Wise sought to restore the honor of his country's flag his very public criticism left no honorable face-saving diplomatic path for the emperor. Brazil may have been more contrite early on had it not been for Wise's very overt public and aggressive call for restitution.

Wise's counterpart, the Brazilian minister to the United States, Gaspar José de Lisboa attempted to heal hard feelings between the two countries and, though separated by thousands of miles and without his emperor's blessing, apologized on behalf of the Brazilian government for his country's handling of the Davis Affair. When the emperor learned what his longtime diplomat had done, he was so angered that he recalled Lisboa in June. This move caught Polk and Secretary of State James Buchanan by surprise. Polk hoped to keep things from escalating and communicated to Lisboa his "desire that the most amicable relations should exist between the Governments of Brazil & the United States."[15]

Secretary of State Buchanan apprised Tod of the delicate situation. The emperor was displeased, said Buchanan, "that the Davis affair was unadjusted . . . in a manner conformable to the dignity of Brazil."[16] Polk hoped that the unseasoned but well-mannered and charming Tod could disarm the emperor and repair the rift. It was a delicate assignment for the inexperienced Tod and the president was anxious to get his new minister "sailing without a moment's delay." But while his ship the *Ohio* underwent repairs Tod was detained in New York. Polk blamed the delay on Tod's preoccupation with "additional accommodations . . . for the unusually large family & attaches which he proposes to take with him, chiefly females." Telegraphed orders from the president instructed Captain Silas Stringham to steer the *Ohio* on a direct course for Rio without stopping at the Portuguese island of Madeira where Tod, it was reported to Polk, had hoped to "obtain wines."[17]

While Tod sailed the Atlantic that August, Senhor Dom Felippe Pereira Leal, acting chargé d'affaires of Brazil, informed Buchanan that Lisboa's aforementioned overture of appeasement had been "disavowed by his government." Furthermore, unless he had the full "authority to treat [the existing] adjustment of difficulty,"[18] the emperor would not permit Tod ashore.

The *Ohio* finally docked in Rio on August 10 where Wise was on hand to greet his successor. News of his arrival "created quite a sensation . . . not only among the American residents, but the natives." Brazilian authorities, however, viewed Tod's presence with "some considerable anxiety." He remained onboard the *Ohio* until the emperor requested the presentation of his credentials to the court.[19]

During the interim, Wise met with Tod onboard over the next two days and provided an extensive review of his recent difficulties. Under the present circumstances Wise requested that Tod delay his request to present his credentials.[20] It was a point of "personal and national pride and honor," Wise explained.[21] After deep reflection and with "unfeigned regret" Tod informed Wise that he intended to press ahead because the Department of State had directed him to do so.[22]

Finally, on August 29, three weeks after landing, Tod was presented to the emperor at the court of Brazil. Adhering to the proper decorum of the moment, Tod addressed the emperor. "I am aware that my charge has commenced at an unfavorable period," he began. "My immediate predecessor involved himself in affairs which were both unpleasant for himself and unfortunate for both governments." Adeptly, he then pledged to "observe a course both honorable and beneficial to both countries" and to purport himself "entirely satisfactory to my own government, and at the same time agreeably to that of your Majesty." He closed with offering prayers for good health to the emperor and his family. The immediate impression of Tod was vastly different from Minister Wise and the emperor appeared satisfied. Dom Pedro's reply, in fact, was more than Tod could have hoped for. "I believe you to be a true interpreter," said the emperor, "who will remove the weighty difficulties in which your immediate predecessor involved himself."[23] The emperor had reason to believe "that the relations between the two governments may continue on the footing of perfect harmony, in which they were always found in former times."[24]

Tod's first official act as the American minister to the court of Brazil was brilliant and regarded as a smashing success. From that moment on, the healing of bruised egos was well under way.

However, Wise was wounded by Tod's public rebuke of his conduct and characterized his replacement's presentation as "bad *in republican spirit,* bad in *grammar* and bad in *taste."*[25] Polk and Buchanan also sent word to Tod that his harsh criticism of Wise had been excessive. In fact, Buchanan relayed that Wise's conduct during the Davis Affair was approved and that the matter "was to be adjusted at Washington and not at Rio."[26] Tod was stung by the administration's rebuke, but he survived. Polk otherwise expressed optimism. The president's December state of the union address acknowledged the "difficulty with the Brazilian Government, which at one time threatened to interrupt the friendly relations between the two countries." But now he expected that tensions would continue to "be speedily adjusted" under Tod's stewardship.[27]

On September 29, 1847, one month after her diplomat son was presented to the Brazilian emperor, Sallie Tod died. She was 69 years old. It would take weeks before news of her passing reached her son in Brazil.[28] David Tod revered his mother and the news hit him hard. One who knew Tod well remembered the genuine affection and regard he held for his mother. "His intense devotion [to her] almost bordered upon idolatry" his friend Samuel Galloway recalled many years later. Among friends the son would regularly refer to her as his "sainted mother" or "precious mother." Later in life he regularly shared that he felt his mother's spirit helping him along in life. And he would often express that because he had looked after her so devotedly, "Providence" justly rewarded him in life.[29]

The new American minister quickly took hold of his official legation. Of immediate and vital importance was the continued healthy commercial intercourse between the two countries. The United States exported agricultural and manufactured goods such as lumber, candles, whaling oil, flour, and lard while importing tropical specialties.[30] One of the most important of these was coffee. Americans had an established love affair with the addictive bean, and they purchased more of it from Brazil than from any other nation.[31] Producers and consumers alike would suffer under strained relations.

The most troubling type of commerce, however, was the Brazilian government's continued participation in the international trade of enslaved Africans. In 1807, the United States and Great Britain abolished the trade, but few countries in the Western Hemisphere like Brazil continued its detestable practice.

Although the US government had outlawed the trade, privateering persisted and in many cases these vessels flew the American flag atop their masts. This was noteworthy because the British navy could not board and search American vessels. What disgusted Tod even more was the subterfuge committed by American citizens involved in the trade. "These men," Tod would learn, "obtain sea-letters, which entitle them to continue in use the United States flag." These ships "take over slave goods and slave crews, under the protection of our flag, and remain nominally American property until a favorable opportunity occurs for receiving a cargo of slaves at Brazilian ports."[32]

When Tod realized the degree of America's participation, he, like Wise, was "mortified" and wasted little time gathering facts before dispatching a gut-wrenching letter to Buchanan. He reported to the secretary of state "that not less than forty-five thousand negroes have been imported into Brazil within the last year," and these "poor creatures are not only separated from their homes and friends; but, on their passage, and frequently after their arrival here, are treated most brutally. More or less of every cargo are murdered on the voyage, and the survivors are too often used as mere beasts of burden." Tod implored Buchanan for assistance while making clear his own position. "This traffic should, at all hazards, be put down; and when I inform you, that by far the greater portion of it is carried on in vessels built in the United States, and under the flag of our country; I trust you will agree with me, that it becomes us to act, and to act promptly. For myself, I will do so with hearty good-will." Little, if any response was returned. And if Tod ever previously waivered or misarticulated his stance on matters related to slavery, there was no mistaking his outrage or his position now.

For the first time, Tod saw up close and personal the cruel effects of the trade and the dehumanizing practice of slavery upon its victims. The closest he had ever come to the South was in Washington, where slavery was legal. There he could not have missed the sight of auctions of enslaved persons, crowded pens, and shackled bondspeople. Due to his limited travels, it is highly unlikely, however, that he ever observed the sheer brutality of a slavery-fueled plantation up close. But these captured

African prisoners unloaded on the docks of Rio helped him understand they were more than inanimate chattel. They were suffering human beings whose families were torn apart at auctions in horrible emotional scenes that played out before his eyes. Public floggings of the poor souls strapped to the whipping post sickened him. He could not avert his eyes from "the blood of the wretched victims, as well as the cry of those who escaped death to enter bondage." These observations had an extraordinary effect on the new American minister and he was determined to end the trade. But he soon learned that this goal would not be easy to attain.

What Minister Tod quickly learned was that the Brazilian economy was totally dependent on enslaved labor, which was used to work the fields and plantations. During the 1840s, enslavers forcibly shipped well over 350,000 Africans to Brazil of which over half that number arrived with American assistance.[33] With such complete dependence on enslaved labor there was no way the Brazilian government could abandon the system without crippling its economy. In addition to the country's economic reliance on enslaved labor, the typical Brazilian philosophy had grown to accept the practice after more than three centuries of use. It was not particularly difficult for Brazilians, explains historian James Oakes: "The basic proposition was startlingly simple." To justify their inhuman practice, Brazilians had learned to see their African captives as less than human. "Nature itself," reasoned the Brazilians, "had determined the place of the African in Brazil."[34] The tough foreign policy work for Tod was before him and he would soon realize that his own government in Washington would provide him no direction in the illegal trade. Like Henry Wise, he would face the issue alone.

As the wife of the new diplomat, Maria Tod settled in and was none too pleased to learn that there was no public education available for her school-age children. This situation was unacceptable and would hasten her departure home the following spring. But first, on December 16, Maria gave birth to the couple's sixth child, a daughter they named Grace. The following April she and the children sailed for home.[35] After a short six-month separation, the couple was finally reunited in October 1848.[36] Together again, the minister and his wife quickly fell into the diplomatic social scene attending balls, festivals, state dinners and receptions.[37] In no time, Minister Tod wrote, "I am getting along very pleasantly with my official business, and doubt not I shall continue to do so."[38]

Indeed, Tod grew comfortable in his new role. Where Wise's irredeemable and unapologetic qualities crippled his effectiveness, Tod offered a fresh approach for both sides. One of his first diplomatic successes was overturning the refueling restrictions placed on American whaling vessels at Ilha Grande, a small island just off the coast of Rio de Janeiro. Tod requested that the constraints be lifted, and this was summarily granted. It was a minor accomplishment but an important sign of his effectiveness and the Brazilian government's willingness to work through him.[39]

During the 1820s, a dispute over navigation rights upon the Plata River between Brazil and Argentina had boiled over into armed conflict. Hostilities between the two nations lasted more than two years. Collateral damages were felt by American citizens residing in harm's way. Casualties took the form of lost or damaged property, mostly in real estate and personal belongings. As late as 1847, American claims remained unsettled. Buchanan directed Tod to reopen discussions with the hope of receiving restitution. Once again, Tod was able to find a resolution. In January 1849, the Brazilian government agreed to pay $300,000 to the United States.[40]

These matters, minor though they were, marked a new spirit of cooperation that had been missing between the two nations. Constructive dialogue had been so curtailed during Wise's tenure but Tod was able to resolve past difficulties. Tod comported himself in such a dignified and honorable way that to say that the Brazilians were pleased would be an understatement. His charming personal traits, his polished sense of decorum, and his good common sense made up for his lack of experience and undoubtedly served him and his government well. Despite Tod's success on mitigating these issues, the dark cloud of American involvement in the Atlantic African trade of enslaved persons continued. Again, he looked to Buchanan to provide formal direction and reassurance, and once again none came.[41]

Secretary of State Buchanan's views on the issue of slavery were clear. The slavery question, the Pennsylvania native once said, and one Tod would have agreed with, was not one "of general morality, affecting the consciences of men, but [rather] a question of *constitutional law*." Even as president, as the nation was unraveling around him during the secession crisis, he was unmoved by the passions that motivated abolitionists. As for the Brazilian trade in enslaved persons, Buchanan lined up with Tod but for varied reasons. Buchanan concurred with Tod on the right of the United States to board and search American vessels for violations though he lacked Tod's moral outrage. He was more concerned that "the British government [would be viewed as] the supreme protector of the rights of humanity... on the ocean or on the land" rather than the United States, for the British Royal Navy was doing just that.[42]

The distinguished historians Don E. Fehrenbacher and Ward M. McAfee reflected on the unsuccessful efforts of both Tod and Wise to convince their government to act. "At home, their words fell on deaf ears. No president or cabinet member showed any signs of being infected with their zeal." The same could be said for the rest of the country back home, write Fehrenbacher and McAfee. Americans were just too "preoccupied with other matters, such as continental expansion and the ulcerating problem of domestic slavery, [and] gave no more than passing thought to the African trade of enslaved persons."[43] It would take a new secretary of state under a new administration before Tod found an ally to work with.

While Tod remained out of the country representing the United States, in 1848, President Polk had decided not to seek reelection. His decision resulted in the election of Zachary Taylor, a Whig who as president appointed Senator John M. Clayton of Delaware to be secretary of state. Taylor kept Tod on at his diplomatic post in Brazil. Clayton shared Tod's view on the trade in enslaved persons, but he, too, was ineffective and could not persuade Brazilian officials to change course.[44]

In 1849, a year after a yellow fever epidemic ravaged the country of Brazil, a new life was added to the local population when Maria gave birth to a daughter Sallie on December 4. Named after David's mother, little Sallie was the seventh and last child born to the family. Her birth brought the number of Tod children residing in Rio to three. Older brother Billie had adapted to his surroundings quite well, even learning to speak the national language, Portuguese.[45]

For the next two years, Secretary Clayton continued to bolster Tod's efforts to fight the Atlantic trade in enslaved persons, beseeching his minister to "adopt any measures which the laws of the United States and that Empire may authorize and which may comport with your official position for the purpose of repressing the illegal traffic."[46] It was not a matter of adopting new measures because there was nothing new to adopt; seemingly all options had been exhausted. Rather, it was a matter of enforcement. "If the Brazilian statutes upon the subject were faithfully enforced," Tod believed, "the trade of enslaved persons could not continue [but] those clothed with their administration and execution, with some honorable exceptions, connive at the traffic, and silently acquiesce in the violation of the laws they are sworn to uphold." By now, Tod realized that the Brazilian economy was too dependent on the enslaved labor system. It could not abandon the practice for fear the economy would collapse. Furthermore, for those intimately involved, for all those with their hand in the mix, the power of profit was too strong to resist. These were "very embarrassing obstacles" and too daunting a task to fight alone.[47]

Historian Gerald Horne notes that the Brazilian trade in enslaved persons was the most "profitable than that of any other national slave trade." Tod was no match without the full backing of the US government, and it would never come.[48]

The eventual collapse of the Brazilian trade in enslaved persons was brought about by forces emanating from within. Fehrenbacher and McAfee explain that the end of the trade was the outcome of several factors. First, they credit aggressive search and seizure measures implemented by the British Royal Navy with no help from the United States. Second, the Brazilian government simply changed economic course. Led by a group of progressively minded citizens and foresighted businessmen pressure came to bear upon the emperor and his class that the benefits of the practice had run its course. Last, the demand for enslaved persons' labor had bottomed out due to a saturated market. In 1849 enslavers delivered close to 60,000 Africans to Brazil. By 1853, the trade had officially ended.[49]

For David Tod to have proclaimed at the end of his tenure in 1851, "I succeeded" in ending the Brazilian trade in enslaved persons was disingenuous.[50] However, history should credit Tod for his dogged efforts to bring it to an end by shining a constant light on the dark business. From the onset, he promptly acted and continued to do so until the end of his mission. Repeatedly he pressed Buchanan with letter after letter asking, pleading, and then demanding intervention. Yet, each time his appeals to Buchanan were ignored. Like an annoying gnat, Tod kept the issue in the diplomatic conscience of both countries.

By the time he left his post in August 1851, David Tod witnessed the beginning of the end of the trade in enslaved persons to Brazil. And if the United States Constitution remained unamended, he was still obliged to adhere to the slavery issue in its present form. Only time would tell, however, just how far politically he was willing to go to effect change.

During his years in Brazil, David Tod served three presidents. This fact alone marked the level of confidence that each successive administration had placed in him. He also served American citizens in residence while there as well as those traveling through. As usual, he befriended many by his acts of kindness and generosity and often opened "his purse to his fellow countrymen" who needed assistance.[51]

More important, his service ushered in a new era of diplomatic relations between the two countries. Emperor Dom Pedro II commended Tod "for the manner in which he always comported himself while exercising the functions under his charge . . . having, moreover, greatly recommended himself by his enlightened views, his circumspection, and other qualities for which he is distinguished, and for the successful manner in which he likewise endeavored to maintain, strengthen and draw closer the relations of good understanding and friendship happily existing between the two countries."[52]

6

Party Patriarch, 1851–1856

THE TOD FAMILY set sail for home on September 14, 1851. Before reaching the United States Tod's ship, the British steamer *Lay*, first stopped in England for a brief visit to the Great Exhibition in London's Hyde Park.[1] After finally reaching New York, Tod proceeded to Washington to present his formal report to the new secretary of state, Daniel Webster, before arriving home on November 25.[2]

He had been gone four years, four months and 14 days.[3] He had missed the simple things, he said, and looked forward to "living in a quiet, unpretending style" at his beloved Brier Hill. Visitors, he said, could find him hard at work at his "true vocation," farming.[4] Like any true Democrat, David Tod still wished to portray himself as a virtuous hardworking farmer behind horse and plow, tilling the soil to plant his crops. Although Brier Hill was a functioning farm it was because of farmhands gainfully employed there. Tod himself committed his hands to farming no more than his father had. His crops were the least of his concerns. Tod's interests during the period would continue to shift between the needs of his expanding coal and iron enterprises and his ongoing preoccupation with politics.

His stately house was "a long wooden building of a story and a half, with a verandah all the length of the west front," which provided a splendid view of the setting sun at day's end .[5] The walls inside the house were soon adorned with "Gancho implements and Brazilian curiosities" that the family brought back from their sojourn. It was not unusual to see the governor, as he was called, standing on his porch in some animated exchange with a small group of visitors or well-wishers.

Tod's businesses performed quite nicely during his time away and the numbers confirm this. During his absence, coal shipments to Cleveland had quadrupled. In 1849 nearly 27,000 tons reached the docks on the Lake Erie shore and by 1853 that number would reach 99,899 tons.[6] Tod soon realized that to keep pace with the growing demand for his coal, he had to look seriously at the new railroad systems that had crept in and through the Mahoning valley. A road from Warren to Cleveland was already in the planning stages by this time. A charter for the Cleveland & Mahoning Railroad was obtained in 1848 not long after Tod landed in Brazil. By 1857, the C&M RR connected Cleveland to Youngstown.[7] His grandson later recorded that Tod "was obliged to devote himself energetically to the task of placing his affairs in good working and profitable condition."[8] With his attention focused on business, he would attempt to put his political interests aside. Although Tod once said that "coal mining is a pretty profitable concern,—much more so . . . than diplomacy," he could not resist the strong appeal of partisan politics.[9] And in an all-too-familiar pattern, in the afterglow of his triumphant homecoming, Democrats summoned Tod back to the political arena. Sometimes he managed the affairs of both concurrently, sometimes not.

During Tod's absence, Ohio had taken progressive measures. Some aspects of the Black Laws were repealed in 1849 "including registration and bond requirements for black immigrants."[10] Ohio had also adopted a new state constitution in 1851 that, among other measures, continued to deny Blacks and women the right to vote.[11] In 1850, while Tod was in Brazil, the US Congress adopted the Fugitive Slave Act, which "required all citizens to assist officials in apprehending black fugitives in their midst." Antislavery proponents, abolitionists, and "somnolent" Northerners were outraged by the congressional overreach.[12]

While he wrestled with the trade in enslaved persons in Brazil, slavery continued to be a growing source of bitter political dispute and sectional resentment in the states. Tod's return brought him back just in time to witness and experience the decade of the 1850s, which saw the United States move inextricably down a self-destructive path fueled by the contentious slavery issue.

Even before the war with Mexico but more so since it ended, the curse of manifest destiny motivated proponents on all sides of the slavery issue to stake claims to newly acquired Western territories. The massive territory acquired from Mexico reignited the slavery issue that had been simmering for three decades. The movement toward statehood for these territories ushered in sectional conflict where "Free-soilers considered the North the aggrieved party" and proslavery Southerners the aggressors.[13] Southerners wanted slavery expanded into the new territories while Northerners and Free-Soilers desired to keep it in check. Each territorial acquisition and each act to chart its future was fraught with dangers and risked upsetting the balance of power in Congress. The Missouri Compromise of 1820 managed to mollify all sides of the slavery issue for a time. By agreement, slavery was prohibited north of the parallel 36° 30'. But Democrats, particularly in the Southern slavery states, clamored for states' rights and the expansion of slavery. The Wilmot Proviso intended to limit the spread of slavery in the territory gained from Mexico and although it passed in the House of Representatives, it failed in the Senate. But the South saw the measure as another threat to its economic and social norms of existence. It also revealed the growing sectional alignment that was taking shape. But the future of the new Western territory still needed a plan.

A series of measures that came to be known as the Compromise of 1850 attempted to placate the sections by bringing California into the Union as a free state while banning the slave trade in the nation's capital. Two of its most controversial features were the strengthening of the Fugitive Slave Law and leaving the fate of slavery in the New Mexico and Utah Territories to popular sovereignty. Abolitionists and antislavery Northerners were outraged by the measure.[14] Far from perfect, it accomplished and sustained a tepid albeit temporary peace.

By 1852, at just 47 years of age, Tod was viewed by Ohio Democrats as "a party patriarch."[15] Campaigning for members of the Democratic Party was a duty he relished and one he was all too familiar with performing. With his finances in excellent shape and with Maria and the children in good health, he was free to travel about the state to help Democratic candidates. His pledge to "labor diligently through the campaign for the election of [Franklin] Pierce" for president in 1852 earned Tod yet another title among Democrats of Ohio: "the noble champion of democracy."[16]

Franklin Pierce, a New Hampshire Democrat with Southern sympathies faced off against the Whig candidate Winfield Scott of Virginia. General Scott was a career soldier who rose to fame during the Mexican War. Although a Southerner by birth Scott had no appeal among Southerners because of his antislavery views. His candidacy was the result of sectional wrangling within the struggling Whig Party as leaders therein denied Millard Fillmore the nomination. Instead, they gave in to the demands of the Southern delegates when the platform endorsed the Fugitive Slave Law. This infuriated the Northern delegates. With such rank disagreement among the Whigs, the party could not last, and Scott would become the last Whig candidate to run for president.[17] Stumping for Pierce in Ohio, Tod attacked Whigs by linking them with the Federalists of old by claiming they supported such measures as the Alien and Sedition Act, the national bank, and protective tariffs. It was old-school rhetoric to be sure but material he found comfortable working with. But it was his aggressive personal attacks on Scott's integrity that riled the general's supporters to rush to their candidate's defense.[18] During a speech at Wooster, Tod claimed that Scott had grown so desperate for the presidency in recent years that his appeals for favor knew no shame. The general, said Tod, was "one day a Native American" and in another "ready to kiss the blarney stone with the Irishman and worship the blessed Virgin." The comment certainly smacked of anti-immigrant and anti–Roman Catholicism sentiment that had recently manifested in the political movement identified as the Know-Nothing Party. One Irishman in the crowd that day sprang to his feet in defense of Scott and shouted at Tod, "You lie sir, Gen. Scott declares that he is a Protestant, and I shall vote for him!"[19] But that sentiment was in the minority that November as Pierce "thoroughly crushed" Scott and the Whigs so much so that the party "would never recover," writes one historian.[20]

It was not too long after Pierce's victory that Tod was rumored to be the next secretary of the interior along with other contenders: James Buchanan, Henry Wise, and Sam Houston of Texas. Tod backers thought the former minister was "a deserving democrat and a gentleman who would bring dignity and talents to any station he might be appointed to."[21] But Pierce settled on Michigan's Robert McClelland.

President Pierce's four-year term helped to accelerate the shift in sectional divide of the country that coalesced around the Democratic Party's cultural and political values. Pierce, writes historian James McPherson, was "acceptable to all factions and safe on slavery despite his Yankee background." The transformation "of southern Whigs into Democrats," explains McPherson, "was made easier by the increasing friendliness of northern Democrats toward the South." This was evident when the party platform guaranteed adherence to the Compromise of 1850 with special emphasis on its support of the Fugitive Slave Law. The Pierce Administration did not disappoint and remained true to its word. Simply put, writes McPherson, "Pierce fulfilled southern expectations."[22]

But Pierce was not alone among his Northern Democratic brethren. He joined such men as Senator Stephen Douglas of Illinois. The zealous lawmaker was an emerging leader of the Democratic Party and a leading voice in Congress when it came to the slavery issue. It was Douglas who brought the Kansas-Nebraska Act to the floor of the US Senate in 1854. The act proposed that new settlers in Kansas should decide the slavery issue through popular sovereignty. Douglas maintained that the plan, which would have nullified the Missouri Compromise, was to help settle the territories quickly so that a transcontinental railroad could be built to California.[23] One thing was for sure: As the nation expanded westward the Slave Power in Congress hoped to spread there with it. Stephen Douglas gave them that chance. On the surface, the use of popular sovereignty was a splendid democratic idea but no one could have predicted the ulterior and coordinated plans to control the outcome. Proslavery and antislavery forces would descend on Kansas to directly influence the outcome. Each congressional measure, despite its intended purposes, seemed only to drive both sides farther apart.

To Ohio's Sen. Salmon P. Chase, a leading member of the Free-Soil Party, the Kansa-Nebraska Act symbolized the assault by pro-slavery advocates upon territories once considered to be safe from its incursion. "Freedom was on the defensive," writes historian Eric Foner, and Chase's observation "was widely accepted in the North."[24] The act had a unifying effect among different quarters. Chase joined fellow Ohioans Joshua Giddings and Rufus Spalding to thwart Douglas's plan and denounced any further effort at compromising with the Slave Power in the south. The anti-Douglas plan brought like-minded Democrats, Whigs, and Free-Soilers together in Columbus in July to "formalize their opposition." And despite Douglas's obvious attachment to the measure, others, writes Stephen E. Maizlish, clearly saw it as a new threat to the current yet delicate equilibrium of power.²⁵ The political events in Ohio were signs of a sectional crisis unfolding upon the land. The notion of permitting slavery beyond the Mississippi River further complicated the political power struggle in Washington and added growing discord among the parties, particularly among the Middle West states.

As the sectional conflict between proslavery and antislavery factions continued to heat up Tod supported Douglas's popular sovereignty plan but just how he felt about the Illinois senator's views on the Kansas-Nebraska Act is difficult to determine at this stage. No speeches or notes of Tod relating to this matter exist. What evidence there is sheds little light on the subject. One journal reported that Tod was wholeheartedly against the bill. "He thinks it anti-Democratic and uncalled for," announced one Ohio newspaper, "and thinks that Douglas could not have more effectually killed himself if he had cut both jugular veins."²⁶ This opinion would prove to be far off the mark on both matters. If any paper could claim to know Tod best, it would be the dependable party standard-bearer the *Trumbull Democrat*. It is most likely to have captured Tod's true positions over the years. Historically protective of Tod, the newspaper reported discussing the matter with his supporters, men who were characterized as "old and particular friends [of Tod], men of good standing truth and integrity . . . and they inform us that he is in favor of the bill."²⁷ This position would be consistent with previous ones in that Tod would rather let the people decide their own course through popular sovereignty instead of Congress ramming through legislation, especially ones dealing with delicate and controversial issues such as slavery. Critics would later claim that all the bill did was nothing more than temporarily interrupt a tenuous coexistence between abolitionists and the slaveocracy held together by the Missouri Compromise of 1820. Yet what Douglas and Pierce and a multitude of other supporters like Tod favored was sure to unleash "turmoil and strife that threatened to tear the country apart."²⁸

During the Ohio gubernatorial campaign of 1855 Tod stayed in front of the public eye as he worked for Gov. William Medill. Medill was a former congressman with a long record of supporting slavery's expansion. He was very much an "old line" Pierce Democrat who was "pro-slavery to the core" or, as the *Meigs County Telegraph* described him, "pro-slavery to the bitter end."²⁹ The governor was up against a formidable antislavery candidate in Salmon P. Chase, head of the new Republican Party in Ohio.

The development of sectional identities within the Democratic Party strained its cohesiveness, but they maintained a fragile existence. The Whig Party, on the other hand, fared far worse. In the words of one distinguished scholar, the Kansas-Nebraska Act cast the Whig Party into "a slow agonizing death." While the Whig party breathed its last "the purely sectional [antislavery] Republican party" emerged to take its place.[30] The Republican Party scored a major victory in Ohio when Chase, the outraged Free-Soiler that he was, defeated Medill.[31] Chase's antislavery message overshadowed Medill's economic development theme. Chase's victory was a major step in the national ascendency of this new sectional party. His success in Ohio catapulted his name to the top of the list for potential presidential consideration in 1856. For the moment, Chase was every bit the sectional candidate in Ohio, capturing a majority of the votes in the northern antislavery part of the state.[32] As Ohio's leading Republican, Chase believed that Congress had the authority to control slavery in the territories. This philosophy was in direct contrast to those like Pierce and Douglas, who wanted the settlers of the territories to decide the slavery issue. It was one of the lasting consequences of Pierce's handling of the Kansas-Nebraska situation.

While typical political rancor befell the country at large, abolitionists and proslavery advocates had rushed to infiltrate the Kansas and Nebraska Territories to control the outcome of the elections. Intimidation, coercion, and violence committed by both sides to affect election results came to bear upon settlers. Threats transformed into unspeakable acts of injury and murder on both sides. In November 1855 1,500 pro-slavery ruffians from Missouri invaded Kansas. Their plan was to overthrow a duly elected state constitution supported by a Free-Soil majority. Overseeing these events was the territorial governor of Kansas, Wilson Shannon. Shannon, the former governor of Ohio appointed by Pierce, tried to convince both sides to stand down and avert further violence. But a bloody standoff in Lawrence between Free-Soilers and slavery proponents would stain the land under Shannon's watch.

So rampant was the violence that Kansas became known as Bleeding Kansas. One of the most celebrated leaders of the Free-Soil movement was the fiery abolitionist John Brown. Before his rise to fanatical fame John Brown spent much of his early life in Ohio's Western Reserve, where he once partnered with Tod's brother-in-law, Col. Simon Perkins in Akron. His antislavery convictions were also learned in the Western Reserve. The restless abolitionist was a man of action and after the passage of the Kansas-Nebraska Act, his mission led him to Kansas. There, Brown and his faithful followers, who included several of his sons, chose five proslavery settlers and mercilessly butchered them in retaliation for the murder of five Free-Soilers by proslavery activists. In Brown's mind, he had served justice in Kansas on that spring day in May 1856. The retaliatory violence continued unchecked on both sides. The events at Lawrence and Pottawatomie, observed McPherson, "escalated the bushwhacking war in Kansas." The uncontrolled civil war within the Kansas Territory continued to inch the country at large toward what seemed an inevitable split.[33]

There was enough blame for the bloodletting at Kansas to go around; from Douglas and those who voted for the Kansas-Nebraska Bill, to Pierce, to the territorial governors he appointed, and to the murderous zealots on both sides of the slavery question. But it was during Wilson Shannon's tenure that so much violence, including Brown's crime spree, occurred. Perhaps Tod had a political ax to grind when he went after his former ally Shannon at a rally in Pittsburgh. Addressing a crowd of thousands Tod criticized Pierce and his Kansas territorial governors for their failed policies. Shannon, said Tod, not only mismanaged affairs but, worse, *"He was a drunkard."* Angry and stung by this personal attack, Shannon denied the allegation in a very public letter to Tod. "You were willing to blast and destroy my character," Shannon hit back, to gain a political favor or an appointment by attempting to place "the whole responsibility of the Kansas difficulties on my shoulders." It was clear, Shannon wrote to Tod, that securing the truth about his character "did not suit your purpose."

The goal of the Democrats of course was to win the presidential contest at any costs. To do so they had to ensure that they distanced themselves entirely from Pierce and the failures associated with his administration even at the risk of losing old friendships. Tod's treatment of Shannon demonstrated his political drive and his indifference to feelings. In his desire to see his party victorious he was not above utilizing "bold and reckless impudence . . . on an old personal and political friend," as Shannon charged.[34] And, it may very well be that Tod just did not approve of Shannon's oversight of Kansas. But Tod certainly was not alone in enlisting this type of aggressive campaign rhetoric during this tumultuous decade.

In June 1856, the new Republican Party nominated John Frémont for president. Without a Whig candidate to support in the presidential contest the *Western Reserve Chronicle* lent its support to Frémont, but it still relished attacking Tod and his Democratic brethren. The Democratic Party was now under the influence of the "slave-ocrats," charged the *Chronicle*. As the *Trumbull Democrat* "summoned the rank and file" to their cause, the *Chronicle* expected that all free-soil loving Northerners would come out for Frémont and the Republicans. The editor of the *Chronicle* warned its readers to get out for Frémont because if the Republicans lost "the burning shame, and the fearful consequences will be ours!" Now was the time that "every freeman vote . . . the cause of freedom and Fremont."[35]

The Democrats selected Pennsylvania's James Buchanan for their presidential candidate, who secured the nomination from Pierce. Prior to Buchanan's selection at the party's convention a who's who of Democratic elites had been surveyed by party leaders to lead the ticket. The names of R. M. T. Hunter and Gov. Henry Wise of Virginia; Douglas of Illinois; Lewis Cass of Michigan; Gov. Andrew Johnson of Tennessee; and William Allen, Samuel Medary, William Medill, and David Tod of Ohio all were given consideration.[36] But it was the former secretary of state, Buchanan, who was acceptable to both Northern and Southern Democrats due to his strong stance on states' rights. Virginia's governor and former minister to Brazil Henry Wise, enthusiastically regarded "Buchanan the choice of the Virginia Slave-breeders."[37] The candidate stood not only for popular-sovereignty, but for the enforcement of the Fugitive Slave Law and Southern "domestic safety and tranquility." He was against "that abolition fusion which once more threaten[ed]" the institution of slavery. Southern Democrats saw James Buchanan as an "uncompromising enemy of their enemies; the devoted advocate of their constitutional rights."[38]

Northerners and Republicans saw the messy, bloody situation in Kansas as proof of Democratic leadership gone wrong. Popular sovereignty, Republicans also feared, would usher in slavery. Pierce's indecisiveness and mismanagement resulted in murder at the hands of guerilla vigilantes on both sides who dispensed their own brand of justice. The violence that occurred in the Kansas Territory, writes historian Jonathan Halperin Earle, "dramatized how significantly the Pierce administration was in thrall to the Slave Power."[39] And Buchanan was no better than Pierce, they argued. Why let Buchanan do to America what Pierce did to Kansas?

With the presidential contest set Ohio's Democratic Party flag bearer David Tod stumped the Buckeye State in support of the ticket. Although as secretary of state, Buchanan demonstrated little diplomatic courtesy toward Tod when the latter sought direction as minister to Brazil, Tod nonetheless exhibited party fidelity and soldiered on for Buchanan.

One of the largest Democratic rallies was held in the antislavery town of Salem, Ohio, where an estimated crowd of 20,000 had gathered. Salem was founded by Quakers and had a reputation as a progressive community; it played an active role on the Underground Railroad and was the home of the *Anti-Slavery Bugle* newspaper. In 1850 the town was also the site of the country's third Women's Rights Convention. On the surface, Salem seemed like an unusual place for a Democratic rally but there had evolved within the party an antislavery faction known as the Barnburners.[40] The Barnburners, led by New York's John Van Buren, son of the nation's eighth president, were "heirs of the Jacksonian political tradition, and were accustomed to couch their political arguments in terms which would appeal to [free] labor." Their feelings were not rooted in morality. Their goal was to support Western expansion with free white labor and contain the spread of slavery and free Black populations. In fact, writes Eric Foner, Barnburners wanted to ensure critics that they cared no more for enslaved Black people than they did for free Black people. If Western expansion were to come about, let the territories fill with white laborers. Besides, the younger Van Buren insisted, the white working class could not coexist in communities where slavery was permitted.[41] Both the younger Van Buren and his father came to believe that their "party must not be permitted to sanction the spread of slavery."[42] But this was a minority position among Northern Democrats and many of their adherents would soon leave the party.

Tod, loyal Martin Van Buren supporter that he was, shared the campaign stump at Salem with "Prince John" Van Buren.[43] Remarks of the speakers went unreported; the size of the crowd drew the headlines. Van Buren's words must have endorsed the containment of slavery relative to the promotion of free soil for white laboring men. And one can only presume that Tod's comments dovetailed with those of the Barnburner Van Buren. Why else would Tod be there? Was he adopting a free soil, free labor position? Perhaps. Later reports, one in Washington's *National Era*, explain that "the burdens of David Tod's speeches" during this campaign was to convince the people that Kansas would enter the Union as a free state and that Buchanan Democrats "were opposed to the extension of Slavery."[44] But Buchanan had advocated no such thing. If Tod was adopting an ideology to contain the spread of slavery it was one based on the expansion of free soil and more important one resolved through popular sovereignty. There were indications that he preferred to see slavery contained because he favored the spread of free labor in the new territories. Without documented evidence we will never know for sure. What we do know is that his position on finances never wavered and would forever remain "radical" because he "demanded a specie currency, strict regulation of banks, individual liability of bank directors, and unlimited liability of corporation stockholders."[45]

Traveling the speaking circuit as much as Tod did, regardless of his message, came with its share of perils. One occurrence may be reason to surmise the lack of documentation regarding Tod's speeches. On the road to Kalida with congressional candidate Alfred P. Edgerton and Common Pleas judge candidate F. C. LeBlond, Tod's satchel was stolen. Not only were his papers gone but so, too, was his wardrobe. Always mindful of his appearance he borrowed a shirt and collar from his companions. Edgerton's shirt "wanted several inches to enable one of the more capacious form of Tod to crowd into." A knife slit up the back of the shirt remedied the tight situation. So, "thus appareled, he appeared upon the stand, and made the best showing he could under the circumstances."[46] While Tod endeared himself to Democratic crowds, critics characterized him as "a very egotistic and much over-rated man."[47] As seasoned as Tod was by this time, he continued to show no hesitancy to go on the political offensive for Buchanan.

The next four years would show that Buchanan's election victory resolved nothing for North, South, Democrats, or Republicans. The Buchanan administration would prove not only disastrous for the Democratic Party but for the nation as well. The South would continue to draw in upon itself while erecting a hardened defensive wall under the banner of the Democratic Party. Northern Democrats, meanwhile, despite capturing the presidency, began to fracture. Prominent figures lost their party identity and abandoned it altogether. Main's Hannibal Hamlin, for one, had proclaimed that he no longer identified with the Democratic Party because it represented nothing more than the preservation and perpetuation of slavery. "I did not learn my principles, and shall not practice," said the future vice president, "in that school."[48]

Northern Democrats saw the slavery issue as a states' rights question whereas Whigs and their successors the new Republicans viewed it in moral terms. Despite his observations and disgust with the practice of slavery in Brazil, Tod continued to avoid moral questions and clung to the law stating, for example, "that the Fugitive [Slave] Law was [sanctioned] by the Constitution, and is therefore Constitutional."[49] One thing was clear in trying to understand the philosophy of his politics: He was a strict Constitutionalist. Stephen Douglas once said; "I deal with slavery as a political question involving questions of public policy."[50] Tod adhered to the same outlook and in Douglas he had found a new champion of the Democratic Party. How long hardcore Democrats like Tod and Douglas would remain attached to a party with factions hell-bent on protecting and expanding slavery at the expense of free labor or even the Union itself remained to be seen. And as the sectional crisis began to heat up the citizenry began to identify itself based upon its geographic location: Northerner, Southerner, Westerner.

7

A Private in the Ranks, 1857–1859

THE ADMINISTRATION OF President-Elect James Buchanan was taking shape as the March 1857 inauguration date approached. Tod's name was mentioned again for a potential cabinet position. But just like four years before when president-elect Pierce was considering Democrats to fill his cabinet Buchanan passed on Tod. If cabinet appointments were based on hard work and effort David Tod's name was as deserving as any. It was to Tod's advantage, however, that he did not end up in the cabinet because Buchanan's term was to end in disaster.[1] Tod was lucky to keep his distance from the fifteenth president. What would become known as the Secession Winter of 1860–1861 occurred during the last months of Buchanan's term and saw the unraveling of the Union that led the country to civil war. Steering clear of Buchanan's administration also gave Tod's political career a new purpose.

In the meantime, in the Mahoning valley, production at Tod's mining operations continued to bring its owner the pecuniary comforts and freedom to travel about the state and country in pursuit of his political interests. As a successful businessman, he was regarded as generous and fair by some but tough and uncaring by others. He had no patience if he thought he was being treated unfairly. A series of coal strikes by miners demanding higher wages, stretching from eastern Pennsylvania to the Mahoning valley took place in 1859. Owners, who were in no mood for such tactics, simply dismissed the strikers outright and hired new men who were willing to work. It was not until November that miners at Brier Hill finally felt "disposed to have a voice in fixing the amount of their wages" and walked off the job, shutting down the operation of Tod's mines.[2]

Tod did not take kindly to these demonstrations, and he moved to ensure that it would not happen again. Through his established political contacts, he sought legislation in the Ohio General Assembly to prevent workers from striking. Specifically, he proposed that such action be considered a felony. But workers across the state rallied behind an effective lobbying campaign coordinated by a conglomeration of Cincinnati unions. Their efforts succeeded in killing any momentum for the bill.[3] Tod's reaction to this strike left a stain on his moniker, "lover of the laboring classes."[4]

However, Tod could be equally unpretentious with workers in his employ. A small group of Englishmen visiting Brier Hill was amazed to observe the social interaction between Tod and the driver of his wagon team. The foreigners were taken aback when Tod's hired hand, during a rest along the roadside, "came down and sat at the fire beside us with perfect freedom, and entered into a conversation with Mr. Tod, which was very amusing to us, displaying as it did the utmost democratic equality, and unfolding a picture of social manners which was new and strange to us. It was continued in the same style in the wagon but was sadly characterized by extreme irreverence."[5]

Tod's connection with the everyday citizen was also on display during his political rallies. After addressing crowds by the thousands, it was common for the distinguished party leader to mingle with the locals. Refreshments and glad tidings were customary after a long day of speech making. Spirits were known to flow fast and freely and the measure of a man was judged by the amount of liquor he consumed. Tod was aware of this and would often put his tolerance to the test. One such instance occurred in Perry Township where Tod and local Democratic candidate William Sawyer, sat down at a table where a "jug and glasses were soon deposited." Sawyer was known among the locals for possessing a "more than ordinary capacity for holding beverages considered intoxicating." After he poured his drink, he handed the jug to Tod who promptly filled his glass to "the very brim!" Tod's ample portion caught the attention of the locals. After he thoroughly consumed his drink, Sawyer expressed his mortification at the public insult leveled by Tod. "Tod, that's the meanest trick I ever had played upon me . . . in the presence of my own constituents, who regard me as one of the best drinkers in the district," the candidate grumbled. Sawyer went on to admonish Tod that if he should lose his election, he would attribute it to "this villainous trick."[6]

Within days of Buchanan's inauguration, the Supreme Court handed down the highly anticipated ruling in *Dred Scott v. Sandford*. Dred Scott was enslaved in Missouri when he sued for his freedom. His enslaver had taken him into free territory for a period of time and Scott believed that the act of residing therein forever changed his status to that of a free man. Forced back to Missouri he then sued for his freedom. Through appeals, the case made its way to the Supreme Court where the Southern-prejudiced bench sided against Scott. In a seven-to-two majority, the court determined that Scott, whether enslaved or free, was not a citizen of the United States and, therefore, had no right to bring suit in federal court. Moreover, the court's decision brought into question the power of Congress to prohibit slavery in the territories. Consequently, measures such as the Missouri Compromise of 1820 were deemed beyond congressional authority and thus unconstitutional. The opinion of the aging Chief Justice Roger Taney, writes historian Kenneth Stampp, did not bring resolution or consensus. Rather, in an act of "judicial activism" the court's decision sanctioned "uncompromising defiance of abolitionists, free soilers, and Republicans" alike.[7] Referring to the court's activism, one Ohio citizen railed that a "great injustice has undoubtedly been done to the 'North.'" But the days of passivity had passed, he wrote. Now "it behooves us to let the oppressors and the world know, that we *silently* submit no longer."[8]

Empowered by the court's decision and a president sympathetic to the mendacious Southern Slave Power in the halls of Congress, a vindicated South felt emboldened. Southerners celebrated the historic "bombshell from the Supreme Court." Congress, proclaimed South Carolina's *Yorkville Enquirer*, was neutralized on the slavery issue and, "henceforth can have nothing to do with the subject." With one final declaration "the precedents of the Missouri compromise, the Wilmot proviso, and all other unconstitutional laws and proceedings of the government during the last forty years on the slavery question," wrote the *Enquirer*, "had its course plainly and authoratively marked out."[9] The court's decision, Southerners and Democrats believed, "put to rest antislavery claptrap about violations of sacred compacts by deciding that the Missouri restriction had always been unconstitutional and, therefore, void."[10] Unfettered Southerners would look to exploit their newfound political freedom as the sectional crisis continued to unfold.

But the North, behind the Republican Party, steadfastly resisted their attempts. Ohio Republicans condemned the *Dred Scott* decision "as anticonstitutional, anti-republican, anti-democratic, incompatible with [state's] rights and destructive of personal security." Senator Ben Wade said the decision was "a disgrace to human nature and as false to the principles of the Constitution as it was to history."[11]

In the three years following the court's decision, Northern Democrats who favored the spread of free labor, like David Tod, watched as their fickle party unity began to unravel. Republicans made political hay out of the Democrats' internal woes. The *Western Reserve Chronicle* accused Northern Democrats of turning "its back upon the Freedom-loving North, and resolved to fight for the South the battle of extending slavery upon free Territory."[12] Stephen Douglas had broken with Buchanan over Kansas, while Ohio Democrats like Tod and Edwin Stanton, remained silent over the Dred Scott decision.[13] Other Northern Democrats publicly applauded the court's decision. Ohio's *Eaton Democrat* believed that the events of March showed that "sectionalism will cease to be a dangerous element in our political contests."[14] It could not have been more wrong. Meanwhile Michigan's Kalamazoo *Gazette* regarded as "the most able and influential of all the interior democratic papers [in the state] bolted its party" over the Dred Scott decision.[15] The differing opinions were testing the unity of the Democratic Party in the North but it had the opposite effect in the South.

In the meantime, the political cycle had no end for Tod the campaigner. From presidential contests to congressional affairs, to gubernatorial races, for Tod the campaign seasons were like the seasonal changes of the year. As each season turned to the next, Tod, ever the cheery party workhorse, put on his harness and readily immersed himself in the next fray to help pull candidates to the finish line. The next race at hand was Ohio's gubernatorial contest of 1857 and the Democrats wondered who could challenge the incumbent Republican governor, Salmon Chase.

With the party convention scheduled in August it was early spring when leaders began to search for potential candidates. The Lancaster *Eagle* and the *Ashland Union* came out early for Tod even though they had remembered his public disdain for seeking elective office. "We all know how averse" he is to this notion, however, "there is no man in Ohio who could command as many Democratic votes . . . who has given so much disinterested and efficient labor here for the service of the party." A recent daguerreotype image of Tod had been in circulation. His "honest face," the *Union* editor warmly wrote, "is engraven upon every Democratic heart, and the echo of his eloquent and logical words are yet upon the ear of every Democratic voter of Ashland county." He was "the best specimen of a Buckeye Statesman . . . and [we] demand that he put on his old harness, and come into the arena."[16]

Tod once again moved quickly to quash any movement on this front. He was not interested in seeking elective office and he fell back on old excuses, mainly that business prevented him from exercising the time required to commit to the responsibilities of the office should he emerge victorious. This excuse, however, seems disingenuous given the time he spent on the road politicking around the state for the party since his return from Brazil.[17]

With Tod out, Democrats chose Henry B. Payne for their gubernatorial candidate. Payne, a seasoned state officeholder and Buchanan supporter, prepared to square off against the incumbent Chase. Sectional issues were sure to take precedence in the campaign. Worse for Chase, economic troubles and failing banks gave the Democratic nominee and his supporters even more ammunition with which to attack him.[18] One Democratic paper believed the selection was an easy one to make. Re-elect Chase and realize more bank failures or vote for Payne and install a strong independent treasury.[19] For those enamored of the sectional crisis over the slavery issue there was plenty of front-page news to go around.

Once again, Tod hit the trail for Payne. But rumors that Tod was not so excited about Payne began to swirl. Payne's unabashed support of Buchanan may have soured Tod. And it did not take long before reports of Tod abandoning the party altogether, at the very least its gubernatorial candidate, began to surface.[20] As whispers of his disdain for Payne increased Tod had to come out with a strong public statement to put the rumor to rest. He had not "abandoned the Democratic party" he said and proclaimed to be "one of Mr. Payne's firmest and warmest supporters."[21] And he was true to his word for Tod stumped tirelessly for Payne as late as September.[22]

Not surprisingly the campaign focused on the issues of slavery: free soil, abolitionism, state's rights, congressional authority, among others. As for Chase, the avowed abolitionist, Democrats labeled him a "Black" Republican due to his calls for racial equality. This last virtue was rare even among progressive Republicans. In the end, Chase narrowly defeated Payne in a race made close due to the third-party candidacy of a Whig, Philadelph Van Trump. For Tod, it would not be the last time he saw Van Trump.

The Chase triumph was not a huge victory for abolitionists. Ohio was much too divided for that assumption. Adam Goodheart reminds us that Ohio resembled the nation where "the upper and lower halves . . . viewed each other with suspicion." Southern Ohioans saw their fellow citizens in the North as "wild-eyed abolitionists" while northern Ohioans viewed the southern half as "lackeys of their slaveholding neighbors."[23]

Although Tod expressed no desire to abandon his party there were growing signs of his and other leading Democrats' discontent with Buchanan. The antecedents of these trace to Buchanan's coercive support of the Lecompton Constitution, a pro-slavery instrument drafted and passed by a fraudulent minority of citizens in Kansas in June 1857 in preparation for statehood. Clauses within this constitution protected slavery. It received the overwhelming support from the nation's 15 Southern slavery states as well as from President Buchanan. Speaking out against its deceitful ratification process that December was the popular-sovereignty senator from Illinois, Stephen Douglas. Whenever Tod was in Washington, he was often spotted with his new political exemplar Douglas.[24]

In a powerful speech on the floor of the US Senate in December 1857, Douglas stated that his objection had nothing to do with the content of the Lecompton Constitution or whether it passed or not. What the people of Kansas decided, asserted Douglas, was their business and not his or anyone else's. He also argued that it was not the responsibility of the US Congress to approve a state constitution. That obligation belonged to the qualified voters of the territory to determine their future course. However, it was overwhelmingly apparent, argued Douglas, that the proceedings in Kansas were fraudulent. Douglas came under attack from members of his own party, namely Buchanan supporters, and especially those in the South. Popular sovereignty must prevail, Douglas insisted, regardless of one's party.[25]

Douglas's stance received overwhelming support from proponents of popular sovereignty and from Democrats in the North like Tod. Republicans like Benjamin Wade and the influential Republican congressman from Indiana, Schuyler Colfax, also gave Douglas's measure support. Douglas's anti-Lecompton efforts eventually gained enough support to get the act back before the voters for ratification. To the Northern states and their antislavery sentiment, the Lecompton fiasco was an alarming example of the depths to which the proslavery power was willing to descend. Douglas would remain a Democrat but he fumed at Buchanan's unscrupulous leadership tactics. An irreparable divide now existed between Douglas and Buchanan, leaving Democrats to support one or the other. If the Democratic Party was not fractured, the divisions were growing more defined. Tod was by now a solid Douglas man.[26]

Douglas's anti-Lecompton/popular sovereignty arguments had resonated with David Tod. State constitutions should be determined by the will of the people. The citizens of each state deserved that reverent bond with their provincial constitution. This had been Tod's position since the beginning of his political career. For as much as Tod agreed with Douglas on the ratification process, he found fault with Buchanan's attempt to force the proslavery measure down the throats of the Kansas majority.

Where supporters of Buchanan planned to address crowds on the Lecompton matter, Tod declined as he came out *"anti-Lecompton up to the hub."*[27] One columnist reported, "We learn from Mr. Tod, personally, that he will not attend . . . any other meeting of the kind. He differs with the administration *only* on the one point of Lecompton, and thinks men may be and are still good democrats, although they happen to differ and think as they please about Kansas affairs. He is not disposed to and will not attempt to embarrass the administration, but he will not address Lecompton meetings. He is sensible in his position."[28] So, Tod, like Douglas, remained loyal to his party and made every effort to help hold Democrats together in Ohio. In January 1858, a majority of the voters in Kansas rejected the Lecompton Constitution. Buchanan's poorly calculated "decision to stake most of his political capital on the Lecompton Constitution in Kansas," writes one historian, "was a blunder of the first magnitude."[29]

In the fall of 1858, longtime congressman Joshua Giddings was relinquishing office. The onetime Whig and founder of the Republican Party was a spirited abolitionist. Republicans and Democrats of the Twentieth

Congressional District, which included Ashtabula, Trumbull, and Mahoning Counties, convened to choose their candidates. Democrats met at Warren and, in his absence, nominated Tod for the seat. The problem was that Tod did not seek the nomination and, more important, did not want it.[30] "Business engagements," wrote the protesting and chagrined candidate again, "forbid me at this time, [from] assuming any new duties."[31] The excuse struck a familiar chord but it was certainly plausible considering the industrial transformation that the Mahoning valley had been undergoing, much of which was connected to Tod's energies. The beehive of activity surrounding Tod's coal enterprises during this time was everywhere apparent. He could have used the excuse with no exaggeration to shun a full-time political career.

"I greatly prefer the position of a private in the ranks of the Democratic party, to that of an officer or leader," Tod admitted. This stunning admonition is one of the most honest expressions made by Tod the politician and supports the assertion made earlier regarding his failed gubernatorial campaigns as well as his single term as a state senator. Campaigning for a fellow candidate had fewer and temporary responsibilities. He could step into and out of any contest at will and return to his family or business concerns whenever he needed. With that flexibility, he believed, "I can be of much greater service to the [party's] cause."[32] Holding office required a much deeper and prolonged commitment of time and service and to this he could not or did not want to pledge himself.

The actions of the Democrats of the Twentieth Congressional District however put Tod in quite a bind. Requesting to have his name removed after the nomination was made was not a straightforward process. To do so the party would have to hold another convention, and this would have been an embarrassment to the party. Reluctantly Tod acquiesced and became nothing more than a paper candidate. Reminiscent of his last campaign for office, he remained idle. His excuse last time was the ill health of his wife. This time it was a lack of will, which he freely admitted. Word of Tod's nomination delighted his old rivals at the *Western Reserve Chronicle*. Sure, Tod was "an able man, and popular with his party"; however, he "has had so much experience in being beaten in popular elections that he will without doubt, bear [another] defeat with resignation."[33] Editors Comfort Adams and George Hapgood also raised the possibility that Tod, who had felt negatively toward Buchanan over the Lecompton mess, found himself in an "unpleasant predicament of being forced to run as the candidate of a convention which was out and out in favor of the policy of Buchanan, when he himself . . . openly favored the Douglas movement."[34] He could not refute the charge.

The Republicans of the Twentieth Congressional District sent forth Tod's former student and law partner, the abolitionist John Hutchins, to replace Giddings. His relations with David Tod had remained friendly and cordial and would continue in this way indefinitely. In fact, in a minor lawsuit in which Tod was the plaintiff in a foreclosure matter, Hutchins's firm had recently represented Tod in the Trumbull County Court of Common Pleas.[35] Now, the two politically opposed each other, directly no less, for the first time. With the ticket set the combatants prepared to square off during the short campaign season. By the first week of October, "the canvass [was] pretty well under way." Hutchins stumped in Ashtabula County while his surrogates fanned out over Trumbull and Mahoning Counties. Tod, however, was "not on the stump, but . . . quietly mining 'black diamonds' [coal] for the Cleveland market." Thus did the interest and the energies of the two campaigns reflect the outcome of the election.[36] Voters came out for Hutchins 2,936 to Tod's 1,664.[37] The Republican's showing represented the strength of the antislavery sentiment in the district. A much-relieved Tod avoided public office.

Despite the results Tod, the solitary voice of the Democrats in the reserve still wrapped himself in his party's banner. But neither he nor any other Democrat could ignore what was happening in the country at large as the recent election revealed a climactic political shift of power in the corridors of Washington. In 1856, the Democrats held a decisive 29-to-21 majority over the greenhorn Republicans in the Congress. The election of 1858, however, demonstrated that the fledgling party was finding its wings. Its message of containment was gaining momentum; Republicans took control of the house 34 to 16.[38] The outcome was cause for concern for the Slave Power.

The Democrats' loss and power shift did nothing to diminish Tod's preference to stay ensconced among the rank and file of his party. Outside of his interests in Ohio, he also followed developments outside the state's borders. In Illinois, Tod's new political hero Stephen Douglas celebrated his reelection after fending off the challenge of the little known but worthy political challenger Abraham Lincoln in their senatorial race.

The two Illinoisans would soon have much to say about the ominous storm clouds rising over the nation's political landscape.

As much as Tod could have remained immersed in the political arena to offer his influence, his businesses also required his influence from time to time. The death of Jacob Perkins, president of the Cleveland & Mahoning Railroad, in January 1859, engendered Tod's rise to the presidency of the company.[39] His additional duties certainly lent credence to his excuse that he was too busy with business affairs to take on the responsibilities of an elective office. While Tod took over the reins handed him after Perkins's death, the country watched another Ohioan march to his own martyrdom and demise.

Since his bloodletting days in Kansas, the radical abolitionist John Brown had gone unnoticed. But he did not remain still. In fact, he had been busy raising funds and assembling a like-minded band of persons who committed themselves to support the radical revolutionary in his bold goal of finally ridding the land of slavery. In October 1859, Brown suddenly and dramatically reemerged in western Virginia. For three days, suspense gripped the nation following Brown's audacious raid upon the federal arsenal at Harper's Ferry. There, Brown hoped to seize munitions and lead a local uprising of enslaved men with plans to turn that into a full-scale revolt. His ill-advised scheme failed miserably. Federal forces under the command of Robert E. Lee apprehended Brown after a brief shoot-out. He was tried, convicted, and sentenced to hang in December. Virginia's governor Henry Wise, Tod's diplomatic predecessor in Brazil, could have commuted Brown's sentence to life in prison but his decision not to intervene sealed Brown's fate and made him a martyr to the abolitionist, antislavery cause.[40] His death provided little solace for Southerners. His raid and his ultimate plan of leading an uprising were just the sort of things that kept Southerners awake at night.

Days after Brown's execution, Democrats of Ohio's Twentieth Congressional District gathered in Warren to choose delegates to attend the national convention at Charleston, South Carolina, scheduled for the following April. There the delegates would select a candidate for president. In a scene that would play out similarly in Charleston, a minority of local Democrats loyal to Buchanan walked out of the Warren convention leaving behind a room filled with Douglas supporters. Promptly, the Douglas men chose Tod and Dr. D. B. Woods "to represent the Douglas wing" at Charleston. The assertion "that Buchananism is defunct in these parts" was premature. Not to be denied, the Buchanan boys chose their own delegates to Charleston.[41] The local split suggests that the district contained its fair share of Douglas Democrats who advocated popular sovereignty like Tod, and Buchanan backers who supported the president's position on slavery.

In the South, the political environment at Charleston was already on a dangerous footing. Radical Southern Democrats known as Fire-Eaters, despite such victories as *Dredd Scott,* felt hopeless about their cause and believed they had no alternative but to call for disunion. The Charleston *Mercury* questioned the sensibility of even holding a convention in the spring because the Democratic Party, it believed, was "under the control of the Northern States. The [upcoming] Charleston Convention ought to be a Convention of the Southern States, or should not assemble at all," it concluded.[42]

In the North, preservation of the Union had become a campaign rallying cry long before it became a battle cry. As Southern threats of secession intensified signs of Northern resistance and determination to hold the Union together began to emerge. Lending credence to political hyperbole was the raising of local militia units. Although local militia units were a long and time-honored tradition, the mood just seemed different these days.

Thus, when the Tod Artillery was "organized in Youngstown, in honor of the distinguished citizen Hon. David Tod" in March 1858 there was no questioning its purpose. There was too much in the political winds not to realize what was happening. When Tod presented a flag to the new unit at Brier Hill, he also delivered a stirring patriotic speech in which he admonished the unit to defend the Union and the Constitution. His words dripped with resistance and sacrifice. "God grant that our beloved country may never require your services in mortal combat," he prayed, but woe to the aggressors who would choose such a destructive, deceitful, and treasonable course. If hostilities should break out, "may the Tod Artillery be assigned the post of danger; and that you will . . . crown yourselves with glory." In such times you must "desert your mother, desert everything near and dear to you, before you desert" our flag. "Wet the dust" with your blood, he said, "before you let the Stars and Stripes of your country" fall upon the soil. "Should you ever meet the enemies of our country," foreign or domestic, he closed, jump into the fight and "let our flag be there."[43] These were not the words of a private in the ranks. These were the impassioned words of a political leader whose devotion to the Union was on full display and who seemed to have risen above sectional and partisan politics. Tod's marching orders that day to the artillery unit named after him were a self-fulfilling pledge to himself because when hostilities did indeed break out, he deserted the bosom of his beloved party and jumped into the fight. Given the circumstances, it was a splendid ceremony and reflected the martial spirit of the day. That spirit would be needed very soon.

8

A Conflict Cometh, 1859–1860

IT WAS ONE thing for politicians like Tod to call for patriotic defense of flag and country. It was another when God-fearing men concluded there was no other alternative left but to take up arms. Patriotic religious leaders from both the North and South claimed that God was on their side. In Cleveland, the Reverend J. C. White had abandoned any hope for peace. His goal, like that of so many others, was not just holding the Union together but a Union without slavery and like John Brown, he believed that it could only be accomplished through force. Abolitionists like Brown were frustrated by the slow pace and advocated violence to bring an end to slavery. His actions may have failed at Harper's Ferry, but they inspired religious leaders like White. "Slavery," White understood, "will not be done away with by oral suasion. It is not to be done away with by the 'Bible argument.'" So "that God might work out his own good purposes," White preached, "sacrifices [will be] needed and called for." In a moment of prescient reflection, he predicted just before Christmas 1859, that "a conflict cometh."[1]

"The link between religion and patriotism," writes J. Matthew Gallman, "took many forms [in the North]. Certainly, many observers had no trouble seeing Southern slaveholders as essentially immoral, leading to the conclusion that God sided with the Union."[2] One New York bishop further tethered religion to "political stability" when he proclaimed that his parishioners stood ready to "fight to the death for support of the Constitution, the Government and the laws."[3]

Not all in the North agreed with this sentiment. For most Northerners, "abolitionism . . . remained a dirty word."[4] Critics, like the *Detroit Free Press*, wrote that after three decades of advocating abolition little had been accomplished. Abolitionism had "not made one negro free . . . has not made one foot of soil free [and] has accomplished no good, but a world of mischief." Critics of abolitionists reckoned that their efforts, well intended as they were, had made matters worse for those held in bondage. "It has made it necessary that greater discipline should be exercised in the government of the slaves" and as for the current political mood of the country, "it has produced a state of feeling between the South and North, which, if it shall not be abated, will cause the dismemberment of the Union."[5] The growing sectional crisis over slavery was causing the whole political world to unravel. The Whig Party was dead, the new Republican Party was far from a single-minded purpose, and the Democratic Party was about to be torn apart.

The leader of the fragmented Democratic Party was James Buchanan, whose presidential term was coming to an ignominious end. Buchanan's intent of serving one term saved himself a world of further embarrassment. His falling out with the popular Stephen Douglas and Douglas men like David Tod led to his difficulties in 1860.

Not only had Buchanan and his men set out to destroy Douglas and his supporters over the disagreement of the Lecompton Constitution, but the president had initiated "an all-out war against anti-Lecompton Democrats in the North." That mission permeated his administration, alienating Democratic loyalists like Tod. The eminent historian William E. Gienapp notes that instead of trying to reconcile before the presidential election of 1860, Buchanan chose instead "to destroy his party opponents, and promot[ed] blatantly pro-Southern policies. The result was the rupture of the party at the 1860 Charleston convention."[6]

With heavy trepidation Democrats of all stripes descended on Charleston. For David Tod and other Northern delegates, it was their first trip to the Deep South and the weather would not be the only thing heating up that spring. But one thing was certain: Warm Southern hospitality was not on display to welcome Northerners. A correspondent for the *New York Herald* walking the streets of Charleston reported, "The mass of people were avowed secessionists." Cries for "disunion" from "hot headed and impulsive" citizens were everywhere. Northern abolitionists were regarded as "deadly enemies" to their way of life and Charlestonians aimed to "stem the tide of abolition fanaticism."[7]

As Northern delegates like Tod entered the lion's den at Charleston, the defiant *Charleston Mercury* underscored the importance of the upcoming Democratic National Convention for the party and the nation. "From these deliberations will be seen whether it stands true to vital constitutional rights of the South, where its strength exists; or whether, by tacit consent, yielding them to anti-slavery allies at the North, where it is almost powerless, it will [eke] official success, devoid of principle, and all under the condemnation of a betrayed South, with a Southern party rising from its disorganization." The ensuing presidential contest will be in every way a "sectional struggle . . . which may turn the scale of Northern mastery in the Government, bringing subjugation for the South beneath the sway of the hostile majority."[8] Such was the mindset of the Southern Slave Power.

Tod and Dr. Daniel B. Woods, a practicing physician with a penchant for politics, represented Ohio's Twentieth Congressional District. Daniel Rhodes, Tod's coal mining partner and a cousin of Stephen Douglas, was there as a delegate-at-large.[9] The railroad executive Henry Payne, who lost his gubernatorial bid to Chase, was also on hand for Douglas. By rejecting the Lecompton Constitution in defense of popular sovereignty Douglas was the overwhelming favorite among the Democrats of the North. Douglas himself believed, inaccurately, that he had greater appeal in the South. But it was Buchanan who was viewed as an outcast in the North and in fact had more followers among Southerners.

Entering the convention, fire-eating delegates of the Southern states made known their demands early on. Entirely distrustful of the Republican Party, they wanted a platform that guaranteed the protection of slavery in the territories as well as a restart of the slave trade. The Slave Power rightly believed that the new Republican Party was innately hostile to the Southern way of life—meaning "the institution of slavery." They also believed that the party was created to make war upon the Constitution and the rights of the Southern states. Emboldened by the Supreme Court's *Dred Scott* decision, delegates from Mississippi, Georgia, Louisiana, Kentucky, Missouri, and even Illinois and Wisconsin would move with coordinated timing one after another to disavow the power of the federal government over slavery in the states and territories.[10] If they held firm to these demands, regardless of securing their nominee, they were sure to ruin the party and any chance of capturing the presidency. But securing these planks within the platform would not come easy. Douglas and his army of supporters were in no mood to compromise their stance on popular sovereignty, and they would not be intimidated by threats from Southern Democrats to break away.[11]

The convention began on April 23 in the Hall of the South Carolina Institute, destined to be remembered as Secession Hall, on Meeting Street. Caleb Cushing of Massachusetts was selected president while each state brought a vice president and secretary. Ohio's delegates announced David Tod as their vice president and W. M. Stark as secretary.[12] They were purely ceremonial roles.

Arkansas's Thompson B. Flournoy, the president pro tem, addressed the convention and pleaded for "moderation and harmony" while reminding the delegates of their common cause and party affiliation and to put sectional divisions aside. "You should regard each other as brothers," he implored, "and not as hostile forces marching forward to hostile music, under different flags.Let us then talk no more about sections. We know no North, no South . . . We come here to consider the good of the great Democratic party." His speech was met with loud and sustained applause.[13] It was one of the last signs of consensus to occur at the convention.

Chairman Caleb Cushing, the "conservative, pro-southern Attorney General" in Franklin Pierce's cabinet[14] reminded delegates of their sacred duty to defend the Constitution against those intent on overthrowing it "to produce in this country a permanent sectional conspiracy." This Democratic Party must stand up to those forces emanating from within that "would hurry our land on to revolution and to civil war." Cushing implored we must "not distrust *ourselves*."[15] Despite his words of caution, unity among the delegates was nonviable. Most were from the North and the majority of those were for Douglas. The Southern sentiment "to destroy Douglas," intense as it was among those delegates, had no chance of success.[16]

One of the few advantages that Southern delegates enjoyed was the convention's location. Local supporters packed the galleries by day while "Fire-eating orators held forth outdoors each evening," verbally assaulting Northern delegates on their way to their nightly lodgings.[17] Despite these tactics of intimidation, the Douglas men resolved to hold firm to their principles. David Tod's son Henry, years later, recollected that his father had gone to Charleston "strongly attached to Stephen A. Douglas" and stood out as one who courageously "resisted the demands of the pro-slavery Southern delegates." When subjected to their threats of secession Henry remembered that his father "bade defiance."[18]

Reporting that "unanimity did not prevail" the convention's platform committee brought forth two separate platforms. The majority platform had been adopted in Cincinnati earlier in the year and included a strong "slave-code plank." Ohio's Henry Payne, with Tod's support, offered the minority platform, which was the same as that adopted by the party in 1856 and which had endorsed Douglas's popular sovereignty covenant and committed to follow laws adopted by territorial governments.[19] Adoption of a platform and the selection of a presidential candidate required a two-thirds majority vote of the delegates. Neither the Douglas men nor the Southern faction could overcome the two-thirds requirement and neither side showed any sign of yielding to the other's demands.[20] Deadlocked, the convention adjourned. But before the delegates departed, Chairman Cushing reminded those who remained of their sacred duty to party and country as well as the Constitution. He also reminded them that, sectional differences aside, their common bonds of history and heritage had been strengthened through revolution and war, "through sunshine and storm." The Union of states had forged a "great Republic." "Shall we cease to be such?" he asked. This Union cannot, must not be "shattered." The delegates needed calm and time to reflect. The plan was to reconvene in Baltimore with the hope that cooler heads would prevail, to unite behind one candidate and one platform, and to "march on [together] forever."[21]

The events at Charleston were unnerving. This feeling undoubtedly increased when the Southern wing of the Democratic Party decided to meet separately at Richmond to adopt its own platform. This development was no mere "*flap*," wrote one Southern newspaper editor, but another sign of the division within the party.[22]

As the second round of conventions neared speculations of all sorts ensued. Tod's name was even rumored to be in the mix for the party's nomination at Baltimore.[23] But Tod had remained faithful to Douglas on all 57 ballots at Charleston and he had no intention of changing course. While the Baltimore attendees were making ready, word from the Richmond assemblage was that they would consider Douglas's candidacy "under no circumstances." Richmond would select its own Southern candidate.[24]

Any hope of reconciliation between Northern and Southern delegates was becoming increasingly improbable. Any sign of unity was all but gone. The open dissent led one *New York Herald* correspondent to foresee that there was "less hope for union and harmony than ever, and greater probability of the election of the Republican candidate."[25] And if in fact more than one Democratic nominee appeared on the general ballot in November the probability of the Republican candidate emerging victorious, as the *Herald* predicted, was certain. The Republican candidate, still a relative unknown, was the trial lawyer from Illinois, Abraham Lincoln. The one-term congressman who had lost his bid for the US Senate to Stephen Douglas in 1858, secured his party's nomination in Chicago in May. The Republican Party quickly coalesced behind its man. Where the Republican's long-shot candidate brought his party together, the fissures within the Democratic Party continued to widen as the odds of Lincoln becoming the next president of the United States increased with each passing day.[26]

When Tod got to the Front Street Theater in Baltimore the feeling was that the convention was doomed from the start. In fact, its imminent failure was already a foregone conclusion. What few Douglas delegates from the upper Southern states attended could not find agreement with their brethren from the lower South. When the lower Southern delegates were unable to get all they wanted onto the platform they marched out of the proceedings, never to return. Realizing the futility of it all most upper South delegates, joined by an assemblage of proslavery Northern delegates, followed suit. By the sixth day the remaining delegates leaked from the convention. A disconcerted Chairman Cushing absorbed the blame, imposed a self-proclaimed no-confidence vote upon himself, resigned his authority, and took his seat with the Massachusetts delegation.[27] "As most of the delegates looked on," writes one historian, "the Democratic party destroyed itself."[28]

David Tod, vice president of Ohio's delegation, was chosen to succeed Cushing as chairman. Tod was as well suited for the chairman role as any other. Described as a conciliator, a compromiser, and loaded with "genial tact,"[29] Tod needed to follow parliamentary procedures and get the plank and candidate secured, a much easier task since the remaining delegates, by now, were far friendlier after the exodus of the separatists. Standing at the dais, Tod was welcomed by the remaining delegates with "hearty and long-continued cheers and applause." It was all they could do to mask the crestfallen and forlorn mood of the remaining crowd. Tod accepted the role "with great diffidence." Once order was restored, he pledged "faithfully to discharge the duties of the Chair."[30]

After this he reminded the delegates that he had carried the Democratic banner for more than three decades and had done political battle in his home district against the likes of such political antagonists as Joshua Giddings and Benjamin Wade.[31] Though a Douglas supporter Tod would nonetheless conduct the proceedings with a sense of fairness, leading one historian to praise the new chairman for his efforts "to heal the breach in his party."[32] Chairman Tod's reign lasted until nightfall, when the convention came to an inglorious conclusion.

The remaining delegates declared Stephen Douglas the party's nominee.[33] Chairman Tod closed the convention but not before reminding his fellow Democrats that achieving success was now in their hands. Electing Douglas president, however, was not going to be easy and he exhorted the party faithful to return to their homes and "continue firmly, nationally, sternly, fairly, [and] honorably" in their efforts to secure victory for the fractured party's official candidate.[34]

Soon after his return home, Tod quickly realized the divisiveness of his own local party and just how dysfunctional the national party was. Historian Joel Silbey describes the Democratic Party after Baltimore as "split bitterly." After the Baltimore gathering two more separate conventions convened. "Three conventions, two candidates for president, two rival national headquarters, two campaigns, and much virulent sniping,"[35] resulted, writes Silbey.

Securing support for Douglas was going to be an arduous task especially since he now had to compete against two other Democratic candidates: current vice president John Breckenridge and John Bell. Breckenridge, a Kentucky native, was the closest ideologically to Buchanan and like Buchanan, he had supported the proslavery Lecompton Constitution for Kansas. Bell, who once served in William Henry Harrison's cabinet, was a Tennessean who enslaved African Americans. He took a neutral position on slavery, however. Their nominations represented the South's dissatisfaction with Douglas and their position on slavery. Douglas stood no chance of gaining Southern support and neither Breckinridge nor Bell would garner any in the North. Their candidacies were sure to further divide the Democrats and ruin what little chance Douglas had at winning the presidency. And among the candidates and their supporters there was no love lost after Baltimore. One observer said there was "no more union between Breckinridge and Douglas than between two naturally repulsive forces."[36] The "fissures" Silbey adds, "were real, the belligerence between the Douglas and Breckinridge men was deep."[37] And deep down Douglas supporters like Tod understood that their mission was lost before it had any chance of getting started. Southerners would never support Douglas and Northerners would never support Breckenridge or Bell.

After Baltimore Tod could not get the name of Douglas atop the masthead of the *Trumbull Democrat*. The local Democrats had grown disillusioned with the events at Charleston and Baltimore and weary of their chance of winning. The Baltimore convention, wrote William Ritezel, editor of the *Trumbull Democrat* "so complicated the affairs of the party, that no man could give unhesitating adherence to the ticket of either wing." A bitter feud between Tod and Ritezel ensued as the editor considered endorsing Breckenridge. Ritezel's view flabbergasted Tod, who then reacted in a very public way by canceling his longtime subscription to the newspaper in protest and encouraged other subscribers to do the same to bring financial ruin to the publication. A nasty rebuttal followed as one critic described Tod's actions as a "degree of malignant meanness ... that we could never have believed Mr. Tod capable of." Tod had even labeled his first law partner Matthew Birchard a traitor to the party for his support of Breckenridge. Ritezel called out Tod's overinflated ego and sense of self-importance and pledged, "we shall not allow Mr. Tod, or any other man, to put a bit into our mouth and guide us at his pleasure."[38] It is hard to fathom that Ritezel would not have supported Douglas who had, among the Democrats, the best chance, futile though it was, to beat Lincoln.[39] Yet, the resistance in the heart of Tod country continued.

A group of local Breckenridge backers vowed that Tod and his Douglas men "cannot brow-beat all the Democrats of Trumbull County." An infuriated Tod, so blinded by his anger, failed to recall the untethered support he had received from the *Trumbull Democrat* for so many years. The *Western Reserve Chronicle* clearly enjoyed the infighting spectacle of their rivals.[40] The animus heaped upon Tod continued. The *Anti-Slavery Bugle* mocked him as a lookalike of Napoleon I and one who operated "the slowest railroad this side of sundown, [but] was president of the fastest National Democratic Convention assembled since the days of Jackson."[41] Coming to Tod's defense, however, was the *Mahoning Sentinel*, which warned that he was not a man who grew "weary or faint in well doing."[42]

While the internecine war of words between Tod and Ritezel continued during the summer of 1860, the Republican campaign for Abraham Lincoln rolled along splendidly. The *Western Reserve Chronicle* wasted no time coming out for Lincoln. After the Whig Party collapsed the *Chronicle* got behind Lincoln and the new Republican Party. Other than his one term in Congress, noted for his opposition to the war with Mexico, critics rhetorically asked, what had Lincoln accomplished? "Absolutely nothing!" came the reply from Ritezel's *Trumbull Democrat*.[43] But the Republicans required a less complicated game plan. Republicans just had to line up their votes behind one candidate and get them to the polls, whereas the Democrats had created an irrepressible three-headed monster in the candidacies of Douglas, Breckenridge, and Bell.

No one doubted that the Democratic Party was in trouble. "The wounds" after Charleston and Baltimore, notes Silbey, "continued to fester."[44] Tod undoubtedly recognized the near-impossible task at hand but ever the true Douglas Democrat he soldiered on for the Northern faction's standard bearer. There was hardly a torch-lit parade or rally that Tod did not attend. Addressing a Douglas "glorification on the Square" in Cleveland in July, Tod told the partisan gathering that he "had never seen a prouder moment" and promised that if Douglas were elected "the slavery question . . . would . . . be settled . . . and settled right." Surely, Tod must have meant that popular sovereignty, a bedrock of the Douglas philosophy, would settle the question of slavery in the territories. In August, Tod addressed crowds in Columbus and Ashland. By then, the *Trumbull Democrat* had passed an olive branch to Tod after it finally came around to endorsing Douglas.[45]

On the attack at Wooster Tod lashed out against Thomas Bartley, the former Democratic governor who had just retired from the Ohio Supreme Court and had recently withdrawn his support for Douglas. But Bartley showed his contempt for Tod all the same calling him a "gump-head and ignoramus" who had become a "bore in private conversation [because of] his Munchausen stories connected with his mission to Brazil, in which he never fails to depict himself as a hero." Tod's intolerant position toward

Bartley, Ritezel, and Birchard was really about his belief that Douglas was the only Democratic candidate who stood any chance of victory. Any breach, faltering, or splintering would further weaken Douglas's chances. Thus, his strident response to these factions earlier in the summer explained his uncompromising stance. Undeterred, Tod finally had the honor to introduce Douglas to a huge gathering on the square in Cleveland.[46]

Tod had never worked so hard for any candidate, and the demanding schedule finally took a physical toll on him. On September 29 Tod was traveling back to Cleveland on his train car when he "was struck with an apoplectic fit from which he suffered severely." How debilitating or what effects the stroke had upon the 55-year-old fatigued campaigner is unknown, but it took Tod weeks of rest at his son John's residence in Cleveland before he recovered well enough to resume his commitment to the Douglas cause.[47]

When voters cast their ballots on November 6 too many obstacles blocked the path to victory for Stephen A. Douglas. Although the contest boiled down to the two Northern candidates from Illinois, Lincoln and Douglas, neither man stood a chance in the South where Lincoln's name appeared on hardly any ballots. Douglas's position on popular sovereignty doomed his chance in the South, while Breckenridge and Bell split the Southern votes. The densely populated Northern states carried the election for Abraham Lincoln. His 1,866,452 popular votes represented just 40 percent of the total votes cast but enough to claim 180 electoral votes and victory despite the efforts of Douglas and his hardworking loyalists like David Tod. Lincoln even captured Tod's coveted Ohio votes.[48] Tod was unable to have any effect in his home counties of Mahoning and Trumbull where Lincoln handily carried both. Voters in Trumbull overwhelmingly came out for Lincoln over Douglas, 4,884 to 1,712. It was much the same in Mahoning, where Lincoln polled 2,907 to 1,989 for Douglas.[49]

After Lincoln's victory, representatives of South Carolina gathered once again in the hall of the South Carolina Institute and voted to secede from the Union. In the days and weeks ahead more were to follow. In comments written for Buchanan but just as appropriate for the new president-elect, the *Western Reserve Chronicle* observed, "There are few that would envy him now; turn which way he will, trouble, perplexity and danger are before him."[50] As Lincoln's inauguration neared, Northern Democrats like Tod and Douglas, who adhered to a peaceful resolution, were now faced with tough personal decisions.

Throughout his entire political career David Tod had represented himself as a Jacksonian Democrat, a dyed-in-the-wool states' rights man. And although his party identity did not change, he and others like Douglas adapted their views as a sign of the challenging times in which they lived. More specifically, the nation was evolving in size, diversity, and political thought. One biographer of Andrew Jackson described his need to change. Jackson, like Douglas and Tod, was a politician. And, as such, he was "subject to his own passions and predilections, and they pressed him to cast his lot with those with whom he agreed on the question at hand."[51] In this way, Tod was "pressed" to modify his outlook when it came to the questions at hand: states' rights, popular sovereignty, and the future of slavery.

Taking the side of popular sovereignty was a compromise even though Tod had hinted at it for years. For Tod, slavery had always been a local matter, one that the people, through the ballot box, should decide. Douglas's popular sovereignty option legitimized that philosophy on a national level. Although Tod would always admire Jackson, he was now a loyal member of the Douglas Democrats. With Tod's long-standing internal conflict resolved, he now wrestled with another. And that conflict was the result of the increasing influence of the Southern Slave Power over that section of the country. "They demand more territory for [their] slaves and more slaves, for their territory." Anyone with "a spoonful of sense," decried the *Western Reserve Chronicle*, "knows that . . . Slavery alone is the cause of all the trouble."[52] And Tod knew that as much as anyone.

9

I Am for My Country, 1861

IN EARLY JANUARY 1861, the annual Ohio Democratic Convention and Jackson Day celebration was held and more than 150 Democrats descended upon Columbus. It was an opportunity to come together and celebrate their common political bonds of affection, or what was left of them. The Democrats that night took their presidential defeat to Lincoln in stride and vainly praised the course, failing as it was, of outgoing President Buchanan whose approach was to permit "each and every State [in the Union], the regulation of its own affairs in its own way." True, the Democrats had been "defeated but [they were] not conquered." They believed their party to be "the guardian protector of the integrity of the constitution" and sent their "best wishes for the whole country [pledging] co-operations in any measure calculated to restore peace, and preserve our happy Union." The state of the Union, however, was anything but happy. Just what was meant by this pledge to cooperate "in any measure" was open for partisan interpretation and it would be. The philosophy of the Democrats was to "hold in check and frustrate the designs of sectionalists, North and South"[1] and abate Southern fears of the Republican designs for the future of slavery and thus save the Union. Southern secessionists had already made up their minds to quit the Union. And Northern Democrats, however, would have to decide if they were going to quit their party.

The day after Ohio's Democratic convention, the secession movement began with Mississippi followed by Florida and Alabama. Georgia and Louisiana concluded the march before the month of January ended while Texas exited on the first of February. The *Ohio Statesman* observed that civil war was "at our doors, and there does not appear to be anything that can prevent it."[2] Northern Democrats continued to cling to the idea that the secession movement could be reversed if some genuine peaceful overtures were made by either the Buchanan administration or the incoming Lincoln administration. Buchanan would do nothing while Lincoln had no authority to do anything until he was sworn in on March 4. The Crittenden Compromise, born in the US Senate, was designed to stem the tide and reverse the secession trend by pledging to preserve the state of slavery in its present form. But the bill failed to make it out of committee.[3] While all eyes shifted to the beleaguered federal troops stationed at Fort Sumter in Charleston, Southern secessionists were meeting in Montgomery, Alabama, to form a Southern confederate government. By their actions the Union had already been dissolved.

Concurrently, Union meetings were held across Ohio. "The time for action," declared the *Statesman*, "immediate and decisive has come." Many in the North agreed with this position. However, the Union's standing army consisted of a mere 16,000 troops. Therefore "taunting the national government as powerless," notes one historian, "had some foundation."[4] There were reports that a disciplined and trained military group of free Black men, armed with muskets, was drilling on the grounds of the new Ohio Statehouse. As much as the martial spirit of this patriotic group could not be subdued, its service would be suppressed for more than two years.[5] Restraint, cautioned the *Statesman*'s editorial, was needed as an act of military aggression would "produce [stronger Southern] unity" with the Ohio River "the line between hostile nations."[6]

Ohio's Governor William Dennison, a member of the Republican Party, had opposed slavery and refused to support the Fugitive Slave Law. Dennison hoped that disagreements could be resolved but he was unwilling to risk the Constitution or the Union. Ohio, he said, was "tied" to both Union and Constitution and was "ready to perform our own appropriate part whenever the occasion may call on us." Ohio would "exert every faculty we possess in aiding to prevent the Constitution from being nullified, destroyed or impaired." Until that call, concluded Dennison, "Ohio calmly awaits the exigencies of the future."[7]

Several days after their first gathering Ohio's Democrats reconvened in Columbus, this time to appraise "the alarming condition of the country." What they resolved was even more alarming: "That the two hundred thousand Democrats of Ohio send to the people of the United States, both North and South, greeting: And when the people of the North shall have fulfilled their duties to the Constitution and the South—then, and not until then, will it be proper for them to take into consideration the question of the right and propriety of coercion."

The Democratic *Daily Ohio Statesman* supported the resolution and encouraged the Republican Party and the entire North to admit that "the free States have done wrong, in our legislation, in the action of our Executives, in the false doctrines we have taught, [so therefore] we must correct our past errors and discharge our duties to the Constitution and the southern portion of the confederacy, and until this be done, the Democratic masses of Ohio will not consider the question of the coercion of a state."[8] David Tod was not in Columbus for these meetings but soon added to the controversy.

State Senator Jacob Dolson Cox, a rising Republican in the Ohio senate, encountered Tod soon after the news of the resolution broke.[9] Cox claimed that the conversation between the two neighbors "turned on the action of the convention." Cox said he did not mince his words and told Tod that the resolution promising to oppose federal troops moving against Southern secessionists, was nothing short of treasonous. When Tod "vehemently reasserted the substance of the resolution," that "Republicans would find the two hundred thousand Ohio Democrats" blocking their attempt "to cross the Ohio River," Cox was further taken aback.[10] Tod's initial threat had "caused a sensation" when he first supported it and he showed no signs of backing down from it now. Andrew Jackson, Cox told Tod, would never have approved such a course of action. Before the two friends went their separate ways, Cox promised Tod that his Democratic resistance could not hold back any national force.[11]

David Tod, like the leader of the wing of his fractured Democratic Party, Stephen Douglas, still hoped for a peaceful resolution. However, violating the Constitution or dividing the country were never serious options for him. For as much as Tod believed in the rights of the states, he did not believe secession to be one of them. Tod held that the Union was indeed bound together by the Constitution and therefore, one and inseparable, making the secession movement illegal. The action of the seceding states amounted to tearing a limb from the body, piece by piece. "To dismember" the Union in this fashion would "destroy it," he said. Therefore, "Secession and Union are incompatible ideas." Secession was in total conflict with Tod's powerful sense of patriotism and love of country. Yet, his most hardened critics called him a secessionist. "We never have admired the political course of Mr. Tod," wrote the editors of the *Western Reserve Chronicle*. "We have often thought that his fidelity to the democratic party, sometimes unconsciously betrayed him into infidelity to the interests of the country."[12] To have his patriotism impugned was devastating but he still hoped that the Northern states and Southern secessionists could resolve their differences.

Another attempt emerged from the South when a group of Virginia congressmen called for a peace conference in Washington. Governor Dennison was persuaded to send representation, but these were "unchartered waters" for governors as historian David Engle points out because they posed potential problems if they worked "independently" from one another. Yet communication did take place between and among some Northern governors to ensure they did not undermine the incoming Lincoln administration.[13] State Senators Cox and James Garfield opposed the idea outright. But Governor Dennison was permitted by the Ohio house to appoint delegates with the senate granting final approval. The governor chose seven in all: six Republicans and one Democrat.[14] Tod was given early consideration to attend as the lone Democrat of the bunch, but his recent controversial comments ended his nomination.[15]

The Border State Convention, as it was also called, came to nothing as the "talk about compromise" turned out to be further concessions from the North to approve the expansion of slavery in the territories. The tired old argument was worn thin and produced nothing of substance.[16] In all 14 free states had sent delegates to the nation's capital. Although it accomplished nothing it served two purposes, writes Engle. First, it momentarily eased tensions by shifting the talk of war to talk of peace, buying more time for the incoming president. Second, and most important for the future, "it previewed the political cooperation among Northern states." Of course, the governors were working within their own states, but they were also leaders of their political parties and they managed to set party politics aside to try to aid the national government.[17]

Meanwhile, president-elect Lincoln's route to the nation's capital, a circuitous journey to greet well-wishers, continued. Crowds turned out in droves at every stop in Ohio. In a display of professional courtesy if not outright political support Tod's Cleveland & Mahoning Railroad offered tickets from Youngstown to Cleveland for half fare. Lincoln's journey traversed Tod's political backyard, stopping in nearby Alliance and Ravenna, where he was enthusiastically greeted. The politically astute Lincoln was aware that thousands of Douglas supporters had turned out to greet him and he asked the crowd to help sustain the country during the trials ahead; "If we all turn in and keep the ship from sinking this voyage, there may be a chance for Douglas on the next; but if we let it go down now, neither he nor anybody else will have an opportunity of sailing in it again."[18] Lincoln's extension of an olive branch to Douglas Democrats bode well for the president-elect. Douglas's acceptance sent a sure sign to Douglas men like Tod to get behind the president and help keep the Union ship from sinking.

Douglas was also present during Lincoln's swearing in. And it had been Douglas who called on Lincoln immediately after Confederate guns let loose on Fort Sumter in April signaling the start of civil war. Douglas, it was reported, expressed to Lincoln his intent "to sustain the President in the exercise of all constitutional functions to preserve the Union, maintain the Government, and defend the Federal Capital." The president, it was reported, "was very much gratified with the interview."[19] Tod's support of Lincoln was now in lockstep with Douglas's.

The attack on Fort Sumter brought matters into clear focus. The North "must face the grave fact that war exists by the act of the insurgent disunionists," wrote one Columbus native. As Jacob Cox fondly remembered, patriots "sprang into vigorous life [as] they crowded to the recruiting stations to enlist for defence [sic] of the national flag and the national Union."[20] That spirit rose in small Ohio towns like Mt. Gilead where partisan sentiments were "buried" underneath a Union pole and replaced with Old Glory attached to porches and balconies. "All are for the Union here," proclaimed one loyal citizen.[21]

As soon as Tod heard the news of the attack his mind, like Douglas's, was instantly made up. He did not need Douglas as his sounding board on this point. It was a good thing, too, for Douglas would be dead in less than two months. Tod's patriotism chartered his own course and critics like Cox were more than pleased to have observed that recently announced party doctrines had been nothing more than "hollow" and "superficial" rhetoric. Cox was delighted to see his friend Tod out front and center for the

Union. Moreover, it became widely reported that even before the attack on Fort Sumter, Tod had urged the new president to reinforce the garrison and promised that the Democrats of Ohio would not try to block any federal advance on the South but would "sustain him" instead.[22]

For David Tod, the attack on Fort Sumter was a heinous, treasonous act. He revered the Constitution, the Union, and the Founders and the moment had arrived that demanded all patriotic Americans to rally around the flag. In taking this position, Tod was one of the first of what became known as the War Democrats.

The War Democrats came to symbolize one of two factions within the Democratic Party of the North. The War Democrats stuck with President Lincoln in his management of the war. Joining Tod and Douglas as War Democrats in Ohio were other party heavyweights like Edwin Stanton.

The other faction, silent at first, became known as the Peace Democrats of the North. This faction remained loyal to the Union but as the war raged on with no end in sight, they would tire of the violence and bloodshed and adopt a "peace at any cost" position even if that peace were arrived at by breaking up the Union and allowing the South to go its own way. During this latter stage they became known as Copperheads. The commonality of the two factions, War Democrats and Peace Democrats, during the initial stages of the war was their "opposition to emancipation."[23]

Less than one week after the surrender of Fort Sumter Tod was before the public exhorting the citizens of the Mahoning valley to support the president. One local recalled Tod making "a most eloquent speech" that resulted "in many enlistments."[24] During "this hour of peril" Tod called for all Democrats to "sustain [President Lincoln] when he calls for support, as readily as though Andrew Jackson had made the demand. Our country, flag and firesides are in peril," implored Tod. "Political organizations should be lost sight of" in the face of "an enemy pledged to disrupt [the] peace, seize upon the federal capital, and dishonor our national ensign."[25] And Tod was ready to lead by example.

When Lincoln called for 75,000 volunteers Tod, holding no official capacity, telegraphed the president to raise the call to 300,000 instead. He then put up $1,000 of his own money to raise and equip the first volunteer company in Youngstown.[26] He also pledged an additional $1,000 to support the families of local volunteer soldiers. And one of the first groups to move out was the Tod Artillery.[27] As president of the Cleveland & Mahoning Railroad he also prohibited any passenger identified as a "secession apologist, sympathizer or abettor" from riding his line. His conductors were given strict orders to remove any passenger expressing anti-Union "sentiments on the trains" and have them "deposited on terra firma at the nearest station."[28]

As one of the leading "Democrat[s] of the old school" Tod became one of the first to publicly shed his party colors in support of the Union. "Away with everything partisan until the war is over," he proclaimed, "and our bleeding nation is saved." It was a stunning attestation for one so rooted in the history and ideology of his party, a real paradigm shift for the lifelong Democrat. By surrendering his political identity, prestige, and influence he must have known that regardless of the war's outcome, there would be no going back. "As I now do," implored Tod, "so do with me. I am for my country."[29] And Tod was not above losing personal friends at the expense of his country. He gained a reputation for being "particularly severe on those Democrats who will not at this critical time, lay aside their partisan feelings and prejudices."[30] In the early days, for example, a neighbor who called on Tod blamed the Republicans for the nation's crisis. They had gotten "the country into trouble and they might get it out," he declared. This demonstrative partisan criticism so angered Tod he admonished his friend to "never darken my door again!"[31]

Tod's speeches were quickly welcomed and embraced by old rivals and supported by like-minded Democrats. Editors Hapgood and Adams, at the *Western Reserve Chronicle,* managed to put aside past quarrels with Tod and they then allied with and supported his efforts. Tod's stance was also just the sort of tonic to heal old friendships once strained by political passions as he and Congressman John Hutchins came together for the sake of recruiting "all men loyal to the Union and the Constitution."[32] Putting aside "party recrimination" Tod helped to unite the "quiet people of the Reserve."[33] One close admirer described Tod's action during this period as an ascension "from the imminence [*sic*] of a party leader to the mountain-height of the loftiest patriotism."[34] Even the Republican *Indiana Journal* picked up and lauded Tod's efforts to unite "all hands, from all parties."[35] He was now a man with no party, but he did have a country, or what remained of it.

Where Tod was fighting to unite parties and factions in Ohio, Stephen Douglas had endeavored the same at the national level, having become an avowed Unionist and die-hard supporter of Lincoln's war efforts. Douglas's unexpected death in June shocked the nation. Even the *Western Reserve Chronicle* set aside past differences and described Douglas's death as "a national misfortune" and worse, "a national calamity."[36] Lincoln's war secretary, Simon Cameron, remembered Douglas as "a man who nobly discarded party for country." These same words were being used to describe David Tod. Whereas in death Douglas was "called from . . . the field of his labors" Tod "had every reason to look forward to a long career of usefulness."[37] By words and deeds Tod was proving to be the most effective Democratic politician in Ohio. Though it was never his goal, little did he realize that his sacrifice would soon gain him the elusive governorship of Ohio.

Just before his death, Douglas stated, "We should never forget that a man cannot be a true Democrat unless he is a loyal patriot."[38] Tod could not have agreed more, and his patriotism was on full display. With no lasting effects from the presumed stroke suffered during the Douglas campaign the previous year, Tod remained active in promoting the administration's war efforts. He answered countless calls from small Ohio towns for purposes of rallying the locals to enlist. Speech making became so frequent and expected wherever he went Tod often found himself speaking "from the impulse of the moment."[39] On one occasion to a crowd that included new recruits he drifted slightly off course alluding to his health. Recalling how hard he worked for Douglas against Lincoln and the physical toll it took on him he admitted to a crowd, "I nearly spent my life." Now with Douglas gone many, at least in Ohio, viewed Tod as the most celebrated Democrat and the "most ardent supporter" of the president. Having already sacrificed his party he was now ready to offer up his own health, his "last child, my last dollar," he said, to see the Union victorious.[40]

Calls to establish a new National Union Party comprising Republicans and pro-war Democrats were raised across the North soon after the events at Fort Sumter.[41] But the movement really gained momentum after the shocking Union defeat at Bull Run in July 1861. Northerners, facing the reality that the war effort was going to take longer than expected, quickly understood that military victory required political unity. Thus, explains historian James Rawley, unifying the parties, Republicans and War Democrats to be specific, was essential and became the goal of a new Union Party movement. Criticism from Peace Democrats, who represented the venerable Democratic Party, claimed that a Union Party was just another name for the nascent Republican Party. So entrenched was political identity in American culture that the goal of universal unity was not realistic.[42] But the effort was undertaken nonetheless, and David Tod led the Ohio War Democrats by joining the Union Party.

By summer's end, the Union movement was described as "sweeping Ohio like a fire on the prairie."[43] With the general elections approaching, names of potential candidates for governor thought to be universally acceptable to Republicans and Democrats alike began to circulate. The *Western Reserve Chronicle* announced its support for Tod who had "been hearty and efficient in his support" of Lincoln's war efforts. As for political differences with Tod, the editors were "willing to let by-gones be by-gones." The *Cleveland Morning Leader* praised Tod for "his late straightforward, earnest and patriotic course." And one Republican liked Tod because "his every thought and feeling is for [restoring] the Union."[44]

Tod was by far the leading Union man in Ohio. Each pro-Union speech he gave further solidified his break from the Democrats, whom he criticized as "grumbling" and who thought the war to be "a Republican war, in which they have no interest or responsibility." Now was not the time to be "calling conventions." But his criticisms were not just leveled at hard-line Democrats. They were also aimed at partisan Radical Republicans whom he called "rabid [and] mischievous" because they "complain[ed] that the slaves are not being set free fast enough."[45]

Historian Adam Goodheart does not think that Ohio was as united as Tod or others thought. Where the "fire of radicalism was burning ever hotter in the Western Reserve" folks living in the counties along the Ohio River would just as soon return all "fugitive slaves ... to their master."[46] These sentiments, Goodheart explains, were irrespective of party affiliations or Union sentiments. For now, these feelings remained under control. But when the war news grew bleak, moderate positions on slavery gave way to extremism from both sides. And Democrats, writes Joel Silbey, would find "it very difficult throughout the crisis to support the Lincoln administration."[47]

In August Ohio Democrats convened and adopted positions that condemned the Lincoln administration while still supporting the war. They also favored peace talks. Tod "pronounced [the platform] a menace to the Union" war effort.[48] For governor they chose Hugh Jewett, an enthusiastic Douglas supporter who was with Tod in Charleston and Baltimore. Until recently Jewett had been a busy railroad officer. He ran unsuccessfully for Congress in the Zanesville district in 1860 and had garnered the endorsement of the *Mahoning Sentinel*, which dropped its support for Tod.[49] Plenty critics of the Jewett-led Peace Democrats and their peace platform existed. Tod and other Union Party supporters asked what value a Democratic victory would hold if it was "celebrated over the ruins of a dismembered Government"?[50] Tod was harsher still, proclaiming that Democrats cast every Union soldier as a murderer; "Can I denounce my own son as a murderer?[51] Under no circumstances would I consent to a dissolution of the Union, or consider terms of separation."[52] Tod quickly denounced Jewett's words, declaring "that *under no circumstances will he support* the pretended Democratic nominations and platform."[53] Whether he intended to or not, he was sounding more and more like a candidate for governor.

Ohio Republicans in the Union Party invited delegates irrespective of party to the Union convention. Invitations exhorted delegates to leave their party stripes at home and substitute "patriotism [in] the place of party spirit."[54] Those that ultimately joined the Union Party, Republicans and Democrats alike, labeled Democrats that remained behind as Southern sympathizers. But the outliers pushed back, especially those in Holmes County who insisted that there already existed a Union Party; its name was the Democratic Party. And it was Lincoln, they insisted, who intended to "destroy" it.[55] The *Forney Press* of Philadelphia countered that true Democrats, Douglas Democrats, that is, were wise to accept the "patriotic proffer" from the Republicans to come together as a Union Party. And David Tod, judged *Forney's* editors, was the "national representative of the Douglas party, and his nomination would be a graceful compliment to the Douglas party, all over the country."[56] It was quite a national endorsement.

When Tod first came out for Lincoln, he had not expressed any desire to be the next governor of Ohio. The thrust of his powerful and patriotic behavior was to support the Union and was not intended to advance his own personal political aspirations. Yet, as the summer of 1861 unfolded, the times called for a candidate who could reach across party lines and unite the varied supporters of the administration's effort to save the Union. Tod was seen by many to be the ideal candidate having already been credited for drawing in "hosts of Democrats to the Union cause." "We do not name him for Governor because he wants the office," wrote the *Mahoning Register*, which now offered its support, "but because [he] is the right man." More followed. The *Cleveland Morning Leader* believed "no choice could be more appropriate . . . Mr. Tod is the national representative of the Douglas party, and his nomination would" help to rally support from Democrats still on the fence.[57] Other Democrats were given passing consideration, but it was Tod who "would strike terror into the hearts of the nation's enemies"[58] and pursue "the war vigorously to an honorable conclusion."[59] There was verily no other serious candidate. "The star of the [upcoming Union] convention," writes the historian Christopher Dell, "was War Democrat David Tod who was virtually assured the gubernatorial nomination before the delegates assembled."[60]

Ohio's current governor, William Dennison, had managed the crisis admirably and efficiently to this point, but his lackluster personality had no appeal during these excitable times. He was viewed as a "suave, well-mannered gentleman" but who came across as "vain and haughty." His placid persona, his genteel style of talk intermixed with his long, passionless speeches failed to excite the crowds.[61] This was no match compared to Tod's patriotic-filled diatribes that called for traitors to be hung from the nearest tree. Furthermore, Dennison was viewed as too extreme for the time because he was so outspoken against slavery. The goal was to save the Union, not to end slavery. What the Union Party was looking far was a moderate who could bring together extremists from both sides of the issue to put country and Constitution above all else. Tod was that person.

Days before the Union convention, "for the benefit of his health" Tod took time to rest at a secluded resort known as Little Mountain in Lake County. The Lake Erie location was not so impenetrable from snooping reporters who called on the candidate to offer remarks. If elected he repeated his promise to aid Lincoln in prosecuting the war to a victorious conclusion after which he would advise the president to hang Jefferson Davis, P. G. T Beauregard, Gov. Henry Wise of Virginia, and "at least thirty [other] traitors."[62] These were not words that could be easily misinterpreted. Enthusiastic Unionists began to convene all over the state. At a rally in Mahoning County in September "the most radical anti-slavery Republicans," it was reported, "are *all* for Tod."[63] There was no other real candidate but Tod.

Exuberant delegates in Columbus unanimously nominated David Tod for governor and Benjamin Stanton, a Republican congressman, for lieutenant governor.[64] For his efforts, Tod was rightfully elevated with such former Democrats turned Unionists as Andrew Johnson of Tennessee,

Lewis Cass of Michigan, Daniel S. Dickinson of New York, and Joseph Holt of Kentucky, all of whom had put the Union's salvation above any political platform or personal goal. Before the war each had been major players in the Democratic Party, with bright political ambitions, but they likewise cast all that aside to fight for the Union. "Their position," wrote the *Chicago Daily Tribune*, was "that political parties and local institutions may be swept away, but the Government must be preserved."[65]

In his letter of acceptance Tod declared, "It shall be my aim to give the utmost support to the National Government, conceiving the doctrine of secession to be entirely destructive of our national existence, without which it will be impossible to govern ourselves." To those firebrands in the South who had orchestrated this crisis his words were unforgiving: "I utterly repudiate the monstrous and wicked plea and petition of the ringleaders of this conspiracy, and would argue for war eternally until they are brought to condign punishment." The world, Tod pointed out, was indeed watching "us as a people in the sanguinary struggle" to prove whether "man's capacity for self-government" would be "settled in such a way that nothing in human power can ever disturb or change it again." The challenge for this generation was every bit as important as that faced by the Founders, if not more. "The struggle of our ancestors was for self-government, our struggle," he exhorted his audience, "is to maintain it." Ohioans must lead in every way to save "the Union, one and inseparable, now and forever!" The Union candidate pledged to "go forward . . . burying all party passions and prejudices, yielding up all political predilections . . . *for the sake of the Union*."[66] Tod's words were powerful.

As the head of the Union ticket, Tod had no illusions about his mission. In fact, it was printed at the top of the paper ticket; "A Vigorous Prosecution of the War, and No Compromise Under the Guns of Rebels."[67] He relentlessly championed the Constitution and demanded unconditional surrender of the rebels "at the cannon's mouth!"[68] "Tod and victory!" became the battle cry in Ohio as Election Day neared.[69]

Supporters of the Tod-Stanton ticket regarded it as "the strongest ever offered."[70] Hard-line Democrats, however, "viewed Tod as a renegade, [a traitor], an opportunist whom the Republicans had bought with thirty pieces of silver." Historian Frank Klement argues that Tod had never really been a true Democrat to begin with and found his true home surrounded by Republicans parading around in some Union masquerade party. His suggestion that Tod was so uncomfortable within the Democratic Party because of the old but lingering spat with Samuel Medary and "looked for greener political pastures" elsewhere is ill supported.[71] Momentum, however, was building for Tod as evidenced by numerous Democratic Party papers moving away from Jewett and toward Tod. Chief among these was the Cleveland *Plain Dealer*, the Toledo *Times & Herald*, the Urbana *Free Press*, and the Hamilton *Telegraph*.[72] The *New York Tribune* also sent along its endorsement for Tod. He received another vote of confidence from New York where friend and returning US minister to Portugal, George Washington Morgan, had just reached shore and sent word of his "earnest support" to his friend. "I understand your position to be of unconditional devotion to the Union," wrote Morgan, "the resistance of all terms of compromise inconsistent with the honor and perpetuity of the nation, and of a vigorous prosecution of the war . . . I am with you and *for the Union*." (italics added)[73]

It was a good thing the campaign season was brief. David Tod was not a healthy man. Whether Tod's setback was related to last year's stroke is uncertain. But he was exhausted from the grueling pace. Tod himself said he had a "chill," which was concern enough for his physician to order his patient to rest. But the order was hard to follow.[74] Calling Tod's health "precarious" the *Ohio Daily Statesman* suggested that he was incapacitated and if elected, would be unable to carry out his duties, thereby ushering into the governor's chair the radical abolitionist Benjamin Stanton.[75] It was a scare tactic used by the Peace Democrats. Yet, Tod had to stay active to disprove these accusations even though he promised his physician a little more than a week before the election that he would keep his speeches brief.[76] After a rousing address in Youngstown, he suffered another apoplectic episode on a train bound for Cleveland almost on the one-year anniversary of his previous attack. Although he rebounded the next day it had become all too apparent that he had a serious chronic health condition.[77] Fortunately, with the election just days away, news of the incident had little time to circulate.

In an election where so little mattered about politics and so much focus was placed on patriotism Tod easily outdistanced Jewett in the election by 55,000 votes.[78] Twice before he tried and failed to capture the state's highest office. In 1861 he was elected governor because he campaigned not to attain the office but to help save his country.

Tod understood that he was elected to help Lincoln save the Union. Exactly what his duties and responsibilities as a war governor would be or how he would administer them, he did not yet know. But he would learn in time. Tod took his orders to heart, and he adhered to them throughout the war, even after the same party would cast him aside after one two-year term.

Even with the election successfully won, Tod's busy pace continued. Before his January inauguration he traveled to Washington to meet President Lincoln for the first time. He did so, according to friend and US Senator John Sherman of Ohio, to ask Lincoln "what a Republican President wanted a Democrat Governor of Ohio to do in aid of the Union cause." Tod was not alone among Union governors as they tried to understand just what their role would be during this unprecedented civil unrest. As events continued to unfold the relationship between the Lincoln administration and the chief executives of the remaining states was one in the making.

It was Tod's first encounter with Lincoln, and he was impressed with the president's "extraordinary firmness" and supportive of the president's intent to either "put down or perpetuate slavery," whichever course would lead to victory. This last sentiment is important because it reinforces the position that Tod, from the beginning, gave emancipation his support as a war measure if it were deemed necessary. When Lincoln finally introduced it as such in 1862, Tod would be unfairly criticized as being soft on the measure. Tod also found Secretary of War Simon Cameron possessed of "reasonable ability," Secretary of State William Seward "a man of extraordinary talent," and General George McClellan a "modest [man] . . . with no political aspirations to minister to . . . He is worthy of applause, and I have not the slightest doubt that our destinies are completely safe in his hands." As the governor-elect prepared to leave for Columbus he believed that the country would be "safely out of this rebellion in a few months" and to have proved the "predictions of our forefathers, that man is capable of self-government."[79]

10

Taking Hold, January–June 1862

ON THE MORNING of January 13, 1862, Ohio governor William Dennison and his successor David Tod walked side by side in a Columbus field inspecting the Ohio Volunteer Infantries (OVI) of the Forty-Sixth, Fifty-Eighth, and Sixty-Ninth Regiments along with two regular companies of US infantry.[1] The inspection was purely ceremonial but symbolic of the military state of affairs in which Ohio found itself. After reviewing the troops, Dennison and Tod were led to the state house by a military escort for the swearing-in ceremony of the governor-elect. Troops from nearby Camp Chase and Fort Lyon paraded in splendid fashion in and around the streets of Columbus, projecting a strong military presence throughout the city. As Dennison and Tod proceeded to the same destination that afternoon, their careers were moving in opposite directions.

During the early days of the conflict the wartime governors found themselves in "a difficult and frustrating position filled with responsibilities [like] the raising and care of troops, [and] the mustering of men and money." No governor had ever experienced such demands before and Dennison did an excellent job when the duties of a war governor were suddenly thrust upon him. When his term ended, he left his successor with a cupboard full of supplies. He did this by calling upon the state legislature to appropriate $450,000 for arms and supplies for the volunteer militia. In less than one month, the legislature authorized Dennison to organize "new regiments to aid the federal government or to fend off invasion, forbidden the transportation of contraband through the state, provided for relief of militia families, passed a measure to define and punish treason . . . reorganized the militia, increased the governor's staff and appointed additional general officers." Steps were also taken to train, house, feed, clothe, pay, and care for the new recruits. And when he found out that Secretary of War Cameron was raising troops within the borders of Ohio, he fumed at the secretary to respect the integrity of Ohio.[2] When Dennison's term ended, ever the patriot, he faced "the avocations of a private life."[3]

Reporters approved Tod's short inaugural address, a compendium of his many speeches from the previous summer. He reiterated his support for Lincoln's war measures and the preservation of the Union under the Constitution. As for domestic institutions such as slavery, Tod said, "we seek, not [its] destruction" but rather the preservation of "the Constitution, as our fathers gave it to us." Tod came back to a specific theme he made the previous summer, one that Lincoln would echo at Gettysburg. This "Union of the States must be preserved," he warned, and "in no other way can we hope to demonstrate to the world that man is fit for self-government. If this Union cannot be preserved, we will be compelled to resort to some other form of government, and thereby confess that our fathers were mistaken, in claiming for their children, [the] ability to govern themselves." As the historian Gary W. Gallagher writes, if the Civil War generation failed to save the Union it would demonstrate that "ordinary people [were] incapable of self-government and [discredit the] political genius of the Revolutionary fathers." Tod could not agree more. To his Ohio constituents he said, "Let us look to [do] it, [and] not disappoint." Every citizen of the state must undergo sacrifice in order "to claim for herself her just share of the . . . glory of putting down this rebellion." He then touched upon the sacrifice of the soldier in the field and his family. He proposed that each of Ohio's 88 counties keep up a tax to provide for "the families of our troops during the war."[4] It was very personal to him especially since his son George, who was on active duty, had already seen combat. Overall, his address was described as "straight-forward and business-like, like its author."[5]

The need for efficient managerial skills would be needed from Tod, whose inaugural appeal to the legislature, "Let the experience of the past year induce us to be ready, at all times," was meant not only for the duration of the present crisis but for future troubles yet unseen. Tod petitioned for an on-call trained state militia of 350,000 to be used "at a moment's warning ... in any portion of the State ... to prevent invasion from any quarter." But the Union Party–led legislature failed to act, and this would force the governor to scramble to acquire new volunteers to defend Cincinnati from invasion before the end of the year.[6] Tod was prepared to act. "The new Governor takes hold with a will," noted one observer, with "an evident determination."[7]

He retained his predecessor's immediate staff, which made for a smooth transition. Adjutant General Catharinus P. Buckingham, Commissary General Columbus Delano, Quartermaster General George Bohan Wright, Judge Advocate General Luther Day, and Surgeon General Gustav Weber agreed to stay on. And reaching for the familiar comforts of home Tod appointed his old law partner Benjamin Hoffman as his private secretary.[8] These selections would prove vital to the success of Tod's administration. Buckingham would be gone in April, however, as the War Department called him forth to Washington to serve "a more extensive field of usefulness," as Tod put it.[9] The experienced staff helped Tod navigate the state establishment while answering the call of the federal government. Thus, the Tod administration was able to quickly get "down to business focusing on the war effort, " writes one historian.[10]

Tod and Quartermaster General Wright first met after Tod's election. Wright was struck by Tod's physical features and provides one of the more concise descriptions of Tod at the time. The governor stood "five feet, ten inches in height, stoutly built, and weighed about one hundred and ninety pounds," recorded Wright. His new boss also possessed "a fine shaped head, with a prominent forehead; bright, dark-brown eyes, with dark hair slightly tinged with gray."[11] The new governor came to rely upon Wright, who earned a reputation as a "faithful and efficient officer."[12] One of Wright's earliest directives from Tod was to construct a prison at Camp Chase in Columbus and to look after the care of captured rebels who were sent there.[13] Wright was a talented and sensible man and able to handle most any assignment including the responsibility of taking indefinite care of prisoners of war, something that was not at all anticipated. General in Chief Henry Halleck had imposed on the new governor the task of housing prisoners captured from the Western theater.[14]

The Tod family moved into a handsome Italianate-style villa on East Town Street just a short walk from the capitol. The mansion was more than accommodating for family and guests. Maria, ever outgoing and supportive, was pleased with its comforts and would host many social functions over the course of her husband's term.[15] The couple was joined by their now teenaged daughter Sallie.[16] Cognizant of judgmental eyes upon her, and not wanting to be outdone by the fashionable gentlewomen of Columbus, Maria was known to dash up the four flights of stairs to the observatory to spy out the attire of the arriving ladies and upgrade her own dress if necessary so as not to be outshone by her guests.[17] She also fulfilled more serious obligations like serving on the executive committee of the Soldiers' Aid Society.[18] As Maria adjusted to her new role so, too, did the new governor. He projected confidence and was described as "a delightful and responsive guest at all social gatherings."[19]

One thing was for sure: The war brought on changes for everyone. Disappointed with his war secretary, President Lincoln decided to replace Simon Cameron. Cameron's short tenure had included charges of incompetence, mismanagement, and corruption. In his place, Lincoln placed Tod's old Democratic Party associate Edwin Stanton, former attorney general in the Buchanan administration. Stanton, writes one historian, possessed "a Radical's mind-set about the war" and like Lincoln wanted action.[20] In Stanton, the fellow Ohioan would provide a familiar face at the White House for the new governor and over the course of Tod's term, the two would exchange a plethora of letters and telegrams dealing with military matters. Stanton encouraged Tod to visit Washington "to consult" on matters and invited the governor to "make my house your home while here."[21] For Tod, with Stanton now in place, there was an intimate conduit to Washington, but this was also so for the other Union governors. Others, like John Andrew of Massachusetts, were jealous of Tod's intimacy with Stanton.[22]

With a new man overseeing the Union's war efforts, Lincoln hoped to get things moving. However, as refreshing as Stanton's presence was to most, the struggle for understanding between the authority of the states and the limits of the federal government continued for new governors like Tod. Although he reached out to Stanton with old familiarity Tod revealed his uncertainties about his role. "I feel myself so much embarrassed for the want of well defined rule or order, in the administration of my military duties, that I am constrained to call your attention to the matter," Tod wrote Stanton.[23] Tod's confusion suggests that the transition between the outgoing Dennison administration and the incoming Tod administration was not as communicative as it should have been. Therefore, the relationship that developed between Tod and Stanton symbolized the relationship between Ohio and the federal government at the time. Tod and Stanton had to get to know each other in their new official capacities. Of pressing need, Stanton required men to build and maintain an army.

"The concept of a national army," writes historian William C. Harris, "independent of the states and the governors, did not become a reality until much later in the war." Once the governors raised, trained, and dispatched their volunteer citizens to the battlefield they were confused about the extent of their "gubernatorial authority." Tod, writes Harris, "reflected this uncertainty" and he was given no clarification from Stanton's office. The answer would become self-evident. Union governors, Harris notes, "conceded tactical authority over their state troops to the War Department and the commanding generals as they became part of a larger federal army."[24] Tod and the other Northern governors really had no other choice but to send troops to the federal government. Nor could they simply set up defensive positions along their borders. The consensus was that an army from the North would have to go on the offensive to bring the seceded states back into the union of states. The governors were expected to be the recruiting agents for this national army. Lincoln and his cabinet desired to see a wave of volunteers come forward rather than having to draft men. When men were needed, as they always were, cabinet members like Secretary of State William Seward were dispatched to gain the assurances of the governors that their volunteers were coming before a national call went out through the press. A poor response could lead to embarrassment. It was one example, Stephen Engle explains, of Lincoln's attempt to gain the cooperation of the governors rather than impose his will.[25] And Tod eventually came to understand his responsibilities.

Governors were also expected to be the patriotic voice inspiring their citizens to aid the cause. This task would prove to be a challenge especially when there was no momentum or positive news from the battlefield. By his first summer in office, Tod began to see more "Northern apathy" as "saving the Union was losing its appeal" absent military success. Though hard-pressed to claim any success under Lincoln's leadership during the first year of the war, Northern governors had to stay on course.

Because of the lack of military progress, in January 1862, the president issued General Order No. 1, which called for a general advance of Union forces under the command of Gen. George Brinton McClellan.

The brash, haughty young commander was a Democrat and a railroad executive before the war. The short winter pause provided little time for the North to regroup under the aggressive Stanton and the pressure was applied to McClellan to get moving. One of the troubles with McClellan was that he was a better organizer than strategist and his stalling tactics and conduct toward the president at times bordered on insubordination. Privately, he disparaged Lincoln. Finally, McClellan started his troops toward Richmond for the war's first large-scale offensive in what became known as the Peninsular Campaign. McClellan believed that capturing the Southern capital would bring an end to the war.[26]

The one bright spot for Lincoln and Stanton that winter was the performance of Maj. Gen. Ulysses Grant. In February 1862, Grant demonstrated dogged tenacity in the Western theater where he forced the surrender of Confederate-held Forts Henry and Donelson. Capturing the two forts opened the Tennessee and Cumberland Rivers to Union control. Union troops, with a strong contingent of Ohioans, would continue to be on the move under Grant and were sure to be in the thick of the fight. It also meant a flood of prisoners of war to Camp Chase. Compelled to accept the prisoners, the accommodations at Camp Chase would be pushed to their limits in no time.[27]

Early in his administration, Tod famously earned a reputation for compassionate and attentive feelings for his men especially if they were wounded in battle. It was a good thing too. The federal government's co-ordinated medical response was adequate but logistically ill prepared to handle the large numbers of casualties of the sick and wounded. It relied heavily on the thousands of volunteers through the US Sanitary Commission, which initially "distributed packages and supplies to soldiers in the camps." Other privately funded volunteer relief organizations came forward in fine patriotic fashion with clothing, bandages, and other homemade first-aid supplies. Church groups of all denominations and benevolent aid societies helped to supplement the needs of the wounded with supplies while administering hands-on care at hospitals in the rear. It would take time before benevolent "groups learned to navigate the war's complex demands." Until an "intricate, multitiered voluntaristic structure evolved," Tod would not sit idle.[28]

Tod showed little patience for these novel systems to work out and he pushed his staff to respond quickly to aid Ohio's wounded soldiers. Although his actions were not necessarily revolutionary, he was one of the first governors to send supplies, first aid, surgeons, and nurses in hospital boats to care for and evacuate injured soldiers. Quartermaster General Wright remembered, "When matters were still somewhat in chaos, and proper system and organization had not been effected, when . . . surgeons and nurses were lacking," Governor Tod acted.[29]

One of Tod's first endeavors to provide care for the wounded occurred in April after the bloody Battle of Shiloh in southwestern Tennessee near the Tennessee River. The two-day battle ended in victory for the Union, but it came with a terrible cost. The casualties from both sides at Shiloh were astonishing, so much so that one participant wrote to his hometown paper days later, "I will not attempt to give the number of killed or wounded of either side. It cannot be told; but it is enormously great."[30] History would record 20,000 killed or wounded. Even before the official number could be verified, those who fought at Shiloh knew that until then this battle was "emphatically the greatest of the civil war, and resulted in a far greater loss of life."[31]

Tod wasted little time responding. On April 9, he directed Surgeon Gen. Gustav Weber and Lt. Gov. Stanton to lead steamboats with 30 surgeons and 50 nurses to the field hospitals. Additional personnel and supplies followed. The injured were treated on-site and those more seriously wounded were loaded aboard the steamships or hospital boats and evacuated to Camp Dennison in Cincinnati for further medical treatment.[32] The wounded were also treated at private hospitals in the Queen City. Of those residences and buildings being used as hospitals, one officer reported, all were "in miserable condition."[33] The care for Ohio's sick and wounded soldiers on display after Shiloh was, if not a novel response, one of the most organized and well-thought-out responses of the war.

Tod renewed the call to Ohioans for help after the carnage at Shiloh. Women were asked to gather up and send medical supplies while Quartermaster General Wright, on behalf of the governor, provided a detailed list of much-needed stores and supplies to the press: "Cotton shirts [and] sheets, Light woolen blankets, Cotton pillow cases, Woolen and cotton drawers, Woolen and cotton shirts, Handkerchiefs and Towels, Lint from old pure linen, Cotton socks, Pillows and cushions, Materials for rags and bandages, Slippers and light shoes, Dried fruit, prepared chickens, Arrow root, Oatmeal, Lemon syrup, [and] Currant jellies," to name a few.

Soldiers' Aid Societies like the Ohio Relief Association helped to lead and coordinate these efforts.[34]

Female nurses were slow to appear in field hospitals but gradually they became a more common fixture. Tod was known to decline the volunteer services of women in a matter-of-fact way. Responding to one group of willing women Tod wrote, "you will regret to learn . . . that I have no authority to employ female nurses. They are not received with much favor by those having charge of our sick and wounded soldiers."[35] Many would go onto find a way around government restrictions until they were finally and fully accepted.

In May, when Tod discovered that "a large number of sick and wounded Ohio soldiers" were laid up at New Albany, Indiana, he turned to Dr. W. L. McMillen. The governor gave the doctor $500 and instructions to charter a steamboat, procure nurses and supplies, and evacuate "all the soldiers whom you find there" to help alleviate "the distresses of these gallant boys." For Dr. S. M. Smith the governor outfitted the steamboat *Tycoon* with medical provisions and instructed the surgeon to seek out "the sick and wounded soldiers of our State" scattered throughout the Tennessee and Cumberland valleys. Then, in anticipation of a battle near Corinth, Mississippi, where Union troops had pursued the retreating Confederates from Shiloh, Tod ordered Wright and Surgeon General Weber to charter a steamboat to extricate "the sick and wounded from the battle-field." By this time Ohio's surgeons had acquired "so much experience in this work of duty, that particular instructions for . . . guidance [became] unnecessary." He also furnished 25 surgeons to attend to the wounded and sent emissaries to Louisville, Kentucky, and Cairo, Illinois, in search of Ohio's wounded. Tod believed it was his paternal duty to look after his soldiers and provide for "their comfort and happiness." He believed that "a great, wealthy and generous State, like Ohio, should take over [the care of] her brave and galiant sons."[36] Earlier in the month, Tod had appointed Robert Harper to meet as many arriving trains and hospital boats as possible to "provide for all sick soldiers whom you may . . . meet [and] minister to all the reasonable wants of our gallant boys."[37]

Tod's efforts naturally garnered great affection from his men. The feedback from Col. George Senter, who had "visited nearly all of the hospitals along the Ohio, Mississippi and Tennessee rivers, for nearly two thousand miles" reassured the governor that his efforts were having the desired effect. With few exceptions, reported Senter, Ohio's wounded were being tended to. Caregivers were working around the clock to administer services. Onboard the *Glendale,* Senter observed surgeons "working for four days and nights, with scarcely an hour's sleep or rest." Senter took a moment, on behalf of the sick and wounded and their families to personally thank Tod for his "promptness, energy and liberality" to see to their needs. He assured the governor that there was hardly a "sick or disabled soldier" who had not "received all possible attention through [Tod's] instrumentality."[38] Tod's continued commitment was demonstrated by the fact that before the end of the year 11 steamboats had been chartered to ply the Tennessee, Ohio, and Mississippi Rivers to treat and retrieve Ohio's fallen fighters.[39]

The *Cleveland Morning Leader* proudly proclaimed that Ohio had "set the example of chartering steamboats to bring home her sick and wounded soldiers from the battle[field]." Indeed, Governor Tod was one of the first to undertake such coordinated action in the war. His progressive medical response undoubtedly saved the lives of countless soldiers. "No state," according to the *Leader,* "has done more for the sick and the wounded soldiers than Ohio."[40] Secretary Stanton lauded Tod's "humane and patriotic service" along with that of Govs. John Andrew of Massachusetts and Oliver Morton of Indiana for similar actions.[41] One historian observed that Tod "had outdone himself in efforts to provide for his constituents serving in the Union armies." By year's end, Tod authorized more than $127,000 to care for Ohio's wounded.[42] The measures put into motion by Governor Tod were sustained for the duration of the war.

Although he was not an overly religious man, Tod believed it was his "Christian duty [to care] for the sick and wounded brave troops of Ohio."[43] And it became his practice to send out religious men such as Rev. James Marvin to minister spiritually to the troops. Rev. A. R. Howbert reported back to Tod later in the year from the Potomac basin that "the Ohio soldiers appreciate your many acts of kind efforts for their comfort. 'God bless Governor Tod!' Is often heard arising from the quivering lips of the afflicted." Some wounded even managed to send their own handwritten notes of thanks to the governor.[44] Regrettably, the demand for more men continued.

In late May, Lincoln called for 500,000 volunteers. It was an extraordinary number and Governor Tod acted quickly to do his part.[45] One of the main reasons for the call for more troops was the apprehensions and misjudgments of George McClellan. The general had gotten into the habit of procrastinating before every planned offensive because he overinflated the strength of the enemy. McClellan's demand for more troops, troops that were not always available, coupled with growing casualties, added to the need for the call of more volunteers. Serious consideration was given to implementing a draft but Tod and other governors were not so keen on the idea and advocated the continued use of volunteers. In fact, throughout the spring and summer, seeking volunteers and furnishing recruits for the Union war machine was Tod's primary responsibility.[46] And the idea certainly weighed on the minds of volunteers in the field. One Ohio infantryman shared his sentiment in a scornful letter home to his mother when he wrote about the excitement surrounding the idea of a draft: "Everybody in our company has somebody that they want drafted."[47]

That same month, Secretary Stanton had been in a state of high anxiety when Confederate forces, under the command of Thomas Jackson, reached striking distance of Washington. Tod was dismayed when he heard of the "astounding" news about the capital's insecurity and promised "one full Regiment" within two days' time. He then sent word to recruiting stations in each county to raise troops for the defense of Washington.[48] On May 26, Tod issued a public-spirited call for volunteers and over the next several days, more than 5,000 answered him. Within a day's time, Tod was proud to report to Stanton that new recruits were "pouring in handsomely."[49]

Major credit must be given to William Dennison. During his last year in office, Governor Dennison had set up recruiting agencies in each of Ohio's 88 counties. Some of these locations also included camps to help muster the volunteers. The system had been so successful under Dennison that Tod kept it in place.[50]

Southern forces had also occupied western Virginia near the town of Martinsburg. Union forces held firm at nearby Harper's Ferry, but they, too, needed reinforcements. "We want as many troops as you can raise," Stanton urgently wrote Tod. "I can furnish arms," Stanton told Tod, if the governor provided the manpower. But the secretary was premature with his promises. In the coming months, he would have to fend off the Ohio governor and his staff over the procurement of proper arms. Unaware of an arms shortage, Tod eagerly sent his Ohio volunteers ahead. The Sixty-First Ohio Volunteer Infantry, stationed at Camp Chase since April 23, was one of the first to ship out via the Baltimore & Ohio Railroad to reinforce the troops in western Virginia. Tod's "stirring [public] appeal," during this recent need, said Stanton, caused a "patriotic feeling" that effected "rapid enlistments," aiding Union efforts needed at Martinsburg.[51]

It was likely during this period that Governor Tod's sincere affection and devotion for the well-being of his young soldiers gained the public's attention. Before his troops were sent off to battle, Tod began the habit of addressing his men with impassioned and patriotic speeches. In addition to a rousing send-off from Camp Chase his remarks were filled with wise, instructive, parental words of advice. At one send-off he "told the boys that if they wished to send their money home," remembered J. J. Parsons of the Sixty-Seventh Regiment, "they could leave it with him, and he would be responsible for its safe delivery."[52] He began to refer to the recruits as "My brothers!" "My boys!" "My sons!" These "terms," said one friend, became "familiar epithets."[53] He "cautioned" them like a father sending his sons off to boarding school "to be careful of their health, to be temperate and always obedient to orders of their officers; to have coolness, patience and courage under all trying circumstances; to save their money and send it to their friends at home." The governor believed they were all "bound on a glorious mission, the protection and preservation of the best government in the world." Tod's words of encouragement were often returned with loud cheers. For as much as Tod believed in the mission to save the Union, for as much as he believed it was the duty of young men to come forward, he must have realized especially after Shiloh, that he was sending them into harm's way. It surely weighed on his mind. How could it not? His feelings for them, his compassion, and his devotion were evident in the medical support that he faithfully sent to the field.[54]

While the governor continued to recruit volunteers (4,000 three-month recruits in June alone) and promised Stanton another five regiments of three-year recruits by the end of September, he grew impatient when proper supplies for his boys were not furnished. One historian described Tod as "a vigorous, forceful man" and never were these traits more on display than when the governor wanted aid for his soldiers.[55] He complained profusely to one supply officer, "I have done every[thing] in my power to procure tents for the Ohio regiments, but as yet without avail . . . I will continue to do all I can to secure tents."[56]

More than once his disappointment was revealed in sternly worded letters to Stanton. "It is important that the State of Ohio should be promptly supplied with arms for the new quota of troops," he lectured Stanton in

July. "I desire that 20,000 . . . should be placed at my disposal at the earliest possible moment, and I trust that, if not all at least a fair proportion of them shall be of the Springfield muskets."

Stanton was not the sort to be lectured to, however. In a measured response, the assistant secretary of war, P. H. Watson, informed Tod on behalf of Stanton that "ten thousand Austrian rifle muskets" were en route to Columbus. Then he reminded the governor of the 10,000 Enfield rifles sent to Ohio back in May and asked curtly, "Where are they?"[57] But Tod would not back down. Of those, he defensively responded that he had only 1,100 remaining after issuing 8,500 to various regiments.[58] When former governor Dennison was in Washington Tod asked his predecessor to investigate "the great deficiency in arms and equipment for our new recruits. We are really destitute of every[thing]," including tents, knapsacks, blankets, and canteens. "Please," Tod implored Dennison, "see to it before you leave . . . that ample supplies of everything are at once provided." The situation, Tod said, lowered troop morale.[59]

Soldiers' morale aside, the war was straining the financial resources of the United States even though they were in the very competent hands of Salmon P. Chase, the efficient secretary of the treasury. Chase's revolutionary ideas—the creation of a national banking system, the issuance of a national paper currency, and the sale of government bonds to subsidize the war effort—were yet to take hold.[60] Until those designs stabilized the nation's finances, money needed to procure pay for personnel, weapons, uniforms, food, horses, and other essentials strained resources. Digging into the country's coffers to pay Tod's discharged soldiers who had only volunteered for three months' service was not a priority for the United States Treasury. But these reasons did not keep Tod from asking.[61]

He was genuinely troubled when he learned that his discharged soldiers experienced problems upon their return to civilian life. Their want for "advice and assistance in the settlement of their accounts and collection of their pay" proved to be such an unbearable "burden" that Tod placed the troubles under the discretion of Quartermaster General Wright. Many soldiers, due to financial hardships, physical setbacks, or both had fallen victim to false agents who offered to work on their behalf but committed "numerous frauds" against them. This compelled Tod to direct Wright to seek some organized protection for the "heroes who have broken down in the service of our country."[62]

Another group that fulfilled its three-month requirement was anxiously awaiting payment at Camp Chase where there was "not a dollar of money here to pay them." Tod implored the War Department to pay his men. An exasperated Stanton wrote back: "It is impossible to pay faster than money can be had from the Treasury." Stanton pleaded with Tod, "Pray do not be impatient for a delay that cannot be helped."[63]

In other instances, wounded or paroled soldiers were left stranded at train stations because they had no money to purchase a ticket home. Under Wright's guidance agencies were soon operating in Cincinnati, Columbus, and Cleveland to aid these destitute men. In time, offices were set up in Louisville; Washington; Memphis; St. Louis; Nashville; New York; and Cairo, Illinois, to assist Ohio soldiers. Though the war was over for these men, it continued for thousands more.

In late June, the president called for another 300,000 three-year men, of which Ohio was expected to provide 74,000. This was on the heels of McClellan's failed Peninsular Campaign. The general's constant call for more troops against superior forces, which existed only in his imagination, worked against recruiting efforts. And the call for more men was irrefutable evidence that the war was not going well.[64] One dispirited volunteer with the First OVI wrote home, "The late call for 300,000 more troops will either bring out a good many cowards or else they will be drafted."[65]

By July, mounting casualties, the lack of military gains, the need for more men, and the reality of a protracted war all contributed to the political angst of the president as critics grew weary with Lincoln's leadership. "How much longer will he allow our brave soldiers to be sacrificed?" asked the *New York Herald*, "How much longer will he permit defeats?" But the paper targeted Stanton for these failures and recommended his removal. Stanton "distracts the confidence of the public, and that his mere retention in office delays enlistments and discourages enthusiasm." It was a time of growing dissension between Stanton and McClellan, and it briefly drew Tod into the fray.

As criticism of the war effort ramped up supporters of McClellan were hard to find within the Lincoln administration. Outside of it was a different story altogether. Partisan politics crept back into things as hardline Democrats took shots indirectly at Lincoln by targeting Stanton. The *New York Herald* did not shy away from doing the party's work, affixing McClellan's setbacks to Stanton himself. This should come as no surprise, read the *New York Herald*, "when we consider that Mr. Stanton, though learned in the profession of the law, knows nothing of the science of war." Under the weight of military failures, Stanton was accused of using the general as his scapegoat.[66]

Unfortunately, the private dissension between Stanton and McClellan was now before the public. McClellan's biographer, Stephen W. Sears, writes: "There was concern that the furious battle going on between the partisans of McClellan and Stanton would jeopardize the Northern war effort."[67] Tod was not alone in his concern for this unfortunate development and likewise embarrassed by its public display. As a result, Stanton again got to experience Tod's force of character. "For God's sake," Tod implored Stanton, "stop the wrangling between the friends of McClellan and yourself in Congress. I ask this as the friend of both."[68]

Shortly after Tod's intercession, McClellan led his troops in flight from the gates of Richmond pursued by Confederate general Robert E. Lee. The failed Seven Days Battles marked another setback for McClellan and the Union. Union defeats dampened recruiting efforts and forced Lincoln to contemplate conscription while Congress considered amending the Militia Act to include the service of free Black men.[69] The Union governors were all under extreme pressure to implement a bounty program using their states' funds.[70]

Tod knew that these types of measures were very unpopular, and he did his best to avoid them by keeping up steady recruiting efforts. But the initial enthusiasm that saw recruits flood into camps during the first year of the war had slowed. There is little doubt that the growing death count and the sight of wounded soldiers returning home with missing limbs contributed to the downward trend. These were just a few "symptoms of war weariness" that began to surface.[71] Although Ohio continued to exceed its quota the overall numbers by July 1862 were down comparatively from the previous year: 58,325 to 84,116.[72] In July Tod informed Lincoln that despite "all my efforts to fill up the old regiments . . . I am meeting with but poor success."[73] And his frustration continued because what new regiments he sent forth were still poorly supplied. As late as August, his troops still deprived of supplies, Tod was again after Stanton for materials, even charging the secretary's quartermaster with "great negligence." He again admonished Stanton for the want of his 20,000 "gallant boys," who were in service without so much as a blanket and proper clothing. "I know not where the fault is, and it is well that I do not," he thundered to Stanton, "for I would whip the fellow were he as strong as Methuselah." Although he remained optimistic in the endeavor to supply more volunteers, Tod's exertions alone could neither sustain nor meet the state's quota.[74]

Tod's experience was not unique, as other Northern governors faced the same challenges. And if they failed to deliver men, the federal government stood ready to assist by implementing a national draft. Tod had to continue to figure out how to satisfy the manpower needs of the federal government.

Governor Tod faced his challenges head-on, faithfully honoring his commitment to assist the efforts of Lincoln and Stanton.[75] More important, he came to understand his role as a war governor. And Stanton learned to further appreciate Tod at this time, writing the Ohio governor, "I shall always be thankful for any suggestions you can make as to the administration of this Department."[76]

In the months ahead, Tod also got a clearer picture of just how fractured Ohio's support of the war was. The lay of the "political land," wrote one loyal citizen to Tod, was filled with "many men [who harbored sentiments of] secession." And they were "doing all they can to" help aid the cause of the South.[77]

"Everything," Tod said, "is valueless to us if our Government is overthrown," as he again called on Ohioans to "help bear aloft the glorious flag unfurled by our fathers."[78] And he continued to do everything in his power to support the war effort.[79] The months ahead would prove no less challenging.

11

Partisans and the Patriot, July 1862–September 1862

THE PROBLEMS THAT plagued Union governors during the first half of 1862 carried over into the second half of the year. Declining enlistments, lack of military progress in the Eastern theater, increased skepticism from the citizenry, the reemergence of partisan politics, and mounting criticism from the fourth estate all cast a dire mood over the Union. These issues alone proved challenging for Northern administrators. However, with the military and thus political fate of the Union still attached to McClellan, it was no wonder that great focus was placed upon the general and the 100,000 stagnant Army of the Potomac under his command. Repeatedly, the general failed to advance or, in Tod's words, was "driven back, merely by the force of overwhelming numbers,"[1] words indicative of a potential crack in his confidence in McClellan. After one of McClellan's recent withdrawals, according to one Cleveland newspaper, Lincoln was reported to have said to his military leader, "Well General, I have heard of people being knocked into the middle of next week, but we are the first people I ever knew who were knocked into the middle of last year."[2] To be sure, Lincoln, Stanton, McClellan, and the loyal governors across the North all needed some military success upon which to reassure Unionists everywhere and to stop the slow leak of confidence pervading the North. This was especially so with Governor Tod.

The month of July brought with it much of the same: McClellan's delays emboldened the enemy and flattened recruitment. Things seemed so desperate for Tod he was compelled to order all soldiers on leave to report back to Columbus or face desertion charges, fit-for-duty status notwithstanding.[3] In the face of these difficulties he continued to put forth his "best endeavors" appealing, almost pleading for volunteers.[4] Tod would have been lucky if finding recruits were his only headache in the coming months. He had other issues to contend with that had even larger national implications, such as protecting Ohio's southern border from invasion while arresting subversives inside the state's borders.

The federal government was given some reprieve when Congress passed the Militia Act, which authorized the president to call on the states to send forth their militias for military service. The most controversial measure of the act was the authorization granted the president to employ self-emancipated Black men to serve in any capacity other than a combat role. They mostly took on camp jobs such as cooking, trench and latrine digging, livery duties, and the like.[5] Assuming these drudgeries helped to free up white soldiers for combat. More important, it was "the first step . . . toward congressional approval for the recruitment of black troops in the army."[6]

Meanwhile, the War Department made plans to implement a draft in October. A draft was viewed by some as another assault by the federal government upon states' rights. Tod thoroughly disagreed with the conscription law but not for this reason. As governor, he was reluctant to employ the draft because he believed he knew the sentiment of his constituents better than did officials in far-off Washington. "The people," it was said, "revolted from the idea of a draft." Fearing strong reactions, Northern governors like Indiana's Oliver Morton, Illinois's Richard Yates, and Pennsylvania's Andrew Curtin joined Tod to forestall the order. Besides, a draft suggested that the men of the state were coerced into fighting and therefore lacked the patriotic spirit to join on their own accord. Tod knew that the draft would "cause [a] diversity of opinion and action among" his fellow citizens so he continued to aggressively seek volunteers.[7] Writing from Cleveland, where he hoped to "stimulate the recruiting" he privately confessed to Stanton his fear that the "harvest" of men was "nearly over."[8] But the governor held out hope that "one more grand effort" from Ohioans would sustain "the proud character of our noble State."[9] Also, Tod did not think it was necessary to institute a state-funded bounty system to induce volunteerism but he eventually gave in to it in hopes of attracting long-term enlistees. He even went as far as to put up the first six months of his salary to help fund the program.[10] He did approve and accept, however, the payment for substitutes. "Conscientious objectors" were able to avoid military service for the hefty sum of $300. Tod could not have been pleased with such conduct. However, he used the $50,000 raised from this practice to hire substitutes and to provide for wounded soldiers.[11] And given his state's reliance on agriculture, he exercised patience by instructing his local recruiting officers to authorize deferments to farmers until after their fields were sufficiently harvested.[12] In August, satisfied with recruiting results the War Department granted Tod a postponement of the draft until September 15.[13] Some success was realized when local communities raised their own regiments.

Most newspapers at this time, regardless of party affiliation, openly solicited support for the draft and gave Tod hearty backing.[14] The draft was certain to lift the enormous burden off Tod's shoulders.[15] And it would allow him to function more as the chief executive of a sovereign state rather than a recruiter for the War Department. However, it was another power surrendered to the national government.

Opponents of the draft were further incensed when rumors of emancipation began to circulate. The news inflamed simmering antiwar sentiments and racial animosities. Support for "the policy of keeping the negro everywhere just where he is" had enjoyed widespread popularity. But as Lincoln looked to emancipation to invigorate the war effort, he also contemplated enlisting free Black men for military service.

Though Lincoln remained silent the very idea of emancipation took on a life of its own. Added to this was the desire to enlist free Black men into the military. These were delicate political propositions. Critics charged that they were now being told that preserving "slavery and the Union" was no longer possible and that exterminating the former would help save the latter.[16] Reports of new volunteers abruptly turning back for home after news that Black soldiers could be joining them was common. Countless Ohioans openly protested, including the editors of the Ashland *Union*, who bemoaned; "The object of the war is now plainly enunciated. Our soldiers are to fight for the niggers."[17] Adding to the despondency was the end of McClellan's command in late July. The president had endured McClellan's failures long enough and replaced him with Henry Halleck.

With the rumor of emancipation, antiwar Democrats and conservatives alike now had a fresh platform from which to preach their opposition to the war. But federal and state authorities were in no mood for questions or criticism. Orders suppressing free speech upon penalty of arrest were issued. More specifically, Secretary Stanton empowered US marshals and local constables to arrest and jail anyone speaking out against or discouraging enlistments.[18] The order was meant to help governors combat political opposition within their states. Accompanying these arrests was the suspension of habeas corpus.[19]

One of the first in Ohio taken into custody for violating Stanton's new order was a Huron County resident named George Fish, who "was arrested in his bed at midnight" and charged with "discouraging enlistments."[20] The most celebrated Ohio case involved Dr. Edson B. Olds, of Lancaster. The physician was a former three-term Congressman and an unabashed Peace Democrat, or Copperhead. His antiwar rhetoric had gnawed at Tod, who described Olds as "a shrewd, cunning man, with capacity for great mischief, [who] should at once be put out of the way."[21] Delivering a speech to local Democrats, Olds blamed the war and "all this bloodshed and ruin upon our country" on abolitionists. No Democrat should continue to support it unless the tyrant Lincoln changed his "policy and war cry." Olds's rhetoric was met with fierce condemnation from Lincoln supporters. The *Cincinnati Commercial* howled that if the government did not "take care of Olds and his squad" then it was up to loyal citizens to "shoot them down like mad dogs."[22] War proponents increasingly grew frustrated with Olds's actions. One self-professed War Democrat in Athens wrote Tod that if Olds weren't stopped "the quota of the state will never be full by the volunteer system."[23] Tod kept Olds under close watch until he had had enough of his mischief. At Tod's request the order to arrest Olds was issued by the assistant secretary of war. On August 12, Olds was seized at gunpoint and charged with disloyalty. He was put away for four months at Fort Lafayette in New York Harbor where he was locked in solitary confinement for more than three weeks. Instantly Olds became a martyr of the Peace Democrats and Tod was accused of violating the doctor's constitutional rights. Olds's ordeal touched off such outrage among the Peace Democrats during the ensuing months that he was elected to the Ohio General Assembly during his incarceration. Olds would not soon forget Tod's role in his arrest and imprisonment and would seek revenge soon after his release.[24]

Tod demonstrated no tolerance for the criticism he received after Olds's arrest. Charles Roland, editor of the *Ohio Eagle,* was invited to the governor's office for an interview. This was after the editor rankled the governor by withdrawing support for Rufus Ranney from his paper's masthead. Ranney, the Democratic nominee for supreme court judge, was an old friend of Tod's. Roland disagreed with Ranney's support of the war.[25] The meeting between Roland and Tod turned contentious when the editor brought up Olds's arrest. Tod reaffirmed his actions then threatened Roland with the same fate if he continued to print columns supporting the conduct of Olds and others. "I HAVE THE BACKBONE TO DO IT!" Tod thundered before an abrupt exit. The Democratic *Logan Gazette* concluded that Tod "must be insane or a traitor." Sane or not, Tod continued to show his resolve against Confederate sympathizers and his support of Lincoln when he ordered the arrest of two more editors for encouraging resistance to the draft.[26]

For as much criticism as they received, Tod and the federal government also enjoyed support for their actions. The *Wyandot Pioneer* wrote, "We are a friend of free speech and a free press, but there are circumstances in which a nation may be placed, when even the indulgence in such sacred rights as these may be subversive of the general good." The *Weekly Perrysburg Journal* also praised Tod as one who was willing to "rise above prejudices of party and to sink the partizan [*sic*] in the patriot." But the Democratic partisan spirit was on the verge of a resurgence.[27]

Two weeks after Olds's arrest the Union suffered another defeat at the Second Battle of Bull Run under the command of John Pope. While Pope's troops were being overrun, McClellan waited . . . and waited. Allegations of duplicity were leveled against McClellan for failing to come to Pope's aid. After the battle Samuel Galloway, judge advocate at Camp Chase, was summoned, along with Governor Tod, to Washington by Lincoln. The president, Galloway later reported, sought the opinion of the two Ohioans on whether to replace Pope with McClellan as the head of the Army of the Potomac.[28] Tod was in favor of giving McClellan another chance. Most of the president's cabinet opposed McClellan's continued service, but Lincoln was more upset with Pope's command. After Pope was dismissed, Lincoln swallowed his pride and reinstated McClellan's command.[29]

Tod managed to remain firm throughout it all but what galled him the most was the political backbiting and self-serving requests for promotions. Records of his official correspondence are filled, particularly during his first year in office, with countless letters from someone, some prejudiced group, or some disgruntled citizen requesting or questioning the promotion or lack thereof of a worthy yet maligned man in uniform. Political rivals would accuse him later of handling promotions based on political favor or even downright incompetence, neither of which is grounded upon any evidence. These letters and telegrams poured into the governor's office, yet he faithfully responded to all.[30]

Tod also managed to work with the state legislature during this time to reduce spending. The savings were then used to offset costs associated with the care of wounded soldiers and their families. The legislature, however, failed to give Tod and his soldiers the absentee voting mechanism he so craved, thus putting the upcoming fall elections at risk.[31] But most disappointing for Tod was the legislature's refusal to give him the militia he had asked for in his inaugural address. The failure to address this issue was infamously highlighted when the state's southern border was threatened with invasion, forcing Tod to scramble to find volunteers to defend his own state.[32]

Tod first received reports about the movement of Confederate cavalry under Gen. John Hunt Morgan in July.[33] Whether Morgan was in search of supplies, or he was trying to draw attention away from other engagements, his force moved quickly through Kentucky and Indiana. Untethered to supply lines they lived freely off their spoils while accumulating war provisions. In addition to supplies, they targeted vital transportation structures like bridges, railroad overpasses, and tunnels for destruction.[34] When the rebel force neared Cincinnati, defending the city and state from invasion became Tod's highest priority.

One of Tod's first decisions was to order 200 soldiers recuperating at Camps Dennison and Chase into defensive positions in Cincinnati.[35] The troops arrived to find a nervous citizenry. Although the Ohio River presented a natural barrier against invasion from the South it was not so impassable at the height of summer's dry season. Morgan had already proved adept at seizing boats to ferry his men back and forth across the 2,000-foot-wide river. Without a defensive force on display at Cincinnati, the raiders would have no trouble getting across the river to infiltrate and plunder before recrossing to safety. To soften defensives, Morgan's artillery, which included Parrott rifles and howitzers, was more than capable of lobbing 6- and 12-pound shells across the water.³⁶ Morgan's threat was averted when Union forces in Lexington, Kentucky, gave chase.

In September, another Confederate threat emerged under the command of Gen. Edmund Kirby Smith. A Mexican-American War veteran Smith was an aggressive yet savvy leader. As Union forces retreated from Lexington to Louisville after the Battle of Richmond, Smith saw an open 50-mile-long swath that led to Cincinnati. He quickly directed his troops to make haste for the city where the Ohio River was still "at a very low stage." But this time, the city and the state had their guard up.³⁷ This was a much more serious development as Smith's force numbered upward of 20,000. Rightfully, Smith's movements in Kentucky "occupied every moment of [Tod's] time for [several] days."³⁸ Fortunately, federal troops under Gen. Don Carlos Buell stood in his way.³⁹ If Buell failed, Ohio was in trouble and if Ohio were invaded, the war could be lost. When Tod found out that troops from Ohio under Buell were still short of supplies, he wired Capt. John Dickerson a one sentence directive, "For God's sake furnish our Ohio troops, now in Kentucky, with canteens."⁴⁰

Despite Buell's presence, a nervous Tod called on Major General Lew Wallace to take command of Cincinnati, where the general immediately declared martial law. Shops closed, fortifications were thrown up, and able-bodied citizens took up defensive positions. The city's African American population also jumped in to assist.⁴¹ Working side by side whites and free Black people came together to shore up the city's defenses. The white citizens of Cincinnati, writes historian Benjamin Quarles, were "given an object lesson in Negro co-operation in a common cause."⁴²

The governor himself arrived in Cincinnati on September 2 to confer with Wallace. Tod found "matters . . . so confused" writing Stanton, "I cannot give you any definite information." But he was confident that if "a large [opposing] force is making toward this place. It will be successfully met."⁴³ A slew of orders quickly helped reinforce the city's defenses. Tod concluded that the town needed more soldiers and called for all armed men residing in the counties along the river to speedily organize.⁴⁴ He also ordered about 600 men stationed at Camp Dayton to make haste for the defense of Cincinnati.⁴⁵ Tod kept Stanton abreast of the unfolding situation.

Tod's public call for volunteers proved enormously effective. From Cleveland, 500 enthusiastic men came forward bearing "rifles, muskets and rusty shot guns." The shops at the Cleveland, Columbus & Cincinnati

Railroad closed because every worker headed for Cincinnati. The Alliance Rangers, a 120-man unit, formed and answered the call. One bullheaded volunteer at Geneva, having no money in his pocket but armed with musket and bayonet, boarded a train for Cincinnati. When the conductor made the ill-advised attempt to try to remove the penniless passenger for want of fare, the determined patriot promised to "serve him as he would a Secesh— run him through with his bayonet." The passenger remained onboard.[46]

Although Stanton believed the "panic in Kentucky" was "exaggerated" he still lauded Tod for mobilizing the citizens of Ohio. He also expressed his gratitude for Tod's "course . . . in calling upon the people to defend themselves. If we in the Northern States cannot guard our borders against marauding bands, but must get into a spasmodic panic on every occasion that threatens, the contest is hopeless."[47] The second threat to Ohio, however, was more than a marauding band. Indiana governor Oliver Morton had also recognized the seriousness of Smith's threat and declared martial law in the river counties while likewise calling for volunteers for the defense of his state.[48] Morton was convinced that the Southern coalition had grand illusions beyond independence. More specifically, he believed that Southern leaders wanted to bring the Middle West states of Ohio, Indiana, and Illinois into its confederation.[49]

Tod kept his guard up and directed Ohio militiamen from Marietta; Wellsville; Chillicothe; Gallipolis; and Falmouth, Kentucky, to head for Cincinnati.[50] Militia Captain Charles W. Smith of the Trumbull Guards, stationed in Gallia County, nervously advised Tod that he had encountered an enemy force of 2,400. The governor attempted to buck up the skittish Captain Smith, exhorting him to "stand firm and show your blood." Tod promised Smith, "Should you fall, I will escort your remains home."[51]

Writing to Major General Horatio G. Wright, the commander of the Department of the Ohio, now in control at Cincinnati, a confident Governor Tod informed him of the additional help on its way. "You will have a very large force of minute-men, or squirrel hunters [who] will make the best soldiers in the world."[52] According to the historian James Bissland, these so-called Squirrel Hunters numbered "nearly sixteen thousand clerks, woodchoppers, and farmers of various sizes, shapes, and ages . . . in overalls and waistcoats . . . lugging ancient muskets, shotguns, horse-pistols, and weapons better suited for shooting rodents."[53] In a letter to Stanton Tod praised the Squirrel Hunters' glorious response.[54]

Assessing the Confederate threat and strength was difficult for several days. Information on Smith was not always dependable. But Cincinnati was now prepared. One eyewitness described defensive "entrenchments for 15 miles round to the river . . . and a great number of heavy cannon planted on the hills [with] two gunboats in the river."[55] The impressive show of force along the riverfront coupled with the presence of Union regulars in Kentucky finally ameliorated the threat of General Smith. On September 13, General Wright wrote Tod that Smith's forces were in full retreat with many thanks to the Squirrel Hunters whose patriotic reaction to the emergency, said Wright, "saved our soil from invasion."[56] Tod regretted that they never had "a chance to shoot" the enemy.[57] Proud as he was of the Squirrel Hunters, an organized state militia could have been deployed along strategic points of the Ohio River to serve as a permanent deterrent. It would also have provided reassurance for all Ohioans. If only the legislature had heeded his request the threat to Ohio might never have materialized.

In Columbus the next day a relieved Tod and West Virginia governor Francis Pierpont turned their focus to the Kanawha River valley, where Ohio troops arrived to prevent the enemy from advancing northward.[58] Admittedly, Tod had been "anxious about Eastern Ohio and Western Virginia for a number of days." The two governors requested that Stanton send troops to the region to deter any Confederate threat.[59]

While Governors Tod and Pierpont worried about West Virginia, Confederate General Robert E. Lee ventured northward across the Potomac into Maryland. Meanwhile Lincoln cautiously proceeded with his thoughts on emancipation. His cabinet convinced him that to issue such an extraordinary measure at this point, after a string of battlefield defeats, would portray an administration in the throes of desperation. A major victory on the battlefield by the army's leader George McClellan would give the president a position of strength from which to issue such a bold measure.

Late that summer, McClellan chased Lee into Maryland. The two powerful armies met near Antietam Creek in Sharpsburg on September 17. The daylong battle resulted in a Union victory and, with more than 26,000 casualties, is remembered as the single bloodiest day in the nation's history. When word of the carnage suffered at Antietam reached Columbus, Tod responded as per usual by sending all available medical personnel and supplies to care for Ohio's wounded.[60]

In Washington, a desperate Lincoln claimed victory at Antietam and used it to announce his intent to issue the Emancipation Proclamation. The measure would take effect on January 1, 1863. The news brought mixed reactions, but it immediately transformed the objective of the war from one based on unification to one that now included the abolition of slavery.[61]

Two days after Lincoln announced the Emancipation Proclamation Tod arrived at Altoona, Pennsylvania, to meet with the governors of Illinois, Iowa, Maine, Maryland, Massachusetts, New Hampshire, New Jersey, Pennsylvania, Rhode Island, West Virginia, and Wisconsin. The administrators had convened at the urging of Pennsylvania's governor Andrew Curtin to discuss Lincoln's handling of the war. Although Curtin spearheaded the gathering, Tod and Pierpont agreed to have their names added to the public invitation alongside Curtin's.[62] Curtin and Governor John Andrew of Massachusetts had conferred with Lincoln beforehand; he made them aware of his planned proclamation. Curtin and Andrew privately gave Lincoln their support. Before he left Columbus, Tod had sought guidance from Secretary Stanton, who had little to offer. The gestures of Curtin, Andrew, and Tod in this instance support historian Stephen D. Engle's assertion that the governors encouraged Lincoln during difficult times specifically on issues like emancipation.[63]

"The governors who converged on Altoona," writes the historian William Hesseltine, "were of many different minds on the nation's problems." The Northern press also represented different minds and monitored events closely even though it was banned from the proceedings. "More sensible newspapers," writes Engle, supported the gathering because they believed that the governors, not members of the president's cabinet, better understood the sentiments of their citizens. Indeed, Engle notes, the populace "identified their governors as their spokesmen" and the meeting was an ideal apparatus "to move the [Lincoln] administration in line with the people it represented."[64]

Although backgrounds were different, their purpose was singular. Republican governor William Buckingham of Connecticut attested to the camaraderie among his colleagues during the summer of 1862. They were "a harmonious family of officials [with] one common and great cause," victory, he asserted.[65] Their desire to save the Union took precedence over all other issues.[66] In addition to debating McClellan's effectiveness the group discussed recruitment, the draft, the overall course of the war, and the president's recently announced Emancipation Proclamation. Tod, described by one observer as a "decided substantial man," strolled about the town in deep conversation with Curtin.[67]

Before the governors could consider the Emancipation Proclamation, they first had to get past the McClellan question.[68] The Radical Governor Andrew of Massachusetts loathed the insolent, do-nothing general and demanded that John Frémont take his place. Andrew was immediately supported by William Sprague of Rhode Island. But Tod sprang to the defense of McClellan "declaring that the people would rise up *en masse* and repudiate" his removal. Curtin also rose to McClellan's defense, pointing to the general's recent victory at Antietam. Tod's opinion was also supported by Maryland's Augustus Bradford, who thought McClellan "the best General in the country."[69] Edward Salomon of Wisconsin and Tod each prepared separate resolutions in support of McClellan, which perhaps helped save the general's tenuous position.[70] McClellan's biographer, Stephen W. Sears, suggests that the general had anticipated an attack by the governors and had probably "importuned [Tod] to speak for him."[71] Conservatives feared that if McClellan was replaced by the abolitionist Frémont, the new commander "would conduct a hard war to save the Union and end slavery," notes William C. Harris.[72] But by this time, emancipation had already redefined the war's objective. McClellan would stay.

With the McClellan issue addressed attention turned toward the Emancipation Proclamation. This was at the real heart of the gathering. Andrew's Radicals erupted with joy when they heard of the president's proclamation and only regretted that it had not come sooner. Bradford had the most cynical response among the governors, believing the measure would "amount to nothing" and "be made a rallying cry" by the enemies of the Union. Although no minutes of the meeting exist the *New York Herald* reported that Tod also advocated caution on the matter and called for "a substitute [plan] of a more conservative nature."[73] Just who provided this tidbit to the *New York Herald* is anyone's guess. Curtin also fell in with Tod. On this issue, however, opinions mattered little as the president's proclamation had already been announced. What did matter in the end was that the governors united behind Lincoln and the Emancipation Proclamation. Practically speaking, Tod was in favor of the measure. His initial hesitation, like Bradford's, was a question of timeliness pertaining to political and military effectiveness. Even though he gave his full support of emancipation at the conference, Tod's inquiry into the timing of the measure was leaked. Once this happened, he had no way to control the narrative. Contemporaries and historians placed too much attention on his initial hesitation on the timing of the announcement.

For Tod, even though his moral opposition to slavery was growing more pronounced, it was still all about a timely war measure. Granted Tod was never an abolitionist but he was also not proslavery. He certainly had no use for it and believed that it would not survive the war should the Union emerge victorious. Tod's name should be included in historian William Zornow's description of Lincoln and his supporters on the issue of slavery: "In their opinion slavery was morally wrong and would probably die as a result of the war, but they refused to tamper with it unless its abolition would directly influence the salvation of the Union."[74] Tod had demonstrated his pragmatism with his focus on winning the war. Emancipation was a war measure. The extinction of slavery, in Tod's mind, was just a matter of time. And that time, Tod realized, had indeed come.

Stephen Engle's study argues there were a handful of state executives like Tod, Curtin, Morton, and Maine's Israel Washburn who fully embraced the measure and offered support for Lincoln's growing "radical measures against slavery" as the president expanded the "Union war aims." Indeed, when Lincoln reached out to Curtin, Curtin "enlisted the counsel of Tod and Andrew . . . to discuss and unite behind a more vigorous prosecution of the war." And when Lincoln "hinted" at emancipation Curtin fulfilled his promise to deliver to the president the support of the governors.[75] Tod's support of emancipation warrants closer analysis.

Tod scholar Delmer J. Trester described the governor as "rather cool towards emancipation."[76] However, the following first-person account refutes that conclusion. Governor Washburn's own description of the Altoona proceedings deserves more attention because it gives a firsthand account of the proceedings just days after the meeting. On his way back to Brunswick, the Maine governor sat with the editors of the *Portland Daily Press*. The journalists "had the pleasure of a long interview with [Washburn] . . . and he was very free and communicative in relation to the purpose, views and acts developed." The Maine governor referred to Tod as "no radical, no abolitionist, nor sorehead" and contended that the Ohio governor was the first to rise in support of the Emancipation Proclamation after careful consideration and discussion. "It was Governor Tod," Washburn described, "who first made a proposition in relation to the Proclamation, and he proposed to tender congratulations to the President, and to express the hope that as he had *spoken the great word*, he would follow it by *striking the great blow;* and to assure him that they, backed by their respective States, were ready, willing and anxious to help him." The editors were incredulous at this news. "The first man to break ground in relation to [emancipation] . . . was not the Executive of 'abolition Vermont,' or 'fanatical Maine,'—as some pro-slavery men would perhaps style those states—but it was David Tod, the *Democratic* Governor of Ohio!"[77]

Washburn's firsthand account requires historians to take a fresh look at Tod's conduct at the Altoona Conference and specifically his reaction to Lincoln's Emancipation Proclamation. Washburn had no ulterior motive for reporting what he did, what he heard, and what he saw. He owed nothing to Tod, nor was he prejudiced by him in any way. He simply sat for an interview with newspaper reporters from his home state of Maine. His observations were current and not made from historical memory and convincingly showed that Tod embraced emancipation as a war measure because it could help bring the war to a successful end. After all, it was Tod who told Lincoln back in December 1861 that he would support the president whether he decided to "put down or perpetuate slavery."[78]

Where conservatives and Democrats rallied against the Emancipation Proclamation, Unionists embraced it and used it to reenergize their work to end slavery and win the war. For War Democrats like Tod, supporting emancipation meant abandoning the original purpose of preserving the Union and the Constitution as they were. One former Democrat and onetime "attorney of the slavecatchers," Brig. Gen. Richard Busteed, publicly proclaimed, "I sincerely believe if slavery lives the republic dies."[79] But if saving the Union meant changing the war objectives men like Busteed and Tod embraced that proposition.

But Tod had to gauge the political climate in Ohio. After all, as a "Middle Border" state Ohio, contends historian Christopher Phillips, was far from unified on the issue of slavery. For as strongly as Tod now supported emancipation as a war measure, he was right to be concerned about the political fallout that emancipation would have on the fall election, further recruitments, and the draft.[80] The anti-administration Democrats grew more emboldened with each military setback and were adept at exploiting unwelcome news. When word of Lincoln's Emancipation Proclamation got out, they used the race issue to drive a wedge between factions and instill fear whenever they had the chance. One of the most vicious of the anti-Lincoln, anti-Tod newspapers in Ohio was the *Cadiz Democratic Sentinel,* in Harrison County. The *Sentinel* warned that white citizens of Ohio had every reason to be "alarmed" with talk of an "emancipation scheme." Should the measure pass, the editor decried, "great numbers of the negroes, without means—lazy, dirty, ignorant [will] continue to come into the State, and become a burden to the people." The state of Ohio "will become Africanized, and the whites driven to the wall."[81] It was this type of rhetoric that Tod feared would inflame emotions, dampen the spirit of volunteers, and embolden resistance to the draft.

After the conclusion of the Altoona Conference the united band of governors traveled to Washington to visit with Lincoln and various cabinet officials. The group presented the president with a vote of confidence and offered a public pledge of their continued support. Lincoln rejoiced and heartily welcomed the gesture.

Tod had accepted Stanton's invitation for lodging. The two men discussed the war. Stanton sought Tod's firsthand details of the conference at Altoona. Stanton must have wanted particulars about the various opinions on McClellan. They also talked about Ohio's recruiting problems and the assistance Stanton could offer. One of the major conclusions Tod gained from the meeting was Stanton's authorization for advance payment and bounties to help encourage recruitment ahead of the October draft.[82] Tod also called on Secy. of the Navy Gideon Welles, to whom he expressed his confidence in McClellan, Lincoln, and the Union war effort in general. Welles also recorded that Tod thought "delay is necessary," a probable reference to the governor's initial opinion that McClellan should be, for the moment, spared.[83]

For Tod, his acceptance of emancipation as a war measure marked the next step in his political evolution. From his last position as a Douglas War Democrat Tod's support of emancipation now positioned him closer to the goals of the radical Republican faction and further away from the conservative Democratic principles that he was reared in. For sure this shift indicates his support of the wartime strategy but, nonetheless, it places Tod deeper inside a Union Party that was under the growing influence of the radical element of the Republican Party.

Though Tod worked extremely hard during his first summer in office, there was little to show for his efforts. The Union still struggled to gain military momentum after the victory at Antietam in large part because

McClellan allowed Lee an unencumbered retreat. Lincoln's new war measure, the Emancipation Proclamation, threatened Northern unity and support for the war. The October 1 draft date for Ohio seemed to be racing toward Tod, bringing with it added political controversy. What political effect all these issues would have on the coming congressional elections was yet unknown.

12

Democratic Thunder, October 1862–May 1863

AFTER THE ALTOONA Conference and his visit to Washington, Governor Tod returned to Columbus reenergized and immediately reaffirmed his commitment to supporting emancipation. Meeting with two acquaintances (probably Gen. Lew Wallace and State Treasurer G. Volney Dorsey), who had come out in support of emancipation, an eager Tod proclaimed, "That's it," a public meeting was needed "and we must all address the people, and appeal to their loyalty."[1] The Emancipation Proclamation rally was held on the east steps of the statehouse on October 6. Tod was the featured speaker along with Dorsey and Wallace. Wallace had recently arrived from his successful defense of Cincinnati. Dorsey told the crowd that "every means [including emancipation] must be used to weaken the hands of the rebels." Wallace, whose job as a soldier he said, "was to kill traitors," proclaimed emancipation to be "the best blow yet struck at the rebellion." When Tod stepped forth, he received an "immense cheer." The necessity of emancipation had been arrived at, he said, because the war "had come to such a pass that the question was forced upon us."[2] And as for the president's proclamation he "heartly endorse[d] every word of it" and believed that its January implementation date "was well timed for Ohio." Far too much Ohio blood had been sacrificed and "must be atoned for in the death of this rebellion!" The enslaved, he said, must be set free because as "long as slaves are allowed to remain at home" to aid their rebel owners, he believed, "so long will rebellion last." As for the president, Tod continued to give his full endorsement. "He was equal to the emergency," he thundered, "and such measures [as emancipation] would end this rebellion in a few months."[3] His words "were enriched with an unusual unction." And he "expressed no doubt as the necessity and propriety of the measure, and avowed it as his conviction, that a just God would never crown our arms with a final victory until we did justice by the emancipation of the enslaved."[4]

Tod's conduct regarding emancipation was too often overlooked. In some instances, words are just as strong as actions, and this is one of them. His political opponents could certainly refer to his inaugural just 10 months previous when he spoke in favor of preserving states' rights and opposed the dismantling of domestic institutions. Lincoln's own inaugural said the same thing. However, when those institutions like slavery were used to make war against the Union then it became imperative to "march over or through the obstruction, whatever it be."[5] No man knew Tod better during this period than Quartermaster Gen. George B. Wright, who said that once the Emancipation Proclamation was announced the governor "never for a moment wavered, but both publicly and privately endorsed and approved it."[6] His words in support of the measure were powerful yet contemporaries ignored them and historians have overlooked them.

Days before the crucial fall election he was again in front of a crowd supporting emancipation. "I have studied it calmly; I have given it my faithful attention," he firmly said, before reaffirming its splendid timing. The blood of Ohio must be acquitted, he charged. "If I have any influence with the Government, I will urge them to ... go on till every one of those infamous leaders are hanged, as an example to all future time. The best blood of Ohio cries from the battlefield and demands the death of these leaders."[7] These stirring remarks and his public endorsement of emancipation, however, would never be enough for the Radical Republicans. Freeing the enslaved as a war measure was one thing but the use of free Black men in the military was another matter.

Tod's refusal to accept free Black volunteers into the military early in the war was expected. To do so as early as 1862 would have jeopardized much of the support for the war at that critical time. But he was under enormous pressure from the Radical Republicans to accept these willing, patriotic, and able-bodied men into the ranks to help meet the state's quota. Infamously, Tod is remembered for lecturing John M. Langston, a Black abolitionist attorney, on the matter of recruiting Black men in August 1862; "Do you not know Mr. Langston that this is a white man's government; that white men are able to defend and protect it . . . ?"[8] These words echoed Stephen Douglas's own when he once said, "I hold that this Government was made on the white basis, by white men, for the benefit of white men and their posterity forever."[9] Langston did not come empty-handed to the statehouse. He offered Tod over 1,000 Black Ohio volunteers who desired to fight because they "recognized that a Confederate victory might mean their own enslavement." But Tod was in no mood to entertain the idea, reportedly concluding his meeting with Langston by stating, "Had the people elected a Colored Lieutenant Governor to serve with me I would not have taken my seat, and I cannot ask the noble men from Ohio who are in the field, to do what I would not do myself."[10]

But Tod was also under pressure from his own family to accept free Black men into the ranks. Julia Ford wrote her brother from her home in Akron, "on the subject of the Colored Regiment that has been tendered you from this part of our state." She asked whether his refusal to accept their service was due to the position of the War Department or her brother's own "lurking prejudice." Either way, she felt it "a very great blunder not to allow any people to fight the Rebels with all their might if inclined to do so." Admittedly, she worried over the fate of her own sons who "may be called upon . . . before this wicked rebellion is put down." She asked her brother therefore to "ponder the subject in your own heart" and to "allow the Blacks to defend their own rights and ours." She closed the letter to Tod with the hopes that their "Heavenly Mother will guide you in the path of duty."[11]

Habitually, in all instances during this period, Tod had fallen back on his old standard excuse when he claimed that the state constitution did not allow him to enlist Black men. This had given the Radicals more cause to oppose Tod. This conviction was rooted in Tod's old Democrat foundation. Democrats, Jean Baker reminds us, "had habits, instincts, and traditions [based] on a white man's government."[12] But Tod was certainly not alone in this thinking. In time, after adopting a more progressive attitude, Tod would advocate the use of Black soldiers but not yet.[13] For the time being, he encouraged their enlistment into the ranks of the state of Massachusetts, where Governor Andrew gladly accepted their service.[14]

General Wallace joined Tod again in the governor's office on the night of the October election to monitor the returns. Wallace had already been the veteran of the Battles of Fort Donelson and Shiloh and he was not easily rattled. His piercing eyes denoted a confident deep thinker but on this night that confidence would be severely shaken. Protests in the weeks leading up to election day sparked concern among Union Party members.

On the night of the election early returns did not look good for the Union Party. As the evening wore on a huge throng of Democrats, with great expectations, began to converge on the grounds of the capitol to celebrate. They were not disappointed. Of the state's 19 congressional districts up for grabs, Democrats captured all but 5. In limited state contests, Ohio Democrats even managed to regain the offices of secretary of state, the attorney general, and a seat on the state supreme court.[15] The Democratic victories sent a message to Governor Tod and in particular the Republican faction that dominated the Union Party; Ohioans seemed to have lost all confidence in the management of the war under Lincoln and by affiliation in Tod. (The feeling was even growing among the troops in the field. One Ohio soldier had recently written home about the increasing sentiment among his comrades in arms, "The boys are getting tired of the way the war is being carried on."[16]) Adding insult to injury, particularly for Tod, was the fact that his incarcerated, anti-war, speech-making antagonist Edson B. Olds won a seat in the state legislature. His scheduled release in December afforded time to take his oath of office in January.

General Wallace turned to Tod after the results were in and said, "I think, Governor, you have got me into a scrape by seducing me to make that speech indorsing [*sic*] the Emancipation Proclamation." Tod replied that the general was not the only one now in a scrape. Celebratory cheers from Democrats outside the governor's office drifted upon the night air. Though it had been some time, the clamor was one he had heard many times before. It was "Democratic thunder," Tod said, harking back to his former days of partisan celebration. "I am familiar with the sound," he said disgustedly.[17]

The Democratic thunder rumbled across the Union. The Union Party took hits in a string of states, "spearheaded," writes historian William C. Harris, "by an aroused Copperhead minority." The Democrats also scored victories in Indiana, Illinois, and New Jersey. And in New York's governor's race, Horatio Seymour defeated the antislavery Republican,

James Wadsworth. "The Democratic surge," said Harris, "created deep concern for Lincoln" and the Union governors. Though most Democrats still "openly supported the war to preserve the Union," added Harris, "the election demonstrated that antiwar sentiment was growing in the party."[18] Even the troops in the far-off field identified the shifting sentiment. Pvt. John L. Hebron, of the 2nd OVI wrote his father from Camp Edgefield Junction outside Nashville in November 1862, "It does look like a political war ... for the states that went strong [for the] Republican[s] before the war now goes Democratic strong."[19] The results of the 1862 election in Ohio was one of the greatest Democratic victories in recent memory. That surge, writes another historian, "repudiated Lincoln" and his loyal governors, like Tod.[20]

If the results of the October election were any indication of things to come, Tod's own chances for reelection the following year were all but lost. Historian Eugene Roseboom writes, "Democrats regarded [the results of the 1862 elections] as a repudiation of the administration, particularly emphasizing arbitrary arrests and emancipation, while the peace element became more open and more vociferous, feeling the State was becoming anti-war." The conservative faction of the Union Party also blamed the missing soldiers' vote for the disappointing outcome. "The star of the Copperheads," Roseboom asserts, "seemed to be in the ascendant."[21] This was particularly so in Ohio, Indiana, and Illinois where "the loudest Copperhead voices" were concentrated.[22] Richard Abbott, in his study *Ohio's Civil War Governors,* also notes that the results strained the cohesiveness of the Union Party. The Radical element of the party was unhappy with McClellan and Lincoln's dismissal of the military abolitionist General John Frémont from his Western command. Conservatives were against emancipation and the use of Black troops. These growing splits within the Union amalgamation aided the Democrats' resurgence.[23] There was a growing sense that the old Republican Party, which had provided the widest base for the Union Party, was showing signs of weakness. The only bright spot for the Union Party in Ohio was the defeat in the Third District of congressional candidate and leading Copperhead Clement Vallandigham.[24]

On New Year's Day 1863 Lincoln signed the Emancipation Proclamation, which in theory freed enslaved people held in bondage in those states in rebellion against the United States. Without federal troops, there was no way to enforce the measure. However Hugh Jewett, the Democrats' nominee for Ohio governor in 1861, brazenly announced that if he occupied the governor's chair, he would have issued an order "countermanding" the proclamation. Ohio's attorney general, Lyman Critchfield, recommended halting the war altogether since the Emancipation Proclamation changed the original goals of the conflict. Tod dismissed this clamor and recommitted his pledge to shut down and arrest any Peace Democrat making treasonous speeches or interfering with recruits. Stanton and Secretary of the Navy Welles lauded Tod for his forceful responses.[25]

In keeping with custom Tod spent the afternoon with Quartermaster General Wright, calling on friends and neighbors. Wright had grown quite fond of Tod, was in his company often, and saw the true side of the governor's nature more than anyone other than Maria Tod. In Wright's estimation of Tod, there was little difference between the public face and the personal side of his chief. "He exhibited," said Wright, "the attributes of kindness to the unfortunate; sagacity and tact combined with unflinching integrity, and with all, a remarkable endowment of common sense." Tod could be "grave and thoughtful" to be sure "but never morose or out of temper." During these grim times Wright said that Tod "endeared himself to all with whom he came in contact, and to the sorrowful and afflicted" victims of the war, "he always had a kind and cheerful word." Tod's letters may not have possessed the poetic style of Lincoln's, but he was more than capable to poignantly express his unfeigned sentiments as in the case to one surviving widow of a slain Ohio soldier. "Dear Madam, I write to assure you of my heartfelt sympathy in the loss of your brave and patriotic husband," he wrote Orpha Annette Hanna, of Mount Pleasant, Ohio, "to express the hope that inasmuch as he sacrificed his life in a most righteous cause, you may enjoy the consolation and receive the honor due to a true soldier's widow."[26] These "were marked features of his character," Wright maintained.[27]

On January 5, Tod published his State of the State Address. His remarks made no mention of Lincoln's Emancipation Proclamation. The omission was another critical error in the eyes of the Radical Republicans who interpreted the exclusion as a continued sign of weak support for emancipation. But it also could have been an attempt by Tod to placate the conservative base of the party. Again, as in years past, he tried to appease both sides, but this time he misjudged the growing influence of the Radical element of the party.

Tod also described his role, and all those Union governors working in support with the federal government. We, "the Executives of the loyal States are co-workers with, and in a great measure agents of, the authorities of the Federal Government in the raising and organizing of Federal forces." This is the best example thus far where Tod knowingly expressed his understanding that the states needed to play a subservient role to keep the war effort on track. The massive effort of raising troops continued to fall upon the states. This issue alone had consumed his time more than any other. "I am in the office every day, Sunday not excepted," he admitted, "from morning until late at night, and patiently and cheerfully devote nine-tenths of my time to the interests of our gallant men in the field.[28] I have promptly rendered them all the aid in my power, cheerfully and diligently." In this same spirit, he completely and willingly supported the president's suspension of the writ of habeas corpus and the arrests of those evil scoundrels, the Peace Democrats, who worked against enlistments and who sought to undermine the draft. "Necessity," asserted Tod, warranted such actions. To justify the denial of "certain privileges" or constitutional rights, Tod reasoned that it was only a temporary "suspension."[29] But contemporary critics and historians alike condemned Tod for his violation of the Constitution that he had held so dear. But the new year, 1863, will see more of this temporary action.

One of the urgent challenges Tod posed to the legislature was to secure for the soldiers fighting on the battlefields the ability to vote. After all, these men were fighting to preserve the Constitution that guaranteed that basic, fundamental right at least for eligible white males. The results of the previous election were missing tens of thousands of votes from Ohio's soldiers that could have changed the outcome of the election but there was no system to furlough troops home to their polling places or to get a ballot to the battlefield. All sides of the political divide pressed the legislature because each believed that the soldiers' vote would be to their advantage. The *Weekly Perrysburg Journal* read it was "the duty of the General Assembly to provide ways and means to carry the ballot box with our Ohio volunteers wherever they go."[30] This issue needed to be remedied. And it was. In April, the state legislature passed An Act to Enable Qualified Voters of This State, in the Military Service of This State, or of the United States, to Exercise the Right of Suffrage. The act enabled active military personnel who were absent from their home polling places on Election Day to cast their vote at the captain's headquarters.[31] The response and the result in the upcoming election would be overwhelming.[32] As for the State of the State Address it should be viewed as the start of Tod's campaign for a second term. His review of his administration's accomplishments during his first year, Tod believed, justified another term.

In response, the *Ohio Democrat* wasted no time attacking Tod's "Democratic manhood," charging the abolition agents in Washington with corralling him into their arms where "in an evil hour" he committed low acts by suppressing free speech, allowing unlawful arrests, and supporting emancipation. In their eyes, Tod had all but forgotten the "name and fame" previously afforded him when he was the leading member of the Ohio Democratic Party.[33]

The *Ashland Union* also criticized Tod's message and his consistent referencing of the Founding Fathers and the question of self-government. The answer would be revealed during the next election, the partisan journal declared, when Ohioans sent "a [Democratic] man of sense and brains to be Governor" to replace the current occupant, who possessed neither.[34]

Within days of the governor's message the Democratic Party convened for the annual Jackson Day commemoration. Among the many attendees were Clement Vallandigham, Samuel Medary, and Edson B. Olds, leading members of the Copperhead faction of the party and notable adversaries of Tod and Lincoln. They were also staunch advocates of "the Constitution as it is, the Union as it was and the Negroes where they are."[35]

A group of Midwest supporters of Lincoln gathered in February. Tod, former Governor Dennison, and General Wallace met Indiana Governor Morton in Cincinnati to address a crowd of Union supporters. Tod railed against the "bastard Democratic party" that hijacked his old Jacksonian institution, defended his arrest of Olds and his ilk, and denounced Southern sympathizers. Wallace warned of conspirators in their midst.[36]

The parties and their factions continued to be fueled by the Emancipation Proclamation. Its effect, writes Engle, "crystalized divisions within political parties."[37] Private clubs and organizations at the grassroots level, particularly during campaign season, supported both Peace Democrats and Unionists. The Knights of the Golden Circle emerged as a secretive society before the war. Their grand plan was a separate slave power of countries encircling the rim of the Gulf of Mexico. During the war, the Knights preached resistance to the "federal war policy" and support of the Peace Democrats.[38] One blatant demonstration of the Knights' intent occurred in the neighboring state of Indiana. When a train car full of Confederate prisoners arrived in Bloomington, coincidentally coinciding with a Democratic rally, the crowd of "copperhead K.G.C.'s [sic]" rushed to press up against the car windows. Peering at the detainees inside the sympathizers pleaded with the prisoners to make a break promising, "We are able to protect you."[39]

Rising to contest the influence of the Knights was the Union League. The popularity of the Union Clubs spread throughout the North and became more vociferous especially as elections neared.[40] Peace Democrats of Ohio looked upon Union League members with great scorn and judged their leaders to be "unscrupulous and corrupt." Union League members, warned the KGC, were "prepared to carry out [dastardly] schemes." Come election time the Knights warned Ohio Democrats to "vigilantly guard the polls on the day of election and see that illegal voters are not permitted to interfere with the election."[41]

Among war governors, Tod led the call for the establishment of a home guard, to stand ready against civil insurrection. General Wallace agreed and came out in February with a strongly worded public warning to the citizens of Ohio. "I solemnly warn you that a wide-spread and insidious conspiracy is on foot," he announced, "which promises revolution and ruin." There were organized forces throughout New England, 80,000 men in Ohio, 70,000 in Indiana, and 100,000 in Illinois, just waiting to strike, announced Wallace, who believed that under the pretext of peace, the goal was to separate the Western states from the Eastern while the South went its own way.[42] It was much more than a bifurcated split of North and South, as the historian Christopher Phillips explains.[43] A near-panicked Wallace warned his fellow citizens, "I have given you the alarm [and] I advise you to *organize*, not politically, but in the style of soldiers. Organize for your lives, for your property, for the peace of society and the Government."[44] What evidence he had and how serious Tod took the warning is not known.

Although Tod believed he earned the right to a second term, his second-year relationship with the state legislature proved to be a "stormy one." Even though Democratic lawmakers in the Ohio General Assembly remained in the minority their victory in the fall emboldened them to challenge the wounded governor and the weakened Union Party. They wasted little time.

A measure was introduced on the second day of the legislative session to create a committee to investigate Tod's role in the military arrests of the previous year. The resolution passed but without the accusatory language aimed at implicating the governor. Rather, it focused on the actions of the military and the suppression of free speech. Tod and the military were cleared of any wrongdoing because Democrats could not show violations of an existing statute.

In addition to the resolution that provided soldiers with the chance to vote, another created the long sought-after state militia. Tod had aggressively sought passage of both measures and should be credited with recognizing their importance as political necessities and military war measures. The latter, however, was passed so late in the session that a militia force was unprepared to face one of the more serious threats to the state's borders. The Ohio Militia would eventually number over 165,000 but was not ready to respond to the reemergence of the raiding forces of Confederate general John Hunt Morgan midyear.

Unable to secure any meaningful victory during the session, Peace Democrats of the assembly showed themselves to be an ongoing irritant to Tod. Resolutions condemning suspension of the writ of habeas corpus, the draft, and the Emancipation Proclamation, among others, lacked support for passage but were supported by the minority, nonetheless.[45]

But Tod did not face these challenges alone. Although he and his fellow war governors remained behind Lincoln's war measures,[46] military victories remained elusive. Each defeat intensified Lincoln's search for the right military leader. Back in November the president for the last time set McClellan aside and replaced him with Ambrose E. Burnside. After he lost the Battle of Fredericksburg in December Burnside was replaced by Joseph Hooker in January. As it would turn out Hooker, like McClellan, "fought excellent campaigns on the map," writes one historian, but could not win battles on the field.[47]

From those battles, on average, 1,000 "disabled soldiers" were discharged from the field per week.[48] Thus, the grinding gears of the federal war machine required more fresh bodies. If more soldiers were needed, Tod counseled Stanton, then bring on national conscription. The governors were nearly spent on the matter of recruiting. As historian Engle puts it, "The time had come to bring the system of raising volunteers under the control of the national government." Congress finally acted to facilitate recruitment by passing a national conscription act in March. Governors were relieved, even though it was another power surrendered to the national government.[49] And if any problems should arise on the home front, the governors were responsible for stopping them. On this point, Tod told Burnside that if the draft came, he would need up to 1,000 troops to enforce it and to suppress any signs of discontent.

The Democratic storm cloud rumbled into the spring casting an ominous forecast over Tod's political future. Not only had he alienated conservative Republicans and Democrats with his support for emancipation, but abolitionists did not think he was radical enough. He was a pawn to all sides as each "used him long enough" and were ready to "lay him on the shelf,"[50] predicted the *Daily Ohio Statesman*. The Union coalition that propelled Tod to victory in 1861 showed signs of coming apart. Old Union Democrats aimed to block his path to a second term come the fall while Republican partisans from within the Union Party attacked him in the spring. Tod was under a two-pronged assault and the outcome would prove disastrous, just as the *Statesman* foretold.

One old Democratic agitator, newly elected State Rep. Edson Olds, managed to turn the tables on the governor. Incredibly, on April 2, a Fairfield County deputy sheriff showed up at the governor's office and handed Tod an arrest warrant for the kidnapping of Olds the previous summer. Tod received word about the warrant and the approach of Sheriff James Miller who "did his business very quietly, stating that it was a painful duty for him to perform, which was doubtless said more for gammon than truth." Fairfield County was none too friendly to Tod in the last election when Hugh Hewitt carried it for the Democrats. Tod surrendered peacefully to Miller, who delivered the governor to the court chamber of Supreme Court Justice William Gholson, a Republican. The governor posted bail in the amount of $2,000 and was granted a writ of habeas corpus. When Olds was arrested, he was issued no such writ or bail. Tod posted bond and was released. It appeared, according to the *Cleveland Morning Leader*, that Olds had hoped to further embarrass Tod not just by the arrest alone but also by incarceration. But Tod's bail postponed his night in jail. The *Fremont Journal* concluded that "the Copperheads failed in their attempt to seek revenge." Nevertheless the arrest of Governor Tod was a brazen act of political resolve on the part of Olds. Word of Tod's arrest caused "quite a sensation ... in the Capitol" but the governor's day in court would have to wait until June.[51]

Battling political opponents was nothing new for David Tod. What was more difficult was dealing with deceptive opponents from within one's own ranks. This was an increasing dilemma for Tod as old Republicans of the Union alliance that once supported his candidacy took issue with his political and military appointments of former Democrats. So upset had some factions grown that there was a movement in the northern part of the state to drop the Union Party label altogether and turn it back to the Republican Party.[52]

One example of Governor Tod's supposed political partisanship occurred with the resignation of Ohio's secretary of state Benjamin Cowen, a former Republican. In his place, Tod named Wilson Kennon, a former Democrat. As if this appointment had not upset old Republicans enough, the Tod-Kennon saga continued when Lincoln tapped Robert W. Tayler, the Republican auditor of the state, to serve in the US Treasury. Tayler was known to Tod from his days back in the Mahoning valley. The death of Elisha Whittlesey, a Canfield native and the comptroller of the US Treasury, created the current need for the new appointment. Secretary of the Treasury Chase strongly recommended Tayler's appointment to Lincoln. Since Whittlesey and Tayler were both Republicans the partisan sentiment was that their replacement should be of the same political stripe. Tod, however, thought otherwise and once again selected Kennon to replace Tayler.[53] Chase, a master of political subterfuge, admonished Tod for his action. But the headstrong governor was unyielding, writing Chase that he had promised voters he would ignore party affiliations and choose the best-qualified candidates. Tod promised to adhere to this principle "during the short time I have yet to remain."[54] The fact that Kennon was a Democrat was just a coincidence and had no bearing on his decision, Tod argued. He had once proclaimed himself "our *no party* Governor," yet he conducted business dressed in his Democratic coat, his critics charged.[55]

Tod's detractors also found fault with his military appointments. County recruiting stations became highly upset when Tod ignored their recommendations for appointments. Promoting officers fell under the authority of the governor's office and Tod's rule was, as much as practicable, "to promote from rank until advised to do otherwise by the commanding officer

George Tod, devoted husband, father, and public servant (The Mahoning Valley Historical Society, Youngstown, Ohio)

President Andrew Jackson, Governor David Tod's political hero (Courtesy of the Library of Congress)

Maria Tod, devoted wife (The Mahoning Valley Historical Society, Youngstown, Ohio)

John Crowell, Governor Tod's Whig rival (1882) (Courtesy of *History of Trumbull and Mahoning Counties, with Illustrations and Biographical Sketches*, vol. 1 [H. Z. Williams and Brother: Cleveland, OH, 1882], 192)

Henry Wise, minister plenipotentiary to Brazil (Courtesy of the Library of Congress)

US Senator Stephen Douglas. Governor Tod worked himself to exhaustion during Douglas's 1860 failed presidential campaign. (Courtesy of the Library of Congress)

Attendees of the Democratic National Convention at Charleston. Governor Tod is standing second from the left, lower balcony. (The Mahoning Valley Historical Society, Youngstown, Ohio)

George Tod, devoted husband, father, and public servant (The Mahoning Valley Historical Society, Youngstown, Ohio)

President Andrew Jackson, Governor David Tod's political hero (Courtesy of the Library of Congress)

Maria Tod, devoted wife (The Mahoning Valley Historical Society, Youngstown, Ohio)

John Crowell, Governor Tod's Whig rival (1882) (Courtesy of *History of Trumbull and Mahoning Counties, with Illustrations and Biographical Sketches*, vol. 1 [H. Z. Williams and Brother: Cleveland, OH, 1882], 192)

Henry Wise, minister plenipotentiary to Brazil (Courtesy of the Library of Congress)

US Senator Stephen Douglas. Governor Tod worked himself to exhaustion during Douglas's 1860 failed presidential campaign. (Courtesy of the Library of Congress)

Attendees of the Democratic National Convention at Charleston. Governor Tod is standing second from the left, lower balcony. (The Mahoning Valley Historical Society, Youngstown, Ohio)

William Dennison, Ohio's dutiful governor at the outbreak of the Civil War (Courtesy of the Ohio History Connection)

The Union candidate's directives are clearly spelled out at the top of the Ohio ticket: "Vigorous Prosecution of the War, and No Compromise." (Author's personal collection)

David Tod, engraved portrait, circa 1860 (Courtesy of the Ohio History Connection)

Secretary of War Edwin M. Stanton (Courtesy of the Library of Congress)

Governor David Tod, artist unknown (The Mahoning Valley Historical Society, Youngstown, Ohio)

Governor David Tod, circa 1863 (Courtesy of the Library of Congress)

Governor David Tod (Courtesy of the Ohio History Connection)

Volunteers soon to be known as Squirrel Hunters answer Governor Tod's call to rush to Cincinnati to defend that city and the state from invasion. Here, they are boarding at the Xenia Railroad Depot in Greene County. This print appeared in *Frank Leslie's Illustrated Newspaper* on September 27, 1862. (Courtesy of the Ohio History Connection)

Squirrel Hunters arriving for the defense of Cincinnati. Illustration by Henri Lovie titled, "The Squirrel Rifles Entertained by the People of Cincinnati in the Fifth Street Market House, Cincinnati, Sept. 6." This print appeared in *Frank Leslie's Illustrated Newspaper* on September 27, 1862. (Courtesy of the Ohio History Connection)

Portrait of Governor David Tod. The portrait was likely created after Tod left office. (Courtesy of the Ohio History Connection)

Portrait of Governor David Tod, 1869, by Jean Claude Crawford, oil on canvas (Capitol Square Review and Advisory Board, Ohio Statehouse. Image courtesy of Garth's Auctioneers & Appraiser, Delaware, Ohio.)

Governor Tod was extremely proud of the 127th Ohio Volunteer Infantry (OVI), Fifth United States Colored Troops. (Courtesy of the Ohio History Connection)

Governor John Brough, Governor Tod's successor. Brough died while in office. (Courtesy of the Ohio History Connection)

President Abraham Lincoln is finished with Secretary of the Treasury Chase and looks for Governor Tod as his replacement. This cartoon ran in *Harper's Weekly,* July 16, 1864 (page 464). (Image published with permission of ProQuest LLC. Further reproduction is prohibited without permission.)

President Abraham Lincoln and Governor David Tod at Gettysburg. Tod is identifiable at the far right by his hair tassel. (Courtesy of the Library of Congress)

A gray-haired Governor David Tod (Courtesy of the Ohio History Connection)

Rufus Spalding, Governor Tod's political mentor (US House of Representatives)

Governor David Tod's grave, Oak Hill Cemetery, Youngstown, Ohio (Photo by Matthew J. Lambert)

of the Regiment." Although he accepted and encouraged opinions from officers in the field, because "the commander of a regiment in the field is the safest source to look to for information to guide me in the discharge of this duty," he was adamant that his office would not be "controlled by [the] recommendation[s]" of anyone. On this point, he did not concede and sternly rebuked one colonel, "I have but to repeat my request, that you promptly make recommendations for all promotions and appointments in your regiment, and to assure you they will receive proper consideration:" nothing more, nothing less.[56] The historian of the 125th Ohio Volunteer Infantry described Tod's policy concerning promotions best when he concluded that the governor "had no specific policy regarding promotions. Some he based on seniority, some on recommendation of the regimental colonel and some were completely political and arbitrary."[57]

Criticism also came from commissary general of prisoners, Col. William H. Hoffman, who condemned Tod for the conditions at Camp Chase and his latitude with the Confederates imprisoned there. When Tod came into office no one could have anticipated the need for the camp to function as a long-term prisoner of war facility. Housing prisoners of war was expected to be a short-term endeavor. But eventually, the evolution of a long, drawn-out war forced the War Department to step in and make accommodations.

The inadequate and unhealthful conditions may be one excuse that Tod permitted paroled Confederate officers the freedom to come and go. He also allowed curious onlookers from the city the chance to view the prisoners and their chattel inside the camp creating what one historian described as a "carnival-like atmosphere."[58] After Fort Donelson fell, captured Confederate officers who had brought along their enslaved persons to the battlefield brought them along to Camp Chase. An Ohio Senate committee assigned to investigate the camp's problems found the situation not only alarming but offensive. The committee concluded that the circumstances all but legalized slavery in Ohio, which would have required an amendment to the state's constitution, of course. The committee also found fault with the War Department and forwarded its findings to Secretary Stanton. In time the problems at the camp were ameliorated but Tod's growing band of critics did not miss the opportunity to lay blame at the governor's feet.[59]

An incredible side note however, surfaced in May 1862 that suggests that Tod was conducting his own acts of liberation at Camp Chase. After an interview by the noted abolitionist Prof. Henry Everard Peck, of Oberlin College, it was revealed that Tod had been quietly but systematically liberating the enslaved of the Confederate prisoners held at Camp Chase. The governor as much intimated to Peck that he had been "sending off the contrabands up at Camp Chase at a rate of three or four a day, with good outfit, and making free men of them." Incredible as it sounded, Peck secured a pass from Tod and visited the governor at the camp to verify such doings. Sure enough, concluded Peck, after seeing with his own eyes, the governor was "elbow deep" in the "contraband business." He claims to have witnessed "four swarthy fellows" accompanied by Tod. "Each one had a new government haversack slung at his side" and a sack full of food and dressed handsomely from head to toe with "hats [and] blankets" to spare. Peck states that Tod presented each of the "jolly rascals" with "a formal deed of manumission . . . and such advice as he needed" before releasing them and sending them off into a new life of freedom.[60] How many enslaved men Tod freed in this way is not known. Remarkably, Peck's public revelation of Tod's activities occurred four months before Lincoln announced his preliminary Emancipation Proclamation.

Tod was also known to visit Camp Chase to look after the welfare of the war prisoners. He saw to it that captives were given medical assistance and that they were sufficiently fed and cared for. He could only hope that Union prisoners, especially those from Ohio, received the same treatment.[61]

One source of staunch support for Tod came from Ohio's troops. That the governor and his troops admired each other's patriotism was true enough. Tod's concern for the well-being of his soldiers was genuine and the troops knew this to be true. He once remarked, "Much of my time every day is spent in battling for the rights of gallant officers and men in the field."[62] In March, a group of soldiers from Camp Chase nearly 100 strong and infuriated by the printing of secession sentiment in the *Crisis*, attacked the office of its publisher Sam Medary.[63] "The soldiers in the field are great admirers of our talented and patriotic Governor," proclaimed the Sixty-First Regiment of Ohio Volunteers stationed at Stafford Court House, Virginia. Left solely to these soldiers to decide the next governor "there is little room for doubt as to who their choice would be."[64]

Tod even looked after his wayward troops who had gone absent without leave or committed outright desertion. In many cases, he was forgiving and tried to create a path back into the service for these men[65] For one deserter who had made his way to Canada he offered "a letter to [his] Colonel, which I think will make [your] punishment, if any, very light."[66] Tod even sought from Stanton a 30-day clemency for the deserters. But it came with a modest price: Just deduct their pay for the period of their absence in exchange for their return, he recommended. Stanton advised Lincoln of Tod's suggestion, who approved it and had the policy implemented throughout the military. Before the 30-day clemency deadline ended Tod took to the press to beseech his wayward boys to come home. "I implore you to avail yourselves of the President's generous offer. Do not listen to those who advise you against returning to duty . . . The man who will advise you to violate your solemn oath, should be shunned as a viper." Railroad ticket agents were authorized to provide free passage to Columbus to all repentant soldiers.[67] Privately, Tod wrote Stanton that the sight of the "collection of deserters and stragglers, scattered throughout our State" was a "constant eye-sore, sickening and discouraging to all loyal men."[68] All things considered, the forgiveness plan was fairly well effective as Tod estimated that "hundreds of good [Ohio] soldiers were returned to their regiments."[69] It was certainly a more enticing approach than that offered by Brig. Gen. Milo S. Hascall, commanding the District of Indiana, in the Department of the Ohio, who promised that all deserters, once apprehended, "will in a few days be shot to death."[70] According to one observer, Tod was "much devoted to the common soldier, and I think he did all in his power for their good."[71]

Traitors were another matter as the governor continued to take a hard-line stance against them. He was approached once by a staff member, Benjamin Runkle, who sought parole for a friend's son detained at the prison camp on Johnson's Island in Lake Erie. "An Ohio boy in the Confederate army. What is he doing in the Confederate army?" Tod asked. When he learned that the young man joined on his own accord Tod dismissed the request and stated that instead he should be executed for treason. On second thought, after much consideration Tod said he would seek Stanton's approval but only if the traitor "will take the oath of allegiance." The "Ohio boy" refused to take the oath.[72]

All this aside, further public incidents testify to the rising discontent across Ohio. At a Peace Democrat meeting in Montgomery County the Stars and Stripes was torn from its mast.[73] In Mahoning County Conservative Democrats were on the rise. Calling for the preservation of the

Constitution and the Union, Democrats of the county demanded an end to the abolition movement.[74] For these incidents and more, the historian Stephen Towne finds that the federal authorities had reason to be concerned. Despite Tod's forgiving gestures many gave up the fight because they were either "homesick, disgusted by the protracted war, dismayed by the Emancipation Proclamation, or all of the above," according to Towne. Deserters in Noble County were prompted by sympathizers to run away to their homes where family and friends promised to hide them. After the "miserable malignants of Noble County [were] gathered from their hiding places"[75] and interrogated, Towne's research found that many had admitted to being members of "secret organizations [Knights of the Golden Circle?] that opposed the Union effort to defeat the Confederate rebellion."[76] In fact, more than a year later (October 1864) the War Department published a detailed report acknowledging the existence of secretive organizations spreading through the Western states at this time.[77]

These were tough challenges for Governor Tod. The political attacks against him increased in frequency as the Democratic convention, scheduled for June 11, 1863, approached. Making matters worse the most recent military debacle occurred in early May when the Army of the Potomac under Hooker's command, with an overwhelming number of troops, was defeated by Lee's Army of Northern Virginia at the Battle of Chancellorsville. It was more of the same disheartening news. Each disaster on the battlefield emboldened Copperhead Democrats to call for peace at any cost while charging the administration with dereliction of duty.

And it just so happened that as Hooker was taking defensive positions at Chancellorsville the leading Copperhead figure in Ohio, Clement Vallandigham, spoke to a massive crowd at Mount Vernon, Ohio. Hidden in the crowd were plainclothes agents who reported back to military authorities.[78] Four days later, Vallandigham was arrested for treason.[79] Tod was said to have known and endorsed Vallandigham's arrest based upon the Copperhead's "seditious utterances."[80] But that is not all Tod was informed of. Evidence shows that the Union had started using military detectives to root out subversives and traitors. The Provost Marshal General's Bureau was created to employ civilians and soldiers to covertly investigate suspected espionage activity. There were signs that a strong antiwar sentiment festered in the Middle West and army commanders, rather than sit idly by, took aggressive actions to infiltrate and shut down treasonous conduct. Governor Tod was made aware of some of the investigations taking place in Ohio and aided in any way he could. But he certainly was not informed of all secret military affairs and was not the only governor in the Middle West troubled by dissidents. Morton of Indiana, with some help from General Wallace and Governor Yates of Illinois, was also on alert. Military arrests of private citizens, like Vallandigham's, became more common. Critics decried these overreaches by Lincoln as further examples of attacks on civil liberties.[81]

Vallandigham was tried before a military tribunal, found guilty of treason, and sentenced to confinement at Fort Warren in Boston. With the advice of his cabinet, Lincoln banished Vallandigham to the Confederacy.[82] More emboldened and defiant as ever, Vallandigham vowed to make a triumphant return to his native soil. "No order of banishment," he promised, "can . . . deprive me of my rights as a citizen of Ohio and of the United States."[83] The exiled leader was the new sound of the Democratic thunder. While Vallandigham vowed to regain a foothold in his country Tod, in the fight of his political life, clung to what little footing he had left.

13

Rising above the Political Muck, May 1863–July 1863

IN LATE MAY 1863, Tod was home in Youngstown where he was given "a grand ovation" by a crowd of well-wishers and a rousing endorsement for a second term "in the approaching Gubernatorial contest!" The warm reception from the friendly faces was just the tonic Tod needed as he prepared for the challenging weeks ahead.[1] On the horizon he had a court date to answer for the kidnapping charges of Edson Olds. Shortly thereafter, the state's Democratic and Union nominating conventions were scheduled for June. Neither of these would offer a positive outcome for Tod let alone any assurance for his future.

When David Tod stood in the courtroom of Judge Philadelph Van Trump to face kidnapping charges of Edson B. Olds on June 1, he was at his most vulnerable. His personal liberty was not assured, and his political career was about to be tossed into the hands of the 400 delegates at the upcoming Union convention. Even more uncertain was the future of the Union itself. It would be a stretch to claim that the survival of both Tod and the Union relied upon the other. But this was certain: David Tod needed to help keep the governor's office of Ohio out of the hands of the Peace Democrats to ensure that his state remained solidly behind Lincoln and the Union war effort even if he were to lose the nomination. Should the Union Party of Ohio lose the governorship to a Peace Democrat, without the full political backing and resources of the Buckeye State, the Union could very well lose the war. For the moment, in this cheerless Fairfield County Court of Common Pleas, with his counsel H. H. Hunter by his side, David Tod had to stand firm for himself and for his beloved country because the trials of both were far from over.

Attorney Hocking Hunter, considered to be "one of the first lawyers and best men of the State," filed a motion on behalf of his client declaring that since Governor Tod was the chief executive of the state he "was not liable to arrest until he vacated his office, either by the expiration of his term or by impeachment."[2] Basing his arguments on the merits of the Indemnity Act, Hunter then tried but failed to get the case moved from the state court to the federal court. Instead, Justice Van Trump granted the continuation of the case to the court's next term.[3] In the clear until he was out of office, Tod and his counselors set out for Columbus with a moral victory in hand. A couple of miles outside of Lancaster, however, the governor and his party were overtaken by the dutiful Sheriff Miller who then served Tod with a new civil suit filed by Olds seeking restitution of $100,000 for damages suffered from his ordeal. Neither suit, however, would ever come to trial.[4] But Olds would not let up and "harassed" Tod "for the remainder of the war."[5] No other chief executive of a loyal state experienced anything like what Tod endured at the hands of Olds. The whole thing seemed like one big waste of the governor's time and a distraction from the critical duties of a war governor.

On June 11, thousands of Democrats gathered for their convention in Columbus. Leading the chorus of Democratic oratory and support for the exiled Copperhead Clement Vallandigham was Edson Olds. Olds denounced the military's role in suppressing freedom of speech under "tyrants" like Tod and his oppressive "military edicts." As governor, Vallandigham would "drive these military orders as chaff before the wind." Also, on the ticket as candidate for the Ohio high court was a familiar face to Tod, Philadelph Van Trump, the presiding judge of the Olds trial. An avowed Democrat, Van Trump was described as "an honest, upright and independent Judiciary," no less.[6]

The Democrats adopted a platform that called for the preservation of and obedience to the US Constitution. It endorsed free government; the protection of life, liberty, and private property a direct reference to the unlawful arrests and imprisonments of the past year; and the attacks on free speech. The platform also indicted Tod for his sanction of and "*active* participations in the violation of these rights."[7] He was called a despot, a disgrace, a "creature [and] a thing that sold himself for a great office, which he has dragged in the dust."[8]

Vallandigham was now a candidate in absentia somewhere in the Confederacy where, opponents hoped, "the disloyal utterings of his wicked heart" were finally silenced.[9] But the South had little use for Vallandigham and frankly did not know what to do with him. Unwanted by Confederates, ever the restless soul, Vallandigham was determined to return home. By the time of his nomination, he had run the Union blockade and found safety in Windsor, Ontario.[10] Vallandigham's nomination energized the peace movement and further emboldened opponents of the war and draft-resisting provocateurs.

Civil unrest indeed was on the rise across the state. Tod had his hands full in June in the Democratic stronghold of Holmes County, where a mob descended on the jail to break out citizens confined for resisting the draft.[11] Another group released prisoners jailed for treason. When local authorities attempted to subdue the mob, they were fired upon. General Ambrose Burnside was dispatched to quell the violence. Through Burnside Tod spoke loud and clear, "I call upon you to at once disperse and return to your quiet home." Disobedience would be met with deadly repercussions: "the consequences to yourselves will be destructive in the extreme." He insisted that the laws of the nation and the state be respected: "I have the will and the power at hand to compel obedience to what I now require of you."[12] But Burnside had no chance to deliver Tod's warning; he and his troops were welcomed with a small volley of fire. Following a brief skirmish order was restored by Burnside's men. In what became known derisively as the Battle of Fort Fizzle, the historian Stephen Towne finds that the men who attempted to free their fellow townsmen were egged on by local politicians and religious leaders. The common thread among the lawbreakers, writes Towne, was their membership in the Democratic Party. Not only had they opposed Lincoln, the war, and Tod, "they feared the threat of military arrests and trials, and raged at military suppression of the Democratic press. Conscription was the last straw, as it meant persons who opposed the war might be forced to fight in it."[13]

Similar reports were received from Crawford County, where draft resisters were urged to "Have a bullet ready for the dastards who order one drafted man to leave his home and County against his will."[14] The rise of domestic dissent against the war and the draft at times seemed like the state itself was on the verge of its own civil war.[15] Tod met these acts head-on and continued to rely on General Burnside's troops to put out these fires.[16] His authority over these local disturbances could not have been carried out if it were not for the help of federal forces who were more than happy to oblige. If only he had had his own state militia to suppress such demonstrations, he could have kept threats of insurrection under tighter control.

Draft resistance, supporting Washington's continued war demands, growing pressure to raise Black troops, and rumors of his impending political demise all weighed on Tod's mind as the Union Party headed to its nominating convention in Columbus on June 17.

Copperheads anticipated Tod's renomination and threw early barbs at the governor days before the convention. Fiery old Dan Tuttle of Bucyrus, an antidraft agitator known for "libelling [sic] everything human and divine," encouraged the citizens of Crawford County to "take up your arms and keep your powder dry" before trudging off to vote come October. Tuttle said he owed "no allegiance to Abe Lincoln, David Tod, or Jesus Christ" and neither should they.[17]

The state Union convention kicked off with great anticipation. "Tod and Victory" proclaimed one banner.[18] "Flags, banners, music, devices and fixings" celebrated the Union Party and other hopeful candidates. A long "procession of carriages, buggies and horsemen ... marched and countermarched through" the streets. The Union Party gathering, observed the Democratic-minded *Daily Ohio Statesman*, attracted "a sort of pleasure-seeking and fun-enjoying gathering of men, women and children, intermixed with a fair sprinkle of Africans, who appeared as if they had gone out for a day of sport and fun."[19] The supportive *Fremont Journal*, described the gathering as "orderly" without "the slightest discord; no drunken men; everything harmonious, enthusiastic, orderly ... a most triumphant and magnificent demonstration."[20]

For David Tod, the affair was a loathsome experience. Though he emerged from the Olds affair unscathed the governor entered the convention a weakened candidate. One supporter from Trumbull County pondered the very real possibility that "Governor Tod [may] be set aside, and a new man be nominated." The writer to the *Western Reserve Chronicle* laid out a thorough review of Tod's performance and urged all to take note before making such a critical decision. To begin with there was the presence of traitors who desired nothing more than the "disruption of the Union [and] the destruction of our government and our liberties." Governor Tod, he insisted, had displayed the backbone to stand up to these discontents who were working at tearing the state asunder. Admittedly, Tod "has made some bad appointments" but most were made "in a hurry" as urgent events required quick action. "What man could have discharged the duties of Chief Magistrate of [a] great State in time of war ... and not commit some error, and make some person angry?" All were reasonable points to ponder. The writer fairly described the political morass Tod was caught up in. "While his old party associates have deserted him, and old friends turned against him, and abused and insulted him, he has like a true and brave patriot stood firm for the Government and putting down this rebellion." Surely, the writer advised, Tod's strong-willed display of determination alone merited support for a second term.[21]

As heartfelt and reasoned a supporter there was for Tod, others were equally unsupportive. The best the *Ashtabula Weekly Telegraph* could offer Tod was, "he has done as well as any one could have" during such trying circumstances.[22] Yet, even with his renomination in doubt, Tod was still regarded as "the representative leader of the War Democracy of the North, and as such, dear to Lincoln," who once complimented the governor as "noble" and "prompt."[23] Having Lincoln's support carried some political weight, but the president's backing alone would not be enough. With his own popularity and support under heavy criticism, Lincoln could ill afford to get mixed up in the political power struggle of the state party.

Not surprisingly, even Tod's relations with the legislature had deteriorated during the election year as Democrats introduced various "resolutions condemning the conduct of the war and emancipation."[24] The political rancor and divisiveness so enraged one Ohio soldier stationed with the Army of the Cumberland in Tennessee, that he poured forth his feelings in a letter home to his brother: "It makes the blood boil in my veins to see so much party feeling in this, the hour of danger. For God's sake, save our country first, and then it will do to talk of parties afterwards."[25]

But there seemed to be some movement afoot. Days before the convention various party newspapers began editorializing about the next Union candidate. On June 6, the *Cleveland Leader* was one of the first to advocate for a change. When the name of John Brough, a former Democrat, surfaced, he represented the change others were looking for. The support of the *Toledo Blade, Cincinnati Gazette, Cleveland Leader,* and *Ohio State Journal* was thrown behind him.[26]

There has been some speculation that secret Radical forces had conspired to oust Tod. The coalition that came together for his election in 1861, conservatives and abolitionists, was weakened. Saving the Union had been the one uniting goal between them but as the war dragged on the philosophical differences over emancipation and the inclusion of free Black men in the military and in society after the death of slavery, and the preservation of the Constitution blunted the alliance. Leaders of these factions, especially the Radicals, looked to replace Tod to advance their political and personal agendas. One of the more influential Radical leaders was the lifelong presidential aspirant, Treas. Secy. Salmon P. Chase. Chase privately confided that there were "some things about [Tod] which are not altogether to my liking." Chase could not deny the fact that Tod "has done as much to sustain the War as any other Governor & I should not like to see him refused the nomination if he or his friends desire it." On the surface Chased appeared to put the needs of the country above his own secret desires when he wrote, "We must be liberal to all who are rowing our boat whether we like them [Tod]—or are liked by them—or not."[27] The Union League clubs were also influenced by the radical faction of the party and looked unfavorably upon Tod. The governor stood little chance of gaining their support.[28] Out of these powerful influences emerged forces that Tod could not overcome.

When Tod left the Democratic Party in 1861, he stepped not into the Republicans' camp but into the Union's, or so he thought. Although he had gained victory as a pro-Union candidate its political effectiveness was limited. After the Democrats turned their backs on him the Republicans, who held political power within the Union Party, never fully embraced him no matter how hard he worked for the Union cause. Invariably, he was bound to offend one of these factions as patriotism gave way to petty politics. One colorful observation described the time as "a day of prejudice; a day in which a little breath could speedily develop into a cyclone and blow a man off the earth."[29] Those winds began to swirl around Tod after the Kennon affair. Once he brushed aside Chase's rebuke over the matter he immediately realized "the short time I have yet to remain" as governor.[30] Tod's efforts on behalf of the Emancipation Proclamation never measured up to the Radical passions of Chase and other like-minded, politicians, like Senator Benjamin Wade. These two men held enormous influence and were strongly suspected of Tod's overthrow.

Chase was attracted to Brough's compelling support for emancipation, quickly moved into his corner, and quietly encouraged his legion of supporters to follow suit.[31] Chase's biographer writes that the treasury secretary "carefully avoided taking sides publicly" against Tod but quietly effected the change he desired. More important for Chase, the secretary had also been advised that Brough would support Chase if he ran for president.[32] Unaware of these backroom deals, Tod must have sensed the hopeless predicament his candidacy was in.

John Brough had been many things during his career. At first he was, like Tod, a Jacksonian Democrat. He and his brother had once owned the *Ohio Eagle* and they used its pages to promote their political views. He spent one term in the general assembly before serving six years as the state auditor. After 1845 his interests continued in newspapers and railroads. When the war broke out, he proclaimed his support for the Union. On June 10, 1863, his political career was reborn after he delivered a strong speech in his hometown of Marietta. With so many questioning Tod's electability Brough was the fresh face political operatives desired to reenergize the Union Party.[33]

On June 17, a large contingent of Brough supporters showed up at the Athenaeum and demanded access to the booked convention. Organizers had little choice but to move the convention outdoors to the east porch of the statehouse. The overwhelming numbers that converged there caused so much chaos that convention chairman, former governor William Dennison, summoned only the delegates back to the Athenaeum to conduct their business. But the crowd followed pressing inside doorways and windows to watch the proceedings. Before accepting nominations, Dennison reminded the crowd of its loyalty to the Union over any party affiliations. Brough was then formally nominated by Nicholas Patterson of Hamilton County while C. L. Little of Carroll County had the honor of nominating Tod. The balloting procedure followed with complete order and decorum.[34]

A majority of the 409.5 possible votes was needed to secure the nomination. Tod took an early lead thanks to Adams, Allen, and Ashland Counties. Cuyahoga County's 8 votes for Tod gave the governor a glimmer of hope. However, the tide turned when Hamilton County cast 27 votes for Brough. His delirious supporters could no longer contain themselves and erupted into "spontaneous and hearty applause." As Brough's lead grew, the enthusiasm of his supporters ascended with each ballot cast until the final tabulations showed Brough 226, Tod 183.5. Upon a motion, the nomination was then made unanimous, followed by "tremendous applause."[35]

After the crowd exercised self-control Senator Benjamin Wade stepped forward to offer several resolutions, which fired up the crowd again. Among these was the continued support for the war, the federal government, and the Union Party, as well as cheers for the soldiers, the president, as well as David Tod.[36] The *Chicago Tribune* observed from afar, "Though there is no cause of dissatisfaction with the policy pursued by Governor Tod of Ohio, the nomination of John Brough as his successor is an event that will give great joy to all union men in the Northwest."[37]

Stung by the most disappointing loss of his political career and before he left the convention floor Governor Tod, composed but sorely hurt, immediately endorsed Brough and pledged his full support. His remarks, reported the *Fremont Journal*, were short "but full of high souled manhood and hightoned patriotism." Tod praised Brough for his integrity and solemnly promised to "do all in his power to promote his candidacy."[38] The party's new nominee could count on David Tod. His trusted confidant George B. Wright noted that Tod's supporters "were moved to tears" after the governor's heartfelt "appeal for unity." There was an immediate sense "that a great injustice had been done to a most worthy citizen in not re-nominating him for a second term," concluded the loyal Wright.[39]

One Democratic newspaper concluded that Tod's defeat was the result of his lack of party affiliation. The *Democratic Press* labeled Tod "a partisan pauper whom nobody owns."[40] The *Detroit Free Press* even weighed in, accusing the Radical Republicans of using Tod to conduct "their dirty work," as in the seizure of Dr. Olds. Because of the support he provided in these arrests and his lingering trial, he was deemed unelectable by too many factions. The *Albany Argus* wrote that the Radical faction made a tool out of Tod and drove him "to extreme party courses."[41]

The historian William Hesseltine introduces yet another cloak-and-dagger theory that led to Tod's ouster. Hesseltine argues that there were powerful railroad executives who were not happy with Tod's reluctance to consolidate various lines that would connect the Alleghenies with the Mississippi River under his personal control. Brough, himself a railroad executive, supposedly supported the consolidation movement. It was a combination of these unnamed party officials and railroad executives in favor of the consolidation, writes Hesseltine, who affected the nomination from Tod to Brough.⁴²

Because the convention's nominating and balloting process had been so orderly and controlled, despite the overflow crowd, it gave credence to the suspicion that the entire affair had been preplanned or even scripted. It certainly had been a harmonious event if it was not orchestrated. "The good order which predominated throughout the entire proceedings of the convention would indicate," writes one historian, "that the party leaders had control at all times and that there was a great degree of unity among the members, as is typified by the reaction of governor Tod who even when defeated was still working for the party."⁴³ And true to his word, Tod would do just that.

The day after he lost Tod telegraphed Lincoln to inform the president of his defeat. He did not want Lincoln to think that his loss was due to the governor's support of the president and his war measures. "Do not for a moment believe it. Personal considerations alone was the cause of my defeat," said Tod. Knowing how important it was to keep Ohio behind the president's war initiatives Tod assured Lincoln that he would work hard to help Brough defeat Vallandigham. "No man will do more to secure the triumphant election of the ticket nominated than I will," promised Tod. Lincoln was disheartened to hear of Tod's political demise, responding, "I deeply regret that you were not re-nominated." But Lincoln would need the support of Tod's successor and carefully responded, "not that I have ought [sic] against Mr. Brough. On the contrary, like yourself, I say, hurrah, for him."⁴⁴ Stanton was more commendatory, "You deserve not only the honor and respect of your great state," Stanton consoled Tod, "but also of every loyal and patriotic heart."⁴⁵

Tod knew that a Brough victory would also vindicate the support his administration gave to Lincoln and every measure he had taken thus far to advance the Union cause. And he understood that a Vallandigham win would renounce the efforts of the president and his tenure in office. If Ohio was lost to Vallandigham it was as much as giving up the Union itself. "All prominent Ohio politicos" from both parties, writes Vallandigham's biographer, "took to the hustings" that election season.⁴⁶

Tod wasted no time and set out to campaign for the Brough ticket. Days after the convention ended, he spoke in Mansfield and New Philadelphia.

The Mansfield region had been an area of concern for Tod just two weeks before when draft officers had been assaulted by antidraft rowdies.[47] But he did not hesitate to campaign there. On June 28 he was in Cleveland imploring "Tod men" to outwork "the Brough Men."[48] He appeared at Somerset on July 4.[49] Recently Tod had said "that the man who is not willing to lay aside his party harness, when the very existence of the Government is periled by keeping it on, is unfit to participate in a free government."[50] Until the election, Tod was as good as his words demonstrating his fitness to participate in the democracy he was so committed to saving. "Tod rose above the political muck," noted historian Engle, "and continued to support Lincoln."[51]

While the politics of war marched on in Ohio the war itself slogged on. This forced Tod to divide his time between political and military battles. Lee's army was on the move again in late June, this time threatening to invade Pennsylvania. Signs of Lee's movements were first detected before the Union Convention. Tod worried about "invasion on our eastern and southern border both." Stanton could not guarantee the placement of federal forces, so he called for help from Pennsylvania, West Virginia, Ohio, and Maryland. Tod hoped for 100,000 sentries for eastern and southern defensives but that was wishful thinking. "I have done all that mortal man can do to arouse the people of Ohio to a sense of their danger, but regret to say with but little avail," he wrote Burnside. Burnside recommended Tod consider a "declaration of martial law."[52]

The state legislature's creation of a standing militia had not yet progressed to the point of deployment and would not be ready until August 17.[53] "As we have but few, if any regularly organized companies of volunteer militia, I can but invite and implore you to duty," Tod announced in newspapers across the state. He called for 30,000 volunteers to secure the Ohio-Pennsylvania line against the advancing "horde of rebels."[54]

Tod hoped to position a sufficient display of force along the border to dissuade Lee from violating Ohio, much as he had done in the defense of Cincinnati.[55] "If the enemy know that we are prepared to give them a warm reception," Tod reasoned, "they may not attempt to invade us." Otherwise, without a show of force "they are certain to do so."[56] He warned his fellow Ohioans that their "sacred homes [were] threatened with pillage and destruction and our wives and daughter with insults."[57] But the response was slow.

On the same day Tod was speaking in Cleveland, June 28, Lincoln replaced his leading general. After the Union defeat at Chancellorsville, Lincoln's confidence in Joseph Hooker vanished. Hooker's every move was supervised by the War Department. General in Chief Henry Halleck's constant and suffocating oversight of Hooker's command was too much for the general to bear. Lincoln welcomed Hooker's resignation and replaced him with Maj. Gen. George Gordon Meade, a West Point graduate. Meade, a veteran of the battles of Antietam and Fredericksburg, was known for his "competent, intelligent leadership." Shocked by his new appointment Meade had little time to waste because Lee crossed into the Union general's home state of Pennsylvania.[58] Lee's movement removed the threat to Ohio therefore relaxing Tod's concern over his state's eastern border.

From July 1 to July 3, Meade's and Lee's armies squared off in the greatest single military battle on the American continent in the tiny hamlet of Gettysburg, Pennsylvania. After three hard days, Meade successfully fended off Lee's forces, highlighted by a valiant but ill-conceived Confederate assault on the last day. It was a momentous and timely military victory for the Union and just as great a moral triumph because it had been so long since the North experienced success. On the heels of Gettysburg news arrived detailing the surrender of Vicksburg and the 30,000 Confederate forces besieged therein to Grant. Great celebrations were held across the North. Tod sent congratulatory wishes to Grant and recalled the "kind relations that existed between our parents."[59] He also wrote a letter to Pennsylvania governor Andrew Curtin offering Ohio surgeons and nurses to help the thousands of wounded at Gettysburg.[60] For the Peace Democrats the news of military success severely undermined their "peace at any cost" platform and weakened Vallandigham's chances at the polls while strengthening Brough's odds.

For David Tod, there was little time to celebrate the recent victories because an old threat reemerged. The rebel raider John Hunt Morgan was back carrying on raids in the North in search of valuable resources, namely horses. He also hoped to draw the attention of federal troops away from Confederate forces in Tennessee. News of the rebel general and his cavalry blazing through Kentucky and into Indiana on his way to Ohio was received as early as June 22. If Tod could not get Ohioans to rally to defend the state once again, he feared the need to follow Burnside's previous recommendation and declare martial law for he was adamant that "Ohio shall not be invaded."[61]

Frantically, Tod implored the patriotic men of Ohio to respond. On July 10 he was "pained to announce . . . that less than (2) thousand men have responded." Crops ready to be harvested can be just "as safe in your fields as they are in your barns," he beseeched the state's farmers.[62] The show of force in Eaton, Ohio, was an exception but just the sort of deterrent Tod had in mind to keep Morgan away. There, "many of the farmers were in the midst of harvesting [but] left" their crops in the field "and shouldered the musket and knapsack" to divert Morgan and his men.[63]

Daily reports tracked Morgan's exploits and plotted his journey of plunder as he slowly but steadily moved toward the Ohio border from Indiana. On July 12, Burnside asked Tod for 20,000 militia. Governor Morton of Indiana sent word on July 13 that Morgan had advanced to the state line on a northeasterly path.[64]

How Morgan was aided by Southern sympathizers along the river is unknown, but Ohioans in the region had been arrested by military authorities for suspicion of guiding the rebel raiders along. Tod acknowledged that Ohio had its fair share of rebel supporters "scattered all over the State."[65] With no organized militia at various points along the southern border the rebel force of 2,500 men eased uncontested into Ohio on July 13 and brought the war to the Buckeye State near Cincinnati. "Ohio invaded!" cried the *Fremont Journal*. "This is no joke, but a stern reality." While tearing up Indiana Morgan destroyed railroad depots, railroads, and telegraph lines and hoped to commit the same "depradations [*sic*]" in Ohio.[66]

By July 14, Morgan had crossed the Little Miami with Gen. Edward H. Hobson giving chase. On July 17 near Pomeroy a number of Morgan's horses and men had been captured after the raiders had "robbed all stores" and stolen "private property" nearby.[67] Morgan made his way eastward through Piketon, Jackson, Vinton, and Berlin but by this time the locals had rallied, pushing the raiders northward.[68]

Once Morgan crossed into the state, local militias finally caught the patriotic spirit and began to assemble once they realized that their towns and villages were at risk. The rising river prevented Morgan an easy escape southward. Now he was on the run.[69] The locals hoped to slow the raiders down, giving Burnside time to chase the rebels from behind.

Along the entire route trees were felled, bridges were destroyed, Burnside gave chase, small skirmishes and bloodshed occurred, rebel prisoners were taken, and Morgan got away. Tod put it mildly when he wrote the day after Morgan entered Ohio, "We have much excitement in the State now, occasioned by Morgan's raid upon us."[70]

Although Morgan remained on the run, the growing militia presence fulfilled its mission by preventing the rebels from resting and recrossing the Ohio and reaching safety in the South. The militia was aided by the river's rising. Thus Morgan was forced to run northeast, heading farther away from escape and toward imminent capture. General Benjamin Franklin Kelley, after having given brief chase to Lee after Gettysburg now worried that Morgan was being flushed toward the lower Kanawha in West Virginia and asked Tod for two regiments.[71] His request was impossible to fill.

Tod worked diligently throughout the drama. As he gathered intelligence information from scouts, he telegraphed local authorities ahead of Morgan to get their militias in place. When Morgan was 50 miles outside Cadiz the local telegraph office frantically tapped a message from the governor ordering ammunition and arms to the small town for use by the 1,000 militiamen on standing. This example of Tod's actions was typical. During the last crisis, he was in every way a hands-on commander in chief.[72]

At the same time, agents informed Tod of trouble brewing among Irish draft resisters in parts of Cleveland and Toledo. Not wanting any more trouble like that in Holmes and Crawford Counties, Tod heeded the warning and called out local militias as a show of force to quash any threats of violence.[73]

As much as he could, Morgan tried in vain to hug the river, attempting to cross back into the South but the militias blocked his route and Union gunboats stood guard on the river. Engagements occurred as "skirmishing and fighting took place all along the route."[74]

Morgan continued northeast and was met by Hobson's troops at the Battle of Buffington Island. It was a brief but important engagement between several thousand troops. About 700 of Morgan's men were taken prisoner while the rebel officer eluded capture. His remaining forces numbered about 400.[75]

Burnside had made steady progress in capturing Morgan's men but not the rebel leader himself. Approximately 350 Confederates were still with Morgan on July 24. The end of Morgan's forays into Ohio came on July

26 in Salineville in Columbiana County approximately 20 miles from the Pennsylvania line and around 25 miles from Tod's Brier Hill estate. Surrounded by militia, with Burnside coming up from the rear, Morgan had no choice but to surrender. Ironically, Salineville was just south of New Lisbon, the birthplace of Clement Vallandigham.

Now prisoners of war, Morgan and his men were transported by rail to Cincinnati. Officers were dropped off, at General Halleck's suggestion, at the Ohio State Penitentiary in Columbus, where the rebel leader's appearance caused quite a stir. Shortly after his arrival Morgan had the audacity to complain about poor conditions at the penitentiary, where the warden had treated the rebels as common prisoners. Governor Tod personally appeared and after listening to Morgan's complaints relaxed the treatment and conditions of the war prisoners, but he could do nothing about the prisoners' hair and beards, which had already been shaved off.[76]

The capture of Morgan was another occasion for celebration in the North and for Tod in particular. He congratulated the citizens of Ohio on their patriotic response in taking down the rebel leader and his band of "marauders." The devoted Tod critic, the *Ohio Democrat*, surprisingly gave the governor credit for the pursuit and capture of Morgan. The governor's nonstop efforts "in urging day and night the lagging generals to their work, deserves more credit . . . He has effected what Rosecrans and all his army failed to do, and what Gen. Burnside and his force was [*sic*] incompetent to accomplish. Therefore let Tod have the honor of circumventing the great rebel leader." Weeks later, the same partisan paper retracted its praise and credited a higher authority. The Ohio River was too high for Morgan to recross. Otherwise, he would have escaped. "God, not Tod, Did It. . . . So then it is God and not Tod who caught Morgan."[77]

As commander in chief of the state of Ohio, Tod performed admirably. "Throughout the entire contest," in Tod's words, he "was in constant communication; both night and day, with Maj.-Gen. Burnside, who had command of the entire forces." True as this statement was Tod knew that it was the soldiers, federal and volunteer militia, who deserved the credit. Tod especially lauded the contribution of the militia of which, it was estimated, over 50,000 had answered the governor's call to action throughout the ordeal.[78] He had been the biggest advocate for such a voluntary force and the performance, marked by "gallantry and bravery" in the face of the enemy, had justified his determination in getting the legislature to finally pass his militia act. Tod would also take steps to make financial reparations to those citizens who suffered stolen or destroyed property at the hands of Morgan and his men.[79]

In August, after the Morgan excitement had died down, Tod wrote Stanton hoping that the secretary of war would agree that a more permanent "protection of the southern border of Ohio [was] now apparent." Stanton authorized Tod to raise a cavalry to guard Ohio's southern border. "The necessity for such a force," Tod concluded to his military committees, "must be apparent to all."[80]

Although the Union Party voted to deny Tod a second term his patriotic commitment to stand firm against this "unholy war," as he had grown accustomed to describing the rebellion, never faltered. When he pledged to work for the Union Party it was a commitment to do all he could to help preserve the Union in political battles as well as military matters. After all the trials he had been through in recent months, the capture of Morgan raised his spirits.

14

A Crumb of Comfort, August 1863–December 1863

IN AUGUST 1863, still in high spirits, Governor Tod was in Washington with "prominent republicans and friends of the administration" to confer with the president on a variety of matters. It was the first time the president had seen Tod since the governor lost his party's nomination. But so much more had gone right for both men in the last six weeks that their confidence in the prospects of the war had grown.

Tod also hoped to see Stanton because he was in search of pay for the militiamen who responded to Morgan's raid. He would also express his concerns with the new Conscription Act and its universal disapproval in Ohio. Of concern to Tod was the violence that had rocked New York City in July. Although the riots in New York City were sparked by the draft and emancipation, lower socioeconomic classes thought that their jobs would be pilfered by a new class of free Blacks who, they feared, would move north and take lower wages for the same work.[1] Tod had faced down similar problems in Ohio though nowhere near the level of violence that occurred in New York City. Although he had successfully persuaded Stanton to postpone the draft in Ohio many wondered if the time had come to finally accept the state's free Black men into the military. This would also help the governors meet their state's quotas. Excluding the border states 180,000 free Black persons lived in the North.[2] This was a huge untapped resource for the Union Army. Tod and Lincoln had come to this conclusion after both had dismissed the idea earlier in the war.[3]

By now Tod and Lincoln had developed a friendly relationship based on mutual respect and admiration. One story Lincoln enjoyed telling was a lighthearted moment he had with Tod. Lincoln leaned into Tod one evening during a visit at the Executive Mansion and noted that the governor shared the same last name with his wife Mary Todd. Lincoln wondered however, why Tod only used one d to spell his name while his wife's Kentucky family used two. George B. Wright, who was present, told the story in his memoir. "Look here, Tod," said the president, "how is it that you spell your name with only one d. I married a Todd, but she spelled her name with two d's. All of her relations do the same. You are the first Tod I ever knew who spelled his name with so few letters." As Lincoln finished his lighthearted interrogation a grinning Tod waited to respond.

"Mr. President," said Tod leaning back, "God spells His name with only one d, and what is good enough for God, is good enough for me." The president laughed heartily.[4]

During the war, Lincoln spent a great deal of time at the War Department's telegraph office. There he anxiously awaited news from the battlefront or sent messages to his generals about the latest developments. One telegraph operator, David Homer Bates, recorded that Tod was often in company with the president. "I remember Governor Tod having come into the War Department Office on several occasions with President Lincoln," said Bates. "I know that Secretary Stanton and President Lincoln had a very high regard for him."[5]

Tod was at ease enough with Lincoln to once question the president on the status of his cabinet with respect to the presidential contest of 1864. Sitting with Wright and Sec. of State William Seward Tod asked Lincoln, "Mr. President, how many candidates are there in your cabinet for President?" It had been the worst-kept secret that supporters of Chase had been surreptitiously promoting a presidential bid for the treasury secretary without any objections from Chase himself. In true Lincoln fashion, the president deflected Tod's question with a yarn about a patent seeker who devised an improvement on an auger, a handheld wood-boring drill. Upon demonstration, the inventor had incorrectly set the screw, explained Lincoln, "and instead of boring itself in, it bored itself *out*." The anecdote would prove prophetic as Chase would one day burrow himself out of Lincoln's cabinet. Tod's inquiry, however, begs the question of whether the one-term governor was attempting to embarrass Chase, the suspected orchestrator of Tod's own political demise.[6]

During the August visit to Washington Tod also had the opportunity to observe the president during his comings and goings to and from the White House. In the course of these occasions Tod was astonished at the lack of security for the country's commander in chief. Not that the president was totally without a personal safety detail, but what Tod saw did not impress him in the least. At one time a cavalry unit from New York known as Scott's Nine Hundred provided presidential security but its service was inconsistent and fell off. Anxious about the president's safety Tod approached Stanton at the War Department and offered his assistance. Stanton had also shared Tod's concern and when the governor volunteered to assemble a proper security detail from Ohio Stanton accepted his offer.

Throughout the coming months Tod raised and delivered what became known as the Union Light Guard, officially referred to as the Seventh Independent Troop of Ohio Volunteer Cavalry. Volunteers, required to stand at least six feet tall, were to serve for three years unless the war ended sooner. Tod considered the confidential project a great privilege for Ohio and a "highly honorable" assignment for those soldiers selected. The Union Light Guard would be the last official recruitment effort of Tod's administration but in August 1863, meeting the state's quota continued to be a concern.[7]

When conscription was postponed recruitment efforts continued. Tod had hoped to have the draft in Ohio postponed until after the upcoming election because he worried that Vallandigham, by this time in Windsor, Canada, and his Peace Democratic supporters at home in Ohio, would use it to their advantage before election day. The *Lorain County News*, for one, suggested that Tod call out his Squirrel Hunters again. Knowing full well how detested a draft would be the newspaper dared government authorities to use it; "if an ARMY is wanted, DRAFT." Medary's *Crisis* challenged critics who claimed that Democrats had discouraged enlistments. Lincoln and Tod were regarded as the worst offenders; "Will either of these dignitaries show by their acts that all their cry against Democrats for discouraging enlistments in [sic] not sheer hypocrisy and political chicanery?" Specifically, the claim was that authorities were conspiring to draft large numbers of Democrats into uniform and onto the battlefields to prevent them from casting ballots in the fall election while keeping "Republicans at home to vote." It was all a part of the bedrock Republican platform. "Coercion and Fraud,"[8] contended Democrats.

Nonetheless, Ohio's contribution of soldiers as of June 10, 1863, was 137,217. As impressive as this figure was the federal government still sought another 8,300 Ohioans for the rank and file. To help recruit the state's draft quota Stanton granted Tod's request to release Ohio officers from the field to return home to help bring in volunteers. Recruiting agents earned $15 for every green recruit and $25 for an experienced recruit with nine months or more of service. If these incentives could not bring in new enlistees, the draft would be implemented.[9]

One group that had been lobbying hard to get into the fight was Ohio's free Black men. From the start of hostilities, they were eager to shoulder weapons and join the ranks. After Sumter fell in April 1861, a group of Black men in Cleveland had rushed forward to volunteer only to be told that Ohio's constitution forbade their enlistment.[10] Dennison and Tod both fell back on this excuse early in their administrations. The widespread sentiment at the time was that the war would be over quickly. Therefore extraordinary measures, like enlisting free Black men, were not needed. As late as August 1862 one diarist recorded Tod as stating that the "war would be over inside of three months."[11] Opponents to enlisting free Black men clung to that position. After emancipation, cries for the use of free Black soldiers became more appealing as a war measure. But there were those who doubted they possessed the fighting spirit, ability, and discipline.

The use of enslaved labor in the Confederate war effort caused some in the North to view things differently. Being a war resource justified the confiscation of those enslaved men. Ohio congressman Carey Trimble said as much: "Every laborer we take from the rebels weakens them that much. Deprive them of their slave labor and their power would depart at once." And in his January 1863 remarks, after acknowledging the successful use of free Black labor, Trimble went further. Why can't the federal government use free Black men "as scouts and spies and soldiers, why may they not be valuable to us?"[12]

However, there was the continued belief that the struggle was "a white man's war" and that white soldiers would never accept fighting alongside Black soldiers. Two years into the war, staunch Democrats like Ohio Congressman Chilton A. White continued to argue, "This is a Government of white men, made by white men for white men to be administered, protected, and defended, and maintained by white men ... and the people of this country will be satisfied with nothing else." White also believed that utilizing Black men in the military, marching them off to help conquer and bring back into the Union the departed states, was part of a grand plan to replace the white ruling class with a new "dominant [Black] race."[13]

In addition, it was said that white soldiers did not join the fight to secure rights for Black men even if they held antislavery feelings. No, white soldiers volunteered to save their country. They did not join a crusade to eradicate the "peculiar institution." These were widely accepted sentiments. Moreover, white soldiers opposed the idea of Black men in uniform because to do so made the latter his equal. Northern governors like Tod, argues one historian, kept "their ears to the ground [and would] not dare act contrary to [these sentiments]." To make soldiers of Black men, it was thought, would discourage the enlistment of white men as well as fly in the face of the widely held belief in racial hierarchy. Public sentiment toward the enlistment of free Black men subtly began to change, however, when emancipation changed the war to liberate the enslaved. These goals caused many to reconsider the idea of using Black soldiers.[14]

With the aid of John M. Langston, the prominent Black attorney, Tod learned that he could send Ohio's Black recruits to Governor John Andrew, who was accepting out-of-state free men to form regiments in Massachusetts. Langston hit the road to deliver his lecture, "The War and the Duty of the Colored Men at this Hour."[15] With over 8,000 Black men of serviceable age, Ohio had the third-largest population after New York and Pennsylvania from which to pull.[16] As for a Black Ohio regiment, as late as May 11 Tod admitted, "I do not propose to raise any colored troops."[17] Instead, they were delivered to Governor Andrew. About 200 of the first group passed through Ohio singing, "We are coming, brother Andrew, several hundred more."[18] Ohio's Democratic newspaper editors were glad to have Massachusetts take the lead and foot the bill; "Surely the tax payers of Massachusetts must be a very patriotic set of fellows to pay out of their State Treasury FIFTY DOLLARS per head to recruit negroes in Ohio."[19]

But newspapers such as the *Toledo Blade* and the *Cincinnati Gazette* began to pressure Tod to change his stance. Earlier in the year, after it was widely known that Tod was in support of the Emancipation Proclamation, Ohio Democrats called him "an abolitionist of the deepest and darkest dye," and his name was detested second only to Lincoln's.[20] It was around the time of the Union Party Convention, when Tod finally sought from Stanton the authority "to organize one or more negro Regiments" from Ohio for three years' service.[21] Stanton conceded. This time Tod appointed Orindatus Simon Bolivar Wall, a successful Black attorney and merchant from Oberlin to be his general recruiting agent. It was Wall who had pressed Tod to contact Stanton.[22] Tod also directed Capt. Lewis McCoy to Camp Delaware to "take charge and supervision of the [new Black] recruits for the 127th O.V.I."[23] But as quick and ready as Tod was in taking these first steps, he sought the advice of Governor Andrew. It was Andrew whom Tod credited with utilizing "the best policy of organizing colored troops" and he planned to "follow closely in [the] footsteps" of his colleague.[24] Tod was delighted to learn that Ohio would indeed receive the "full benefit of all enlistments from the State" to help meet Ohio's quota.[25]

Meanwhile, Tod asked Wall to raise a minimum of 640 men.[26] Tod had fumed when he learned that his Black troops would receive not only less bounty but less pay than his white soldiers, especially after assurances were made that they would receive equal pay. Black soldiers of the United States Colored Troops (USCT) were to be paid $10 per month while white soldiers received $13.[27] His complaints to Stanton were ignored. "The men are expecting the usual pay and bounty allowed white soldiers—will they get it?" When he did finally respond Stanton further disappointed Tod by referring the governor back to Ohio for the extra pay he sought.[28] Check your state coffers or ask the next Congress, advised Stanton. When Tod realized the inequity would stand and that his Black troops were not eligible for federal funds to help support their families, he tried vigorously to raise extra money through private and public donations.[29] One newspaper suggested to the men that pay was not everything. Rather, more important, they had the chance "to help lift the load of oppression and degradation which has weighed down his race."[30] Despite all this, Tod still hoped to raise one regiment in 30 days with the aid of Wall.

To his credit, Tod's opinion had changed, and he took an unashamedly hardline approach in support of Ohio's Black soldiers. "The colored soldier fill [sic] the place of a white man," Tod said and "his risks are as great, if not greater" especially if captured by Southern troops who had the habit of executing Black soldiers. Langston encouraged recruits to enlist, "pay or no pay."[31] Tod was so pleased and proud of Ohio's Black recruits that he proudly boasted to Stanton, "The colored regiment is progressing handsomely."[32]

Much can be said of Tod's metamorphosis and newfound devotion to Ohio's Black soldiers. Whether pay, bounty, uniforms, or Springfield rifles, he did his best to secure these essentials for his Black troops.[33] On one occasion, Tod "adopted a radical tone" when he addressed a group of Black men considering enlistment. He lectured them that the only way to attain the "rights and privileges" of white men was to "fight for them." And for the energy he put forth for these men, Langston and his recruits began to warmly refer to Tod as "our old friend, Governor Tod."[34] His fight for equality on their behalf softened criticism from Republican Radicals.

The *New York Herald* tossed faint praise at Governors Andrew and Tod for their efforts. Blacks "should lend a hand in such work. The blood of white men has been shed very copiously in the cause of the negroes. Let the negroes themselves now bleed a little," the newspaper suggested. The editor's words dripped with its heavy racist viewpoint when it gave its true opinion of Black men; "We shall thus get rid of the blacks ... We have no need of negroes at the North. Let the whole race be sent South"[35] to fight.

Proponents, like the *Cleveland Morning Leader*, took a more pragmatic view. As a race African Americans had "long been oppressed and down-trodden." But after emancipation that yoke was now cast off. At this time more than any other, said the *Leader*, they "must *show* that they are worthy of the inheritance of liberty and equality." "They have now an opportunity to show that they are patriotic, manly and heroic." Moreover, "If the colored citizens of Ohio are such men as they aspire to be, now is the time to show it."[36] Although there were those who supported social and civil advancements for Black soldiers, many were not ready to see these changes take place. Even though the *Cincinnati Commercial* supported the raising of Black troops, it decried that the war was still "a war for the restoration of the Union as it was" and it was not a war for Black equality. "The negro [was just] a mere incident in its progress."[37] And when free Blacks were finally given the opportunity, they welcomed the chance to demonstrate their bravery and worthiness in the struggle for their country with an eye toward justifying their own rightful claims to citizenship.

By the time Tod returned to Columbus from Washington in August 1863, there were 700 Black soldiers making up the Fifth USCT drilling at Camp Delaware. The regiment was described as "a fine one" needing "only a little timely assistance" during training. The Fifth USCT would finally deploy in November to Fort Monroe after a splendid send-off ceremony that included the Chillicothe brass band; a flag presentation; and speeches by Tod, Dennison, and Langston, among others. Tod relied on the use of paternal affection by warmly referring to the men as his "boys." It had been his parlance to affectionately refer to all his recruits, Black men and white men, in this way. It should not be interpreted as insensitive. In fact, at the beginning of this speech, he asked the recruits for the "privilege of calling them 'his boys'" as a sign of "'fatherly counsel.'" The men responded "with a roar" of approval. They were as dear to him, Tod said, as if they were his own sons. His warm remarks were loudly and energetically received. In content and feeling, Tod's words to the Fifth USCT were no less honorable, stirring, and patriotic than any he gave to white troops preparing to embark on their maiden missions. They were certainly not the utterances of a man only concerned with meeting his state's quota. Rather, they were heartfelt and sincere. As for Tod's transformation in his new acceptance of and support for Black troops, one journalist wryly remarked after the November speech, "The world moves, verily."[38]

The Fifth USCT would go on to proudly represent themselves and Ohio by participating in at least 10 battles in Virginia. Any doubts about the fighting spirit and ability of Ohio's Black troops were quickly dispelled. Union officers in the field observed these traits firsthand and their reports helped to reinforce supporters of the experiment and change the sentiment of naysayers.[39] Tod beamed. One thing was certain: The enlistment of Black men undoubtedly helped Ohio to meet its quota and postpone the draft.

Peace Democrats of Ohio however used the expanding role of Black people to excite and instill fear in their members. They warned that matters like advancement for African Americans were moving irreversibly forward in the wrong direction. The only way to save the country and to protect the prewar values of the nation was to vote for Vallandigham. "Upon the success of the Democratic party depends the perpetuity of our Republican form of Government. If the Democracy are [*sic*] defeated at the ballot-box, then farewell to every vestige of freedom in the State of Ohio. Free Speech, a Free press and a Free Ballot, will be among the things that were." A vote for Vallandigham and the Democrats will demonstrate that "white man's freedom is more ardent than their love for the freedom of the negro."[40]

Moreover, Vallandigham's candidacy was considered to be more than that. James A. Rawley speculates that getting Vallandigham elected was part of a larger Democratic plan to wrest the Middle West's support of the war away from Lincoln. It would not take much. War weariness, emancipation, the use of Black soldiers, and the growing consolidation of power by the federal government contributed to the increasing discontent. The southern geographic portions of the states of Ohio, Indiana, and Illinois had shown sympathetic sentiments to Southern values and came to symbolize the very real concern of greater sectional divide among the Middle West states. Even the president's home state of Illinois had already repudiated his leadership in 1862 when voters turned the state legislature over to the Democrats. Indiana's state legislature was also dominated by Democrats whereas the party had made gains in Ohio in 1862. Rumors of spies and secret societies emerging in the Middle West had troubled governors and the president. Lincoln, writes Rawley, was right to fear these Democratic machinations.[41] Tod had already arrested Olds, threatened the Democratic press, supported Vallandigham's arrest, and subdued protesters so he knew full well what Lincoln feared. Morton in Indiana and Yates in Illinois all had similar experiences.

Although their private worries over the election's outcome were misplaced Brough and other politicians, who included Tod, Senators Wade and John Sherman, as well as Governors Morton and Yates, worked hard to canvass the state of Ohio right up to the election. Even though Vallandigham was stranded in Canada he also had supporters like Congressmen Samuel Cox and George Pendleton campaigning for him. Tod was feeling good about the outcome and telegraphed Lincoln that Brough's victory was all but certain.[42]

When Ohio voters went to the polls on October 13, they did so with a commitment to see the war through to the end. Overwhelmingly they heeded the alarms of sensational editorials warning of the movement underfoot led by Vallandigham "to break the Union into fragments."[43] In what was then the largest turnout in the state's history voter support for Brough was astounding. The Union candidate received 288,856 votes compared to 187,728 for Vallandigham, the Peace Democrat. Even more telling was the all-important soldiers' vote. It revealed even deeper support for the course of the war.[44]

Earlier in the year the legislature had moved on Tod's request for a system of absentee balloting, which enabled soldiers to cast votes from the field. As the election neared, Tod privately expressed confidence that Ohio's men in blue would deliver for Brough. The campaign, he said, was "waxing warm" and he was sure "the gallant men in the field will swell the Union majority."[45] Of the more than 43,700 votes cast by men in uniform, 94.8 percent or 41,467, went to Brough. One Ohio soldier nearly predicted the outcome when, in September, he forecast, "I do not think Vallandigham will get a single vote among Ohio troops," so loathsome was the "Canadian pony."[46] Although Democrats cried that the soldier vote was suppressed Brough's margin of victory was so great the soldiers' vote was irrelevant in terms of the final tally. Indeed, one historian of the Copperhead movement writes that the disparity of soldier votes for Brough and the Union was a sign that the fighting men knew "what was best for the nation."[47] One N. S. Westcott, of the Western Sharp-Shooters, stationed at Camp Davies in the Western theater, disclosed, "I have heard the opinion of a great many of the soldiers, and we all agree on the policy of the war. We are in for the emancipation proclamation; for we believe it to be the quickest way to end the war, and restore the Union . . . for we believe it to be the only way to gain an honorable peace. And we are willing to do the fighting."[48] "God be praised," Tod wrote to Lincoln.[49]

The state elections were just as revealing. Republicans garnered 30 senate seats versus 4 for the Democrats. In the house, the Republicans captured 76 seats to the Democrats' 21. On a personal note, Tod was gladdened to learn that his defense attorney Hocking Hunter defeated Philadelph Van Trump for a spot on the state supreme court.[50]

Vallandigham's biographer brushed aside the results as just "an unlucky day for Vallandigham."[51] He could not have been more wrong. Democrats found solace in the fact that Brough's margin of victory was not as great as Tod's in 1861. It was "a crumb of comfort," not only for Democrats but for Tod as well.[52]

Although Lincoln's name was not on any ballot, as head of the Union Party he represented all others listed. If there were any doubt of where Ohioans stood on the war and the president's leadership before the election, it was made clear after the results were counted. They were with Lincoln, the Union, Tod, and Brough. So elated and relieved was Lincoln with the election results that the president wired Tod, "Glory to God in the highest; Ohio has saved the Union." Historian Roseboom aptly concludes that the wide disparity of Brough's victory "was . . . a ringing indorsement [sic] of the war." Democrats cried foul about the results charging, on weak grounds, that the margin of victory was inconceivable, and that the election was stolen, attained through fraudulent means. But the news was just as glorious for the Union in Pennsylvania, where Andrew Curtin fended off his Democratic challenger in a much tighter race.[53] Victories were also claimed in Iowa and Indiana.

Joining Brough were four neophyte pro-Lincoln governors, Samuel Cony of Maine, Frederick Low of California, J. Gregory Smith of Vermont, and William Stone of Iowa. These victories ensured that there would be cohesiveness to aid the president's continued efforts. He would miss the outgoing state executives, like Tod, who supported the president through the darkest days of the war. The governors who served during this period had all grown to understand their roles relative to working with and supporting the federal government. Long gone were the days when an unsure Tod blindly reached out to Stanton looking for direction. The political demise of this group was not because of Lincoln but was due to the political backbiting in its own states. Engle shows that although the governors became "agents" for the federal government, it was "not at the expense of losing prestige or political sovereignty over state affairs."[54]

To think that the last 75 days of Tod's administration would wind down in quiet relaxation was unrealistic. Even Tod realized that. The "cozy little cottage" he had built the previous summer at Little Mountain near Lake Erie had stood empty. The turbulent last 12 months, accompanied by "the pressure of official business has not permitted him to enjoy it and it never has been furnished," reported the *Ashtabula Weekly Telegraph*.[55] In a letter to his son Henry, Tod lamented, "I am so much oppressed with official duties that it is impossible for me to give any attention to my private affairs." He looked forward, he wrote, to when "my time here . . . will soon be out [and] I will again be able to attend to my private matters."[56]

In a separate letter to "Hen" that summer he wrote that his health was "quite good although the weather is extremely hot. I take my meals at the Neil House [Hotel across from the State House] but sleep at home, where I have a very quiet time."[57] Whenever in Cleveland, he would try to spend time at the home of his son John and his family for a little relaxation. This he did a week after the election but not before riding in Brough's torch-lit victory parade through the streets of Cleveland. One correspondent at the time observed Tod to be tired. "Worn and weary from the labor and excitement of this campaign," reported the *Cleveland Morning Leader*, "from the cares and burdens of executive duties." Each challenge of the past year would have been hard on anyone let alone on one who suffered health issues like Tod. From Cleveland, he managed a short visit home to Brier Hill only to be back at his duties the next day. Any thoughts of riding out the last days of his term undisturbed by war duties were quickly dispelled.[58]

Four days after the Union electoral victory in Ohio, Lincoln declared that the state's quota had been met and therefore the draft was no longer necessary. But this quota filled old regiments in the field. Lincoln needed more and soon thereafter he announced that another 300,000 soldiers were needed. And Ohio was expected to supply 32,000 of these men. States falling short of their new quotas would compel the president to reinstitute a draft on January 5, 1864. Ever the optimist, Tod believed Ohio volunteers would again come forward. Recruiting officers were sent to their respective districts across the state as the governor once again asked citizens for their "hearty co-operation."[59] The lure of the bounty proved too tempting a prize. Bedeviling Tod and other Northern governors were individuals who took advantage of the bounty system. These "bounty jumpers" enlisted in one state, collected their reward, and then struck out to the next state for another payoff. In states where the draft had already been instituted, substitute brokers or agents showed up to help find another to stand in for one who was conscripted. Of course, this came with a price. To Tod's chagrin, many of Ohio's eligible males were recruited and hired away by agents to serve in other states. Tod considered this practice a "great evil" and it gave him "much trouble and anxiety," but he would not infringe on the rights of his citizens to freely "go where they please." As for the brokers or agents, said Tod, "These devils are about as hard to head off as counterfeiters and horse-thieves are."[60]

Tod still had other troubles to look after. For one, he had to deal with a new threat to the state's border but this time, one emanating from the North. In mid-November, the War Department had been alerted to what was then referred to as the Rebel Plot or the Canadian Conspiracy or the Lake Erie Plot, among other names. Secretary Stanton was alerted at midnight on November 11 by the British diplomat in Washington, Lord Richard Lyons, who had received information from the Canadian governor general of a scheme to raid the federal prisoner of war camp on Johnson's Island in Lake Erie, where 2,330 rebels were held. The daring stratagem was much more than raiding the island fortress and springing a bunch of prisoners.[61]

Although Great Britain and its Canadian dominion had remained neutral during the war there existed small pockets of Confederate sympathizers north of the border. Southern rebels also managed to establish a presence in Canada. One report claimed that 15,000 secessionists lived there.[62] At any rate, these "disaffected skedaddlers from the North" and a band of "rebel refugees," as one correspondent described them, had a broader plan to bring terror to all reaches of the American side of the Lake Erie shoreline.[63]

The first objective was to land an armed steamer on Johnson's Island and overwhelm the 500 Union guards stationed there. Once the 2,300 rebel prisoners were freed, they were to seize steamships, then make their way to Buffalo to sack the city. After turning Buffalo into "a heap of ashes" Cleveland and Detroit were targeted to suffer the same fate. The destruction of these three major port cities would effectively destroy the lake commerce from Chicago to western New York.[64]

Stanton committed the federal government to "employ all the means in its power to suppress any hostile attacks from Canada."[65] Maj. Gen. John Dix arrived in Buffalo to help oversee defenses.[66] Tod advised doubling the guards at the prison. When details of the plot became clearer Tod rerouted 400 rebel prisoners heading from Columbus to Johnson's Island by train back to the capital and called out 600 militia to report to Cleveland, Toledo, and Sandusky.[67]

As quickly as the threat emerged it just as quickly disappeared. The word from Detroit was that a Rebel presence, realizing the surprise was gone, returned to Windsor, Ontario, from where it came. Within a week of the scare Tod reassured Stanton, "With the force we now have [deployed] we have nothing to fear." The *Weekly Ottumwa Courier* concluded, "Exactly how [real and] formidable this great Canadian naval raid in its design and execution was to be, is not known, and perhaps never will be except to those engaged in it." With another threat to Ohio behind him Tod was free to travel to Gettysburg, where a new cemetery was ready to be dedicated.[68]

There, preparations were under way with the support of Governor Curtin and David Wills, a Gettysburg attorney, to dedicate a new national cemetery for the Union dead buried on the battlefield.[69] Tod had sent D. W. Brown, an attorney, to travel to Gettysburg to function as his "agent" and look after the interests of Ohio's fallen soldiers. He was to remain at Gettysburg on Tod's behalf until the dedication ceremony scheduled for November 19.[70]

Union states that suffered losses were invited to send delegates to the ceremony. Edward Everett was asked to deliver the keynote address. President Lincoln was added as an afterthought. Tod would lead Ohio's delegation, which included former governor William Dennison, Governor-Elect Brough, Lieutenant Governor–Elect Charles Anderson, and a handful of other officials. Tod had asked Anderson to deliver remarks at Ohio's evening reception after the dedication ceremony. Tod told Anderson that it would be "very agreeable to the gentlemen from Ohio who may be there to an address from one of their own [and] we can think of no one better fitted for that duty than yourself."[71] Anderson, a colonel during the war, was wounded at the Battle of Stones River. His older brother was Robert Anderson, commander of Fort Sumter when the bastion fell in April 1861, which started the war.[72]

With the Lake Erie plot satisfactorily resolved, Tod went ahead with his plans to attend the Gettysburg dedication. The dedication day found Tod leading the Ohio delegation down Baltimore Street, passing right by Ohio's graves before the distinguished guests took their assigned seats within the cemetery walls.[73] Tod and Brough sat behind the president. When Lincoln finally made his way through the dense crowd and onto the platform to his seat he reportedly quipped to Tod and Brough, "Why, I have just seen Governor Dennison of Ohio—how many more governors has Ohio?" For the next two hours, Everett delivered the keynote speech detailing the battle and the war.[74] In comparison, Lincoln delivered his immortal words in just three minutes. Though brief, Lincoln's eloquent terms honored the soldiers of the battle, gave meaning to their deeds, and defined a new purpose for the war. The test of this Union of States he said, as Tod had alluded to during his inaugural and State of the State Address, was whether the Founders "were mistaken, in claiming for their children, [the] ability to govern themselves." Lincoln believed they were not mistaken and committed this current generation to save self-governing for the succeeding generations to come.

When the ceremony ended, Tod invited Lincoln to the Ohio reception at the Presbyterian church. With Lincoln and Sec. State Seward in attendance Tod called the meeting to order at 5 P.M., at which time he introduced Dennison. The former governor then presented the featured speaker, Ohio's newly elected lieutenant governor Charles Anderson. Anderson proceeded to deliver a long and "provocative" discourse on the necessity to see this war to a victorious and decisive conclusion.[75]

While Tod honored the dead at Gettysburg, the *Ashland Union* labeled him a notorious "*drunkard,* and a profane man [who] aided in electing to the same position one of the most *notorious sots* in the land [Brough]; a man who was so drunk at several of his appointments that he was unable to speak." Although both men enjoyed a social drink from time to time, there is no record of either failing to report to duty due to inebriation. The *Union* was not finished with its character assassinations. One week later it scorned the outgoing governor in "his last hours and last energies to the demoniac spirit of abolitionism, anarchy and civil strife. He dies [a political] death of the wicked. He ends his days, after crucifying the sovereignty of his State, and acting as the mere viceroy of the Federal Government."[76] Once back in Columbus Tod prepared for the end of his term. He could not help but come to the realization that he was "soon to surrender the highly responsible duties now resting upon" him. As early as November he was offering his "profound thanks" to members of the public who had sustained him "in the discharge of the arduous duties" during his trying term.[77]

As the last day of his term drew closer, Tod continued to press on. The necessities of war demanded that he faithfully fulfill his duties until the very end. The federal government still needed him. Much as he did at the beginning of his term, Tod called on the loyal citizens of Ohio to join the fight. Lincoln needed more men and Tod did his best to rally them. Under the threat of the new draft date, January 5, Ohio needed to reach its quota. Otherwise, the process of conscription would descend upon our "homes," he warned.[78]

Tod would not forget the selflessness of his soldiers, especially those suffering in hospitals, imprisoned at the hands of the enemy, and those who gave the last full measure of devotion. Tod's efforts to provide medical treatment and care for the state's wounded have been noted. He also sought to send supplies to captured Ohio soldiers lingering in dreadful, inadequately supplied Confederate prisons. Knowing that their sufferings were great, he endeavored to alleviate their misery; he was "still doing all in my power for the relief of these gallant men." The federal and state governments possessed "abundant supplies, but as yet we have not been permitted to forward them to our suffering soldiers."[79] The *Western Reserve Chronicle* heaped praise on Tod for his unending efforts to aid the prisoners, noting those especially incarcerated in Libby Prison in Richmond.[80]

The year did not end on a high note for Tod—or Ohio, for that matter. In fact, he suffered the most embarrassing event of his governorship. On November 27, John Morgan and six of his fellow officers crawled through a seven-foot-long ventilator shaft under the cells at the state penitentiary, then dug a short tunnel under the main wall that led them into the prison yard. From there, in the dark and rainy night they managed to sneak past distracted guards and with the use of bedsheets fashioned into a braided rope scaled the prison's walls to freedom. Initial reports falsely said that Morgan escaped to Toronto, Canada. But his getaway route was due south. He was reunited with his wife at Danville, Virginia, on Christmas Day.[81] Morgan had the last laugh and blighted the administration of Gov. David Tod, who admittedly was "deeply chagrined and mortified . . . to hear of the escape." The *Western Reserve Chronicle* labeled the incident "a disgrace to the State."[82]

15

Shin Plaster and Pot Metal, January 1864–June 1864

THE COUNTLESS DECISIONS that Governor Tod made during his exciting but tumultuous two-year term had impactful and historic effects on people and events. Once out of office, the authority he once wielded would be replaced by hope and a bit of relief. David Tod believed that he had done his best to advance the causes of the national government and to bring ultimate victory and restoration to the Union, all worthy of a second term.

Tod's children gathered in Columbus to be with their father on his last day in office. Unfortunately, Charlotte, George, William, and Sallie were so ill they were confined to their rooms where they "require[d] the constant attention of their mother." The governor could not wait for the last day to come declaring, "It is my intention to go immediately home" to Brier Hill.[1]

Before David Tod "lay down the robes of office and retire to private life" he released his outgoing message on January 4, one week before the end of his term.[2] He used this last message to highlight the accomplishments of Ohio and its soldiers under his leadership during the war. He also defended his actions in putting down the antidraft violence in Holmes and Montgomery Counties. The state's finances were sound despite the costs of the war, which included the pursuit, capture, and reparations paid for damages caused by Morgan's raid. As for the rebel officer's recent escape Tod continued to publicly sidestep any responsibility and blamed it on the "negligence of those having him in custody and [a] misunderstanding with the United States military authorities." He was especially proud of the progress of the militia. Not surprisingly he made special mention of the more than 200,000 Ohio troops who had thus far taken the field and wished that none of their families should suffer hardships. Therefore, he asked for a tax increase to support them and their families. Of their service, he added, no state could be prouder.[3]

Of course, Tod's words were not universally well received. State Sen. William Lang, a Democrat from Holmes County, thought the Governor's contingency fund of $100,000 was twice the amount required. His itemized statement, said Lang, was full of waste and a nauseating example of "useless and extravagant throwing away of money." State Senator John Connell, another "life-long Democrat," could not have agreed more. The newly elected officeholder thought the governor's participation at the Gettysburg dedication, for instance, was driven by his "excess zeal for the good of the soldier" and further evidence of Tod's frivolous spending.[4]

Governor Tod worked up to his last day in office wanting to thoroughly tie up loose ends in preparation for the transfer of authority to his successor. And he also wanted to ensure that the official record of his administration accurately reflected his efforts. He was a proud man, even vain, and he made no secret about his desire to leave a positive legacy. Though he was denied a second term tributes and accolades from friends poured in. The *Western Reserve Chronicle* commended their favorite son for his "effective measures" and "wise administration of the State Government" and believed that every loyal citizen of the state owed him a debt of gratitude. As far as the editor was concerned, Tod had "won a proud name and place in the record of the State and Nation."

As complimentary as the *Chronicle* was it objectively and accurately pointed out Tod's mistakes. He was criticized for pardons, promotions, and "some bad appointments," especially in choosing recruiting agents. He had not taken the advice of the community leaders within the recruiting districts and instead named his own agents. Not only would local leaders have had a more positive effect on recruitment, but Tod was viewed as an arrogant outsider uninterested in the opinion of community influencers and he could also come across as condescending. Of course, Republicans had charged Tod with giving "his old party friends" political appointments. But in the end, the local paper was more than forgiving of

Tod considering the pressures he faced during two years of nonstop war. Mistakes were bound to happen.[5]

The journalist and historian Whitelaw Reid later described Governor Tod's efforts as "zealous, watchful, and pains-taking."[6] No one, not even his political adversaries, questioned Tod's patriotic spirit and devotion to saving the Union. His optimism about the country's future remained rooted in its past. The principles upon which the nation was founded would continue to serve as his beacon. He never wavered in his belief that persons could govern themselves and that if the Union lost this war it also lost the great experiment of a republican form of self-governance.

Tod also brought closure to personal affairs. He bid farewell to his faithful inner circle, especially to George B. Wright, to whom he had grown quite close. The pair had been known to visit wounded soldiers in the hospitals and make weekly inspections of Camp Chase.[7] As a token of affection for their old boss Wright and his fellow staffers presented Tod with a gold and diamond encrusted snuffbox engraved with the letter *T*.[8] The *Daily Ohio Statesman* contemptuously pointed to the facial likeness between "His retiring Excellency" Governor Tod, with his hair "combed *a la* that of the First Consul of France" Napoleon Bonaparte, his look-alike.[9]

Inauguration day, January 11, 1864, finally arrived. Sitting on the platform, dressed in an "old worn hat and faded brown overcoat,"[10] Tod watched Brough take the oath and then listened attentively to his inaugural address. Tod must have felt terribly cheated out of a second term. The *Urbana Union* ventured that "it would be nothing strange if he felt something of resentment at the treatment he [had] received at the hands of the Combination party."[11] When Brough finished taking the oath of office Governor Tod became private citizen David Tod. In that moment he was unburdened of the duties of the highest office in the state. But no person having served in the same capacity under the same challenging circumstances could just shut down the cares and worries that had consumed his every day for the last two years. He was anxious to see his country reunited and peace restored.

Critics like the Radical wing of the Union Party of course were glad to see him go. He never measured up to their expectations when it came to emancipation. Others criticized him for his blind trust in Lincoln and Stanton. Every time Lincoln called for more troops Tod was there to rally Ohio's young men to the call. Tod knew that the might of the nation must be concentrated behind the national government if this war was to end successfully. And it was only after Lincoln appointed Ulysses S. Grant commanding general of the army that the fortunes of war begin to shift in the Union's favor and eventually to victory.

Tod never vacillated in his support of the president, even after mounting defeats. He once told Wright during one difficult stretch, "We must stand by Mr. Lincoln; he knows better than any of us what is best."[12] But Lincoln did not always know what was best and neither did Tod. Tod once called for Grant's removal from command when rumors of his drunkenness reached a fever pitch after the Battle of Shiloh in April 1862 just three months into Tod's tenure. In his eagerness to see military success Tod was often guilty of overreaching into military affairs. History does not look at Tod's support of McClellan and his quick criticism of Grant fondly. His limited service in the militia hardly provided the requisite experience on such matters. In "his zeal in the cause of the Union" he was too trusting in the unproven federal war machine.[13] Fortunately, Lincoln ignored some of the military recommendations made by Tod and others.[14] In 1863, however, after a year in office, Tod more than adequately displayed sharpened military instincts as he effected the defense of Cincinnati and, later that summer, strategically called out the militia that kept Morgan on the run until his eventual capture by the local militia. He also helped to erect a defensive deterrent on Lake Erie to protect the prison on Johnson's Island.

But Tod's military problems were not confined to the riverfront or the lakeshore; they carried over onto the field of battle. Disagreements between various officers and Tod arose over the issue of promotions. The problem, observes Reid, was that the governor adopted no consistent approach to this sacred military tradition. "Sometimes he promoted in accordance with rank, sometimes against it; sometimes in accordance with the wishes of the Colonel, sometimes against him." And more than one colonel formerly expressed his dissatisfaction when Tod promoted soldiers in the field. Tod was also known to show leniency toward enlistees; "certain privates" were not to be punished for being absent without leave. Officers complained that this undermined discipline. But Tod had a soft spot for the young soldiers. Incidents like these created embarrassing situations for all involved.[15]

For as much as Tod and old Democrats and Republicans wanted to shed themselves of their former partisan identifications to come together as true Unionists at the beginning of the war, it was not so easy to do. Many of Tod's appointments were viewed as political payback or favoritism to old friends. Wright suggests on this point that Tod was simply trying to include Democratic "friends in the cause of the Union." Partisan bloodlines ran deep however, and Tod's disregard of this loud criticism only served to reinforce the charges against him.[16]

Tod's tenure also revealed the traits of a private businessman. As the leader of several successful private industrial enterprises, such as the Brier Hill Iron and Coal Company, the Cleveland & Mahoning Railroad, and his numerous coal operations before he took office, he was used to wielding unlimited authority and influence. Even George Wright noted that his boss was sometimes "accused of being arbitrary and despotic." This criticism was especially fitting during the arrests of Olds and Vallandigham and on at least 11 other occasions when habeas corpus was suspended. These incidents garnered Tod all kinds of tyrannical adjectives from justified critics.[17] In the politically charged climate of Columbus, these traits were not warmly welcomed. His straightforward manners were received coolly, especially by officials who were not subordinate to the executive branch. Military officers, however, had to accept his direct orders. Tod also introduced various "reforms [and] adopted careful business methods" that did not go over well, observed Wright.[18]

One of the most initiative-taking measures in which Tod moved with alacrity was his response to aid Ohio's wounded. In this area, Tod showed remarkable leadership. He spared no expense for the care of the wounded, yet he was roundly criticized for his public expenditures. Even more he hoped to provide for the permanently wounded and their families, a novel concept that gained little momentum. What Ohio could not furnish Tod sought from various volunteer organizations to remedy the petitions of his injured troops. Of all Tod's shortcomings and successes, "the most beautiful feature of his work," writes Reid, was his "watchful care for the wounded."[19]

As straightforward as Tod could be no one could claim that he was not a charitable man. When empathy and compassion were required, few could match his comforting words or his kindly display of affection. He had received numerous letters from private citizens including women, young and old, who wished to offer their services as nurses in hospitals. He could have easily ignored these requests in the face of other mounting duties but instead he often took the time to gently decline their offers. He also had to fight his own emotional urge to allow mothers, wives, and beloved to visit their wounded loved ones in hospitals, informing one soldier's beloved that her "pleading letter" nearly convinced him to let her in. He thought it was in the best "interest of the service" however, to decline the request.[20]

It was easy to criticize Tod for the mistakes he made especially with his "peculiarities." One contemporary observer said that Tod could be "a trifle pompous in his style—somewhat . . . egotistic," for example "in habitually referring to the soldiers as 'my gallant boys.'"[21] True, he could be a bit haughty or patronizing, but when it came to the welfare of his gallant boys, he spared no energy or cost no matter what color their skin. For these young men, who stepped forward to risk life and limb to save the Union, Tod brushed aside the criticism and worked tirelessly for their welfare. Overall, despite being turned out of office, one objective onlooker believed that Tod "left [Ohio's] affairs in good order, her contributions to the Nation fully made up, her duties to her soldier sons jealously watched, and her honor untarnished."[22] If nothing else he was an efficient and effective administrator.

Lincoln had valued Tod's constant support, but he was fortunate that Brough would be equally as protective if not more helpful. Lincoln had invested much in building relationships with governors like Tod, who was not the only Lincoln supporter leaving the governor's office that year. Frederick Holbrook of Vermont, James Robinson of Kentucky, Leland Stanford of California, and Samuel Kirkwood of Iowa all joined Tod on the way out. Overall, a strong Union coalition prevailed among the loyal states in the North. Excluding the border states, of the 11 gubernatorial elections held in 1863, all remained squarely in Union hands.[23]

Once out of office, Tod found it difficult to fade from the day's events. Former governors seemed to have a level of expectation placed upon them once out of office. As governor, Tod had involved William Dennison in unofficial as well as official assignments. Dennison cheerfully and patriotically accepted duties like electioneering or fact-finding missions involving the troops. During the Brough administration Tod, at the governor's request or on behalf of the Union Party, would do whatever he could to help win the war as well as the political battles in support of that cause.

Maria Tod had been a source of strength and support for her husband especially during the darkest days of his term. One of her last gestures occurred after Brough's inauguration when she opened her residence to well-wishers for a "farewell reception" in honor of her husband. The *Cleveland Morning Leader* could not help but pity the incoming governor. Awaiting Brough, as surely Tod could attest, were "the thousand annoyances of the public pillory of power, and to work night and day for a Republic, the most ungrateful of mistresses." The *Leader* had been a great supporter of Tod and paid homage to his service and sacrifice and wished him rest, love, and admiration. Brier Hill wine, it was said, flowed freely the night of Tod's send-off.[24] When he left Youngstown two long years before, he arrived in Columbus a War Democrat turned Union Party man. He returned home a staunch member of the Union Party but with serious leanings toward the Republican Party. The ideological shift in his political philosophy had been in the making as a direct effect of his solemn responsibilities as a war governor and they continued to evolve as the war dragged on.

For now, in early 1864, the Tods looked forward to quieter days at Brier Hill. Maria and David both needed the rest. The former governor's health had demanded it. The burdens of office afforded no respite and the weight of responsibilities had been enough to exhaust an otherwise healthy man approaching his sixtieth birthday. His fatigued and weary appearance had come under scrutiny in recent weeks. The physical signs of his declining health were hard to ignore. George Wright had thought his boss looked "much worn and with great labor."[25] Uncharacteristically, Tod had passed on an occasion to deliver a celebratory speech after Brough's election the previous October at the Angier Hotel in Cleveland. When called to address the crowd that fall day he declared "that there [was] a point beyond which human endurance cannot go" and asked to be excused.[26] Medical practice during the period was primitive compared to today's standards and it is likely that Tod's symptoms were incorrectly treated, untreated, or undetected. He had aged noticeably during his "very toilsome" two-year term and the antagonist partisan press eagerly took note.[27] The *Cadiz Sentinel* for one, hearkened back to his "Pot Metal Davey" nickname from the 1840s to reapply it to what they observed to be his enlarged "abdominal proportions."[28] What the press actually knew about his health is hard to determine but those friendly to Tod's administration wished him a "speedy restoration of his health, and for a calm and quiet life . . . in his retirement."[29]

Tod's business interests in the Mahoning valley—coal mining, iron production, and railroad operations—had been in the able hands of his sons and trusted business partners during his absence. Tod's eldest son

John had married Sarah Keys Little in 1858 and started a successful coal firm in Cleveland that same year. Henry, 24, ran the iron furnaces at Brier Hill. George had been the only son to answer the call of duty in May 1861 and served his country until stricken with rheumatism before he was discharged. Once back on his feet he studied law like his father. He passed the bar in 1865 but unlike his father George never practiced law and instead followed his brothers into the family business.[30] William, the youngest son, attended school in Columbus while his father was governor and got into the manufacture of metal castings and machinery.[31] The winter months back in Youngstown passed quickly and when the important political events of the coming season beckoned to him, David Tod faithfully answered their calls.

The year 1864 was a presidential election year and the Union Party gathered to renominate Lincoln in Baltimore in June. Ohio's Union Party met in May and selected Tod, William Dennison, and State Legislator Columbus Delano to attend and pitch their votes for Lincoln at the convention. Their selection followed the publication of the Pomeroy Circular, a political hit job on the president promoted by the supporters of Salmon P. Chase.

Chase and the Radical ideologues were not happy with the president's lenient reconstruction plans for a conquered South once the war was won. They wanted nothing more than to secure the candidacy for Chase, their Radical leader. Not only was the Pomeroy Circular critical of the president's leadership, it endorsed Chase to replace Lincoln on the ticket. Although Chase was aware of the pamphlet's origins, he took no active role in promoting or quashing the scheme. But the president's supporters rallied to his side. His more "moderate course on race and reconstruction issues was much preferred to Chase's more liberal position." The damage to Chase's political aspirations, caused by the imbroglio, however, was irreparable. His biographer described the action of his supporters as "ill-timed, [and] intemperate" and "precipitated a rush of politicians to join the Lincoln bandwagon and urge his renomination." With Tod a member of the Ohio delegation in Baltimore, writes historian Frederick J. Blue, "no amount of parliamentary maneuvering by Chase partisans could prevent an endorsement of Lincoln's renomination." Naming Tod a delegate was also a sign that the Moderate wing within the party had wrested control from the Radical faction. Furthermore, Tod's place within the delegation secured for Lincoln Ohio's support and provided the death knell of a

Chase nomination. If Chase had played any role in scuttling Tod's chances for renomination for the governorship one year before, the political retribution was duly returned. The irony was hard to miss; the same party that cast Tod aside now revived his political career for one more assignment.[32]

On a rainy June evening in Baltimore, the Seventh Ohio Regiment marched four miles from its post at Ft. McHenry to greet the Ohio delegation at Barnum's City Hotel on Monument Square. As the soldiers stood at attention in the light drizzle the Ohio delegates stood under cover upon a hotel balcony to deliver short addresses praising Lincoln. Tod, it was said, took to "Speechifying" during which he paid tribute to Lincoln's humble beginnings and his leadership during this critical juncture in the nation's history. Ohio, he said, would not forsake the president or his efforts to save the nation. Shouts of "Old Abe!" answered Tod when he asked the troops whom they wanted as their next president.[33] When the proceedings opened on June 7, Dennison was chosen president of the convention and Tod one of a handful of elected vice presidents.[34] With Lincoln's renomination now a foregone conclusion the interest turned to selecting a new vice presidential candidate. Before the delegates settled upon the loyal Democratic war governor of Tennessee, Andrew Johnson, to replace Hannibal Hamlin, there was feeble and faint talk of a Tod vice presidency among Ohio's sons but nothing serious came of it.[35] With the Lincoln-Johnson ticket set, Tod made plans to join Brough and Dennison in Cleveland for a Fourth of July celebration.[36] But the political excitement of the moment was far from over.

The strained relationship between the president and his egotistical, yet extraordinarily competent treasurer Salmon Chase had grown more uncomfortable after the publication of the Pomeroy Circular and once the Republican Convention ended. It seemed as if any time the president questioned Chase or there was even a hint of disagreement between the two Chase was ready to resign. Prior to June, in fact, the secretary had submitted his resignation on three previous occasions, all of which were declined by the president. But Lincoln's patience had finally run out.

What brought the matter to a head occurred in late June when Chase requested an opportunity to discuss his recommendation with the president for the replacement of John J. Cisco, assistant treasurer of the United States, who intended to resign. Lincoln's reaction was blunt when he informed Chase that his request to suggest a successor was out of the bounds of his office and therefore, did not "lie within the range of a conversation between you and me." Stung by Lincoln's terse reply, Chase explained that in his action he "sought" merely "to get the best man for the places to be filled." Reeling from Lincoln's censure a conciliatory Chase wrote, "I cannot help feeling that my position here is not altogether agreeable to you" any longer. Embarrassed, pained, or disgruntled Chase once again resigned. This time the president accepted. Although Lincoln had had great confidence in Chase's abilities to finance the war, he believed their personal association had "reached a point of mutual embarrassment in [their] official relation" and it could no "longer [be] sustained."[37] So indignant yet so predisposed was Lincoln to accept Chase's most recent action he simultaneously sent both the news of Chase's resignation and the name of his choice to replace the secretary to the senate.

David Tod was in his office at the Brier Hill Iron and Coal Company on June 30 when a telegram from Lincoln arrived. "I have nominated you to be Secretary of the Treasury in place of Gov. Chase who has resigned. Please come without a moment's delay."[38] Shock waves traveled throughout political Washington. Most could not decide if they were more astounded by the news of Chase's resignation, and that Lincoln accepted it, or of the president's nomination of Tod to take his place.

Choosing Tod could not have been decided in haste. Lincoln's was a busy mind and prone to thoughtful, deep contemplation; hardly one to make emotional decisions. But based upon the reaction of his inner circle he chose Tod on a whim. Only one of the president's cabinet members, William Seward, claimed to have had knowledge beforehand. In fact, the secretary of state had advised the president to select Tod for the office. Said Seward, "It was the patriotic services thus rendered the nation which induced President Lincoln, upon my suggestion, to tender to Mr. Tod the office of Secretary of the Treasury when Mr. Salmon P. Chase resigned."[39]

Attorney General Edward Bates penned in his diary that the news "took us all by surprise."[40] The diarist Gideon Welles, secretary of the navy, concurred wholeheartedly and recorded a more detailed entry for June 30: "All were surprised to-day with the resignation of Secretary Chase and the nomination of Governor David Tod as his successor. I knew nothing of it till the fact was told me by Senator [James] Doolittle, [Wisconsin], who came to see and advise with me, supposing I knew something of the circumstances. But I was wholly ignorant."[41] The most stunned cabinet member was Chase himself who had been working at the capitol when he learned that Lincoln had accepted his resignation.[42] "So my official life closes," a dejected Chase recorded in his diary that night.[43]

In three years, with the passage of the National Banking Acts of 1863 and 1864, Chase introduced and implemented a huge, sound system for funding the war by acquiring loans that were then financed through taxes and the sale of interest-yielding bonds. Chase never would have endorsed it had it not been for the nation's troubles. Although the system of soft or paper money massively expanded the national debt, there was no other way to keep up with the nation's war needs.[44] This method of deficit spending was a major philosophical shift for Chase, but the survival of the Union depended on it. Some wondered if Tod could demonstrate such flexibility; few remembered that before he assumed the governorship, he had encouraged citizens to purchase Chase's government bonds. Chase brought in the Philadelphia financier Jay Cooke whose company helped the federal treasury finance the war's efforts. After Tod "investigated the character of the security" of the bond plan put up by Chase, he touted the program as "safer than bank stock" and invested accordingly.[45] It is extremely doubtful that had Tod taken over the US Treasury he would have introduced any changes to Chase's successful system.

Although Seward would one day pay tribute to Tod's service, he made no mention of Tod's financial abilities. This was the problem with Tod's nomination. Those who opposed it based their opinion "on the ground that he was unrecognized as a man of any financial ability," said the *New York World*.[46] He had no hands-on experience with governmental finances (but neither had Chase) and was known for his long-standing opposition to paper currency—this at a time when over $600 million in greenbacks was in circulation and when the war's expenditures had brought the nation's debt to a record $1.7 billion, with each day adding another $3 million to it.[47] The negative reaction was overwhelming. Frantic and confused senators like Wisconsin's Doolittle "were struck dumb with amazement" at the news, wrote the journalist Noah Brooks.[48] One correspondent of the *Daily Ohio Statesman* wrote, Tod "knows as little of finances as a cow does of arithmetic."[49] Another paper wryly asked "what amount of brains was really needed to manage this immense department" if someone like Tod was nominated? The *Saint Paul Press* referred to Tod as "a man of . . . inferior calibre."[50] The *New York Herald* called Tod a "highly respectable [but] broken down politician."[51] One upset and unnamed congressman went so far as to describe the day as one of the "gloomiest . . . seen in Washington since the first Bull Run."[52] And one recent historian has described Tod as "supremely unqualified."[53]

There were exceptions to the criticism of course. The influential Republican stalwart Thurlow Weed, who was no admirer of Chase, regarded Tod's nomination a "gleam of national sunshine."[54] The *Evening Star* in Washington said Tod was "able, loyal and energetic."[55] But these words of support were rare.

In the US Senate John Conness of California summarized that Secretary Chase "had done valuable work" and that to replace him at this critical moment "would be a public misfortune." And although Tod had a reputation as a "sterling patriot" Conness said he did not possess the talents to head up the government's finances.[56] The issue was immediately turned over to the Senate Finance Committee under the leadership of William Fessenden of Maine. Fessenden marched his committeemen to the White House to see the president for answers. Congressman Elihu Washburne had already declared to Lincoln that Tod's selection was "a great disaster."[57] Fessenden pressed the president hard for an explanation.

More than Tod's lack of experience was his contrasting view on currency compared to Chase's. Tod had long ago established his conservative hard money stance that earned him the nickname "Pot Metal Tod." Chase, however, had embraced soft or paper currency and was nicknamed, Shin Plaster Chase, a reference to paper money and a takeoff on his initials.[58] Tod believed in the gold standard. Chase could not have financed the war on gold alone. Tod sought higher taxes to support the war and the troops and believed that they should "be somewhat increased until the rebellion is put down."[59] The crisis had forced both Secretary Chase and Governor Tod to take unprecedented steps to finance the war.

Choosing Tod, therefore, would lead one to believe that Lincoln was proposing a major philosophical shift in the way the war was financed. Even more so Chase had proven to be an evolving yet effective risk taker while Tod, ever the financial conservative, remained so. To make that switch now, with no end to the war in sight, was indeed a "radical departure" from what had sustained the Union war machine to this point. The concern on everyone's mind was whether a Treasury Secretary Tod would modify his conservative economic viewpoint as necessitated by the war. Would he adhere to Chase's system or retreat from it?[60] Secretary Welles's thoughts represented much of the confusion. "I have my doubts" he recorded, that the president selected Tod with "sufficient study." To Welles, Lincoln was a man who had "given but little attention to finance and the currency, but yet he can hardly be ignorant of the fact that Chase and Tod are opposites." Welles feared that Tod's confirmation would "disturb . . . the paper-money men."[61] What the Fessenden committee wanted was to reinstate Chase. But Lincoln, according to the *New York Times* "was immovable, and declared the separation [with Chase] irrevocable."[62]

According to Lincoln's personal secretaries John Nicolay and John Hay, Welles was correct. Although the president had given Tod's nomination consideration it was a decision not based upon his economic philosophy but rather "on account of the high opinion he had formed of him as governor of Ohio." And, being a man of his word, Lincoln refused to rescind the offer. The president, said Nicolay and Hay, "could not, in justice to himself or to Tod, withdraw the nomination."[63] A troubled Lincoln sought out the opinion of Governor Brough, who happened to be in Washington. Brough enlightened the president about Tod's poor health and therefore prophetically suggested that his predecessor would decline the offer. Besides, Brough ventured that the offer alone would provide Tod "all the honor" he needed to soothe hurt feelings since his gubernatorial defeat orchestrated by the Radical Republicans. As it turned out, Lincoln's nomination vindicated Tod's patriotic service and was enough to heal the injury his ego sustained after he was denied a chance at a second term.[64]

Another historian, Joseph Martin Heron, suggests that Lincoln was attempting to assemble an administration that appeared even more aggressive in prosecuting the war and thus more appealing to the pro-war electorate. Lincoln would have to fend off the serious challenge posed by the retired general George McClellan at the head of the Democratic peace ticket. The promise of peace from McClellan presented an attractive alternative to the more than three years of bloodshed. To many, Lincoln was heading for "certain defeat"[65] because his military forces had not been aggressive enough. Therefore, adding former War Democrats like Andrew Johnson and Tod, both known for their use of harsh and unforgiving rhetoric against traitorous rebels, might help to create a more aggressive image.[66]

The distinguished Lincoln historian Richard N. Current offers yet another opinion. Current writes that in choosing Tod the president was more "concerned about appeasing the Ohio Republican organization rather than Congress or Wall Street." Ohio was vital to the president's reelection bid. If removing Chase from his cabinet upset voters in Ohio, the president hoped to appease hurt feelings by replacing one Ohioan for another.[67]

After Tod read the telegram from Lincoln, having given the proposition little thought, he handed it to a young business associate who happened to be in his Brier Hill office. When asked if he would accept, Tod responded coolly, "No. It means if I accept, I will soon be brought back from Washington in a coffin."[68] This was not only an allusion to the expected demands of the job but also to Tod's fragile state of health. Therefore he responded to the president, "The condition of my health forbids the acceptance of the distinguished position you offer me."[69] Tod's decision saved the president from a potentially embarrassing situation and effectively ended his own political career. Tod's hurt feelings were assuaged however by the president's gesture, as "the tribute was nonetheless appreciated." Lincoln knew that he needed Tod's campaign help to carry Ohio in the upcoming election. Christopher Dell explains that Tod was still extremely popular in Ohio and that Lincoln's offer kept the old War Democrat and the former governor's followers securely in the president's corner.[70]

So Brough was right. In one fell swoop Lincoln retired Chase, restored Tod's pride, retained the loyalty of Ohio's War Democrats, and kept the nation's financial system on course when he named Fessenden to replace Chase after Tod declined. Politically, it was a much safer choice. Even Chase agreed that Fessenden's selection had the greater "confidence of the country."[71]

The political spectacle did not go unnoticed. The following month, *Harper's Weekly* printed a cartoon depicting Lincoln seated at a dining table. On his plate is the skeletal remains of a fully devoured piece of fish bearing the facial features of Salmon P. Chase. The carcass was stripped to the bones; used up. The president told his waiter, "remove the Salmon and bring me a Tod." But the servant responded instantly, "The Tod's out; but can't I fitch something else, Sir?"[72]

With the all-important presidential election fast approaching, Tod, his spirits boosted by Lincoln's distinguished offer, would find himself back on the campaign trail, poor health and all. The fate of the nation would be decided by the outcome of the election. Without a Lincoln victory, the Union was sure to be dissolved under a Democratic peace plan. Tod recommitted his energy to get Lincoln reelected.

16

The Condition of My Crops, July 1864–December 1865

THE REELECTION OF Abraham Lincoln in 1864 was not a foregone conclusion. In fact, it looked downright unlikely. Military victories again eluded Union troops despite Ulysses Grant's elevation to the head of the army in March. For several days in July Confederate troops under the command of Jubal Early threatened to overrun Washington, throwing the city into panic. Confidence and morale once again sank to new lows. After some courting, George McClellan consented to head the Democratic ticket. Frustrated by more than three years of war the Democratic peace platform, with the former general at its head, looked mighty appealing to some in the North. As ominous as things looked for Lincoln it was even more so for the Union itself. "The coming election season," observes the historian Charles Bracelen Flood, "was indeed to be a referendum on the war."[1]

A McClellan victory promised to bring an end to the Union that David Tod and countless other Unionists knew and loved. To save the Republic, wrote the *Cleveland Morning Leader* in September, "all the manly and heroic efforts that belong to great souls" were needed "to stand by [her] in this hour of trial and peril."[2] Despite his health issues Tod continued his efforts to save the Union by working to reelect Lincoln to a second term. Even though his physician had "forbidden" him to make any more speeches in October, Tod continued to travel about the region addressing

Union rallies.³ A Lincoln victory would see the Union fight continue until victory was certain.

Tod could have easily eluded public life secluded in the peace and security of his adoring family at Brier Hill, which became "the center of [local] public interest" now that the famous former governor had returned home to take up residence at his estate.⁴ Tod had written to Lincoln earlier in the year that he was "quite contented with my present happy condition of private life,"⁵ which had been anything but quiet. In fact, it was in a constant state of motion. He was always coming and going, devoting his time and energies to various projects. And he enjoyed the public notoriety and the well wishes of friends and admirers. Although he did not lack for confidence, from time to time his self-esteem needed reassurance.

But David Tod had a large ego to be sure. One critic said of him, "If Lord Almighty were to resign on the morrow Tod would attempt to fill the place and believe that he could improve on the administration of his predecessor."⁶ But he was not a selfish or insensitive man. In fact, he was known as being very generous despite the troubles with labor unrest at his mines over the years. Once, in 1856, the Warren Gun Squad was conducting training exercises when a horrific accident "resulted in the shattering and loss of the arms of two" of the gunners. Tod led a donation drive by contributing 500 dollars for their benefit. He was lauded as "second to none where deeds of charity and kindness were demanded."⁷ When the Catholic diocese made plans to build a new church in Youngstown in 1863 Tod, "with his characteristic liberality," donated 200 dollars.⁸ And little effort was needed to persuade the former governor from donating his time to help the Union during the upcoming political battle.

In September, thousands of Union supporters gathered around the speakers' platform in Warren to listen to Tod, and Congressmen James Garfield and Robert Schenck. Thousands more converged at Ravenna and in Ashtabula County. They took aim not at *"The Rebels in front . . . But . . . the Traitors in the rear."* The *Cleveland Leader* captured the essence of the message of the Union Party as the troop traveled about soliciting support for Lincoln. The *Leader* described "two classes of citizens in the North." One's goal was to simply save the "Republic at all hazards. This is the . . . whole ground of the Union party." The goal of the Democrats was simply opposed to this. "While the Union party has the rebel down, with knee upon his breast and fingers upon his throat, the so-called Democrats, the

Copperheads, wish to drag us off and let him up."⁹ Tod, reported the reliably friendly *Western Reserve Chronicle*, "addressed the people at some length, in his usual logical and convincing manner."¹⁰

Tod pushed himself and kept up a grueling pace addressing crowds across northeastern Ohio. He spoke at Cleveland with US Sen. John Sherman in front of an audience of 50,000 on October 5. Two days later, he delivered a speech at Lancaster and the next day, October 8, he was in Youngstown, where a driving thunderstorm moved the event inside. His message was simple: Elect Lincoln to save the Union or McClellan to dismember it. Tod reveled in the warm embrace of the crowds. Any leftover feelings of dejection were long gone as the party clearly rediscovered its appreciation for him. Party leaders needed to keep him in front of loyal crowds where he could excite the voters. Both parties deployed their best campaigners throughout the state to address intensely partisan crowds as the election neared.¹¹

On the other side the Democrats even paraded out the venomous Copperhead, Clement Vallandigham at the nominating convention at Chicago. From there he was then sent forth to rally the passions of the Peace fanatics. But his presence on the stage and the campaign trail was cut short because his advocacy of the Peace plank was proving to be a major liability for McClellan, who rejected it altogether. The Peace plan was regarded as wildly unpopular among the soldiers, who would not concede the deaths and sacrifice of their comrades without a final military victory.¹² McClellan the old soldier, writes historian John Waugh, was "a firm War Democrat" who "despised" anyone who looked upon the war as "a failure." To appease the other faction of their party and add balance to the ticket Ohio Congressman George Pendleton, a Peace Democrat, was chosen as McClellan's running mate.¹³ From the onset, because of these divergent views, the Democrats had a tough time gaining any momentum.

Matters got worse for the Democrats when Union victories on the field of battle finally began to turn the tide of the war and public opinion. In early September, Gen. William Tecumseh Sherman, brother of Sen. John Sherman, sent word to Lincoln that his troops had taken Atlanta. It was part of Lincoln's and Grant's policy of executing a calculated war, and not one of destruction of the South as called for by radical editors in the North. Their zeal, like Tod's, sometimes got the best of them. Tod had often expressed a desire to see "the death or surrender of every rebel in arms against the Government." But Lincoln knew that such a policy would not bode well for reunifying the country when the time came. And Grant knew he had to keep a short rein on the fiery General Sherman.[14] Surely the leaders of rebellion must be taught a lesson they would not soon forget but Lincoln knew that the object was to eventually entice the citizens of the South to want to come back into the Union fold. News of the capture of Atlanta was the shot in the arm that the Lincoln campaign needed. In addition to Sherman's joyous news, word of the death of Tod's and Ohio's old nemesis, John Hunt Morgan, arrived the day after the fall of Atlanta. Morgan had been killed in Tennessee after Federal troops surprised the usually vigilant marauder.[15]

After the fall of Atlanta, the Democrats' message was snuffed out while Lincoln rode the military's momentum on to victory in November. Lincoln's reelection assured that the Union war effort would be carried through to a successful conclusion. By Christmas, Sherman presented the city of Savannah as a gift to Lincoln. The course of the war was now fixed and with the election over, Tod could once again slip away from politics and resume his business life.

In February 1865 Tod was elected president of the Cleveland & Mahoning Railroad Company, a position he would hold until his death. The C&M RR had been under construction since 1848 and had reached Youngstown in 1856. The railroad enabled the delivery of freight, raw materials, and passengers from the steamships on the Great Lakes to the Mahoning valley with links to Pittsburgh and the Ohio River. The speed of travel upon the iron rails and the train's ability to move gross tonnage easily surpassed the capabilities of canal boats. Not only was the railroad a more fruitful endeavor of its own accord but it also helped to link the various business interests that made up Tod's industrial empire. Tod's coal mining operations continued to bring in enormous profits and his natural business inclinations, with encouragement from his enterprising sons, had led him into the manufacture of iron at Brier Hill.[16]

Over the winter months, Tod had been absent from the national scene ever since the president's reelection. Even the adversarial *Dayton Daily Empire* missed him, noting that he had seemingly "disappeared from public view some months ago, and has not been heard of since."[17] But, his reemergence occurred just over a month later in great celebratory fashion.

During the spring of 1865, Union troops under Grant and Sherman proved to be an unstoppable tandem. The Confederate capital at Richmond fell in the early days of April and realizing the cause was over, Lee surrendered to Grant soon after on April 8 at Appomattox, Virginia. On April 14, four years after the fall of Fort Sumter, a Union victory celebration was held within the damaged walls of the garrison at Charleston. Tod was in attendance that day, a guest of Lt. Gov. Charles Anderson, whose brother Robert had surrendered the fort four years earlier. So much had changed in the four years since Tod's last visit. The last time he was in the cradle of the Confederacy, he was a leading figure in the Democratic Party that was trying to get Stephen Douglas elected president. Now Tod returned as a member of a conquering delegation representing another party over another country, exalting over a humiliated and defeated foe.

The highlight of the day occurred when Major Anderson raised Old Glory triumphantly up the flagpole. It was the very same banner that he had lowered when he surrendered the fort to Confederate troops in 1861. Of the ceremonies and with total victory all but assured the *Highland Weekly News* reflected, "We have proved to the world that our Government, though founded on the will of the people, has the strength to maintain itself not only against foreign enemies but against those of its own household." Most importantly, the reporter wrote, "The UNION, established by our Revolutionary fathers, has been preserved."[18] David Tod could not have expressed it any better. Tragically, the high spirits of the occasion came crashing down the next day with the stunning news that the Union could not preserve the life of its commander in chief.

News of the assassination of Pres. Abraham Lincoln quickly spread across the nation, North and South. Just when the news reached David Tod is not known but he was either still in Charleston or traveling north by rail. He departed Charleston late Friday night after the flag raising festivities because the next day, April 15, Tod and Governor Brough were in Cleveland addressing the tragedy in front of thousands of mourners.[19] In the days ahead, shocked citizens of the North made funeral preparations for their martyred leader instead of immersing themselves in wild victory celebrations.

Plans were made to return Lincoln's remains to his final resting place in Springfield following the same train route, in reverse order from

Washington back to Illinois, that Lincoln first made when he set off for his inauguration in 1861. Important cities like Cleveland and Columbus were selected to hold public viewings of the martyred president. Tod and Governor Brough, among others, were chosen to board the train outside Cleveland to function as honorary pallbearers and to accompany the president's remains into the city.

Although Lincoln did not survive, the United States emerged from its civil war as one nation, in name at least. As the nation adjusted to the new leadership of Pres. Andrew Johnson, Ohio made plans for a new governor. Citing poor health, Gov. John Brough announced that he would not seek the Union Party's nomination for a second term.[20] Once again Tod's name was one of many mentioned as a potential replacement but the party settled on Jacob D. Cox, who would go on to face the Democrat George Morgan.[21]

Before Tod was drawn into the campaign for Cox, he first had to dispel rumors that a reconciliation with the Democratic Party was under way. Even with the war over, there was no way Tod could ever return to the party of his upbringing after all the treasonous chaos it had created during the war. Nor was he interested. The break between Tod and the Democratic Party that occurred in 1861 was permanent, despite recent stories to the contrary. Tod himself, in a speech at a Cox rally in Wooster, summarily dismissed any suggestion of detente. The Democratic Party in Ohio, Tod said, "couldn't be trusted." If it were returned to power, Tod believed, "the national debt would be in danger of repudiation . . . and justice would not be done the soldier or the soldiers' wives and widows." For at least one more election, Tod said, "it was the patriotic duty of every patriot to stand by the Union Party" and deny the Democrats a seat of power.[22]

When his health permitted, Tod still enjoyed delivering a good old-fashioned campaign speech like no other. His rousing, carefree approach fed off the energy of the crowds and sometimes his sense of humor invited criticism. In front of a Union rally in Warren, Tod pointed to the fact that with the war over, the end of the Union Party was inevitable. For the same reason, the Republican Party would enjoy a rebirth. And when those developments should happen Tod sarcastically said that he would then rejoin the Democratic Party to help *"make it pure."* Taking the bait, the *Jefferson Democrat* mockingly encouraged its "Desponding Democrats" to "cheer up! There is yet hope for your party [because] A Good Samaritan is coming to heal its moral infirmities."[23] The *Dayton Daily Empire* had also taken notice of Tod's return to active duty for the Union Party and questioned his moral state. The Democratic tool wrote that Tod, the "lifelong Democrat, disappeared from public view some months ago" but had since reemerged after engaging in excessive drinking and as a result "is subject to fits."[24] The *Cadiz Sentinel* joined in reminding all that when Tod "left our party to be made Governor," the Republicans all but "turned [him] out in disgrace, and his name is about forgotten."[25] These attacks were baseless and harmless. Tod made good on his commitment to the Union-Republican Party by faithfully campaigning for Cox's election.

Tod's comments about the future of the Union Party were not far off the mark. With the war over, the unity of Republicans and Democrats throughout the North was no longer needed, and the old days of party politics would soon creep back into the public mainstream. Tod's political destiny, however, was tied to the Union Party. It was the Union Party that elected him governor (and summarily turned him out). At times he must have felt like a man with no party. At least the Republican faction of the Union Party put its arms around him once again and gave him a role in the Cox campaign. The lukewarm embrace that the Union Party extended was because of Tod's views regarding social advancement of Black persons. Tod still did not accept the ideology of the Radical faction of the party. The contrast between the two really became known during the gubernatorial campaign of 1865.

Although Tod was for Cox, he disagreed with the candidate on Black suffrage, the new question of the day since the passage of the Thirteenth Amendment. Ohio had recently cleaned up its past by passing legislation that ended voting restrictions based upon the color of one's skin. The State's infamous Black Laws that "disgraced the state by odious and arbitrary political discriminations [were] wiped off the statute book." Elated with recent developments, an overly optimistic *Cleveland Morning Leader* prematurely proclaimed, "Henceforward the colored citizens of Ohio, who have proven themselves as public-spirited and patriotic as any class of the community, will not be debarred the privileges of the polls."[26] Although the Republican-controlled Ohio General Assembly would ratify the Fourteenth Amendment, granting citizenship to former slaves among others in 1867, the decision was reversed the following year after the Democrats regained control. And it would take five years and the passage of the Fifteenth Amendment before Black men were granted the right to vote. During the current gubernatorial campaign candidate Cox supported social advancement of Black persons, including the right of males to vote, but Tod opposed these "in decided terms."[27]

At this time, David Tod believed that although Black men could fight for their freedom and help save the Union, he had little faith in "the capacity of [former] slaves to exercise the right to vote." He also said that he would oppose amending Ohio's constitution granting them that right.[28] Before the war, while serving in Brazil, Tod learned to abhor slavery and the slave trade through firsthand observations of the brutal and heartless institution. During the war, Tod had accepted emancipation and the enlistment of Black males to fight as soldiers but only out of military necessity. He gladly welcomed them into the ranks once he realized that their numbers would count towards Ohio's quota. Although he supported equal pay for Black soldiers, he was not ready to support equal rights, let alone greater participation in the democracy they had fought for, bled for, and died to help save. Although he was morally opposed to slavery the efforts of successful Black men like O. S. B. Wall, John Mercer Langston, and Medal of Honor recipient Powhatan Beatty, himself formerly enslaved, and countless others did not change his opinion.[29]

The truth of the matter was Tod could not, at this stage, justify greater civic participation. But if not now, when? Of course, there were those who believed never. Others held firm to social and political limits. Although he was not alone in adhering to these social mores, the position Tod took on the matter clearly shows that he believed in the prevailing stereotypical prejudices of the day. However, for Tod, it had always been a constitutional matter. The Thirteenth Amendment was on its irrevocable path of ratification by the states. And there he drew his line. For Tod to support any further advancements he would need to rely on additional changes to the Constitution. The Constitution as it was always defined the limits of his support, whereas amendments helped to rationalize his evolving positions and explain the evolution of his progressive thinking.

For Tod, the opportunity to take the moral high ground without fear of political reprisals, for certainly his political career was over, was at hand. He had nothing to fear and even less to lose. He had wealth beyond his wildest dreams and was surrounded by a loving family and an adoring community that would have followed his lead. His legacy of patriotic service to the country he loved was already legendary. Yet, he just could not come to terms with the progressive social movement stirring around him, at least not until constitutional changes led him to advanced positions. Consequently, one is led to believe that the limited progressive notions he supported only applied to matters of military exigencies. But it is slightly more complicated than that.

As governor, Tod's attitude toward his troops, both white and Black, can be characterized as paternalistic. We saw evidence of his benevolent sentiments when he warmly sent off freshly trained soldiers from camp to their first assignments or, when he respectfully asked troops of the Fifth USCT permission to address them as "his boys." This display of affection and this bond would carry over after he left office and even after the war ended. And this was especially true when it came to disabled veterans or widowed wives. He was genuinely concerned for the future of Black and formerly enslaved persons in the South. After they proved their courage in the heat of battle he believed that "the poor slave made free by the rebellion, must be protected and cared for by the Government." He said this because he believed they could not protect themselves from political, legal, social, and physical predators in their midst. In time, they could enjoy the rights of full citizenship, including the franchise but these changes could only come about under the protection and stewardship of the Union-Republican Party. Given the chance the Democrats, Tod believed, would reverse what limited progress had thus far been made. Of that progress, it was Tod's opinion that much had already been attained "to secure to the African race prosperity and happiness."[30] And he found great satisfaction in this and did not want to see progress reversed, especially if left to the states.

At the time Tod expressed these sentiments, he had not been fully in support of the Fourteenth and Fifteenth Amendments, it is true. As Eric Foner explains, "Most Republicans assumed that freedom," as proclaimed by the Thirteenth Amendment, "meant more than not being chained and that abolition would [eventually] expand the rights [of] blacks." However, Republicans also believed that any further rights would come by way of state governments and therefore preventing Democrats from taking control of state governments was critical for further advancement of freed people.[31] Tod and his contemporaries would soon come to recognize this danger and act upon the threat.

In August 1865, news of Governor Brough's death took Ohioans by surprise even though his poor health was a matter of public record. Charles Anderson succeeded Brough and completed the five months remaining on the deceased governor's term of office. In October, Jacob Cox was elected governor, the last from the Union Party to be so honored.[32]

Although Cox was the last to wear the banner of the soon-to-be-defunct Union Party, he talked like a true reformer. His social views contrasted sharply with Tod's, whose position represented those of a different generation. Where Tod's words offered limited and cautionary advancement, Cox's ideas promised a fresh new outlook. It was freedom, the governor-elect had said, that would pave the way. Freedom, he said, "shall give them the fullest opportunity to make such advancement in civilization and enlightenment as they are capable of, which shall open for them a future in which the only limit to their progress shall be such as they themselves, in their own notion, shall impose." It would not be an easy road, and how these things shall occur he did not know. It was "one of the great questions which the successful end of the war is bringing upon us," he acknowledged. "I recognize," he conceded, "as fully as any one can the fact revolutions do not go backward. The question is in what direction is the truest progress for both races and by what course can the greatest degree of happiness ultimately be secured for all[?]"[33] Tod shared the same stage when Cox made these powerful remarks but did not share the same sentiments. One cannot help but think how Tod failed to recognize that the war itself had brought about transformative measures and that its success demanded even more changes ahead, changes that he was unwilling, at this moment, to support.

Retirement life for David Tod was decidedly less demanding, his pace less grueling, and he believed that life at Brier Hill was having a positive effect on his health.[34] All the same, he was in a constant state of motion and, he quickly assimilated back into the world of industry, where he found an audience willing to give him the attention and adulation that a former governor had grown accustomed to receiving. Tod, either in politics or private enterprise, was a relevant force with a big personality. He was an affluent member of a new and growing socioeconomic class of capitalists and the seat of his economic empire was found in the Mahoning valley, home base of his successful coal and railroad interests. His businesses were profitable and continued to add to his wealth. Brier Hill, the center of his business world, was proving to be a financially "better thing than the Governorship," observed the *Cadiz Sentinel*.[35]

Tod's business decisions earned him a small fortune; "my crops look well and my pork barrel is in good condition," he said of his financial situation.[36] His 1865 net income alone was reported to be $65,209.[37] The combination of wealth and once holding the highest office in the state brought invitations to many events, not all political. As a stockholder in the Atlantic & Great Western Railway, Tod was one of several to entertain a group of English capitalists touring the United States. At Cleveland, they gathered to hear speeches by the English entrepreneur and railroad builder, Sir Morton Peto. Congressman Garfield and Tod also delivered addresses from the Americans. Tod's remarks extolled the agricultural, industrial, and financial prosperity of Ohio.[38] The Cleveland Board of Trades arranged carriages to take the group around the city to observe its "manufactories, foundries, and forges."[39] Tod may have slowed a step or two because of his health but his enthusiasm for life and business was as strong as ever. It was clear that he had no interest in sitting still.

About this time, George B. Wright asked his old boss his age. "You will be surprised," replied Tod for as "youthful and active as I appear, the old family Bible makes me 60." The truth of the matter was that he had aged. The stress of the war and the nagging reminder of his delicate health accentuated the deepening lines upon his face. A touch of gray had also crept in and dusted his dark head of hair, which added to his distinguished appearance. Despite his poor health, he remained resolute in his determination to live life to the fullest. His colorful description of the steady speed of his railcars was an amusing metaphor for his own careful and stable approach to business competition and life in general: "We run at a rate of speed only to keep out of the way of cows; that is, we neither overtake any cattle, nor permit any to overtake us." He added; "My staid habits and extreme caution have thus far in life given me protection and ... I would continue to rely upon them."[40]

17

Duties Discharged, 1866–1868

ALTHOUGH HIS HEALTH was indeed slowing him down, David Tod's enthusiasm for new and exciting business projects, guided by his staid habits, remained strong. But he learned to listen attentively to the orders of his personal physician and therefore he had given up on his goal to one day serve in the United States Senate; the responsibilities of the political morass that was Washington would have been too strenuous. The truth of the matter is that he just did not possess the physical stamina for stressful responsibilities. His troubling health problems effectively ended his desire for higher office. Where he found personal satisfaction, where he could come and go at his leisure, and most important where he possessed influence was back among his family, friends, and business colleagues, who included his capable sons. The citizens of the Mahoning valley by and large gladly reclaimed their famous son and all the economic action he stirred up. Within this friendly environment Governor Tod, as he was warmly called, and who still possessed an "energy and restless spirit," got things moving in the valley beginning with the building of a modern iron plant named the Girard Iron Company.[1] The next three years, beginning in 1866 until his death, would see the return of the entrepreneurial spirit of David Tod and with it one last opportunity at political relevance.

Everyone was anxious to get on with life free from the worries of a horrific war. And the residents of the Mahoning valley were optimistic about the future for the first time in a long while. This included David Tod. However, for as much as Tod was focused on business, political forces were at work trying to lure the former governor along with his influence back into the arena where Republican leaders once again desired his service. Supporters of Pres. Andrew Johnson, looking ahead to the 1868 election, organized the National Johnson Club in Washington, which was said to be made up of Northern Copperheads and Conservatives and reconstructed rebels whose goal was to put to rest the old Democratic Party and emerge as a new party of Johnsonians. Johnson, the old military governor of Tennessee, was at odds with the Republican-led Congress over his reconstruction plans. The president wanted a quick and painless restoration of the Southern states, whereas Congress was in no mood for leniency. Likewise, Tod was in no mood for mercy and supported the reconstruction plans of Congress. Friends of Tod said that the ex-governor had "no sympathy for any organization of rebels, Copperheads or men of doubtful political character and disturbers of the harmony of our country."[2] Nonetheless Tod was listed as a vice president and Ohio's representative of the National Johnson Club. But this was done without Tod's consent and he moved quickly to discredit the unauthorized coalition. Tod "spiked that gun," reported the *Gallipolis Journal;* "he has no sympathy with any such movement."[3]

What had become quite the custom, Tod's name was floated as a candidate for governor of Ohio. It had become a biennial tradition that his name would surface for the office. The *Wyandot Pioneer* eagerly recommended his candidacy in 1867 proclaiming, "He would demolish the one-horse-Confederate-Rump-Copperhead-ticket so bad that it would never see day-light again."[4] But again, Tod's days of occupying political office were over even though his name remained perpetually popular among Ohioans. He was to say one year later, "Political position has no charms for me now . . . I am getting too gray to think of accepting any more honors."[5]

When Tod was invited to address a group in Cuyahoga County in the fall of 1867, he took "the advice of his physician" and declined. Shortly thereafter, he turned down another request for the same reason. For David Tod to decline to make a political speech, let alone two, was news on its own and a strong indicator of just how much his health concerned him. As for the upcoming gubernatorial contest, Tod offered his "hearty support" to any "gentleman who [had] pledged his life to save our Government" during the war.[6] Ohio Republicans nominated Civil War veteran and congressman Rutherford B. Hayes.

Though Tod lacked the stamina to deliver one of his celebrated and lengthy speeches of old, he possessed the energy to submit for public consumption a wordy discourse to his friends in Cleveland explaining his latest views on the state of things. It was one of Tod's last efforts to address the public and it was full of his usual patriotic political dogma. Now was not the time, he said, to disband the Union Party because there was important work for the members to do, namely to safeguard that which was won during the war. Although the armies and their soldiers of both sides had returned to their homes, the political opponents of the government, many entrenched within Ohio's borders, were still searching for "an opportunity to do [political] mischief, to again strike." The Union Party, said Tod, was needed to look after the soldiers' widows, and the "fatherless children of the brave and gallant men who fell in the great conflict." These families "demand the protection, assistance and sympathy of the men of this party." They needed protection from old adversaries like Vallandigham and Olds, who were still actively lurking about attempting to sow social discord and political discontent, said Tod. God forbid, he said, that the wounded patriot soldier should suffer further to see traitors occupying places of public power in the government. The Union Party, wrote Tod, was also needed to protect former enslaved and free Blacks of the North and to help usher in the social and political reforms taking shape for their benefit: "the question of equal suffrage."[7] Simply stated, he said, "I am not willing to trust the democratic party."[8]

He could not have been more right. When Ohio legislators ratified the Fourteenth Amendment in January 1867, Democrats took back control of the general assembly one year later and rescinded the previous legislature's monumental work. In Ohio, Democrats also fought progress on the Fifteenth Amendment, which would have bestowed Black suffrage. They opposed these measures based on the belief that to allow Black participation in civic affairs "would incorporate a defective civic population into American politics," writes Jean Baker, "thereby threatening the harmony of the republic."[9] But change was coming.

The Fourteenth Amendment, for one, bestowed citizenship upon Black males, thus invalidating archaic legal decisions like Taney's *Dredd*

Scott. And as these changes were made to the Constitution, Tod adapted. His evolution was guided by his adherence to constitutional law. The Constitution changed to correct and safeguard the nation's shortcomings and Tod followed suit.

Progressive thinking at the time affected everyone differently. Abraham Lincoln's view of Blacks before and during the war was one of spiritual transformation. Much has been written about the Great Emancipator's spiritual journey over the question of slavery, freedom, citizenship, and suffrage.[10] Tod's views of Blacks and their role in American society were more conservative and evolved slowly over his lifetime toward a more radical position. His arrival at the idea of citizenship and equal suffrage for them appears to have been more of a logical, political, and legally interpretive journey versus a spiritual one but it was one he finally completed all the same. However, a close friend of Tod's, Samuel Galloway, who had known Tod intimately, asserted that the governor, beginning with emancipation, developed an "advanced attitude" on civil rights that was helped by "the light of God's guidance." According to Galloway, Tod "had triumphed over [his] prejudices" because he accepted "the coming kingdom and reign of universal freedom."[11] Either way, the views he began to espouse were those promulgated by the Radical Republicans. It was nearly a 180-degree turn from the Democratic David Tod of old. The prewar Tod of early 1861 would not have recognized the postwar Tod of 1867.

One historian has charged that David Tod was "never noted for adhering to one view for any length of time."[12] This charge plagued him during his political life dating all the way back to his first campaign for the Ohio senate. Critics have accused Tod of being nothing more than a political opportunist riding the current on the political winds. However, since Tod had by now given up any desire to seek political office due to health reasons, what political reward was he after at this juncture? None. As much as this criticism sticks to Tod for past decisions, there is no evidence to support it during the last years of his life. It may have been for political gain but surely not his own.

With an embattled President Johnson neutralized by his impeachment, Congress stepped in to fill the vacuum by passing the Reconstruction Act, of 1867 to 1868. The act aimed to return the seceded states conditionally back into the Union with the US military present to ensure conformity and maintain peace. According to historian Eric Foner, the act "looked to a new political order for the South" but that order did not apply to the loyal states of the North.[13] One provision forced returning states to adopt Black suffrage. Thus, social advancements for Black people were now taking place faster in the South than they were in the North. Citizenship and suffrage for Black males would not be universally granted until the adoption of the Fourteenth and Fifteenth Amendments in 1868 and 1870, respectively. This stipulation alone, Tod said, made the issue of suffrage for northern Black males "a different question entirely."[14] If the North saved the Union, progressive changes should be emanating from the loyal states. If formerly enslaved Blacks were enfranchised by the tens of thousands in the South, while the North stood still on the matter, it was just a matter of time before political power was wrested from the loyal states and the Union Party and shifted to the South.

For these reasons, the work of the Union Party was "not yet finished," said Tod. For surely if the South, and Democrats in particular, regained political power, he rightly believed the political and civil advances of Black males would be reversed. Now more than ever, the Union Party was needed to protect the modest "prosperity and happiness" that they had thus far experienced, limited as it was. Moreover, men of the Union Party were obligated to "maintain our good old Government, and hand it down to our children."[15] As for rehabilitating his former Democratic Party, still under the influence of former Peace Democrats in the North and Secessionists in the South Tod said, "I would not do it just yet."[16]

In addition to the major developments taking place with Tod's political philosophy and the growth of his business interests, plans to build a second house for his family were also under way. Although he was quite comfortable at his Brier Hill estate, he purchased a lot close to downtown Youngstown. Having a residence closer to the business district, particularly during the harsh winter months, had its advantages, especially for entertaining.

In 1867, Tod hired Plympton Ross Berry, an African American bricklayer and stonemason, to build his new mansion. Berry arrived in Youngstown with his wife and young family in 1861 from New Castle, Pennsylvania. Berry was no ordinary bricklayer. In the years shortly after his arrival he established a reputation as an expert builder and architect and was awarded contracts to perform work on many notable local buildings. At six feet, six inches tall the handsome 26-year-old Berry was an imposing figure.[17] Tod was immediately impressed with the master builder and his accomplished résumé and wanted no one else but Berry for his project. Whether or not Tod's respect for Berry's intelligence and skill helped to advance and shape his opinion of African Americans and their place in society is hard to say. The community's respect for the talents of the young builder did not hurt.

The cost to construct Tod's new mansion was $50,000, ($900 thousand in today's dollars). The two-story mansion would have 20 rooms, plenty of space to accommodate family and guests. Berry and his crew, many of whom were Civil War veterans, both Black and white, began work in 1867. As the mansion neared completion in early 1868, it was regarded as "one of the most complete and expensive dwelling houses in the State."[18]

The new year looked to be as promising as any other for David Tod. Business was booming, the city was growing, and Berry was applying the finishing touches to the new mansion. Tod received a singular honor in late February when Ohio Republicans chose him to be one of two presidential electors for the upcoming presidential election. Former congressman Samuel Galloway was also chosen.[19]

On the heels of this noteworthy honor disaster struck on the morning of February 28 when fire tore through the recently completed Tod mansion. Although no one was hurt the grand house was destroyed.[20] By the time the flames were extinguished only one wing of the residence was left standing and it was so structurally compromised it could not be saved.[21] Fortunately, Tod had recently purchased a $15,000 insurance policy, which allowed him "to go promptly forward with the work of rebuilding, without sacrifice of raising money."

Tod's personal setback helped to spark a movement that led to the community's first volunteer fire department, replete with modern equipment. Rather than sit idly by the governor took charge. Despite the best of intentions local leaders realized that funding such a project through private donations was cost prohibitive. Modern fire equipment was estimated to cost every bit of $20,000. It did not take much to convince the new progressive city council to authorize a bond issue to fund the project. With funding secured, 60 volunteer firefighters were organized and the proud recipients of a brand-new red and brass Silsby steam fire engine complete with a reel hose wagon. The horse-drawn engine was dubbed the "Governor Tod."[22]

As the spring season gave hope for renewal, tragedy again struck the Tod family. In June, Charlotte Tod, the eldest child of David and Maria, and wife of Gen. August V. Kautz died suddenly in Columbus, Mississippi, where her husband was stationed. She was 35 years old. Her sudden death crushed the family and it hit the governor particularly hard. A news report of Charlotte's death being "a very severe" shock to her father was an understatement. There had existed between the father and daughter an "affection of extraordinary warmth and tenderness" and her sudden and tragic passing brought Tod tremendous grief.[23] He would never be the same after the death of his eldest child.

The dog days of summer were now approaching, bringing with them another campaign season. No one could have predicted it would be Tod's last. Still mourning Charlotte's death, he stayed busy despite failing health. Indications are that he suffered from high blood pressure and in all probability was afflicted by the common symptoms associated with hypertension such as headaches, anxiety, and shortness of breath. He also experienced bouts of what was described as "congestive chills."[24] Up to now, he had followed his physician's order to avoid unnecessary exertion but he intended to honor his commitment to help get Ulysses Grant elected president.

Tod's connection with Grant was known but it was a story he enjoyed telling during his latest speeches. "I have known his family well," he said before detailing the families' common bond. As for the candidate, Tod said at a stop in Orwell, "He possesses every element of character which should attach you to him."[25] He is a "great and good man who led our soldiers to victory," proclaimed Tod and as far he was concerned, "there was not a man in all the country that I prefer to General Grant."[26]

In contrast, Grant's opponent, Gov. Horatio Seymour of New York, was a Peace Democrat who, according to Tod, "lacked moral courage." If Seymour were to win, the Democratic nominee would be nothing more than a "tool" to be used and manipulated by such characters as the cunning Vallandigham.[27]

Tod "was in a happy humor" as he enjoyed taking "palpable hits" at Democrats.[28] He teamed up with James Garfield in the Mahoning valley. The speakers were greeted by large crowds, brass bands, old cannons, and "an excellent Glee Club." The speeches of both men "were frequently interrupted with the heartiest applause." The duo of Tod and Garfield proved so popular that they were in demand from as far away as St. Louis. If "those giants Gov. Tod and General Garfield" could spend a week campaigning in Missouri they "would make such an impression upon the enemy as would make the balance of the canvass just a bagatelle."[29] In addition to taking jabs at his old party while supporting Grant, Tod's remarks continued to reveal his political progression and support for expanding the rights of Blacks.

In Cleveland, on September 11, Tod was introduced to a great crowd of Grant supporters. For one hour, Tod praised the heroics and integrity of Grant while he assailed the treacherous behavior of the Democratic Party. Why, if Seymour won the presidency and Vallandigham won a seat in Congress, General Lee might as well "take a seat beside him." Now was not the time to "let bygones be bygones."

No abolitionist, Tod declared, "rejoices more sincerely than I do in the abolition of slavery." At that, he went on in a most convincing manner to explain his new position of granting Black Americans the right to vote. He began by recounting with great clarity the exhilaration he felt after he voted for the very first time. It was an uplifting experience, one that gave him a sense of value. "The idea has tended from that hour to this to elevate me; and I tell you that the strongest argument in favor of permitting all men to participate in the right of suffrage—negroes and foreigners—is based upon the principle that it tends to elevate the man who exercises this privilege of freemen." Not only that, but it also brought one closer to the designs of the Almighty as Tod invoked a religious argument. Granting the "negroes of Ohio" lawful access to the ballot box he observed, "would elevate them and bring them nearer what their Maker designs them to be." To deny them this transcendent journey was contemptible in the eyes of Heaven. Tod's last public comments on social reforms for Black Americans, at least the suffrage question, were complete. His own spiritual journey pertaining to these questions had reached its peak. But why now, what had changed? The answer was that the Constitution had changed.

After Blacks were granted citizenship with the ratification of the Fourteenth Amendment in July 1868, Tod could now base his arguments on moral grounds. Before the Thirteenth and Fourteenth Amendments, he did not inject moral opinions into public policy because he relied on the US Constitution, not the Bible, for guidance. Slavery had been legal based on the Constitution. When the amendments eradicated slavery and granted citizenship, the Constitution was forever changed, and the political Tod was forced to deal with it. With these changes he was free to insert his moral arguments. Suffrage was inevitable; it was just a matter of time. The

Constitution and the nation evolved, and David Tod evolved. How far he was willing to advance the liberty of Black Americans remains unanswered because Tod would not live to see the passage of the Fifteenth Amendment granting Black suffrage in February 1869.

The hour-long Cleveland address was one of Tod's last public appearances, where he urged the crowd to keep the faith in the Republican Party by supporting Grant who, he believed, was the best man to address the troubles that now afflicted the country. "Put Grant in the Presidential chair," he said, "and justice will be done to all."[30] Reunification with the Southern states was one thing, but reconciliation would elude the nation for generations to come.

A portion of Tod's Cleveland speech was part autobiographical. "They call me pretty well over there" in Youngstown, he explained, although his early life was not always that way. But he spoke passionately of his birthplace. "I would not have been born anywhere else than in Youngstown if I could," he said, nor would he have been reared in or made his home anywhere else. "Youngstown, the township in which I have spent my life . . . is a town a man may be proud of having been born in," he said. It was also the place, Tod said, "in which I hope to die, and in which I shall be buried, no matter where I die."

He hearkened back to his humble beginnings and modest upbringing by his "dear old mother" and his "honored father." He talked about his political rise within the Democratic Party and listed his service to the country, which was highlighted by his term as governor. He also reviewed his 24 years as a businessman and the jobs he helped to create for workers in his coal mines and iron foundries and the more than $9 million dollars in wages he paid them during that span.[31] (He made no mention of the incidents of labor unrest at his mines.)

On November 3, the people of Ohio turned out and gave their 21 electoral votes to Ulysses S. Grant, helping the Republican defeat the Democrat Seymour by an electoral margin of 214 to 80 to become the eighteenth President of the United States. Tod, however, would not have the opportunity to fulfill his duties as a presidential elector for Grant.

Ten days after the presidential election, Friday, November 13, Tod had plans to take the train from his Brier Hill estate to Cleveland. He awoke early that morning but not with his usual appetite. After he finished a light breakfast, he stood to retrieve his coat. At that moment, he placed his head in his hands as "another of those congestive chills," he said, "was coming on again." He asked for his wife. When Maria came to his side her husband was resting in bed complaining of nausea. "Spirits of some kind were administered, without affording relief." Tod lay restless while Maria kept a nervous vigil at his bedside, praying for his recovery. At 7:00 A.M., after an hour had passed, David Tod sat up in bed "without uttering a word." As quickly as he sat up, he slumped lifeless upon the bed. The former governor of Ohio was dead.[32] He was 63 years old. The official cause of death was attributed to an apoplectic stroke.[33]

His close friend George Wright tells us Tod "had more than once been threatened with the malady that finally ended his life."[34] The malady, which he referred to as "congestive chills," seems to have plagued Tod chronically during his last years. An 1868 description of congestive chills is found in an edition of the *New York Tribune:* "the blood rushes to the heart, and leaves the extremities chilled and paralyzed" and can be accompanied by an attack of a severe fever.[35] An acute attack could prove fatal.

The historian Stephen B. Oates graphically describes one victim's untreated flare-up; "the poor victim suffered from ever-worsening chill, diarrhea and abdominal cramps . . . vomiting, extreme thirst, jaundice, declining pulse, back pain, excruciating headaches . . . and, in the disease's fatal stages, coughing, profuse sweating, 'involuntary discharges,' and delirium, until the victim lapsed into a coma and died."[36] This does not appear to be Tod's experience, however.

One physician attributed a Civil War veteran's heart disease and rheumatism to malaria. But this same soldier had also suffered chronically from congestive chills, and it was said to have caused "a sudden and severe paralysis, most probably the result of a stroke." Death claimed this patient a brief time later after having lived with malaria for more than 20 years.[37]

During the nineteenth century, *congestive chills* was another name for malaria. Doctors did not know that malaria was passed on by mosquitos and mistakenly thought it was spread through bad air. It is possible that Tod contracted malaria at some point in his life; during the war more than three million people were afflicted with the disease, while 30,000 troops succumbed to it.[38]

The death of David Tod, it was reported, was caused by a stroke. But did Wright mean to suggest that Tod suffered from paralysis, the common side effect of strokes? It is impossible to determine. To those who were unaware of his hidden health issues he appeared to be "a man apparently in robust health." Reports that he "dropped dead without exhibiting any previous signs of sickness" suggests that he had no lasting visible effects of paralysis.[39] The *Fremont Weekly Journal* sorrowfully contemplated, "Who can tell what a day may bring forth." On the day before he died, Tod was in good health during a visit to Warren.[40] Another report, from that same day (November 12), observed Tod "unusually cheerful and buoyant, regaling his genial nature with the sports and amusements of children."[41] Without the benefit of an autopsy, attributing Tod's death to an apoplectic stroke was made on the best possible information available.

When the news was transmitted over telegraph wires, it so "startled" citizens that it was at first deemed incredible. But once the announcement was indeed verified the people responded with appropriate measures. Later in the morning, word had not yet reached Warren, where court was in session. During questioning of a witness, one attorney was interrupted by whispers of the news of Tod's passing. The lawyer's "half-uttered question was left unfinished, all business stopped, Court, Counsel, Jury, witness, all seemed paralyzed." The presiding judge, after a moment of consultation, adjourned the court. Immediately, a meeting was called by the members of the Trumbull County Bar. Tod's first law partner, Matthew Birchard, was made chairman. Later that evening, resolutions were adopted that expressed the body's grief and utmost respect, as well as condolences and plans to attend the funeral. The next evening, Warren mayor Isaac Dawson gathered with citizens to remember the life and service of David Tod.[42]

The citizens of the Mahoning valley were shocked; their state of disbelief gave way to grief. "His loss," predicted the *Belmont Chronicle*, "will be especially felt by the residents of his section of the State, for he was alive to all its interests."[43] As the leading businessman in the valley and the region's most celebrated figure, David Tod touched everything of major significance from politics to the local economy and therefore, affected countless lives. The day after his death, "a poor Irish woman" was walking along a set of railroad tracks near Brier Hill and commented to a reporter, "I am sorry he is dead, *he was so good.*"[44]

In Columbus, flags flying atop the Ohio Statehouse and around the city were lowered to half-mast.[45] Once the unexpected news reached the four corners of the state the reaction was much the same.

For all his faults, David Tod was a much-beloved and popular figure throughout the state of Ohio, especially during the troubling and uncertain times that were the Civil War era. Regardless of how depressing and unnerving the latest war news could be, Tod's consistent patriotic fervor shown like a beacon of light in the darkness, calling on his fellow citizens to keep the faith and rally around the Union and the flag. It is hard to imagine today but at the time it was no exaggeration for one Ohio journal to claim that David Tod's name "had become a household word in almost every school district" in the state.[46] To illustrate just how much his life and death effected Ohioans, a newspaper in Findlay, the *Hancock Jeffersonian*, wrote a simple yet touching tribute to honor the memory of the now deceased former governor: "Since the death of the lamented Lincoln we doubt whether the hearts of the people have been so much stirred within them as when the wires flashed over the length and breadth of the State the short but sad message, 'David Tod is no more.'"[47]

Despite his notoriety, David Tod was an approachable "man of the people," said Ohio state Sen. William Stedman, in his eulogy on the senate floor.[48] He had this innate ability throughout his life to connect with people whether with those he encountered as a young boy, an aspiring lawyer, or as a personable businessman visiting his coal mines. Even Tod the partisan politician stumping across Ohio had friendships that crossed party lines. As a US ambassador, he developed close relations not only with his royal foreign hosts but also with the local citizens. No newspaper had covered the life and career of Tod more closely than the *Western Reserve Chronicle* and who better to describe his endearing traits than its editor, William Ritezel. The editor, who was once a fiery critic of David Tod, now wrote admiringly that he

> was loved and honored for his honesty, frankness and pre-eminent executive ability, but the traits of character which endeared him more than all these rare qualities to the social, business and political circles in which he moved, were his kind, cordial and genial disposition, and his royal munificence. He never met a friend or an acquaintance without a word of cheer and a friendly greeting. His benignant countenance seemed like perpetual sunshine to those around him. It was constantly lit up with a genial flow of spirits, which perennially welled from his great heart.[49]

Even if Tod possessed half the qualities Ritzel described, he would have been a captivating and attractive figure all the same.

Similar tributes were offered by friends, neighbors, and even strangers. "It was in the circle of his own home and in his immediate neighborhood where he was most deeply and fully appreciated," concluded one friend.[50] The overwhelming number of people in attendance at Tod's funeral were everyday, ordinary citizens, the majority of whom hailed from in and around the Mahoning valley. David Tod was synonymous with the Mahoning valley and the majority felt a sense of pride with that connection.

So many of the local mourners could recall a simple gesture, a word of encouragement, or an act of charity that Tod discreetly provided. The *Chronicle* saw Tod up close as "an unselfish man" who lent a hand to countless young men by doing an act of "kindness and generosity."[51] One local Welshman, a teenager at the time of Tod's death, recalled the personal obligation he felt to attend the funeral to pay his respects: "I wanted to go, because the governor had been like a father to me. When he came to his mines at Weathersfield I used to hold his horses. He never failed to give me something for my time but he did more than that. He'd bring me something that showed he was thinking about me, a picture, a book or some little thing."[52]

The *Chronicle* also cited Tod's benevolence to the less fortunate. "How many poor people have been encouraged by his kind words and aided by the kinder charities of his hand?"[53] Tod, said the *Columbus Journal,* "did every thing largely and generously. Hundreds of incidents come to mind illustrative of this."[54] One poor widow shared her experience with Tod's generosity. While Tod employed the best carpenters and craftsmen to work on his mansions, he observed that the widow's simple dwelling was in a state of disrepair. Rather than ignore her hardship he sent his work crew to fix up her rundown structure. The grateful woman told Tod she had no means to pay him for his generosity. "All I ask of you," he replied, "is that you will attend my funeral." She fulfilled his request.[55] His appeal to the plain masses of citizens, one admirer said, was due to the "toils and struggles of his boyhood." Suffering "privations and disadvantages of comparative poverty, brought him into close companionship" with the common laborers.[56]

Arguably, nowhere were these qualities more appreciated than among the young men of Ohio's troops during the Civil War. Even after he left office Tod made the occasional visit to see his former soldiers mustering out of service, like he did in June 1865 when he thanked the soldiers at Camp Taylor in Cleveland "for helping to preserve the Union."[57] A simple act but long remembered by the troops.

From all over the Union, the news of David Tod's death sparked immediate reaction. Tributes honoring his life poured in. Indiana's *Liberty Herald* described the feeling of reassurance that Tod's election in 1861 had on the electorate. During the uncertain times that characterized 1861, Tod the stalwart Democrat emerged as a unifying figure because of his rush to defend the Union once it came under attack. His victory as the Union Party candidate, wrote the *Herald*'s editor, "gave courage and joy to all in an hour of great darkness."[58] The *Cincinnati Gazette* called Tod "a true friend of his country" who "had not soft words for traitors. His outspoken Unionism won him the respect and good will of those who had been his political opponents."[59] Not even Tod's critics within the disunited Union Party could find fault with his unceasing devotion to the Union and his efforts to support the war. No one, recalled the *Wyandot Pioneer*, "hated treason, in any form, with more undying hatred than Governor Tod."[60]

The *New York Times* also lauded Tod's "doctrine of war until every rebel was cut off or made to surrender." The *Times* remembered him for his "faithful, zealous, and generally able" leadership during the "darkest hours" of the struggle. His administration, said the *Times,* left Ohio's "affairs in good order, her contributions to the nation fully made up, her duties to her soldiers jealously watched, and her honor untarnished."[61]

Secretary of State William Seward recalled Tod's "invaluable service to our Union administration. He gave me full confidence on the spot, and he never failed, afterwards, to yield to the most vigorous and energetic support to the Government." No doubt Seward's remarks represented the sentiments of the deceased President Lincoln. "Few citizens of the United States," concluded Seward, "left a purer or nobler record."[62] Had Tod lived, Seward was sure that President Grant was prepared to offer him a place in his cabinet, the secretary of the treasury perhaps.[63]

Although the tributes were overwhelmingly positive, hard-core partisan enemies had long memories. Just days after his death, Tod's opponents, dismissive of the mourning family, could not wait to attack his memory. From Ashland, the *States and Union* said Tod was "born a tyrant," as governor ruled like an "Autocrat," and did "much evil in his time," namely arresting free speech.[64] From nearby Canton, the *Stark County Democrat* also did not mince words, labeling Tod a "hateful, cowardly, cruel, arrogant braggart and tyrant" and falsely accused the deceased of enriching his own finances and using them to construct his new mansion. Tod, according to the editor, Archibald McGregor, had a passion for opulence and therefore needed a grand "palace" to satisfy his "avarice." But alas, there is a vengeful God who "interposed, and burned it to ashes." The Almighty was not yet finished with the "wicked" Tod for soon after, He "smote the War Governor so that he died." Three weeks later, McGregor tamped down his characterization of Tod calling him "a vain egotist and braggart."[65]

Accounts from the working class also testified to Tod's charity and the record showed that he donated liberally to many causes. This study does not focus on Tod's relations with his employees. Undoubtedly, he was remembered fondly but it is fair to state that relations between Tod and his coal miners were stormy at times. Miners and ironworkers, suffice it to say, respectfully attended Tod's funeral services. Others may have been compelled to go. But they came, all the same.

Funeral services were held at noon on Sunday, November 15, at Tod's Brier Hill estate. In less than 48 hours from the time of his death, the grieving Tod family lined up speakers and established a parade route for the funeral services to honor its patriarch. Dignitaries such as Gov. Rutherford B. Hayes, Congressman James A. Garfield, and former congressman Samuel Galloway adjusted their schedules, made travel arrangements, and worked on eulogies to celebrate their friend's life and his years of distinguished service to his country and his state. A large crowd was anticipated, even on short notice, especially if the weather cooperated.[66]

Indeed, the weather did cooperate on the day of the funeral. Temperatures were unseasonably warm and made for a pleasant day in northeastern Ohio. The mild temperatures helped to draw out an estimated 15,000 mourners who had gathered for the funeral. Estimates ranged as high as 20,000. It was by far the largest crowd ever assembled for such an occasion in Youngstown. His old boss's funeral "was the largest assembly of the kind," said George Wright, Tod's loyal assistant, "except that of President Lincoln, that I have ever witnessed."[67] The size of the crowd swelled at different points along the procession route to the cemetery. One thing for sure was that the number of mourners could have been greater. More were left stranded at the depots in Columbus, Cleveland, and Canton because the train cars were filled. The steam engines that pulled in were "appropriately draped in mourning." The grounds at Brier Hill were described by the *New York Tribune* as "probably the most beautiful farm in the United States" and easily accommodated the enormous crowd.[68]

Conducting the services that day was Rev. Samuel Maxwell, of St. John's Episcopal Church. From inside the mansion Tod's remains were brought outside and placed under a canopy. This gave mourners a chance to file past to pay their last respects. The procession to the cemetery was led by a local band, followed by the Tod Fire Department and attorneys representing the bars of Mahoning and Trumbull Counties. The stream of horse-drawn carriages of thousands of mourners made its way to Oak Hill Cemetery to lay the governor to rest.[69] Once through the gates, family, friends, and dignitaries ascended the worn path to the top of a hill. There, on the northern edge of the cemetery, a family plot personally chosen by the governor himself already contained the remains of his daughter Charlotte. It was the highest point of the cemetery and gave a commanding view of the growing city. In time, the Tod family erected a simple greenhouse adjoining the plot where fresh flowers would be easily accessible to decorate the grave sites of the deceased.

Surely David Tod had his faults but no matter where his travels took him, he never outgrew his humble beginnings. What he did outgrow was his lifelong ties to the Democratic Party. But before he was a Democrat, before he was a Unionist, and before he joined the Republican Party, David Tod was an American patriot. "Among his many virtues," judged the *Hancock Jeffersonian*, "none were more prominent than his love of country."[70]

As a matter of personal pride, he hoped to leave a legacy that his children and descendants could be proud of, and he was certain that he had. In the waning hours of his term as governor of Ohio he confided to his devoted wife, "You will be glad to know that in the discharge of the responsible duties thrown upon me, I have won for myself and children a reputation of which any man may be proud."[71] One year after the funeral, the pedestal monument that Tod had personally selected was installed at the family plot.[72] At the top of the flat marble column he had ordered to be carved, *Hon. David Tod*. Few could disagree with the simple epitaph. At a time in which the nation was most severely tested, when it needed patriots more than partisan politicians, when it needed men of honor, it was fortunate to have such nationalists, such Unionists as David Tod.

Epilogue

At the time of his death, David Tod's estate was valued at over $500,000.[1] It was vastly different from his father's financial legacy. David Tod's fortune would benefit his descendants for generations to come.

Maria Tod would join her husband in death in 1901 at the ripe age of 88. A picture of Maria emerges as the typical nineteenth-century wife, dutifully devoted to her husband's aspirations. Though she had thoroughly enjoyed the excitement of the social scene on the arm of her distinguished husband she just as quickly retreated from the public eye after David's death.

Every indication suggests that Maria was a nurturing and loving wife, mother, and grandmother. Though she would go on to survive her husband by more than 30 years and missed him terribly, she had no time for loneliness for she was in the constant company of her children and grandchildren, who looked after the endearing family matriarch. Grandma "Janny," as she was called, loved to read, especially to her grandchildren. She attended Episcopalian services for as long as she was physically able before the crippling effects of rheumatism made her an invalid. Her life, and those of her children, was lived in relative comfort thanks to the business success of her husband and their father.[2] She lived the rest of her days with her devoted daughter Sallie and son George. Both offspring never married. Sallie remained her mother's abiding companion. Maria was the unfortunate victim of criminal mischief just one year after her husband's death when a thief broke into her residence and made off with a piece of silver jewelry. The dim-witted bandit was apprehended in Sharon, Pennsylvania, where he tried to unload the keepsake, a silver piece of jewelry engraved to Maria from her daughters Grace and Sallie.[3]

David Tod's sons were successful businessmen in their own right. John remained a distinguished figure in Cleveland until his death in 1896. Henry and partners added to the cultural scene of Youngstown by building a luxury hotel and an opera house. In 1872, a fire severely damaged Henry's residence at Brier Hill. Fortunately, his home was insured by the same insurance company that covered his father's house fire.[4] Henry also had a lengthy and successful career in banking before his death in 1905.

Son George, the only Civil War veteran of the family, eventually became president of the Brier Hill Iron and Coal Company, a position he held until his death in 1908. George also preserved the Brier Hill estate of his parents, maintaining the upkeep for years. Upon his death, he directed that the grounds be used for a cemetery, today known as the Tod Homestead Cemetery. George's will disposed of more than $2 million. Nine nieces and nephews received nearly one quarter of a million dollars each from their uncle. The city hospital also received $40,000 from the estate.[5]

William married Frances Barnhisel of Girard. He presided over the William Tod Company, specialists in building engines and heavy machinery. He also died in 1905.

Daughter Grace married George Arrel in 1875 at Brier Hill. She died in 1921 having outlived all her siblings.

Sallie, the youngest child of David and Maria, died in 1911, 10 years after her mother's death.[6]

David Tod's name and service remained fresh in the minds of citizens in the years immediately after his death. Two years after his passing, the Sixth Ohio Cavalry held a reunion and remembered Tod as "A champion of Freedom."[7] The local Grand Army of the Republic fraternal lodge number 29 named itself the Tod Post.

Invariably, Tod's name was trotted out during political campaigns to support Ohio Republican candidates.[8] In 1892, Governor William McKinley honored his predecessor when he said that Governor Tod "behaved handsomely and most patriotically under very trying circumstances" during the Civil War. "He was an able, honest, and fearless Executive, a public servant whose official conduct deserved, as it received, the approbation of all loyal people."[9]

On July 4, 1894, McKinley was on hand again to help dedicate a beautiful Civil War monument in Cleveland. The concept for what became known as the Soldiers' and Sailors' Monument originated with a small group of local veterans in 1879 who desired to pay tribute to the thousands of military and private civilians from Cuyahoga County who had served their country during the war. The state legislature agreed to fund the project in 1888. The outside of the completed monument pays homage to the men who served in the infantry, cavalry, artillery, and navy. Inside the walk-in monument the tablet room depicts several themes. "Beginning of the War in Ohio" portrays the state's three war time governors: Dennison, Tod, and Brough. They are flanked on the right by Generals James A. Garfield, Jacob D. Cox, George B. McClellan, and on the left by William Rosecrans, Rutherford B. Hayes, and Quincy A. Gilmore. Standing prominently in the middle of the raised bronze relief panel is Gov. David Tod. In the background, fresh recruits are shown on one side and on the other, they appear as sharply dressed troops heading off to battle. This scene accurately highlights the most pressing of responsibilities the governors faced: finding enlistees for the Union war effort, training them, then sending them off to battle.[10]

In 1905, the hundredth year of his birth, there was no commemoration to mark the occasion. In 1909, Governor Tod's old official carriage was located, dusted off, spruced up, and sent to Washington to lead Ohio's delegation in President-Elect William Howard Taft's inaugural parade.[11] Later that year, 47 years after the fact, Tod's call to the Squirrel Hunters to defend Cincinnati was remembered. This was because the Ohio General Assembly finally decided to compensate the legendary volunteer soldiers for their one month's service. They or their descendants received $13.[12] Plans for a new courthouse for Mahoning County were finalized in 1910. The [George?] "Tod estate" proposed to fund a statue of David Tod to "adorn" one of the columns.[13] The statue never materialized.

In 1914, another David Tod made a run for the governorship of Ohio. This Tod was the son of William and Frances. Like his grandfather, he also served in the Ohio senate but lost his bid for the Republican nomination for governor. Nonetheless, his name revived fond memories of his grandfather.[14]

Historical memory of David Tod has faded over the decades. The mansion that he and Maria occupied in Columbus during his term still stands with a historical marker outside denoting it as Governor Tod's Civil War residence. There are few reminders of David Tod in the Mahoning valley. There are streets and a small park named after him. His bust sits in silent gaze at the McKinley Birthplace Memorial in Niles. His Brier Hill Estate was given to the public by his son George to be used as a cemetery. A portrait of the late governor hangs in the cemetery's office. His official portrait silently hangs in the State House in Columbus alongside those of his peers.

When he died, the *Western Reserve Chronicle* concluded, "A truly great and good man has fallen, and all the people mourn."[15] Those people, those that knew him best indeed mourned, honored, and remembered. But they, too, are gone. This author, some 20-odd years ago, reached out to a direct descendent to see if something more could be done to keep Governor Tod's memory alive. Modestly, he declined, believing that there were enough reminders throughout the community.

I respectfully disagreed. David Tod needs to be a part of our historical conversation and our historical memory. His official term as governor of Ohio lasted just two years, but what a dangerous and exciting period it was. His brief term does not diminish his importance. The Civil War era is filled with many more figures like Tod whose limited role on the stage of that epic drama was limited but whose contributions deserve to be remembered. More studies of these relevant historical individuals are needed to help fully understand the challenges of the time. In this regard, there is much to uncover. Samuel Galloway also earnestly, almost pleadingly, said of Governor Tod, and should be applied to many more, "the thoughts, the affections, the deeds, which were so brightly embodied in useful action . . . cannot die."[16] I hope that this study will help to shed light on the relevancy of Tod's service to the nation and keep alive the important role he played in helping to preserve the Union, and his place in American history.

Notes

PREFACE

1. Richard Abbott, *Civil War Governors*, 4. Brough died before his term ended.
2. See Goodheart, *1861*.
3. See Phillips, *Rivers Ran Backward*.
4. See Goodheart, *1861*. See also Stanley's *The Loyal West*.
5. Silbey, *A Respectable Minority*, 5–6
6. Silbey, *A Respectable Minority*, 5–6.
7. Trester, "David Tod, 1862–1864." Ohio's Governors, *Fundamental Documents*, Ohio Historical Society's Searchable Database. Copyright 1996–2008. Retrieved on-line 4/22/2008.
8. Johannsen, *The Lincoln-Douglas Debates*, 7.
9. Baker, *Affairs of Party*, 321.
10. Wilson, "The Man for the Hour," 31.
11. Engle, *Gathering to Save*, 1–3.
12. Harris, *Lincoln*, 3.
13. Catton, *Army of the Potomac*, 82. 2
14. Harris, *Lincoln*, 3.
15. Gallagher, *The Union War*, Cambridge, 2–5.
16. David Tod To the Military Committee, Nov.7, 1863, *Message 1865*.
17. Abbott, "Lives."
18. Flood, *1864*, 166; Dell, *Lincoln*, 281; Hesseltine, *Lincoln*, 359; *Collected Works of Abraham Lincoln*, Lincoln to Tod, vol. 7.
19. Sherman, *Recollections*, 284.

20. Mathews, *Ohio*, 194
21. Stewart, *History*, 353.
22. Rawley, *Politics of Union*, 17, 185, 187.
23. Engle, *Gathering*, 1–3.
24. Butler, *Recollections*, 296, 297, 305. See also Lambert and Shale, *First Citizen*, chaps. 8, 13.
25. Rawley, *Politics of Union*, 1.
26. Fuller, *Oliver P. Morton*. Morton was the only man to serve as Indiana's war governor, from 1861 to 1867.

1. A DEMOCRAT IN THE MAKING, 1800–1838

1. *Annals of the Early Settlers*, no. 1, 66, Also see the *New York Times*, July 25, 1884, regarding a speech Spalding had just given in Cleveland. There are slight variations to this story, namely the song sung by David Tod, but the premise of Spalding's offer remains unchanged. Also, there are two variations of the spelling of Spalding's last name. The second is *Spaulding*. Both spellings have been used and, continue to be used inconsistently. This author has decided to use *Spalding*.
2. *Annals of the Early Settlers*, no. 1, 66
3. *Mahoning Dispatch*, Sept. 28, 1877. In this account, Spalding remembered differently and said that David Tod sang, "Old Grimes Is Dead." He also said that George Tod, lacking money, requested that Spalding, from time to time, take "a piece of beef, etc. from the farm" in exchange.
4. Melhorn, "Lest We Be Marshall'd," 40–41, where George Tod's dilemma is discussed. *History of Trumbull and Mahoning Counties*, vol. 1, 172.
5. *New York Times*, Feb. 14, 1881.
6. *Biographical Directory of the United States Congress*.
7. *Weekly Law Bulletin and Ohio Law Journal*, vol. 16, July 1–Dec. 31, 1886, "In Memoriam—Judge Spaulding," 180. This comment was made by the Honorable F. J. Dickman.
8. Strahan, "David Tod House." http://lostnewengland.com/2017/08/david-tod-house-suffield-connecticut/ retrieved 1/15/2018. This online article shows two pictures of the David Tod House in Suffield, Connecticut, one dated 2017. This David Tod is the grandfather of the subject of this work. The house dates to between 1773 and 1795. David and Rachel did not build this house. It has undergone extensive remodeling over the years and still "stands as one of the many elegant 18th century homes in the center of Suffield."
9. Hatcher, *The Western Reserve*, 16.
10. Hatcher, *Western Reserve*, 75.
11. Phillips, *Rivers Ran Backward*, 22, 41, 65, 85.
12. Melhorn, "Lest We Be Marshall'd," 175.
13. Stewart, *History of Northeastern Ohio*, vol.1, 345.

14. John Tod, *Some Account*, 7, 15.
15. MVHS, Tod Collection, box 1, 65.29.45, letter from George Tod to Charlotte Tod, Feb. 26, 1814, box 1, 65.29.45.
16. John Tod, *Some Account*, 69.
17. *History of Trumbull and Mahoning Counties*, 171.
18. Ferguson, *America by River and Rail*, 257.
19. *Mahoning Dispatch*, Jan. 8, 1915.
20. Richardson, *Ulysses S. Grant*, 43.
21. *Cleveland Leader*, Sept. 11, 1868.
22. *Grant Network Newsletter*, "To the Editor."
23. Grant, *Personal Memoirs*, 4.
24. John Tod, *Some Account*, 70, 89
25. MVHS, Tod Collection, box 1, 65.29.44, letter from Grace Ingersoll to Sallie Tod, Feb. 24, 1813, b.
26. Hinsdale, "The History of Popular Education," 48.
27. MVHS, Tod Collection box 1, folder 21, John Ford Bill for boarding, Ingersoll & David, Apr. 10, 1822.
28. *Pioneer and General History*, 481–82, 533.
29. *New York Times*, Sept. 7, 1868.
30. So remembered by Alexander M'Kinney, *Historical Collections*, 93.
31. *Cleveland Leader*, Sept. 11, 1868.
32. Quotation from Eben Newton, *Historical Collections*, 82.
33. Wright, *Honorable David Tod*, vol. 8, 111. Tod's height was noted by Wright in the fall of 1861 upon his first introduction to the then governor-elect.
34. John Tod, *Some Account*, 176.
35. Joseph G. Butler, *History of Youngstown*, vol. 1, 340.
36. *Report of the Convention*, 162.
37. Wright, *Honorable David Tod*, 103.
38. Chase, *The Statutes of Ohio*, vol. 2, 800–801.
39. Galloway, *Eulogy*.
40. Biographical History of Northeastern Ohio, 160.
41. John Tod, *Some Account*, 176.
42. Galloway, *Eulogy*.
43. Wright, *Honorable David Tod*, 103, 111.
44. John Tod, *Some Account*, 121–22.
45. John Tod, *Some Account*, 97.
46. Upton, *History of the Western Reserve*, 176.
47. John Tod, *Some Account*, 130.
48. Butler, *History of Youngstown*, vol. 1, 456.
49. Prechel-Kluskens, "The Nineteenth-Century Postmaster," 35.
50. *Register of All Officers and Agents, on 30 Sept. 1835*, 251; *Register of All Officers and Agents, on 30 Sept. 1831*, 183.
51. *Western Reserve Chronicle*, Aug. 31, 1870.

52. Howe, *What Hath God Wrought*, 503.
53. Howe, *What Hath God Wrought*, 504–5.
54. *Western Reserve Chronicle*, Apr. 10, 1838.
55. John Tod, *Some Account*, 176, 130. Quotation is from a written notarized agreement in David Tod's hand recorded April 11, 1838, MVHS Tod Collection.
56. Baker, *Affairs of Party*, 24, 27, 43.
57. Jon Meacham, *American Lion*, 59–60.
58. Baker, *Affairs of Party*, 32.
59. Stewart, *History of Northeastern Ohio*, vol. 1, 346.

2. THE COOLEST, MOST COLLECTED GENTLEMAN, 1838–1840

1. *History of Trumbull and Mahoning Counties*, vol. 1, 172, 281, 192.
2. *History of Trumbull and Mahoning Counties*, vol. 1, 172, 281, 192.
3. For a good explanation of the origin of the term *Loco Focos*, see Schlesinger, *Age of Jackson*, 191.
4. Sellers, *Market Revolution*, 167, 321.
5. Brown and Cayton, *Pursuit of Public Power*, 99–116.
6. *Western Reserve Chronicle*, Sept. 25, 1838.
7. Printed in the *Maumee City Express*, Sept. 15, 1838.
8. Brown and Cayton, *Pursuit of Public Power*, 106.
9. Two excellent studies on the antislavery, abolitionist movement in the community of Oberlin for further reference are Morris, *Oberlin*, and, Nat Brandt, *Town*. Both works help to highlight the important role that the then Western states, Ohio in particular and the Western Reserve in it, played in the abolition and antislavery movement before the Civil War.
10. Silbey, *Storm Over Texas*, 49.
11. Volpe, "Ohio Election," 85–100.
12. Phillips, *Rivers Ran Backward*, 24.
13. Nye, "Marius Robinson, 138–54.
14. Howe, *What Hath God Wrought*, 433.
15. Brown and Cayton, *Pursuit of Public Power*, 117–43.
16. *Western Reserve Chronicle*, Oct. 2, 1838.
17. *Western Reserve Chronicle*, Sept. 25, 1838.
18. *Western Reserve Chronicle*, Sept. 25, 1838.
19. Hammond, "The Most Free," 35–57, 49.
20. *Western Reserve Chronicle*, Sept. 25, 1838.
21. Brown and Cayton, *Pursuit of Public Power*, 111.
22. *Western Reserve Chronicle*, Oct. 16, 1838. This was not the end of John Crowell's political career. He would replace Tod as mayor and he was elected to the Ohio senate in 1840 when Tod decided not to seek another term. Crowell would go onto to serve two terms in the US Congress. While in the Congress Crowell would

work intimately with Whig figures such as Congressmen Robert Winthrop, Hugh White, Joseph Mullin, Artemas Hale, John Crisfield, and Abraham Lincoln. (See DeRose, *Congressman Lincoln*, 148.)

23. *Ohio State Journal and Register*, Dec. 18, 1838.

24. *Ohio State Journal and Register*, Dec. 18, 1838.

25. *State and National Banking Eras, A Chapter in the History of Central Banking*, 3.

26. The Panic of 1837 refers to a financial crisis that lasted into the 1840s. The panic was touched off by a number of domestic and international events that led to a major recession. Unemployment and bank and business failures, among others, led to a major economic collapse.

27. Trefousse, "Ben Wade." Wade would lead the Radical Republican branch of the party during the Civil War, which pushed Lincoln and his administration to abolish slavery.

28. *Ohio State Journal*, Jan. 25, 1839.

29. *Western Reserve Chronicle*, Oct. 2, 1838.

30. Brandt, *The Town*, 48–49.

31. Vance, *State of the State Address*. See also Reid and Reeder, "Trial of Rev. John B. Mahan."

32. See Trester, *Political Career of David Tod*, 16–17. Trester discusses these types of measures in ensuing years. The *Ohio Statesman* quotations are from February 8, 1839.

33. Phillips, *Rivers Ran Backward*, 3.

34. Trester, *Political Career of David Tod*, 19.

35. Phillips, *Rivers Ran Backward*, 4.

36. *Biographical Directory of the United States Congress, 1774 to the Present*.

37. Feller. "Brother in Arms," 54.

38. See Trester, *Political Career of David Tod*, 16–17. Trester discusses these types of measures in ensuing years. The *Ohio Statesman* quotations are from February 8, 1839.

39. *Journal of the Senate of Ohio, 37th General Assembly*, 594, 486.

40. Foner, *Free Soil*, 18–19.

41. Wittke, *History of Ohio*, vol. 3, 351–52.

42. Hammond, "The Most Free," 57.

43. Abbott, *Ohio's Civil War Governors*, 22, 23.

3. A HARD MONEY MAN, 1840–1844

1. *Trumbull Democrat*, May 26, 1840.
2. Butler, *History of Youngstown*, vol. 1, 463.
3. *Trumbull Democrat*, Aug. 25, 1840.
4. Baker, *Affairs of Party*, 181.

5. Baker, *Affairs of Party*, 276.
6. Rezneck, "Social History," 668, 669.
7. Baker, *Affairs of Party*, 130.
8. Foner, *Free Soil*, 169.
9. *Ohio Democrat and Dover Advertiser*, July 10, 1840.
10. Baker, *Affairs of Party*, 269.
11. *Trumbull County Democrat*, June 23, 30, 1840.
12. Phillips, *Rivers Ran Backward*, 70.
13. *Trumbull Democrat*, Aug. 4, 1840, July 14, 1840, Apr. 21, 1840.
14. Marvel, *Lincoln's Autocrat*, 27.
15. *Western Reserve Chronicle*, Oct. 6, 1840. Joshua R. Giddings "To the Honest Electors of the Sixteenth Congressional District," is "An Answer to Communication by David Tod Charging Giddings with Having Overcharged the Distance to Washington," 8277.
16. *Western Reserve Chronicle*.
17. Biography of George Tod, OhioLINK Finding Aid Repository, Finding Aid for the George Tod Papers, Sept. 10, 2018.
18. John Tod, *Some Account*, 130.
19. See Curtin, *Ohio Politics Almanac*. The *Democratic Standard*, November 24, 1840, count is Corwin 144,054 to 127,964 for Shannon.
20. Reid, *Ohio in the War*, 1020.
21. Trester, *David Tod*. "Ohio's Governors, *Fundamental Documents*, Ohio Historical Society's Searchable Database."
22. *History of Trumbull and Mahoning Counties*, 72–76.
23. *Trumbull Democrat*, Apr. 3, 1841.
24. https://www.supremecourt.ohio.gov/SCO/formerjustices/bios/tod.asp7/3/18. The quotation is from the *Trumbull Democrat*, Apr. 20, 1841 but cited in John Tod's work, 50–51.
25. Rice, *Founder of Cleveland*, 147.
26. Untitled biography of David Tod written on *Henry Tod* letterhead and dated April 11, 1889. MVHS
27. *Western Reserve Chronicle*, Mar. 10, 1858.
28. *Ohio Cemetery Journal*, vol. 3, issue 1, Apr. 2013, 4; John Tod, *Some Account*, 94.
29. *Vindicator*, June 12, 1910.
30. Howe. *Historical Collections*, 113.
31. Butler, *History of Youngstown*, vol. 1, 181.
32. John Tod, *Some Account*, 97; *Vindicator*, June 12, 1910.
33. Brown and Cayton, *Pursuit of Public Power*, 118.
34. Rezneck, "Social History," 662–87.
35. Holt, *Party Politics*,. vol. 38, no. 1, Jan. 1929, 515–17.
36. Trester. *David Tod*, 165. The term *Coonskinner* originated during the campaign of 1840 where William Henry Harrison was portrayed in a raccoon-skin cap,

emblematic of the common man. Democrats aptly applied the symbol to represent Whigs.

37. Trester, *David Tod*, 168,163.
38. Trester, *David Tod*, 166.
39. Quoted in Trester, *Political Career*, 34.
40. *Ohio Democrat*, Jan. 18, 1844.
41. Quoted in Trester, *David Tod and the Gubernatorial Campaign of 1844*, 166,167.
42. Borneman, *Polk*, 90–93.
43. *Ohio Democrat*, May 30, 1844.
44. Quoted in Trester, *David Tod*, 169.
45. *Coon Dissector*, Aug. 16, 1844.
46. Baker, *Affairs of Party*, 271.
47. *Whig Standard*, Aug. 13, 1844.
48. *Coon Dissector*, Sept. 20, 1844.
49. Quoted in Francis D. Nichol's "Midnight Cry," 290n. The original quotation appeared in the *Cincinnati Daily Gazette*, Oct. 7, 1844.
50. Quoted in Wright, "Hon. David Tod," 107–31.
51. Trester, *David Tod*, 169, 170.
52. Quoted in Trester, *David Tod*, 170, 171.
53. Holt, *Party Politics*, vol. 38, no. 1, Jan. 1929.
54. *Carroll Free Press*, Mar. 22, 1844.
55. Quoted in Trester, *David Tod*, 178.
56. Trester, *David Tod*, 172.
57. Wittke, *History of Ohio;* Weisenburger, *Passing of Frontier*, 418, 420.
58. Taylor, *Ohio Statesmen*, 528.
59. *Ohio State Journal*, Oct. 15, 1844.

4. NOT AN OFFICE SEEKER, 1844–1846

1. Trester, *David Tod*, 178. Quotations are from *James K. Polk Papers: Series 2, General Correspondence and Related Items, 1775-1849; 1844, November 18-1844, Dec. 11*. Library of Congress, Image 821.
2. Holt, *Party Politics*, 439–591. Ohio History Connection, Columbus, Ohio, 507.
3. Holt, *Party Politics*, 559, 560, Bartley quotation, 562.
4. Holt, *Party Politics*, 565, 567, 569.
5. *Governors of Ohio*, 55.
6. *Daily Commonwealth*, Feb. 10, 1846.
7. Holt, *Party Politics*, 571, 572, quotation, 572.
8. Quoted in Holt, *Party Politics*, 575.
9. Holt, *Party Politics in Ohio*, vol. 37, no. 3, 576; *Daily Union*, Jan. 13, 1846.
10. *Kalida Venture*, Mar. 12, 1846.

11. *Governors of Ohio*, 55, 58.
12. Quoted in Polk, 242.
13. Morrison, *Slavery*, 33.
14. Morrison, *Slavery*, 31.
15. Foner, *Free Soil*, 73.
16. *Cadiz Democratic Sentinel*, Feb. 11, 1846.
17. *Cadiz Democratic Sentinel*, Apr. 1, 1846.
18. *Cadiz Democratic Sentinel*, Mar. 11, 1846.
19. *Democratic Pioneer*, Mar. 20, 1846.
20. *Cadiz Democratic Sentinel*, Apr. 1, 1846.
21. *Spirit of Democracy*, June 13, 1846.
22. Brandt, *Town That Started*, 48.
23. Blue, *The Free Soilers*, 4.
24. *New York Daily Tribune*, July 3, 1846.
25. *Carroll Free Press*, Aug. 28, 1846.
26. *Trumbull Democrat*, Sept.18, 1846.
27. Trester, "Political Career," 74.
28. *Salmon P. Chase: Correspondence*, 134.
29. Trester, *The Political Career of David Tod*, 75.
30. Edwin Stanton to Salmon P. Chase, Nov. 30, 1846. *The Salmon P. Chase Papers, volume 2, Correspondence, 1823–1857*. Edited by John Nivens, Kent State university Press, Kent, Ohio, 1994, 136.
31. Trester, "Political Career," 70, 71.
32. John Tod, *Some Account*, 104. David Todd Papers: To Jane Shaler, Oct. 26, 1848.
33. Quoted in *New York Herald*, Aug. 26, 1846.
34. Tochtenhagen, "Mine Subsidence," 13.
35. *Carroll Free Press*, Oct. 9, 1846.
36. *Ohio Statesman*, Jan. 8, 1847. The date of Tod's letter is November 8, 1846.

5. IT BECOMES US TO ACT, 1847–1851

1. See Borneman, *Polk*.
2. *New York Herald*, Nov. 28, 1846. Note that the dateline is November 26, 1846.
3. *Daily Union*, Oct. 26, 1846.
4. John Tod, *Some Account*, 98.
5. Polk, *Diary*, 456, 464.
6. *Richmond Enquirer*, Mar. 9, 1847.
7. *National Whig*, May 12, 1847.
8. *Carroll Free Press*, Mar. 12, 1847.
9. Tod File, 3.
10. Holt, *Party Politics*, vol. 38, 109.

11. Quoted in Custis. "Henry Alexander Wise," 478, 18, 6, 8, 9, 17.
12. *New York Herald*, Mar. 5, 1847.
13. *Daily Union*, Jan. 18, 1847.
14. *Daily Union*, Feb. 2, 1847.
15. Polk, *Diary*, 97.
16. John Tod, *Some Account*, 98.
17. Polk, *Diary*, 66.
18. Polk, *Diary*, 109.
19. *New York Herald*, Oct. 11, 1847.
20. Wise, *Correspondence*, 127.
21. Wise, *Correspondence*, 100.
22. Wise, *Correspondence*, 131.
23. *New York Herald*, Oct.11, 1847.
24. Tod Collection, *Speech of Emperor Dom Pedro II*, Sept. 18, 1847.
25. *Baltimore Patriot*, printed in *Lancaster Gazette*, Oct. 22, 1847.
26. James Buchanan to David Tod, Nov. 22, 1847; Manning, *Diplomatic Correspondence of the United States*, vol. 2, 1946.
27. Polk, *State of the Union Address*.
28. John Tod, *Some Account*, 55.
29. Galloway, *Eulogy*.
30. *New York Herald*, Oct. 11, 1847.
31. *New York Herald*, Nov. 30, 1847.
32. Quoted in Lawrence F. Hill, *Diplomatic Relations*, 129.
33. Fehrenbacher and McAfee, *Slaveholding Republic*, 179.
34. Oakes, *Slavery and Freedom*, 29.
35. John Tod, *Some Account*,102–5.
36. John Tod, *Some Account*, 105.
37. Trester, "Political Career," 82–83.
38. John Tod, *Some Account*, 104–6.
39. Trester, "Political Career," 83.
40. Trester, "Political Career," 84.
41. David Tod, *Exposition*, 103–4.
42. Rank, "Attitude of James Buchanan Towards Slavery," 126–42.
43. Fehrenbacher and McAfee, *Slaveholding Republic*, 178.
44. Smith, *History of Brazil*.
45. John Tod, *Some Account*, 130, 155. The entire poem can be found on pages 170–71.
46. Manning, *Diplomatic Correspondence*, 477.
47. *New York Tribune*, Jan. 21, 1851.
48. Horne, *Deepest South*, 1–24.
49. Fehrenbacher and McAfee, *Slaveholding Republic*, 179–80. It was not until 1888 that Brazil finally ended the practice of enslaved labor.
50. *Trumbull Democrat*, Dec. 15, 1851.

51. John Tod, *Some Account*, 109.
52. John Tod, *Some Account*, 108–9. The emperor's reign lasted until 1889. He died in 1891.

6. PARTY PATRIARCH, 1851–1856

1. *Spirit of Democracy*, Jan. 7, 1852.
2. John Tod, *Some Account*, 111–12.
3. *Alexandria Gazette*, Sept. 25, 1852.
4. John Tod, *Some Account*, 111.
5. *Vindicator*, July 23, 1916.
6. *Annual Report of C&M RR*, 21.
7. Rose. *Cleveland*, 250.
8. John Tod, *Some Account*, 112.
9. Ferguson, *America by River and Rail*, 256.
10. Phillips, *Rivers Ran Backward*, 73.
11. George W. Knepper, *Ohio*, 212–14.
12. Phillips, *Rivers Ran Backward*, 88.
13. Morrison, *Slavery*, 113.
14. See Blue, *The Free Soilers*.
15. OhioHistoricalSociety\OhioGovernors,ohiohistory.org/onlinedoc/ohgovernment/governors/tod.html.
16. *Portage Sentinel*, July 7, 1852.
17. Blue, *The Free Soilers*, 238.
18. *Ohio Star*, Sept. 1, 1852.
19. *Des Moines Courier*, Oct. 14, 1852.
20. Blue, *The Free Soilers*, 256–57.
21. *Mountain Sentinel*, Dec. 9, 1852.
22. James M. McPherson, *Battle Cry*, 118–19.
23. Fuller, *Oliver P. Morton*, 21.
24. Foner, *Free Soil*, 95.
25. Brown and Cayton, *Pursuit of Public Power*, 137.
26. *Perrysburg Journal*, Apr. 10, 1854.
27. Reported in *Portage Sentinel*, Apr. 12, 1854.
28. Fuller, *Oliver P. Morton*, 68.
29. *Meigs County Telegraph*, Oct. 2, 1855.
30. Blue, *No Taint*, 220–21.
31. Blue, *Salmon P. Chase*, 102; Phillips, *Rivers Ran Backward*, 88.
32. Blue, *Salmon P. Chase*, 102–3.
33. McPherson, *Battle Cry*, 148, 152–53.
34. *Spirit of Democracy*, Oct. 15, 1856
35. *Western Reserve Chronicle*, Oct. 8, 1856.

36. *Ashland Union*, Nov. 28, 1855.
37. *James Buchanan*, 13.
38. *Memoir of James Buchanan*, 7–15.
39. Earle, *Jacksonian Antislavery*, 195.
40. Blue describes the term's origin in *The Free Soilers*, 31. Democrats of the Barnburner persuasion were concerned with one issue: the containment of the spread of slavery. Critics within the party charged that they would ruin the whole party, or burn the barn down, as they raised the importance of their plank above the whole party platform.
41. Foner, *Free Soil*, 60–61.
42. Blue, *The Free Soilers*, 66. See also Donald, *Charles Sumner*, 138–39.
43. *M'arthur Democrat*, Sept. 4, 1856.
44. *National Era*, Dec. 25, 1856.
45. Foner, *Free Soil*, 169.
46. Knapp, *History*, 269–70. Edgerton served in the US House of Representative from 1851 to 1855.
47. *Portage Sentinel*, Sept. 15, 1855.
48. Quoted in Michael A. Morrison, *Slavery*, 181.
49. *Ohio Star*, Sept. 1, 1852.
50. Quoted in Baker, *Affairs of Party*, 192.

7. A PRIVATE IN THE RANKS, 1857–1859

1. Trester, "Political Career," 91.
2. *Cincinnati Daily Press*, Mar. 9, 1859; *Cleveland Daily Leader*, Sept. 13, 1859, as reported in the *Mahoning Register* on events in Pennsylvania and Ohio. The *Cleveland Daily Leader*, November 7, 1859, reported the Brier Hill strike though no details emerge for the reason of the miners' strike or its extent. But the *Jeffersonian Democrat*, March 2, 1860, picked up a report in the *Toledo Blade* that the miners were "disposed to have a voice."
3. Boryczka and Carey, *No Strength*, 79.
4. *Toledo Blade*, reported in *Jeffersonian Democrat*, Mar. 2, 1860.
5. Ferguson, *America by River and Rail*, 252.
6. Knapp, *History of the Maumee Valley*, 269. Sawyer represented Ohio's Fifth Congressional District from 1845 to 1849.
7. Stampp, *America in 1857*, 93.
8. *Western Reserve Chronicle*, May 13, 1857.
9. *Yorkville Enquirer*, Mar. 26, 1857.
10. Morrison, *Slavery*, 193.
11. *Ohio State Journal and Register*, reported in *Western Reserve Chronicle*, Aug. 19, 1857.
12. *Western Reserve Chronicle*, Aug. 26, 1857.
13. Walter Stahr, *Stanton, Lincoln's War Secretary*, 80.

14. *Eaton Democrat,* Mar. 26, 1857.
15. *Western Reserve Chronicle,* Apr. 29, 1857.
16. *Ashland Union,* May 13, 1857.
17. *M'arthur Democrat* June 25, 1857, July 2, 1857; Trester, "Political Career," 91–92; *Evening Star,* June 29, 1857.
18. Blue, *Life in Politics,* 116.
19. *Portage Sentinel,* Oct. 8, 1857.
20. *Western Reserve Chronicle,* Sept. 23, 1857.
21. *Portage Sentinel,* Oct. 8, 1857.
22. *Western Reserve Chronicle,* Sept. 23, 1857.
23. Goodheart, *1861,* 99.
24. Birkner, *James Buchanan,* 29; *Evening Star,* May 5, 1857.
25. Stampp, *America in 1857,* 252–53, 272, 302.
26. Stampp, *America in 1857,* 307.
27. *True American,* Mar. 10, 1858, as reported in the *Cleveland Plain Dealer.*
28. Quoted in *Portage Sentinel,* Mar. 18, 1858.
29. Birkner, *James Buchanan,* 29.
30. *Portage Sentinel,* Sept. 16, 1858.
31. Tod to the Democrats of the Twentieth Congressional District, printed in *Western Reserve Chronicle,* Sept. 22, 1858.
32. Tod to the Democrats of the Twentieth Congressional District, printed in *Western Reserve Chronicle,* Sept. 22, 1858.
33. *Western Reserve Chronicle,* Sept. 8, 1858.
34. *Western Reserve Chronicle,* Sept. 22, 1858. Hapgood and Adams regained control of the newspaper in 1855.
35. *Western Reserve Chronicle,* Nov. 27, 1858. The newspaper is filled with cases involving Tod or his companies pertaining to legal matters dealing with the purchase of properties or contested sales of properties. The substance of these matters is well beyond the scope of this work.
36. *Cleveland Daily Leader,* Oct. 7, 1858.
37. Trester, "Political Career," 94.
38. McPherson, *Battle Cry,* 188.
39. *Western Reserve Chronicle,* Jan. 26, 1859.
40. McPherson, *Battle Cry,* 201–6. See also Horwitz, *Midnight Rising.*
41. *Western Reserve Chronicle,* Dec. 7, 1859.
42. Quoted in *Cincinnati Daily Press,* Dec. 9, 1859.
43. *Western Reserve Chronicle,* Mar. 10, 1858.

8. A CONFLICT COMETH, 1859–1860

1. *Cleveland Daily Leader,* Dec. 3, 1859.
2. J. Matthew Gallman, *The North Fights,* 89.
3. Quoted in Gallman's *The North Fights,* 89.

4. Goodheart, *1861*, 113.
5. Reported in *Weekly Portage Sentinel*, Mar. 7, 1860.
6. Birkner, *James Buchanan*, 108-9.
7. Printed in *Abbeville Press and Banner*, Mar. 9, 1860.
8. Printed in *Abbeville Press and Banner*, Mar. 9, 1860.
9. Smith, 100.
10. *Official Proceedings of Democratic National Convention, Held in 1860*, 31-34. Wisconsin Democrats likely joined the Southern walkout due in part to their shared support of personal liberty laws. These were adopted to counter the effects of the Fugitive Slave Law. See Current, *History of Wisconsin*, 290.
11. Guelzo, *Fateful Lightning*, 120-21.
12. The North was represented by 17 states and the South was represented by 15 states.
13. *Official Proceedings of the Democratic National Convention*, 16.
14. Stampp, *America in 1857*, 32.
15. *Official Proceedings of the Democratic National Convention*, 17.
16. McPherson, *Battle Cry of Freedom*, 213.
17. McPherson, *Battle Cry of Freedom*, 214.
18. Tod Collection, MVHS, box 1, folder 5, 65.29.95A, Apr. 11, 1889.
19. McPherson, *Battle Cry*, 214.
20. *Official Proceedings of the Democratic National Convention*, 37.
21. *Official Proceedings of the Democratic National Convention*, , 14, 52-70, 90-91
22. *Yorkville Enquirer*, May 10, 1860.
23. *Wyandot Pioneer*, June 7, 1860.
24. *New York Herald*, quoted in *Daily Exchange*, June 12, 1860; *Daily Exchange*, June 13, 1860.
25. *Daily Exchange*, June 16, 1860.
26. See Holzer, *Lincoln*.
27. *Official Proceedings of the Democratic National Convention*, 155-56.
28. Johannsen, *Stephen A. Douglas*, 771.
29. Richard Abbott, *Ohio's War Governors*, 22.
30. *Daily Exchange*, June 25, 1860, *Official Proceedings of the Democratic National Convention, Held in 1860*, 156; *Daily Exchange*, June 25, 1860.
31. *Official Proceedings of the Democratic National Convention, Held in 1860*, 156.
32. Abbott, *Ohio's Civil War Governors*, 22.
33. Trester, "Political Career," 97-99.
34. *Official Proceedings of the Democratic National Convention*, 156, 181.
35. Silbey, *Respectable Minority*, 21.
36. *Jeffersonian Democrat*, Oct. 19, 1860.
37. Silbey, *Respectable Minority*, 22-23.
38. *Trumbull Democrat*, July 12, 1860.
39. Only later did it come to pass that Ritezel would support President Abraham Lincoln by opposing secession. He also joined the Republican Party and was elected to local as well as state offices. His dedication to the party would continue

as he supported James Garfield and William McKinley in their candidacies for the presidency. See Butler, *History of Youngstown*, vol. 3, 717.

40. *Western Reserve Chronicle*, July 18, 1860.
41. *Anti-Slavery Bugle*, Aug. 4, 1860.
42. Reported in *Trumbull Democrat*, July 19, 1860.
43. *Trumbull Democrat*, June 21, 1860.
44. Silbey, *Respectable Minority*, 4.
45. *Cleveland Morning Leader*, July 24, 1860, Aug. 10, 1860; *Ashland Union*, Aug. 15, 1860; *Trumbull Democrat*, Aug. 9, 16, 1860.
46. Thomas Bartley was the son of Mordecai Bartley who had defeated Tod for Governor in 1843. *Cleveland Morning Leader*, Sept. 5, 24, 1860.
47. *Cleveland Morning Leader*, Sept. 24, 1860, Oct. 1, 1860, Oct. 20, 1860.
48. Holzer, *Lincoln*, 41-42.
49. *Cleveland Morning Leader*, Nov. 10, 1860. Breckinridge polled 286 in Trumbull and 132 in Mahoning. Bell polled 24 in Trumbull and 26 in Mahoning.
50. *Western Reserve Chronicle*, Dec. 5, 1860.
51. Meacham, *American Lion*, 304.
52. *Western Reserve Chronicle*, Oct. 9, 1861.

9. I AM FOR MY COUNTRY, 1861

1. *Ohio Statesman*, Jan. 9, 1861.
2. *Ohio Statesman*, Jan. 5, 1861.
3. McPherson, *Battle Cry*, 252-54; *Ohio Statesman*, Jan. 7, 1861.
4. Engle, *Gathering*, 165.
5. In the spring and summer of 1863, Governor Tod would finally begin to organize Free Blacks for military service. This will be reviewed in a later chapter.
6. *Ohio Statesman*, Jan. 9, 1861.
7. Gov. William Dennison's Annual Message, printed in full in the *Holmes County Farmer*, Jan. 7, 1861. See also Abbott, *Ohio's Civil War Governors*, 9-10.
8. *Daily Ohio Statesman*, Jan. 24, 1861.
9. Jacob D. Cox, *Military Reminiscences*, vol. 1, 4. Cox would go on to become the twenty-eighth governor of Ohio and secretary of the interior in the Grant administration.
10. Cox, *Military Reminiscences*, 3-5. See also Dell, *Lincoln*, 64.
11. Cox, *Military Reminiscences*, 3-5.
12. *Western Reserve Chronicle*, Jan. 16, 1861, May 31, 1861.
13. Engle, *Gathering*, 21.
14. Abbott, *Ohio's Civil War Governors*, 10.
15. *Pomeroy Weekly Telegraph*, Feb. 1, 1861. Tod's support of popular sovereignty relative to the expansion of slavery in the territories did not sit well with those opposed to slavery on moral grounds for the sake of free labor.
16. *Jeffersonian Democrat*, Feb. 8, 1861; *Western Reserve Chronicle*, Feb. 6, 1861;

Engle, *Gathering*, 20–21. According to Abbott's *Ohio's Civil War Governors*, surprisingly, "the Ohioans approved every section of the compromise resolutions," 10.

17. Engle, *Gathering*, 20–22. See also Tooley, *Peace*.
18. *Western Reserve Chronicle*, Feb. 13, 20, 1861.
19. *New York Times*, Apr. 15, 1861.
20. *Western Reserve Chronicle*, Apr. 17, 1861; Cox, *Military Reminiscences*, 4.
21. *Cleveland Moring Leader*, Apr. 20, 1861. The name of the loyal citizen was Jacob Bruce.
22. Cox, *Military Reminiscences*, 4; *Chicago Daily Tribune*, Apr. 19, 1861.
23. McPherson, *Battle Cry*, 506.
24. Butler, Jr, *Recollections*, 82.
25. *Cleveland Morning Leader*, Apr. 20, 1861.
26. Wright, "Hon. David Tod," 113–14.
27. *Western Reserve Chronicle*, Apr. 24, 1861.
28. *Western Reserve Chronicle*, May 14, 1861.
29. Wilson, "The Man for the Hour," 31.
30. *Holmes County Republican*, May 30, 1861.
31. *Western Reserve Chronicle*, May 28, 1861.
32. *Western Reserve Chronicle*, Apr. 24, 1861.
33. Taylor, *Supply*, 8–9. The nephews and their cousin George Tod were 90-day volunteers in Company B of the Nineteenth Ohio Infantry, which Governor Tod formed and financed. Simon Jr. would go on to become a quartermaster for the War Department. George Tod was commissioned a first lieutenant, Second Regiment, Ohio Volunteer Infantry (OVI). John Tod, *Some Account*, 149.
34. Galloway, *Eulogy*.
35. Quoted in *Marshall County Republican*, Apr. 25, 1861.
36. *Western Reserve Chronicle*, June 7, 1861.
37. *Western Reserve Chronicle*, June 4, 1861.
38. Douglas's last letter was dated May 10, 1861, and reprinted in the *Highland Weekly News*, Sept. 18, 1862.
39. *Ohio Statesman*, June 21, 1861.
40. *Western Reserve Chronicle*, May 28, 1861.
41. *Ohio Statesman*, Apr. 30, 1861.
42. James A. Rawley, *Politics of Union*, 41–42.
43. *Tiffin Weekly Tribune*, Aug. 23, 1861. Tod's other three sons, all of age at some point during the war, did not serve.
44. *Western Reserve Chronicle*, May 31, 1861, June 10, 1861; *Cleveland Leader*, June 1, 1861.
45. *Mahoning Sentinel*, quoted in *Western Reserve Chronicle*, July 31, 1861.
46. Goodheart, *1861*, 119, 121.
47. Silbey, *Respectable Minority*, 45, 48.
48. Christopher Dell, *Lincoln*, 110.
49. *Ohio Statesman*, Sept. 22, 1861.
50. *Jeffersonian Democrat*, Aug. 23, 1861.

51. *Cincinnati Daily Press,* Aug. 31, 1861.
52. *Ohio Statesman,* Aug. 16, 1861.
53. *Belmont Chronicle,* Aug. 22, 1861.
54. *Belmont Chronicle,* Aug. 22, 1861.
55. *Holmes County Farmer,* June 6, 1861. The early anti-Lincoln/antiwar sentiment in Holmes County rose to near-rebellion during Governor Tod's administration.
56. *Forney Press,* printed in *Gallipolis Journal,* Aug. 29, 1861. The *Forney Press* was published by John W. Forney.
57. *Cleveland Morning Leader,* Sept. 4, 1861, Aug. 12, 1861, Aug. 24, 1861. Tod was so enamored of the location that he had ordered the construction of a little cottage for him and Maria to enjoy. Construction was completed in June 1862. The couple would never use the structure. Tod had no time as governor to retreat there and sold it after he left office. William Reynolds to Gov. David Tod, May 12, 1862; A. S. Hale to Gov. David Tod, June 14, 1862. Both letters are found in Ohio Governors Papers, David Tod, Jan. 13, 1862, to Jan. 11, 1864.
58. *Marshall County Republican,* Aug. 29, 1861, *Cleveland Morning Leader,* Aug. 30, 1861.
59. *Canton Republican,* printed in *Ashtabula Weekly,* Aug. 31, 1861.
60. Dell, *Lincoln,* 111.
61. Abbott. *Ohio's Civil War Governors,* 7.
62. *Chardon Democrat,* in *Cincinnati Daily Press,* Aug. 31, 1861.
63. *Cleveland Morning Leader,* Aug. 26, 1861.
64. *Fremont Journal,* Sept. 6, 1861.
65. *Chicago Daily Tribune,* Sept. 14, 1861.
66. *Proceedings of the Great Union Convention,* "Governor Tod's Letter of Acceptance."
67. The author is in possession of an original ticket.
68. *Fremont Journal,* Sept. 27, 1861.
69. *Western Reserve Chronicle,* Dec. 9, 1868.
70. *Gallipolis Journal,* Sept. 12, 1861.
71. Klement, *Limits,* 81. 81.
72. *Tiffin Weekly Tribune,* Sept. 13, 1861.
73. Printed in *Cleveland Morning Leader,* Sept. 17, 14, 1861.
74. Quoted in Trester, "Political Career," 119.
75. *Ohio Statesman,* Sept. 26, 1861.
76. *Cleveland Morning Leader,* Oct. 2, 1861.
77. Trester, "Political Career," 121.
78. *Governors of Ohio,* 81.
79. *Delaware Gazette,* Dec. 6, 1861; *Chicago Daily Tribune,* Dec. 24, 1861. Suffice it to say that Tod's ability to read men's talent took a hit in these observations. McClellan had replaced Winfield Scott, a move Tod described as, "a painful act rendered necessary by evident causes."

10. TAKING HOLD, JANUARY–JUNE 1862

1. Joseph Patterson Smith, *History of the Republican Party*, 145.
2. Abbott, *Ohio's War Governors*, 3, 4, 12, 15.
3. *Holmes County Republican*, Jan. 16, 1862.
4. *Ohio Statesman*, Jan. 14, 1862; Gallagher, *Union War*, 2.
5. *Cleveland Morning Leader*, Jan. 14, 1862.
6. *Ohio Statesman*, Jan. 14, 1862.
7. *Belmont Chronicle*, Jan. 23, 1862; Poland, *Army Register*, 20.
8. *Belmont Chronicle*, Jan. 23, 1862; Poland, *Army Register*, 20.
9. Ohio Governors Papers, David Tod Jan. 13, 1862, to Jan. 11, 1864. Gov. David Tod to Gen. C. P. Buckingham, Apr. 26, 1862.
10. Bissland, *Blood, Tears, & Glory*, 189.
11. Wright, "Hon. David Tod," 111.
12. *Ohio Statesman*, Jan. 16, 1862.
13. "Old Northwest" Genealogical Society, *"Old Northwest" Genealogical Quarterly*, 8.
14. Miller, *States at War*, 149.
15. *Belmont Chronicle*, Feb. 6, 1862.
16. John Tod, *Some Account*, 169. Sallie would not marry and remained a devoted companion to her widowed mother. Sallie Tod died in 1911.
17. The house is now known as the Snowden Gray Mansion and is open to the public for private events. www.snowdengraymansion.com.
18. *Ohio Statesman*, May 21, 1862.
19. Wright, "Hon. David Tod," 118.
20. Waugh, *Lincoln and McClellan*, 66.
21. US War Department, *War of the Rebellion*, vol. 2, 580.
22. Abbott, *Ohio's War Governors*, 25.
23. Quoted in Engle, *Gathering*, 152.
24. Harris, *Lincoln*, 38–39.
25. Engle, *Gathering*, 186.
26. See Waugh, *Lincoln and McClellan*, for a fascinating account of the tumultuous relationship between the president and his general.
27. Miller, *States at War*, 149. See also Ohio History Connection, series 147-42, 118.
28. Gallman, *North Fights Civil War*, 94, 110, 112–13. See also Oates, *Woman of Valor*.
29. Seventy-Six to editor, *Fremont Journal*, Apr. 25, 1862.
30. Seventy-Six to editor, *Fremont Journal*, Apr. 25, 1862.
31. Seventy-Six to editor, *Fremont Journal*, Apr. 25, 1862.
32. Trester, "Political Career," 131–32.
33. *Messages and Reports to General Assembly and Governor* (hereafter MR1862P1); Miller, *States at War*, 153.
34. *Cleveland Morning Leader*, Apr. 19, 1862, May 17, 1862, Dec. 29, 1862.

35. MR1864P1, Governor Tod to Mrs. Emily Burnham, Feb. 24, 1863. In Tod's annual message the following year he would praise "the efficient aid of the good women of Ohio" for their services to the wounded, MR1864P1.

36. MR1862P1, Governor Tod to Dr. S. M. Smith, May 2, 1862, 58, 60.

37. Miller, *States at War*, 155.

38. MR1862P1, Col. George B. Senter to Governor Tod, May 12, 1862.

39. Trester, "Political Career," 132.

40. *Cleveland Morning Leader*, May 17, 1862.

41. "Acknowledgment of Offers of Assistance," by Edwin M. Stanton, Apr. 11, 1862, *War of the Rebellion* (hereafter OR), series 3, vol. 2, 14.

42. Abbott, *Ohio's War Governors*, 34, 35.

43. MR1862P1, Governor Tod to Col. S. Bliss, June 12, 1862.

44. MR1862P1, Governor Tod to Rev. James Marvin, July 2, 1862, Rev. A. R. Howbert to Governor Tod, Dec. 29, 1862. See also Ohio Governors Papers Jan. 13 to Jan. 11, 1864.

45. Bissland, *Blood, Tears, & Glory*, 139.

46. See Waugh, *Lincoln and McClellan*.

47. John L. Hebron (2nd OVI) to Dear Mother (Lydia Hebron) Aug. 11, 1862, Spared & Shared, Letters of John L. Hebron, John L. Hebron (2nd OVI) to Dear Mother (Lydia Hebron) Aug. 11, 1862.

48. MR1862P1, Governor Tod to Reuben C. Lemon, chairman of Military Committee, Toledo, May 25, 1862, and Governor Tod to Secretary of War Stanton, May 25, 1862,19.

49. OR, Governor Tod to Edwin M. Stanton, May 27, 1862, vol. 2, 87.

50. Trester, "Political Career of David Tod," 130.

51. OR, Edwin Stanton to Governor Tod, May 26, 1862; Edwin Stanton to Tod, May 26, 1862; Edwin Stanton to Governor Tod, May 26, 1862; Edwin Stanton to Governor Tod, May 30, 1862; Series 3, vol. 2, 78, 79, 100; and, Reid, *Ohio in the War*, vol. 2, pt. 1, 363.

52. *Weekly Perrysburg Journal*, Feb. 6, 1862.

53. Galloway, *Eulogy*.

54. Wright, "Hon. David Tod," 116–17.

55. Roseboom, *History of Ohio*, 394.

56. MR1862P1, Governor Tod to Brig. Gen. John Love, Covington, Kentucky, Sept. 12, 1862.

57. Governor Tod to Edwin Stanton, June 11, 1862; Governor Tod to Edwin Stanton, June 27, 1862; Governor Tod to Edwin Stanton, July 14, 1862; OR, series 3, vol. 2, 145, 179, 223; and Garrison Sr. and Garrison, *Civil War Dictionary;* 307 defines a *stand* as "the complete equipment of a single soldier." OR, P. H. Watson to Governor Tod, July 19, 1862; OR, series 3, vol. 2, 234.

58. MR1862P1, George B. Wright to P. H. Watson, July 21, 1862.

59. MR1862P1, Governor Tod to William Dennison, Aug. 15, 1862, and Governor Tod to William Dennison, Aug. 28, 1862.

254 · NOTES TO PAGES 124–129

60. See Blue, *Salmon P. Chase, A Life in Politics*, 129–72.
61. Trester, "Political Career," 132.
62. Governor Tod to George B. Wright, July 14, 1862; Tod to James E. Lewis, July 14, 1862, MR1862P1, 18, 19.
63. Governor Tod to C. P. Buckingham, Sept. 16, 1862, Edwin Stanton to Tod, Sept. 16, 1862, OR, series 3, vol. 2, 549.
64. Reid, *Ohio in the War*, vol. 1, 67, 70.
65. Spared & Shared, Letters of George Washington Fawcett, George Washington Fawcett to Clara Lucretia Strieby, Aug. 5, 1862.
66. *New York Herald*, July 7, 20, 10, 1862.
67. Sears, *George B. McClellan*, 232.
68. Governor Tod to Edwin Stanton, July 11, 1862, OR, series 3, vol. 2, 219.
69. Allan Nevins, *War for the Union*, 145.
70. Guelzo, *Fateful Lightning*, 458; *Ohio Statesman*, July 7, 1862.
71. Roseboom, *History of Ohio*, 395.
72. Reid, *Ohio in the War*, vol. 2, 4.
73. David Tod to The President [Abraham Lincoln], July 28, 1862, OR, Series III, Vol. 2, 269.
74. Tod to Edwin Stanton, Aug. 11, 1862; and Tod to Edwin Stanton, Aug. 14, 1862; OR, series 3, vol. 2, 355, 386.
75. Tom Wheeler, *Mr. Lincoln's T-Mails*. Wheeler's work provides great insight into how Lincoln's war department received communication instantaneously from the fields of battle and returned praise, encouragement, orders, etc. The telegraph system also helped the war department to communicate with the loyal governors. Tod was able to communicate directly as a telegraph line stretched from Columbus to Washington.
76. Miller, *States at War*, 158–59.
77. J. M. Lee to Governor David Tod, June 29, 1862, Ohio Governors Papers, David Tod Jan. 13, 1862, to Jan. 11, 1864.
78. *Daily Evansville Journal*, May 27, 1862.
79. Miller, *States at War*, 161.

11. PARTISANS AND THE PATRIOT, JULY 1862–SEPTEMBER 1862

1. *Pomeroy Weekly Telegraph*, July 11, 1862
2. *Cleveland Morning Leader*, Nov. 19, 1862.
3. *Democratic Press*, July 3, 1862.
4. *Holmes County Farmer*, July 10, 1862.
5. *New York Daily Tribune*, July 17, 1862.
6. Harris, *Lincoln*, 48–49.
7. *Ohio Statesman*, Aug. 7, 1862.
8. Reid, *Ohio in the War*, vol. 1, 71. Tod to General Buckingham Aug. 23, 1862, Tod to Edwin Stanton, July 30, 1862, OR, series 3III, vol. 2, 449, 285.

9. *Cleveland Morning Leader*, Aug. 15, 1862.
10. Reid, *Ohio in the War*, vol. 1, 70–71; Wright, "Hon. David Tod," 177.
11. Hesseltine, *Lincoln and War Governors*, 279.
12. Trester, "Political Career," 134–35.
13. OR, Governor Tod to General C. P. Buckingham, Aug. 30, 1862, series 3, vol. 2, 493.
14. Reprinted from *New York Times*, Aug. 15, 1862.
15. Reid, *Ohio in the War*, vol. 1, 80.
16. *Cleveland Morning Leader*, July 21, 1862.
17. Reprinted in *Fremont Journal*, Aug. 1, 1862.
18. Miller, *States a War, vol. 5*, 30.
19. The Habeas Corpus Act was not signed until March 1862.
20. *Cleveland Morning Leader*, Aug. 15, 1862.
21. Governor Tod to William H. Seward, July 29, 1862, printed in the *Crisis*, Mar. 25, 1863.
22. Printed in *Belmont Chronicle*, Aug. 7, 1862.
23. Ohio Governors Papers, David Tod Jan. 13, 1862 to Jan. 11, 1864, A Democrat to Gov. David Tod, July 30, 1862.
24. *Ohio Statesman*, Sept. 11, 1862; *Biographical Directory of US Congress; Dayton Daily Empire*, Dec. 17, 1862; *New York Times*, Aug. 17, 1862.
25. Trester, "Political Career,", 141.
26. "Backbone" from *Ohio Statesman*, Sept. 11, 1862; "Insane" printed in *Ohio Statesman*, July 30, 1862; Trester, "Political Career," 140.
27. *Wyandot Pioneer*, Aug. 15, 1862; *Gallipolis Journal*, Aug. 28, 1862; *Weekly Perrysburg Journal*, Oct. 1, 1862.
28. Hertz, *Lincoln Talks*, 347–49.
29. McPherson, *Battle Cry*, 528–33.
30. These letters are found at Ohio History Connection (OHC SA 147), Correspondence: Correspondence to the Governor and Adjutant General of Ohio.
31. Trester, "Political Career," 148–49.
32. Trester, "Political Career," 148–49.
33. OR, Governor Tod to Edwin Stanton, July 30, 1862, series 3, vol. 2, 285.
34. McPherson, *Battle Cry*, 513–16.
35. MR1862P1, Governor Tod to William Dennison, July 14, 1862.
36. Horwitz, *Longest Raid*, 46.
37. Trester, "Political Career," 43, 144; *Highland Weekly News*, Sept. 11, 1862.
38. MR1862P1, Governor Tod to R. C. Lemmon, Esq., Sept. 6, 1862.
39. McPherson, *Battle Cry*, 517–20.
40. MR1862P1, Governor Tod to J. H. Dickerson, Sept. 8, 1862.
41. Bissland, *Blood, Tears*, 239.
42. Quarles, *The Negro*, 192, 30.
43. OR, Governor Tod to Edwin Stanton, Sept. 2, 1862, series 1, pt. 2, vol. 16, 476.
44. MR1862P1, Governor Tod to Loyal People of River Counties, Sept. 2, 1862.
45. Miller, *States at War*, 182.

46. *Cleveland Morning Leader,* Sept. 5, 1862.
47. OR, Edwin Stanton to David Tod, Sept. 3, 1862, series 1, pt. 2, vol. 16, 479.
48. Miller, *States at War,* 183.
49. A. James Fuller, *Oliver P. Morton,* 125. For an in-depth study of this theme see Phillips, *Rivers.*
50. Miller, *States at War,* 182.
51. MR1862P1, Governor Tod to Maj. Gen. Horatio Wright, Sept. 7, 1862, and Tod to Captain C. W. Smith, Sept. 7, 1862, 13; and Miller, *States at War,* 184.
52. MR1862P1, Governor Tod to Maj. Gen. Horatio Wright, Sept. 12, 1862; MS, Tod to Edwin Stanton, Sept. 12, 1862, 14, 15.
53. Bissland, *Blood, Tears,* 240.
54. MR1862P1, Governor Tod to Maj. Gen. Horatio Wright, Sept. 12, 1862; MS, Tod to Edwin Stanton, Sept. 12, 1862, 14, 15.
55. Dee, *Ohio's War,* 86–87.
56. MS, 15. Wright to Tod,
57. MS, Tod to Dennison, 15; *Cleveland Morning Leader,* Sept. 15, 1862.
58. Miller, *States at War,* 185, 186, 188. West Virginia was admitted into the Union on December 31, 1862.
59. MR1862P1, Governor Tod to Governor Pierpont, Sept. 12, 1862, and Governor Tod to Stanton, Sept. 14, 1862.
60. MR1862P1, Governor Tod to Col. Charles W. Doubleday, Sept. 21, 1862.
61. *Hancock Jeffersonian,* Oct. 3, 1862; *Western Reserve Chronicle,* Oct. 8, 1862; *Ohio Statesman,* Sept. 25, 1862.
62. Invitation published in *Cleveland Morning Leader,* Sept. 18, 1862.
63. Engle, *Gathering,* 230, 225. Governor Morton was unable to attend the conference in Altoona and sent D. G. Rose in his place.
64. Hesseltine, *Lincoln and the War Governors,* 224, 225, 227, 255; Engle, *Gathering,* 235.
65. Quoted in Engle, *Gathering,* 225.
66. Ridderbusch, "The Lincoln Reminiscence Manuscript," 75–92.
67. Egle, *Life and Times,* 309.
68. Governor Bradford did not sign the address to President Lincoln.
69. *New York Herald,* Sept. 25, 1862.
70. Hesseltine, *Lincoln and the War Governors,* 258.
71. Sears, *George B. McClellan,* 324.
72. Harris, *Lincoln and the Union Governors,* 60.
73. *New York Herald,* Sept. 25, 1862.
74. William Frank Zornow, "Lincoln, Chase," 5.
75. Engle, *Gathering,* 165, 185.
76. *Governors of Ohio,* 82.
77. *Portland Daily Press,* Sept. 30, 1862.
78. *Delaware Gazette,* Dec. 6, 1861.
79. *Newark American* printed in *Jeffersonian Democrat,* Oct. 10, 1862.

80. See Phillips, *Rivers*.
81. *Cadiz Democratic Sentinel*, Apr. 23, 1862. The editors were worried about emancipation five months before Lincoln announced it in September.
82. Miller, *States at War*, 190.
83. *Diary of Gideon Welles*, 153.

12. DEMOCRATIC THUNDER, OCTOBER 1862–MAY 1863

1. Galloway, *Eulogy*.
2. *Cleveland Morning Leader*, Jan. 14, 1862.
3. *Fremont Journal*, Oct. 17, 1862.
4. Galloway, *Eulogy*.
5. *Cleveland Morning Leader*, Jan. 14, 1862.
6. Wright, "Hon. David Tod," 116.
7. *Cleveland Morning Leader*, Oct. 9, 1862.
8. David A. Gerber, *Black Ohio*, 34.
9. *Daily Ohio Statesman*, Oct. 15, 1862.
10. Cheek and Cheek. *John Mercer Langston*, 387, 383. The quote, "Had the people" was reported in the *Lorain County News*, Aug. 6, 1862.
11. Ohio Governors Papers, David Tod Jan. 13, 1862, To Jan. 11, 1864, Julia Ford (sister) to Governor David Tod, July 28, 1862.
12. Baker, *Affairs of Party*, 145.
13. Gerber, *Black Ohio*, 34.
14. Reid, *Ohio in the War*, vol. 1, 176.
15. Miller, *States at War*, 193–94.
16. Spared & Shared, the Letters of John L. Hebron, John L. Hebron to Dear Mother (Lydia Hebron), Oct. 25, 1862..
17. *Ohio Statesman*, Nov. 6, 1862.
18. Harris, *Lincoln and the Union Governors*, 87–88.
19. Spare & Share, the Letters of John L. Hebron, John L. Hebron to Dear Pap, Nov. 24, 1862.
20. Klement, *Limits of Dissent*, 124.
21. Roseboom, *The History of Ohio*, 403.
22. Gallman, *North Fights Civil War*, 52.
23. Abbott, *Ohio's War Governors*, 26.
24. Printed in *Western Reserve Chronicle*, Mar. 25, 1863.
25. Dell, *Lincoln and War Democrats*, 200, 223n.
26. MR1864P1, Governor Tod to Mrs. Orpha Annette Hanna, Mount Pleasant, Ohio, June 15, 1863.
27. Wright, "Hon. David Tod," 116.
28. MR1864P1, Governor Tod to Major General William S. Rosecrans, Mar. 8, 1863.
29. David Tod, *Message of Governor*.

30. *Weekly Perrysburg Journal,* Feb. 4, 1863.
31. Miller, *States at War,* 250.
32. David Tod, *Message of Governor.*
33. *Ohio Democrat,* Jan. 16, 1863.
34. *Ashland Union,* Feb. 11, 1863.
35. Quoted in Weisenburger, *Columbus,* 24.
36. Quoted in Abbott, *Ohio's Civil War Governors,* 33.
37. Engle, *Gathering,* 264.
38. Dell, *Lincoln and War Democrats,* 151.
39. *Western Reserve Chronicle,* Apr. 1, 1863.
40. *Cleveland Morning Leader,* Mar. 28, 1863.
41. *Cadiz Democratic Sentinel,* Sept. 30, 1863.
42. *Daily Ohio Statesman,* Feb. 26, 1863.
43. See Phillips, *The Rivers Ran Backward.*
44. *Daily Ohio Statesman,* Feb. 26, 1863.
45. Trester, "Political Career," 158–60. Trester provides a good but brief overview of these issues. See also Miller, *States at War,* 252–53.
46. Engle, *Gathering,* 264.
47. Stackpole, *They Met,* 6.
48. *Daily Ohio Statesman,* Feb. 12, 1863.
49. Engle, *Gathering,* 277; MR1864P1, Governor Tod to Major General Burnside, Mar. 27, 1863.
50. *Daily Ohio Statesman,* Jan. 30, 1863.
51. *Cleveland Morning Leader,* Apr. 6,1863; *Fremont Journal,* Apr. 10, 1863; Miller, *States at War,* 217. See also Scott, *Complete History,* 145, 155.
52. Roseboom, *History of Ohio,* 399.
53. *History of Trumbull and Mahoning Counties,* 213–15.
54. Quoted in,Trester, "Political Career," 161–62.
55. *Cadiz Democratic Sentinel,* Jan. 28, 1863.
56. MR1864P1, Governor Tod to Col. A. C. Voris, 67th Reg't, Folly Island, S.C., May 10, 1863; Governor Tod to Col. T. Heath, Mar. 1, 1863; Governor Tod to Col. Anson G. McCook, 2d OVI, May 16, 1863; Governor Tod to Col. P. P. Lane, 11th Reg't, OVI, July 18, 1863; Governor Tod to Col. William T. Wilson, Apr. 20, 1863.
57. Crowl, *Opdycke's Tigers,* 110.
58. Robert Ernest Miller, "War within Walls, 42.
59. Many Confederate officers brought along to the battlefield their enslaved Blacks to act as body servants to look after their personal needs in camp. See Levin's *Searching.* See also *Holmes County Republican,* Apr. 3, 1863.
60. *Fremont Journal,* May 16, 1862. See also *Daily Ohio Statesman,* Apr. 29, 1862. For more information on Professor Peck, see Brandt, *Town.*
61. Wright, "Hon. David Tod," 117.
62. MR1864P1, Governor Tod to Lt. James A. Clark, May 25, 1863.
63. Weisenburger, *Columbus,* 24–25.

64. *Delaware Gazette*, Apr. 24, 1863.

65. MR1864P1, Governor Tod to Col. M. D. Leggett, 78th Regt. Memphis, TN, Feb. 28, 1863.

66. MR1864P1, Governor Tod to Orson Sells, Esq. Garrettsville, Ohio, Feb. 27, 1863.

67. Miller, *States at War*, 214–15; *Belmont Chronicle*, Apr. 2, 1863.

68. MR1864P1, Governor Tod to Hon. E. M. Stanton, Sec. of War, Feb. 1, 1863.

69. MR1864P1, Governor Tod to Alex McConnell, Esq., Warren, Ohio, Apr. 20, 1863.

70. *Daily Ohio Statesman*, Mar. 28, 1863.

71. Howbert, *Reminiscences, of the War*, 289.

72. Runkle, "James Parks Caldwell," 323–25.

73. *Western Reserve Chronicle*, Mar. 25, 1863.

74. *Daily Ohio Statesman*, Apr. 16, 1863.

75. Printed in *Western Reserve Chronicle*, Apr. 1, 1863.

76. Stephen E. Towne, "Lesson for Rebels," 5–37.

77. *Report of Judge Advocate General*, 3.

78. Michael Kent Curtis, "Lincoln, Vallandingham, and Anti-War Speech in the Civil War," 7; *Wm. & Mary Bill Rts. J.*, 105 (1998), https://scholarship.llaw.wm.edu/wmborj/vo17/iss1/3, 121.

79. Engle, *Gathering*, 282.

80. John Tod, *Some Account*, 63.

81. Towne, *Surveillance and Spies*, 82.

82. Miller, *States at War*, 218–20.

83. *Cadiz Democratic Sentinel*, June 3, 1863.

13. RISING ABOVE THE POLITICAL MUCK, MAY 1863–JULY 1863

1. *Portage County Democrat*, May 20, 1863.

2. *Delaware Gazette*, June 19, 1863; *Ohio Democrat*, June 5, 1863.

3. *Daily Ohio Statesman*, Apr. 17, 1863. The Act "allows the transfer of the case of all persons suing the parties thus arresting them, from the State Courts to the US Courts." Flamen Ball, US district attorney for Ohio's Southern District, applied for an "allowance of a writ of peremptory mandamus, to compel the Court of Common Pleas of [Fairfield] County to make an order for the removal to the Circuit Court of the United States, within and for the Southern District of Ohio." In part the application was made based upon Tod acting as an agent for the secretary of war, whose conduct was sanctioned by a previous standing act of Congress. Therefore, Ball maintained that Van Trump refused Tod's right to have the case removed from the state court to a federal court. See *State of Ohio, Ex. Rel. David Tod v. Circuit of Common Pleas of Fairfield Co., O.*, brief in behalf of relator, by Flamen Ball, attorney, US, December Term, 1863.

4. *Cleveland Morning Leader*, June 3, 1863.

5. Engle, *Gathering*, 282.
6. *Daily Ohio Statesman*, June 12, 1863 ; *M'arthur Democrat*, June 18, 1863.
7. *M'arthur Democrat*, July 9, 1863.
8. Pugh's comments were made at the Ohio Democratic Convention and printed in the *Democrat and Sentinel*, courtesy of the *New York Daily News*.
9. *Weekly Perrysburg Journal*, May 20, 1863.
10. Blue, *Salmon P. Chase*, 213.
11. *Delaware Gazette*, June 19, 1863.
12. Tod's order is dated June 16, 1863. It was reprinted in the *National Tribune*, June 11, 1908.
13. Stephen E. Towne, "Lesson for Rebels," 303.
14. *Wyandot Pioneer*, May 29, 1863.
15. Randall and Ryan, *History of Ohio*, 181.
16. Engle, *Gathering*, 303.
17. *Wyandot Pioneer*, May 29, 1863.
18. *Cadiz Democratic Sentinel*, July 1, 1863.
19. *Daily Ohio Statesman*, June 18, 1863.
20. *Fremont Journal*, June 26, 1863.
21. *Western Reserve Chronicle*, June 3, 1863.
22. *Ashtabula Weekly Telegraph*, May 9, 1863.
23. Engle, *Gathering*, 310 and Howbert, 288.
24. George H. Porter, "Ohio Politics," 93, 110.
25. Letter of Capt. D. C. Wadsworth, of Co. C, 24th OVI, published in the *Fremont Journal*, May 15, 1863.
26. Harold L. Naragon, "Ohio Gubernatorial," 23–24.
27. Nivens, *Salmon P. Chase Papers*, vol. 1, 66–67.
28. Roseboom, *History of Ohio*, 417.
29. Powell. *Democratic Party of Ohio*, 179, 147.
30. Porter. "Ohio Politics," 114.
31. Dell, *Lincoln and War Democrats*, 244.
32. Blue, *Salmon P. Chase*, 212.
33. Powell, *The Democratic Party*, 147; *Governors of Ohio*, 83–85.
34. Naragon, *Ohio Gubernatorial*, 24–26.
35. *Cleveland Morning Leader*, June 19, 1863; *Jefferson Democrat*, June 26, 1863.
36. Naragon, *Ohio Gubernatorial*, 26.
37. Printed in *Cleveland Morning Leader*, June 23, 1863.
38. *Fremont Journal*, June 26, 1863.
39. Wright, "Hon. David Tod," 123.
40. *Democratic Press*, July 9, 1863.
41. Both newspapers quoted in *Cadiz Democratic Sentinel*, July 1, 1863.
42. Hesseltine, *Lincoln and War Governors*, 331–32.
43. Naragon, *Ohio Gubernatorial*, 27.

44. MR1864P1, Governor Tod to His Excellency, John A. Andrews, Governor, Boston, Mass., June 22, 1863. All other quotes in this paragraph from Lincoln to Tod, June 18, 1863. *The Collected Works of Abraham Lincoln,* volume 6, 287.

45. John Tod, *Some Account,* 117.

46. Klement, *Limits,* 238.

47. Miller, *States at War,* 223–24.

48. *Cleveland Morning Leader,* June 29, 1863, and quoted in Naragon, *Ohio Gubernatorial,* 29.

49. *Lancaster Gazette,* June 25, 1863.

50. *Daily Ohio Statesman,* Sept. 16, 1863.

51. Engle, *Gathering,* 306

52. MR1864P1, Governor Tod to Hon E. M. Stanton, Secretary of War, Apr. 28, 1863; Governor Tod to Major General Burnside, June 23, 1863; A. E. Burnside to Governor Tod, July 6, 1863.

53. Lester V. Horwitz, *Longest Raid,* 173; *Cleveland Morning Leader,* Aug. 10, 1863; Miller, States at War, 232.

54. *Weekly Perrysburg Journal,* June 17, 1863.

55. *Delaware Gazette,* June 26, 1863.

56. *Cleveland Morning Leader,* June 29, 1863.

57. Quoted in Hesseltine, *Lincoln and War Governors,* 296.

58. Stackpole. *They Met,* 269. Meade suffered a severe wound at the Battle of Glendale on June 30, 1862.

59. MR1864P1, Governor Tod to Major General U. S. Grant, Vicksburg, Miss., July 23, 1863.

60. MR1864P1, Governor Tod to Governor Andrew G. Curtin, July 6, 1863. Curtin declined the offer of help.

61. *Daily Ohio Statesman,* June 23, 1863. Quotation is from MR1864P1, Governor Tod to John H. Young, Urbana, Ohio, July 5, 1863.

62. *Crisis,* July 11, 1863.

63. *Democratic Press,* July 16, 1863.

64. Miller, *States at War,* 233–34.

65. Towne, *Surveillance and Spies,* 112. Quotation is from MR1864P1, Governor Tod to Major W. T. Sherman, Mar. 1, 1863.

66. *Fremont Journal,* July 17, 1863.

67. MR1864P1, A. E. Burnside to Governor Tod, July 12, 1863, O. P. Morton, Governor of Indiana to Governor David Tod, July 13, 1863, A. E. Burnside to Governor Tod, July 14, 1863, C. Carpenter to Governor Tod, July 17, 1863.

68. Miller, *States at War,* 233–34.

69. MR1864P1, G. W. Neff, Lt. Col. Comd'g, to Governor Tod, July 14, 1863.

70. MR1864P1., Governor Tod to F. W. Bingham, July 18, 1863.

71. MR1864P1, B. F. Kelley, Brig. Gen. to Governor Tod, June 24, 1863; MR1864P1, B. F. Kelley, Brig. Gen. to Governor Tod, July 15, 1863.

72. Lester V. Horwitz, 256, 258, 264, 291, 297.
73. Towne, *Surveillance and Spies*, 113.
74. *Belmont Chronicle*, Aug. 6, 1863.
75. Miller, *States at War*, 234.
76. Horowitz, *Longest Raid*, 333–35, 346, 354; MR1864P1, Governor Tod to Major General Burnside, July 27, 1863.
77. *Ohio Democrat*, July 31, 1863, Aug. 7, 1863.
78. Miller, *States at War*, 255.
79. *Belmont Chronicle*, Aug. 6, 1863.
80. MR1864P1, Governor Tod to Edwin Stanton, Aug. 14, 1863; *Cleveland Morning Leader*, Aug. 25, 1863.

14. A CRUMB OF COMFORT, AUGUST 1863–DECEMBER 1863

1. Quarles, *The Negro*, 235.
2. Gallman, *North Fights*, 23.
3. *Cleveland Morning Leader*, Aug. 14, 1863.
4. Wright, "Hon. David Tod," 119–20.
5. Butler, *Memorandum*, 13.
6. Wright, "Hon. David Tod," 119–20.
7. McBride. *Lincoln's Body Guard*; 5, 20, 21; Kallina, "George Ashmun," 1–3. Quotation is from Tod to the military committee of _____ County, Nov. 5, 1863, MR1864P1.
8. References to *Lorain County News* and *Crisis* are reprinted in *Cadiz Democratic Sentinel*, Aug. 12, 1863.
9. Miller, *States at War*, 236, 237, 238.
10. Quarles, *The Negro*, 29.
11. Ira F. Mansfield. *Ohio and Pennsylvania*, 191.
12. Speech of Hon. C. A. Trimble, in the House of Representatives, Jan. 31, 1863, printed in *Highland Weekly News*, Mar. 12, 1863. Little did Trimble and others know that free Black people as spies were being used by the federal government. Waller, *Lincoln's Spies*, offers a fresh and comprehensive study of covert operations.
13. White's speech was delivered on the floor of the House of Representatives on February 2, 1863. Printed in *Columbia Democrat and Bloomberg General Advertiser*, Feb. 28, 1863.
14. Quarles, *The Negro*, 30, 31, 64, 107.
15. *Cleveland Morning Leader*, Apr. 29, 1863; *Tiffin Weekly*, May 22, 1863.
16. Douglas R. Egerton. *Thunder*, 72; *Western Reserve Chronicle*, May 20, 1863.
17. Quoted in Reid, *Ohio in War*, vol. 1, 176.
18. *Urbana Union*, May 13, 1863.
19. *Cadiz Democratic Sentinel*, June 3, 1863.

20. Comments by Congressman Chilton A. White, *Columbia Democrat and Bloomberg General Advertiser,* Feb. 28, 1863.
21. MR1864P1, Governor Tod to Jacob T. Johnson, Esq., Circleville, Ohio, June 15, 1863.
22. *Cleveland Morning Leader,* June 25, 1863, July 4, 1863.
23. MR1864P1, Governor Tod to Capt. Lewis McCoy, June 18, 1863.
24. MR1864P1, Governor Tod to His Excellency John A. Andrew, Governor, Boston, Mass., June 22, 1863.
25. Egerton. *Thunder.*
26. *Cleveland Morning Leader,* June 25, 1863, July 4, 1863.
27. Quarles, *The Negro,* 200.
28. Abraham Lincoln Papers, Governor David Tod to Edwin M. Stanton, June 27, 1863.
29. *Ashtabula Weekly Telegraph,* May 23, 1863; MR1864P1, Governor Tod to the State of Ohio, Executive Department_____, 1863, Order No. 143, Governor Tod to the People of Ohio, June 22, 1863, E. M. Stanton, Secretary of War to Governor Tod, June 26, 1863.
30. *Cleveland Morning Leader,* June 24, 1863, July 4, 1863.
31. *Cleveland Morning Leader,* June 29, 1863; *Highland Weekly News,* July 23, 1864.
32. Abraham Lincoln Papers, Governor David Tod to Edwin M. Stanton, June 27, 1863.
33. MR1864P1, Governor Tod to Messrs. Charles J. Starks and Others, Colored Regiment, Delaware, Ohio, July 17, 1863, Governor Tod to Edwin Stanton, Aug. 14, 1863, Governor Tod to C. W. Foster, A.A.G., Washington, D.C., Sept. 22, 1863, MR1864P1.
34. Quoted in Cheek and Cheek, *John Mercer Langston,* 397, 401.
35. Printed in *Ohio Democrat,* June 5, 1863.
36. *Cleveland Morning Leader,* June 25, 1863, Aug. 21, 1863.
37. Printed in the *Delaware Gazette,* June 19, 1863.
38. *Cleveland Morning Leader,* Oct. 22, 1863, and Nov. 12, 1863. The quotes that include "privilege," "fatherly counsel," "roar," and "verily" are found in Cheek and Cheek, *John Mercer Langston,* 407.
39. Quarles, *The Negro,* 193.
40. *Daily Ohio Statesman,* Oct. 7, 1863.
41. Rawley, *Politics of Union,* 121.
42. Trester, "Political Career," 196–98.
43. *Western Reserve Chronicle,* Aug. 5, 1863.
44. *Hancock Jeffersonian,* July 17, 1863.
45. MR1864P1, Governor Tod to Lt. Col. Durbin Ward, 17 Regt., OVI, Sept. 17, 1863.
46. *Columbus Journal,* printed in *Fremont Journal,* Sept. 25, 1863.
47. Jennifer Weber, *Copperheads,* 122.
48. *Hancock Jeffersonian,* July 17, 1863.

49. Quoted in Engle, *Gathering*, 338.

50. The vote totals in this and the preceding paragraph are from Miller, *States at War*, 240 and Trester, "Political Career," 201.

51. Klement, *Limits of Dissent*, 252.

52. *Belmont Chronicle*, Oct. 29, 1863.

53. Roseboom writes in *History of Ohio*, 421, that the telegram was sent to Brough. Others note Tod as the recipient. Author David Dixon notes in *Lost Gettysburg Address* that though the telegram has been referenced ad nauseam by historians it is not found among Lincoln's letters (151). That Lincoln was extremely concerned about the elections in Ohio and Pennsylvania is fact. Dixon also states that Lincoln responded to Tod. See *Spirit of Democracy*, Nov. 4, 1863, for charges of fraud.

54. Engle, *Gathering*, 339, 340, 351.

55. *Ashtabula Weekly Telegraph*, Aug. 15, 1863.

56. MVHS, Tod to Henry Tod, Sept. 6, 1863.

57. MVHS, Tod to Henry Tod, July 5, 1863.

58. *Cleveland Morning Leader*, Oct. 19, 20, 1863.

59. MR1864P1, James B. Fry, Provost Marshal General to Governor Tod, Oct. 25, 1863; *Fremont Journal*, Oct. 30, 1863.

60. MR1864P1, Governor Tod to Capt. F. A. Nash, Cleveland, Ohio, Nov. 7, 1863, Governor Tod to Col. Geo. W. McCook, Steubenville, Ohio, Oct. 28, 1863. See also Guelzo, *Fateful Lightning*, 458–59.

61. *Western Reserve Chronicle*. Nov. 18, 1863; *Weekly Ottumwa Courier*, Nov. 26, 1863; *Jeffersonian Democrat*, Nov. 20, 1863.

62. *Cleveland Morning Leader*, Nov. 16, 1863.

63. *Cleveland Herald*, quoted in *Western Reserve Chronicle*, Nov. 18, 1863.

64. *Jeffersonian Democrat*, Nov. 20, 1863.

65. *Western Reserve Chronicle*, Nov. 18, 1863.

66. *Cleveland Morning Leader*, Nov. 16, 1863.

67. *Weekly Ottumwa Courier*, Nov. 26, 1863; Miller, *States at War*, 242; *Western Reserve Chronicle*, Nov. 18, 1863.

68. Miller, *States at War*, 242–43; *Weekly Ottumwa Courier*, Nov. 26, 1863.

69. Miller, *States at War*, 240.

70. *Lancaster Gazette*, Oct. 29, 1863; MR1864P1, Governor Tod to D. W. Brown, Esq., Oct. 25, 1863.

71. Dixon, *Lost Gettysburg Address*, 152–53; MR1864P1, Governor Tod to Col. Charles Anderson, Dayton, Ohio, Oct. 27, 1863.

72. Baumgartner, *Buckeye Blood*, 207.

73. *Highland Weekly News*, Nov. 26, 1863.

74. Baumgartner, *Buckeye Blood*, 209, 210.

75. Dixon, *Lost Gettysburg Address*, 156–57, 161.

76. First quotation printed in *Western Reserve Chronicle*, Nov. 11, 1863; the second quotation is printed in *Ashland Union*, Nov. 18, 1863.

77. *Portage County Democrat*, Nov. 18, 1863.
78. MR1864P1, Governor Tod to Military Committee of _____ County, Nov. 7, 1863.
79. *Cleveland Tri-Weekly Leader*, Nov. 17, 1863.
80. *Western Reserve Chronicle*, Dec. 2, 1863.
81. Horwitz, *Longest Raid*, 356–65.
82. MR1864P1, William Wallace, Col. 15th O.V.I., Com'dg to Brig. Gen. John S. Mason, Nov. 28, 1863, Nathaniel Merion, Warden to Col. Wm. Wallace, Nov. 28, 1863; MR1864P1, Tod quotation from Governor Tod to Nathaniel Merion, Warden of Penitentiary, Dec. 11, 1863; *Western Reserve Chronicle*, Dec. 2, 1863.

15. SHIN PLASTER AND POT METAL, JANUARY 1864–JUNE 1864

1. MVHS, Tod to Dear Mother, Jan. 7, 1864.
2. *Daily Ohio Statesman*, Jan. 5, 1864.
3. *Cleveland Morning Leader*, Jan. 5, 1864.
4. *Daily Ohio Statesman*, Mar. 11, 1864.
5. *Western Reserve Chronicle*, Aug. 5, 1863, June 3, 1863.
6. Reid, *Ohio in the War*, vol. 1, 172.
7. Wright, "Hon. David Tod," 114.
8. *Western Reserve Chronicle*, Jan. 6, 1864.
9. *Daily Ohio Statesman*, Jan. 3, 1864.
10. *Cleveland Morning Leader*, Jan. 13, 1864.
11. *Urbana Union*, Jan. 13, 1864.
12. Wright, "Hon. David Tod," 113, 116.
13. Wright, "Hon. David Tod," 113, 116.
14. Perret, *Ulysses S. Grant*, 206.
15. Reid, *Ohio in the War*, vol. 1, 179.
16. Wright, "Hon. David Tod," 115, 122.
17. Neely, *Fate of Liberty*, 113; Wright, "Hon. David Tod," 115–16.
18. Wright, "Hon. David Tod," 115.
19. Reid, *Ohio in the War*, vol. 1, 177, 178, 179.
20. MR1864P1, David Tod to Rosella Rice, Jan. 24, 1863, and Governor Tod to C. L. Boult, Apr. 28, 1863.
21. Reid, *Ohio in the War*, vol. 1, 181.
22. Reid, *Ohio in the War*, vol. 1, 181.
23. Engle, *Gathering*, 351.
24. *Cleveland Morning Leader*, Jan. 13, 1864.
25. Wright, "Hon. David Tod," 109.
26. *Cleveland Morning Leader*, Oct. 19, 1863.
27. *Cleveland Morning Leader*, Jan. 5, 1864.
28. *Cadiz Sentinel*, June 22, 1864.

29. *Daily Ohio Statesman*, Jan. 5, 1864.

30. John Tod, *Some Account*, 135, 139, 149.

31. Butler, *History of Youngstown*, vol. 2, 221.

32. Blue, *Salmon P. Chase*, 223-24.

33. *Daily Ohio Statesman*, June 9, 1864; *Urbana Union*, June 15, 1864.

34. *Delaware Gazette*, June 17, 1864.

35. *Cadiz Sentinel*, June 22, 1864.

36. *Cleveland Morning Leader*, June 30, 1864.

37. Lincoln to Chase, June 28, 1864; 408, Chase to Lincoln, June 29, 1864; 409, Lincoln to Chase, June 30, 1864, 411; Nivens, *Salmon P. Chase Papers*, vol. 1, *Journals, 1829-1872*.

38. Lincoln to Tod, June 30, 1864, *Collected Works of Abraham Lincoln, volume 7*, 420. Also, *Telegram from President Abraham Lincoln to David Tod of Youngstown, Ohio Nominating Him as Secretary of Treasury, June 30, 1864*, National Archives.

39. *Wyandot Pioneer*, Dec. 3, 1868, William H. Seward to George B. Senter, Nov. 17, 1868. . Seward was paying tribute to Tod, who had died the previous month.

40. Bates, Howard K. Beale,Ragatz, *Diary of Edward Bates*. Entry is from July 1, 1864, 381.

41. *Diary of Gideon Welles*, 62.

42. Nicolay and Hay, "Abraham Lincoln," 295.

43. *Salmon P. Chase Papers: Diaries*, June 24-July 6, 1864..

44. Blue, *Salmon P. Chase*, 170.

45. *Cleveland Morning Leader*, Oct. 2, 1861.

46. Published in *Daily Ohio Statesman*, July 4, 1864.

47. Hearn, *Lincoln*, 228.

48. Noah Brooks, "Lincoln, Chase, and Grant," 612.

49. *Daily Ohio Statesman*, July 4, 1864.

50. *Saint Paul Press*, July 1, 1864 and, *Cleveland Morning Leader*, July 1, 1864.

51. *New York Herald*, July 1, 1864.

52. *Cleveland Morning Leader*, July 1, 1864.

53. Roger Lowenstein, *Ways and Means*, 285. Lowenstein's study is a critical contribution to the history of the financing of the Civil War, led by Salmon P. Chase's financial strategy. However, his two-word criticism of Tod is based solely on Welles's June 30, 1864, diary entry. See endnote #285 in Lowenstein's book.

54. *Spirit of Democracy*, July 20, 1864.

55. *Evening Star*, June 30, 1864.

56. Quoted in Rice, *Reminiscences*, 62.

57. Quoted in Hearn, *Lincoln*, 228.

58. *Daily Register*, July 1, 1864.

59. *Cleveland Morning Leader*, Oct. 2, 1861.

60. *Daily Ohio Statesman*, July 6, 1864.

61. *Diary of Gideon Welles*, vol. 1, 62.

62. *New York Times*, July 1, 1864.

63. Nicolay and Hay, "Abraham Lincoln," 296.
64. Current, "Lincoln's Plan; *American Heritage*, Vol. 6, Issue 4, June 1955; *Daily Ohio Statesman*, July 4, 1864.
65. Heron, *Profiles; Daily Ohio Statesman*, July 4, 1864.
66. Heron, *Profiles*, 73.
67. Current, "Lincoln's Plan."
68. Butler to R. J. Kaylor, memorandum, Oct. 11, 1924, vertical files on David Tod, Public Library of Youngstown and Mahoning County, Ohio, 14. *Memorandum for R. J. Kaylor*, 14. See page 404.
69. Tod to Lincoln, June 30, 1864, *Collected Works of Abraham Lincoln*, vol. 7, 420.
70. Dell, *Lincoln*, 299–300.
71. *Salmon P. Chase Papers*, June 24–July 6, 1864.
72. *Harper's Weekly*, July 16, 1864.

16. THE CONDITION OF MY CROPS, JULY 1864–DECEMBER 1865

1. Flood, *1864*, 281.
2. *Cleveland Morning Leader*, Sept. 19, 1864.
3. *Cleveland Morning Leader*, Oct. 1, 1864. Tod was scheduled to stop at Alliance on Oct. 1, and Mansfield on Oct. 4.
4. Butler, *Recollections*, 304.
5. Quoted in Trester, "Political Career," 206.
6. Quoted in Trester, "Political Career," 207.
7. *Portage Sentinel*, Sept. 11, 1856.
8. *Cleveland Morning Leader*, Aug. 17, 1863.
9. *Cleveland Morning Leader*, Sept. 19, 1864.
10. *Western Reserve Chronicle*, Sept. 21, 1864.
11. *Lancaster Gazette*, Sept. 29, 1864, quoted in *Cleveland Morning Leader*, Oct. 15, 1864
12. Flood, *1864*, 274–79, 377.
13. Waugh, *Lincoln*, 191, 202.
14. MR1864P1, Governor Tod to Col. B. F. Potts, 32d Reg't OVI, June 29, 1863. For more information on the Union's military policy, particularly during the invasion of the South during the closing days of the Civil War, see Mark Grimsley's *Hard Hand;* Mark E. Neely Jr., *Civil War;* Noah Andre Trudeau, *Southern Storm*.
15. Lester V. Horwitz, *Longest Raid*, 372–73.
16. *Tiffin Weekly Tribune*, Feb. 9, 1865. See also Butler, *History of Youngstown*, for a broad history of Tod's business undertakings.
17. *Dayton Daily Empire*, Mar. 17, 1865.
18. *Highland Weekly News*, Apr. 13, 1865.
19. *Cleveland Leader*, Apr. 17, 1865.
20. *Governors of Ohio*, 85.

21. *Cleveland Leader*, May 11, 1865.
22. *Fremont Journal*, Sept. 8, 1865.
23. *Jeffersonian Democrat*, Aug. 25, 1865.
24. *Dayton Daily Empire*, Mar. 17, 1865.
25. *Cadiz Sentinel*, Sept. 27, 1865.
26. *Cleveland Morning Leader*, Mar. 9, 1865.
27. *Cleveland Leader*, Aug. 16, 1865.
28. *Jeffersonian Democrat*, Aug. 25, 1865.
29. Charles W. Hanna, *African American Recipients*, 16, 17.
30. *Belmont Chronicle*, July 11, 1867.
31. Eric Foner, *Second Founding*, 40–41.
32. *Governors of Ohio*, 85–86.
33. *Ashtabula Weekly Telegraph*, Sept. 9, 1865.
34. Trester, "Political Career," 213.
35. *Cadiz Sentinel*, Aug. 9, 1865.
36. Tod to George B. Wright, May 27, 1865, printed in *Daily Ohio Statesman*, June 1, 1865.
37. *Cadiz Sentinel*, Aug. 9, 1865.
38. *Fremont Journal*, Sept. 22, 1865.
39. *New York Herald*, Sept. 30, 1865.
40. Tod to George B. Wright, May 27, 1865, printed in *Daily Ohio Statesman*, June 1, 1865.

17. DUTIES DISCHARGED, 1866–1868

1. Butler, *Recollections*, 298.
2. *Ashland Union*, May 9, 1866; *Cleveland Daily Leader*, Apr. 19, 1866.
3. *Gallipolis Journal*, Apr. 26, 1866; *Cleveland Daily Leader*, Apr. 7, 1866.
4. *Wyandot Pioneer*, Apr. 18, 1867.
5. *Belmont Chronicle*, Sept. 10, 1868.
6. *Belmont Chronicle*, July 11, 1867. The second incident is related in a letter from David Tod to Dr. James Williams, in Columbus, Ohio, Aug. 16, 1867, Ohio History Connection Notes, MSS 8277. The Republicans nominated Rutherford B. Hayes, who went on to defeat the Democratic nominee, Allen G. Thurman.
7. *Belmont Chronicle*, July 11, 1867.
8. *Fremont Journal*, Apr. 27, 1866.
9. Jean H. Baker, *Affairs of Party*, 183.
10. Ronald C. White Jr., *A. Lincoln*, examines Lincoln's increasing acceptance of religion and God in his life and the life and fate of the nation. See pages 180–82, 512, 523, which touch upon examples of Lincoln's coming to accept God's role in the war and the trials of the war-torn country.
11. Galloway, *Eulogy*.

12. Abbott, *Ohio's Civil War Governors*, 46.
13. Eric Foner, *Reconstruction*, 276–77.
14. *Belmont Chronicle*, July 11, 1867.
15. *Belmont Chronicle*, July 11, 1867.
16. *Fremont Journal*, Apr. 27, 1866.
17. Aley, *Heritage to Share*, 82–83.
18. Blue, Jenkins, Lawson, and Reedy. *Mahoning Memories*, 38. Wilson, *African American Architects*. Quotation in this paragraph is from *Western Reserve Chronicle*, Mar. 4, 1868.
19. *Daily Ohio Statesman*, Mar. 5, 1868.
20. *Daily Ohio Statesman*, Feb. 29, 1868.
21. Aley, *Heritage to Share*, 83.
22. Butler, *History of Youngstown*, vol. 1, 278.
23. Quotes are from the *Wyandot Pioneer*, June 18, 1868, and *Western Reserve Chronicle*, June 10, 1868.
24. *Lancaster Gazette*, Nov. 19, 1868.
25. Brooks D. Simpson, *Let Us Have Peace*, 248.
26. *Belmont Chronicle*, Sept. 10, 1868.
27. *Western Reserve Chronicle*, Sept. 2, 1868.
28. *Mahoning Register*, Sept. 17, 1868.
29. *Western Reserve Chronicle*, Sept. 9, 1868, Oct. 21, 1868.
30. *Cleveland Leader*, Sept. 11, 1868.
31. *Daily Ohio Statesman*, July 23, 1868.
32. *Lancaster Gazette*, Nov. 19, 1868.
33. *Stark County Democrat*, Nov. 18, 1868.
34. Wright, "Hon. David Tod," 124.
35. *New York Tribune*, May 25, 1868.
36. Oates, *Woman of Valor*, 48–49, 166, 274, 309.
37. Gansler, *Sarah Emma Edmonds*, 203, 219.
38. See Faust, This *Republic of Suffering*. Of the more than 650,000 deaths, 30,000 troops succumbed to malaria. See *Civil War Diseases*, found in CivilWarAcademy.com (accessed Apr. 5, 2022).
39. *Daily Ohio Statesman*, Nov. 16, 1868.
40. *Fremont Weekly Journal*, Nov. 20, 1868; *Democratic Press*, Nov. 19, 1868.
41. Galloway, *Eulogy*. Galloway said that these observations were made "but a few hours before" Tod's death.
42. *Democratic Press*, Nov. 19, 1868; *Western Reserve Chronicle*, Nov. 18, 1868. The trial noted was the case of *Hutchins v. Curtis & Boyee*. The article reported that Tod had been a witness in the case in the court of common pleas of Trumbull County the day before, which testifies to his presence and appearance in Warren on November 12, 1868, one day before his death.
43. *Belmont Chronicle*, Nov. 19, 1868.
44. *Western Reserve Chronicle*, Nov. 18, 1868.

45. *Fremont Weekly Journal*, Nov. 20, 1868; *Daily Ohio Statesman*, Nov. 14, 1868.
46. *Hancock Jeffersonian*, Nov. 20, 1868.
47. *Hancock Jeffersonian*, Nov. 20, 1868.
48. *Western Reserve Chronicle*, Dec. 9, 1868.
49. *Western Reserve Chronicle*, Nov. 18, 1868.
50. Quotation by State Senator William Stedman in *Western Reserve Chronicle*, Dec. 9, 1868.
51. *Western Reserve Chronicle*, Nov. 18, 1868.
52. *Vindicator*, Mar. 19, 1938.
53. *Western Reserve Chronicle*, Nov. 18, 1868.
54. Printed in the *Wyandot Pioneer*, Nov. 19, 1868.
55. Galloway, *Eulogy*, and quoted in John S. C. Abbot, "Lives of the Governors."
56. Galloway, *Eulogy*.
57. Mansfield, diary entry from Camp Taylor, Cleveland, OH, June 8, 1865; Mansfield, *Reminiscences*, 191.
58. Quoted in *Indiana American*, Dec. 4, 1868.
59. Quoted in the *Richmond Palladium*, Nov. 24, 1868.
60. *Wyandot Pioneer*, Nov. 19, 1868.
61. *New York Times*, Nov. 14, 1868.
62. William Seward to George B. Senter, Nov. 17, 1868, printed in the *Wyandot Pioneer*, Dec. 3, 1868.
63. *Belmont Chronicle*, Dec. 17, 1868.
64. *States and Union*, Nov. 18, 1868.
65. *Stark County Democrat*, Dec. 23, 1868, and Dec. 2, 1868.
66. *Democratic Press*, Nov. 19, 1868; *Western Reserve Chronicle*, Nov. 18, 1868. Galloway was the judge advocate at Camp Chase during the war. During Reconstruction, he was asked by President Andrew Johnson to investigate various conditions in the South.
67. Wright, "Hon. David Tod," 125. The *Ashtabula Weekly Telegraph* of November 21, 1868, put the number of mourners at "about 15,000."
68. Printed in the *Hancock Jeffersonian*, Nov. 20, 1868. Engines "draped in mourning" from *Western Reserve Chronicle*, Nov. 18, 1868.
69. *Western Reserve Chronicle*, Nov. 18, 1868.
70. *Hancock Jeffersonian*, Nov. 20, 1868.
71. MVHS, Tod to Dear Mother, Jan. 7, 1864. The letter was likely written to Maria.
72. *Spirit of Democracy*, Nov. 2, 1869.

EPILOGUE

1. *Western Reserve Chronicle*, Dec. 9, 1868. In today's value, one half of $1million dollars is worth more than $8,800,000.
2. John Tod, *Some Account*, 122.

3. *Democratic Press*, Dec. 16, 1869, and *Western Reserve Chronicle*, Dec. 15, 1869.
4. *Western Reserve Chronicle*, June 12, 1872.
5. *Mahoning Dispatch*, Nov. 27, 1908.
6. John Tod, *Some Account*, 135, 139, 149–50, 165.
7. *Western Reserve Chronicle*, Jan. 13, 1869, Oct. 13, 1868.
8. *Highland Weekly News*, Oct. 7, 1869.
9. *Speeches and Addresses of William McKinley*, 566.
10. *Rock Island Argus*, July 5, 1895; "Soldiers' and Sailors' Monument," *Encyclopedia of Cleveland History*, Case Western Reserve University, https://case.edu/ech/; *Brief Historical Sketch of the Cuyahoga County Soldiers' and Sailors' Monument. Complete Description of the Memorial Structure. Dedication Programme*, Cuyahoga County Soldiers' and Sailors' Monument Commission (Cleveland, OH), 1896.
11. *Omaha Daily Bee*, Feb. 18, 1909.
12. *Point Pleasant Register*, Nov. 17, 1909.
13. *Mahoning Dispatch*, Apr. 22, 1910. The estate passed into the hands of George Tod.
14. *Mahoning Dispatch*, July 1, 1910, and Feb. 23, 1912.
15. *Western Reserve Chronicle*, Nov. 18, 1868.
16. Galloway, *Eulogy*.

Bibliography

MANUSCRIPT COLLECTIONS

Buchanan, James. *James Buchanan, His Doctrines and Policy Exhibited by Himself and Friends.* Collection of Univ. of Illinois, Urbana-Champaign. Original publication date, 1856.

Buchanan, James. *Memoir of James Buchanan, of Pennsylvania: Democratic Party (PA).* Library of Congress Collection. Philadelphia: C. Sherman and Son, Philadelphia, 1856.

Calhoun, John C. *The Papers of John C. Calhoun.* Columbia: Univ. of South Carolina Press, 1996.

Chase, Salmon P. *Salmon P. Chase Papers, 1755–1898, Diaries, 1829–1870.* Library of Congress, Manuscript Division, online format.

Grant, U. S. *Personal Memoirs of U. S. Grant, in Two Volumes.* New York: Bonanza Boks, 1885 (facsimile of 1885 original edition, published by Charles L. Webster and Co.).

Lincoln, Abraham, The Collected Works of. 9 vols. Abraham Lincoln Association. New York: Rutgers Univ. Press, 1953.

Nivens, John, ed. *The Salmon P. Chase Papers.* Vol. 1, *Journals, 1829–1872.* Kent, OH: Kent State Univ. Press, 1994.

———. *The Salmon P. Chase Papers.* Vol. 2, *Correspondence, 1823–1857.* Kent, OH: Kent State Univ. Press, Kent, Ohio, 1994.

Ohio History Connection Notes, MSS 8277.

Polk, James K., Paper, series 2, *General Correspondence and Related Items, 1775–1849; 1844, Nov. 18–Dec. 11.* Washington, DC: Library of Congress, image 821.

Quaife, Milo Milton, ed. *The Diary of James K. Polk during His Presidency, 1845–1849: Now Printed from the Original Manuscript in the Collections of the Chicago Historical Society.* Vol. 1. (Chicago: A. C. McClurg, 1910).

Telegram from President Abraham Lincoln to David Tod of Youngstown, Ohio, Nominating Him as Secretary of Treasury, June 30, 1864. Washington, DC: National Archives.

Tod, David. *Ohio Governors Papers,* Jan. 13, 1862–Jan. 11, 1864.

Tod, David, Papers, Ohio History Connection, MSS 306.

NEWSPAPERS

Abbeville (SC) Press and Banner
Alexandria Gazette (Washington, DC)
Anti-Slavery Bugle
Ashland (OH) Union
Ashtabula (OH) Weekly
Ashtabula (OH) Weekly Telegraph
Belmont Chronicle (St. Clairsville, OH)
Cadiz (OH) Democratic Sentinel
Canton (OH) Republican
Carroll Free Press (Carrolton, OH)
Chardon (OH) Democrat
Chicago Daily Tribune.
Cincinnati Daily Press
Cleveland Daily Leader
Cleveland Leader
Cleveland Morning Leader
Cleveland Plain Dealer
Columbia Democrat and Bloomberg General Advertiser (Bloomberg, PA)
Coon Dissector (Dayton, OH)
Crisis (Columbus OH)
Daily Commonwealth (Frankfort, KY)
Daily Evansville (IN) Journal
Daily Exchange (Baltimore, MD)
Daily Ohio Statesman
Daily Union (Washington, DC)
Dayton Daily Empire
Delaware (OH) Gazette
Democrat and Sentinel (Ebensburg, PA)
Democratic Pioneer (Upper Sandusky, OH)
Democratic Press (Ravenna, OH)
Des Moines Courier

Eaton (OH) Democrat
Evening Star (Washington, DC)
Fremont Journal (Sandusky County, OH)
Gallipolis (OH) Journal
Hancock Jeffersonian (Findley, OH)
Highland Weekly News (Hillsborough, OH)
Holmes County Farmer
Holmes County Republican
Indiana American (Brookville, IN)
Jeffersonian Democrat (Chardon, OH)
Kalida (OH) Venture
Lancaster (OH) Gazette
Lorain County News
Mahoning Dispatch (Youngstown, OH)
Mahoning Register (Youngstown, OH)
Mahoning Sentinel (Youngstown, OH)
Marshall County Republican (Plymouth, IN)
M'arthur Democrat (Vinton County, OH)
Maumee City (OH) Express
Meigs County Telegraph (Pomeroy, OH)
Mountain Sentinel (Ebensburg, PA)
National Era (Washington, DC)
National Tribune (Washington, DC)
National Whig (Washington, DC)
New York Daily News
New York Daily Tribune
New York Herald
New York Times
Ohio Democrat (New Philadelphia, OH)
Ohio Democrat and Dover Advertiser (Canal Dover, OH)
Ohio Star (Ravenna, OH)
Ohio State Journal (Columbus, OH)
Ohio Statesman (Columbus, OH)
Omaha (NE) Daily Bee
Perrysburg (OH) Journal
Point Pleasant (WV) Register
Pomeroy Weekly Telegraph (Meigs County, Ohio)
Portage County (OH) Democrat
Portage Sentinel
Portland (ME) Daily Press
Richmond (VA) Enquirer
Richmond (IN) Palladium
Rock Island (IL) Argus

Saint Paul (MN) Press
Somerset (PA) Herald
Spirit of Democracy (Woodsfield, OH)
Stark County (OH) Democrat
States and Union (Ashland, OH)
Tiffin (OH) Weekly Tribune
True American (Steubenville, OH)
Trumbull Democrat (Warren, OH)
Urbana (OH) Union
Vindicator (Youngstown, OH)
Weekly Ottumwa (IA) Courier
Weekly Perrysburg (OH) Journal
Weekly Portage Sentinel
Western Reserve Chronicle (Warren, OH)
Whig Standard (Washington, DC)
Wyandot Pioneer (Upper Sandusky, OH)
Yorkville Enquirer (York, SC)

SECONDARY SOURCES (BOOKS, DISSERTATIONS, THESIS)

Abbott, John S. C. "Lives of the Governors." Chap. 42 in Ohio Statewide Files (1875). File contributed for use in USGenWeb Archives by Kay L. Mason, keziah63@yahoo.com, Jan. 23, 2012.

Abbott, Richard H. *Ohio's War Governors*. Columbus: Ohio State Univ. Press, 1962.

Aley, Howard C. *A Heritage to Share: The Bicentennial History of Youngstown and Mahoning County, Ohio. Youngstown and Mahoning County, Ohio, from Prehistoric Times to the National Bicentennial Year*. Youngstown, Ohio: Youngstown Lithographing Company, 1975.

Baker, Jean H. *Affairs of Party, the Political Culture of Northern Democrats in the Mid-Nineteenth Century*. Ithaca, NY: Cornell Univ. Press, 1983.

Baumgartner, Richard A. *Buckeye Blood: Ohio at Gettysburg*. Huntington, WV: Blue Acorn Press, 2003.

Biographical Directory of the United States Congress 1774–Present.

Biographical History of Northeastern Ohio, Embracing the Counties of Ashtabula, Trumbull and Mahoning. Chicago: Lewis Publishing Co., 1893.

Biography of George Tod, OhioLINK Finding Aid Repository, Finding Aid for the George Tod Papers 9/10/18.

Birkner, Michael, ed. *James Buchanan and the Political Crisis of the 1850s*. Selinsgrove, PA: Susquehanna Univ., 1996.

Bissland, James H. *Blood, Tears, and Glory: How Ohioans Won the Civil War*. Wilmington, OH: Orange Frazer Press, 2007.

Blue, Frederick J. *The Free Soilers: Third Party Politics 1848–54.* Urbana: Univ. of Illinois Press, 1973.

———. *No Taint of Compromise: Crusaders in Antislavery Politics,* Baton Rouge: Louisiana State Univ. Press, 2005.

———. *Salmon P. Chase: A Life in Politics.* Kent, OH: Kent State Univ. Press, 1987.

Blue, Frederick J., William D. Jenkins, H. William Lawson, and Joan M. Reedy. *Mahoning Memories: A History of Youngstown and Mahoning County.* Virginia Beach, VA: Donning Co., 1995

Borneman, Walter R. *Polk: The Man Who Transformed the Presidency and America.* New York: Random House, 2006.

Boryczka, Raymond, and Lorin Lee Cary. *No Strength without Union: An Illustrated History of Ohio Workers, 1803–1980.* Columbus: Ohio Historical Society, 1982.

Brandt, Nat. *The Town That Started the Civil War.* Syracuse, NY: Syracuse Univ. Press, 1990.

Brooks, Noah. "Lincoln, Chase, and Grant." *The Century* 49, no. 4 (Feb. 1895): 607–20.

Brown, Jeffrey P., and Andrew R. L. Cayton, eds. *The Pursuit of Public Power: Political Culture in Ohio, 1878–1861.* Kent, Ohio: Kent State Univ. Press, 1994.

Butler, Joseph G., Jr. *History of Youngstown and the Mahoning Valley, Ohio.* 3 vols. Chicago: American Historical Society, 1921.

———. *Recollections of Men and Events: An Autobiography.* New York: G. P. Putnam's Sons, 1925.

Catton, Bruce. *The Army of the Potomac: Mr. Lincoln's Army.* Garden City, NY: Doubleday and Company, 1951.

Cheek, William F., and Aimee Lee Cheek. *John Mercer Langston and the Fight for Black Freedom.* Champaign: Univ. of Illinois Press, 1989.

Crowl, Thomas. *Opdycke's Tigers in the Civil War: A History of the 125th Ohio Volunteer Infantry.* Jefferson, NC: McFarland & Co., 2019.

Current, Richard N. *The History of Wisconsin.* Vol. 2, *The Civil War Era, 1848–1873.* Madison: State Historical Society of Wisconsin, 1976.

Current, Richard N. "Lincoln's Plan for Reconstruction." *American Heritage* 6, no. 4 (June 1955).

Curtin, Michael F. *The Ohio Politics Almanac.* Kent, OH: Kent State Univ. Press, 1996.

Curtis, Michael Kent. "Lincoln, Vallandingham, and Anti-War Speech in the Civil War," 7 *Wm. & Mary Bill Rts. J.* 105 (1998). https://scholarship.llaw.wm.edu/wmborj/vo17/iss1/3.

Custis, Denis Rodgers. "Henry Alexander Wise, Minister to Brazil, 1844–1847." Master's thesis, Univ. of Richmond, 1983.

Dee, Christine, ed. *Ohio's War: The Civil War in Documents, the Civil War in the Great Interior.* Athens: Ohio Univ. Press, 2006.

Dell, Christopher. *Lincoln and the War Democrats: The Grand Erosion of Conservative Tradition.* Milwaukee, WI: Associated Univ. Presses, 1975.

DeRose, Chris. *Congressman Lincoln: The Making of America's Greatest President.* New York: Threshold Editions, 2013.

Dixon, David. *The Lost Gettysburg Address*. Santa Barbara, CA: B-List History, 2015.
Donald, David Herbert. *Charles Sumner and the Coming of the Civil War*. New York: Alfred A. Knopf, 1960.
Earle, Jonathan Halperin. *Jacksonian Antislavery and the Politics of Free Soil, 1824–1854*. Chapel Hill: Univ. of North Carolina Press, 2004.
Egerton, Douglas R. *Thunder at the Gates: The Black Civil War Regiments that Redeemed America*. New York: Basic Books, 2016.
Egle, William Henry. *Life and Times of Andrew Gregg Curtin*. Philadelphia: Thompson Publishing Co., 1896.
Engle, Stephen D. *Gathering to Save a Nation: Lincoln and the Union's War Governors*. Chapel Hill: Univ. of North Carolina Press, 2016.
Faust, Drew Gilpin. *This Republic of Suffering: Death and the American Civil War*. New York: Alfred A. Knopf, 2008.
Fehrenbacher, Don E., and Ward M. McAfee. *The Slaveholding Republic: An Account of the United States Government's Relations to Slavery*. New York: Oxford Univ. Press, 2002.
Feller, Daniel. "A Brother in Arms: Benjamin Tappan and the Antislavery Democracy." *Journal of American History* (June 2001): 48–74.
Ferguson, William. *America By River and Rail; or, Notes by the Way of the New World and Its People*. London: James Nisbet and Co., 1856.
Flood, Charles Bracelen. *1864: Lincoln at the Gates of History*. New York: Simon and Schuster, 2009.
Foner, Eric. *Free Soil, Free Labor, Free Men: The Ideology of the Republican Party before the Civil War*. New York: Oxford Univ. Press, 1970.
———. *Reconstruction: America's Unfinished Revolution: 1863–1877*. New York: Harper Collins, 1988.
———. *The Second Founding: How the Civil War and Reconstruction Remade the Constitution*. New York: W. W. Norton & Co., 2019.
Fuller, A. James. *Oliver P. Morton and the Politics of the Civil War and Reconstruction*. Kent, OH: Kent State University Press, 2017.
Gallagher, Gary W. *The Union War*. Cambridge, MA: Harvard Univ. Press, 2011.
Gallman, J. Matthew. *The North Fights the Civil War: The Home Front*. Chicago: Ivan R. Dee, 1994.
Gansler, Laura Leedy. *The Double Life of Sarah Emma Edmonds, Civil War Soldier*. New York: Free Press, 2005.
Garrison, Webb, Sr., and Cheryl Garrison. *Webb Garrison's Civil War Dictionary: An Illustrated Guide to the Everyday Language of Soldiers and Civilians*. Nashville, TN: Cumberland House, 2008.
Gerber, David A. *Black Ohio and the Color Line, 1860–1915*. Urbana: Univ. of Illinois Press, 1976.
Goodheart, Adam. *1861: The Civil War Awakening*. New York: Alfred A. Knopf, 2012.
Governors of Ohio. Columbus: Ohio Historical Society, 1969.
Grimsley, Mark. *The Hard Hand of War: Union Military Policy toward Southern Civilians, 1861–1865*. Cambridge, UK: Cambridge Univ. Press, 1995.

Guelzo, Allen C. *Fateful Lightning: A New History of the Civil War and Reconstruction.* New York: Oxford Univ. Press, 2012.

Hammond, John Craig. "'The Most Free of the Free States': Politics, Slavery, Race, and Regional Identity in Early Ohio, 1790–1820." *Ohio History* 121 (2014): 35–57.

Hanna, Charles W. *African American Recipients of the Medal of Honor: A Biographical Dictionary, Civil War through Vietnam.* Jefferson, NC: McFarland & Co., 2002.

Harris, William C. *Lincoln and the Union Governors.* Carbondale: Southern Illinois Univ. Press, 2013.

Hatcher, Harlan. *The Western Reserve: The Story of New Connecticut in Ohio.* New York: Bobbs-Merrill Co., 1949.

Hearn, Chester G. *Lincoln, the Cabinet, and the Generals.* Baton Rouge: Louisiana State Univ. Press, 2010.

Heron, Joseph Martin. *Profiles in Character, Hubris and Heroism in the US Senate, 1789–1990.* Armonk, NY: M. E. Sharpe, 1997.

Hertz, Emanuel, ed. *Lincoln Talks: An Oral Biography.* New York: Bramhall House, 1986.

Hesseltine, William B. *Lincoln and the War Governors.* New York: Alfred A. Knopf, 1948.

Hill, Lawrence F. *Diplomatic Relations between the United States and Brazil.* New York: Kraus Reprint Co., 1969. First published by Duke Univ. Press (Durham, NC).

Hinsdale, B. A. "'The History of Popular Education on the Western Reserve': An Address Delivered in the Series of Educational Conferences Held in Association Hall, Cleveland, September 7 and 8, 1896. *Ohio History* 6: 35–58.

Historical Society of Geauga County. *Pioneer and General History of Geauga County, with Sketches of Some of the Pioneers and Prominent Men.* Vols. 1 and 2, 1880.

History of Trumbull and Mahoning Counties with Illustrations and Biographical Sketches. Vol. 1. Cleveland, OH: H. Z. Williams & Bro., 1882.

Holt, Edgar Allen. "Party Politics in Ohio, 1840–1850." *Ohio History Journal* 38, no. 1 (Jan. 1929): 47–182.

Holzer, Harold. *Lincoln President-Elect: Abraham Lincoln and the Great Secession Winter 1860–1861.* New York: Simon and Schuster, 2008.

Horne, Gerald. *The Deepest South: The United States, Brazil, and the African Slave Trade.* New York: New York Univ. Press, 2001.

Horwitz, Lester V. *The Longest Raid of the Civil War: Little Known and Untold Stories of Morgan's Raid into Kentucky, Indiana, and Ohio.* Lester V. Horwitz, 2001.

Horwitz, Tony. *Midnight Rising: John Brown and the Raid That Sparked the Civil War.* New York: Henry Holt and Co., 2011.

Howbert, Abraham R. *Reminiscences of the War.* Springfield, OH: Globe Printing and Publishing Co., 1888.

Howe, Daniel Walker. *What Hath God Wrought: The Transformation of America, 1815–1848.* New York: Oxford Univ. Press, 2007.

Howe, Henry. *Historical Collections of Ohio: An Encyclopedia of the State; History Both General and Local, Geography with Descriptions of Its Counties, Cities, Villages, Its Agricultural, Manufacturing, Mining and Business Development, Sketches of Eminent and Interesting Characters, Etc., with Notes of a Tour over It in 1886*. Vol. 1. Cincinnati, OH: C. J. Krehbiel, 1900.

Johannsen, Robert W. *The Lincoln-Douglas Debates of 1858: 150th Anniversary Edition*. New York: Oxford Univ. Press, 2008.

———. *Stephen A. Douglas*. New York: Oxford Univ. Press, 1973.

Kallina, Paul. "The Other George Ashmun." *The Lincolnian* 5, no. 4 (Mar.–Apr. 1987).

Klement, Frank L. *The Limits of Dissent: Clement L. Vallandigham and the Civil War*. Lexington: Univ. of Kentucky Press, 1970.

Knapp, Horace S. *History of the Maumee Valley: Commencing with Its Occupation by the French in 1680, to Which Is Added Sketches of Some of Its Moral and Material Resources as They Exist in 1872*. Toledo, OH: Blade, Mammoth Printing and Publishing House, 1872.

Knepper, George W. *Ohio and Its People*. Kent, OH: Kent State Univ. Press, 1989.

Lambert, Joseph, Jr., and Rick Shale. *First Citizen: The Industrious Life of Joseph G. Butler Jr.* Jefferson, NC: McFarland and Co., 2022.

Levin, Kevin M. *Searching for Black Confederates: The Civil War's Most Persistent Myth*. Chapel Hill: Univ. of North Carolina Press, 2019.

Library Company of Philadelphia. *"The State and National Banking Eras: A Chapter in the History of Central Banking."* Philadelphia: Federal Reserve Bank of Philadelphia (Dec. 2016).

Lowenstein, Roger. *Ways and Means: Lincoln and His Cabinet and the Finance of the Civil War*. New York: Penguin Press, 2022.

Mansfield, Ira F. *Ohio and Pennsylvania Reminiscences: Illustrations from Photographs Taken Mainly in Mahoning, Columbiana, and Beaver Counties, 1880–1916*. Beaver Falls, PA: Tribune Printing Co., 1916.

Marvel, William. *Lincoln's Autocrat: The Life of Edwin Stanton*. Chapel Hill: Univ. of North Carolina Press, 2003.

Mathews, Alfred. *Ohio and Her Western Reserve, with a Story of Three States, Leading to the Latter, from Connecticut, by Way of Wyoming, Its Indian Wars and Massacres*. New York: D. Appleton and Co., 1902.

McBride, Robert W. *Lincoln's Body Guard: The Union Light Guard of Ohio, with Some Personal Recollections of Abraham Lincoln*. Indianapolis: E. J. Hecker, 1911.

McPherson, James M. *Battle Cry of Freedom: The Civil War Era*. New York: Oxford Univ. Press, 1988.

Meacham, Jon. *American Lion: Andrew Jackson in the White House*. New York: Random House, 2008.

Melhorn, Donald F., Jr. *"Lest We Be Marshall'd": Judicial Power and Politics in Ohio, 1806–1812*. Akron, OH: Univ. of Akron Press, 2003.

Miller, Richard F., ed. *States at War*. Vol. 5, *A Reference Guide for Ohio in the Civil War*. Hanover, NH, and London: Univ. Press of New England, 2015.

Miller, Robert Ernest, "War Within Walls: Camp Chase and the Search for Administrative Reform." *Ohio History* 96 (1998): 33–56.
Morris, J. Brent. *Oberlin, Hotbed of Abolitionism: College, Community, and the Fight for Freedom and Equality in Antebellum America*. Chapel Hill: Univ. of North Carolina Press, 2014.
Morrison, Michael A. *Slavery and the American West. The Eclipse of Manifest Destiny and the Coming of the Civil War*. Chapel Hill: Univ. of North Carolina Press,, 1997.
Naragon, Harold L. "The Ohio Gubernatorial Campaign of 1863." Master's thesis, Ohio State Univ., 1934.
Neely, Mark E., Jr. *The Civil War and the Limits of Destruction*. Cambridge, MA: Harvard Univ. Press, 2007.
———. *The Fate of Liberty: Abraham Lincoln and Civil Liberties*. New York: Barnes and Noble, 1991.
Nevins, Allan. *The War for the Union*. Vol. 2, *War Becomes Revolution, 1862–1863*. New York: Charles Scribner's Sons, 1960.
Nichol, Francis D. "The Midnight Cry, A Defense of the Character and Conduct of William Miller and the Millerites, Who Mistakenly Believed That the Second Coming of Christ Would Take Place in the Year 1844." Washington, DC: Review and Herald Association, 1944.
Nye, Russel B. "Marius Robinson: A Forgotten Abolitionist Leader." *Ohio History Journal* 55, no. 2 (Apr.–June 1946): 138–54.
Oakes, James. *Slavery and Freedom: An Interpretation of the Old South*. New York: W. W. Norton and Co., 1990.
Oates, Stephen B. *A Woman of Valor: Clara Barton and the Civil War*. New York: Free Press, 1994.
Ohio Cemetery Journal 3, no. 1 (Apr. 2013).
Perret, Geoffrey. *Ulysses S. Grant, Soldier and President*. New York: Random House, 1997.
Phillips, Christopher. *The Rivers Ran Backward: The Civil War and the Remaking of the American Middle Border*. New York: Oxford Univ. Press, 2016.
Poland, Charles A. *Army Register of Ohio Volunteers in the Service of the United States*. Columbus, OH: State Journal Printing Co., 1862.
Porter, George H. "Ohio Politics During the Civil War Period." PhD diss., Columbia Univ., 1911.
Powell, Thomas Edward. *The Democratic Party of the State of Ohio: A Comprehensive History of Democracy in Ohio from 1803 to 1912, Including Democratic Legislation in the State, the Campaigns of a Century, History of Democratic Conventions, the Reverses and Successes of the Party, etc*. Columbus: Ohio Publishing Co., 1913.
Prechel-Kluskens, Claire. "The Nineteenth-Century Postmaster and His Duties." *NGS News Magazine* (Jan.–Mar. 2007): 33–37.
Quarles, Benjamin. *The Negro in the Civil War*. New York: De Capo Press, 1989.

Rank, James B. "The Attitude of James Buchanan Towards Slavery." *Pennsylvania Magazine of History and Biography* 1.51, no. 2 (Apr. 1927): 126–42.

Rawley, James A. *The Politics of Union: Northern Politics during the Civil War.* Lincoln: Univ. of Nebraska Press, 1974.

Reid, Joseph B., and Henry R. Reeder. "Trial of Rev. John B. Mahan, for Felony: In the Mason Circuit Court of Kentucky, Commencing on Tuesday, the 13th, and Terminating on Monday, the 19th of Nov., 1838. Reported by Joseph B. Reid and Henry R. Reeder, Esqs." Cincinnati: Samuel A. Alley, Printer, 1838.

Reid, Whitelaw. *Ohio in the War: Her Statesmen, Generals and Soldiers.* Vols. 1–2. Cincinnati: Robert Clarke Co., 1895.

Rezneck, Samuel, "The Social History of an American Depression, 1837–1843." *American Historical Review* 40, no. 4 (July 1935): 662–87.

Rice, Allen Thorndike. *Reminiscences of Abraham Lincoln by Distinguished Men of His Time. Collected and edited by William Blackwood and Sons, Edinburgh and London.* New York: North American Publishing Co., 1886.

Rice, Harvey. *The Founder of the City of Cleveland, and Other Sketches.* Boston: Lee and Shepard, 1892.

Richardson, Albert D. *A Personal History of Ulysses S. Grant, Illustrated by Twenty-Six Engravings, Eight Facsimiles of Letters from Grant, Lincoln, Sheridan, Buckner, Lee, Etc. and Six Maps. With a Portrait and Sketch of Schuyler Colfax.* Chicago: G. and C. W. Sherwood, 1868.

Ridderbusch, Michael R. "The Lincoln Reminiscence Manuscript in the Francis Harrison Pierpont Papers." *West Virginia History* 1, no. 1 (Spring 2007): 75–92.

Rose, William Ganson. *Cleveland: The Making of a City.* New York: World Publishing Co., 1950.

Roseboom, Eugene H. *The History of the State of Ohio.* Vol. 4, *The Civil War Era, 1850–1873.* Columbus: Ohio State Archaeological and Historical Society, 1944.

Runkle, Benjamin Piatt. "James Parks Caldwell, March 27, 1841 to April 5, 1912." *Sigma Chi Quarterly* 16, no. 4 (July 1896): 323–25.

Schlesinger, Arthur M., Jr. *The Age of Jackson.* Boston: Little, Brown and Co., 1946.

Scott, Hervey. *A Complete History of Fairfield County, Ohio, 1795–1876.* Columbus, OH: Sibert and Lilley, 1877.

Sears, Stephen W. *George B. McClellan: The Young Napoleon.* New York: Ticknor and Fields, 1988.

Sellers, Charles. *The Market Revolution: Jacksonian America, 1815–1846.* New York: Oxford Univ. Press, 1991.

Silbey, Joel H. *A Respectable Minority: The Democratic Party in the Civil War Era, 1860–1868.* New York: W. W. Norton and Co., 1977.

———. *Storm Over Texas: The Annexation Controversy and the Road to Civil War.* New York: Oxford Univ. Press, 2005.

Simpson, Brooks D. *Let Us Have Peace: Ulysses S. Grant and the Politics of War and Reconstruction, 1861–1868.* Chapel Hill: Univ. of North Carolina Press, 1991.

Smith, Joseph. *A History of Brazil.* Taylor and Francis, 2014.

Smith, Joseph Patterson, ed. *History of the Republican Party in Ohio and Memoirs of Its Representative Supporters in Two Imperial Quarto Volumes.* Chicago: Lewis Publishing Co., 1898.

Snowden Gray Mansion. 2019. www.snowdengraymansion.com

Stackpole, General Edward J. *They Met at Gettysburg: A Step-by-Step Retelling of the Battle with Maps, Photos, Firsthand Accounts,* 3rd ed. Harrisburg, PA: Stackpole Books, 1982.

Stahr, Walter. *Stanton: Lincoln's War Secretary.* New York: Simon and Schuster, 2017.

Stampp, Kenneth M. *America in 1857: A Nation on the Brink.* New York: Oxford University Press, 1990.

Stanley, Matthew E. *The Loyal West. Civil War and Reunion in Middle America.* Urbana: Univ. of Illinois Press, 2016.

State and National Banking Eras: A Chapter in the History of Central Banking. Federal Reserve Bank of Philadelphia, December 2016. www.philadelphiafed.org

Stewart, John Struthers. *History of Northeastern Ohio.* Indianapolis: Historical Publishing Co., 1935.

Strahan, Derk. "David Tod House, Suffield, Connecticut." *Lost New England* (Aug. 24, 2017).

Taylor, Lenette S. *"The Supply for Tomorrow Must Not Fail": The Civil War of Captain Simon Perkins Jr., Union Quartermaster.* Kent, Ohio: Kent State University Press, 2014.

Taylor, William Alexander. *Ohio Statesmen and Hundred Year Book: From 1788 to 1892.* Columbus, OH: Westbote Co., 1892.

Tochtenhagen, Mark S. "Mine Subsidence and the History of Coal Mining in the Mahoning Valley." Bachelor of Science, Ohio State Univ., 1985.

Tod, John. *Some Account of the History of the Tod Family and Connections.* Compiled and printed by John Tod, 1917.

Tooley, Mark. *The Peace That Almost Was: The Forgotten Story of the 1861 Washington Peace Conference and the Final Attempt to Avert the Civil War.* Nashville: Nelson Books, 2015.

Towne, Stephen E. "A Lesson for All Rebels at Home: The Holmes County, Ohio, Rebellion of 1863 Revisited." *Ohio History* 126, no. 2 (2019): 5–37.

———. *Surveillance and Spies in the Civil War: Exposing Confederate Conspiracies in American's Heartland.* Athens: Ohio Univ. Press, 2015.

Trefousse, Hans L. "Ben Wade and the Negro." *Ohio History Journal* 68, no. 2 (Apr. 1959): 161–76.

Trester, Delmer J. "David Tod and the Gubernatorial Campaign of 1844." *Ohio History Journal* 62, no.2 (Apr. 1953): 162–78.

———. "The Political Career of David Tod." Master's thesis, Ohio State Univ., 1950.

Trudeau, Noah Andre. *Southern Storm: Sherman's March to the Sea.* New York: Harper Collins, 2008.

Upton, Harriet Taylor. *History of the Western Reserve.* Chicago: Lewis Publishing Co., 1910.

Volpe, Vernon L. "The Ohio Election of 1838: A Study in the Historical Method?" *Ohio History Connection* 95 (Summer–Autumn 1986): 85–100.
Waugh, John C. *Lincoln and McClellan: The Troubled Partnership between a President and His General*. New York: Palgrave MacMillan, 2010.
Waller, Douglas. *Lincoln's Spies: Their Secret War to Save a Nation*. New York: Simon and Schuster, 2019.
Weber, Jennifer L. *Copperheads: The Rise and Fall of Lincoln's Opponents in the North*. New York: Oxford Univ. Press, 2006.
Weekly Law Bulletin and Ohio Law Journal 16 (July 1–Dec. 31 1886).
Weisenburger, Francis Phelps. *Columbus during the Civil War*. Columbus: Ohio State Univ. Press, 1963.
Wheeler, Tom. *Mr. Lincoln's T-Mails: The Untold Story of How Abraham Lincoln Used the Telegraph to Win the Civil War*. New York: Harper Collins, 2006.
White, Ronald C., Jr. *A. Lincoln: A Biography*. New York: Random House, 2009.
Wilson, Dreck Spurlock, ed. *African American Architects: A Biographical Dictionary, 1865–1945*. New York: Routledge, 2004.
Wilson, William. "The Man for the Hour: A Sermon." Cincinnati: Printed by Franklin & Tidball, 1863.
Wittke, Carl, ed. *The History of the State of Ohio*. Vol. 3, *Weisenburger*. Columbus: Ohio State Archaeological and Historical Society, 1941.
Wright, George B. "Hon. David Tod. Biography of David Tod." *Ohio Archaeological and Historical Quarterly* 8: 107–31.
Zornow, William Frank. "Lincoln, Chase, and the Ohio Radicals in 1864." *Bulletin of the Historical and Philosophical Society of Ohio* 9, no. 1: 3–32.

US CONGRESSIONAL DOCUMENTS

Department of State, *Register of All Officers and Agents, Civil, Military, and Naval, in the Service of the United States, on the Thirtieth September, 1831, 1835, 1847*. Washington, DC: J. and G. S. Gideon, 1831, 1835, 1847.
Manning, William R. *Diplomatic Correspondence of the United States*. Vol. 2. Washington, DC: US Government Printing Office, 1946.
Polk, James K. *State of the Union Address*, December 7, 1847.
United States Congress, *House Documents, Otherwise Published as Executive Documents*.
United States Congressional Serial Set, issue 3790. Governor David Tod to Edwin M. Stanton, September 16, 1862.
United States War Department. *The War of the Rebellion: A Compilation of the Official Records of the Union and Confederate Armies*, US Government Printing Office, 1880–1901. This compilation comprises 70 volumes of letters and reports written by both armies, in 128 parts.
Wise, Henry A. "The Correspondence of Mr. Wise, Late Minister to Brazil, in Relation to the Imprisonment of Lieutenant Davis, of the Navy, and Three American

Seaman, by the Police Authority at Rio de Janiero." March 22, 1848. Submitted to the United States Senate in "Message from the President of the United States Communicating." Thirtieth Congress, 1st session, executive no. 29.

STATE GOVERNMENT DOCUMENTS

Acts of a General Nature, Passed by the Forty First General Assembly of the State of Ohio, Begun and Held in the City of Columbus, Commencing December 5, 1842. Vol. 41. Columbus, OH: State Printer, 1843.

Chase, Salmon P., ed. *The Statutes of Ohio and of the Northwestern Territory Adopted or Enacted from 1788 to 1833 Inclusive Together with the Ordinance of 1787; the Constitution of Ohio and of the United States and Various Public Instruments and Acts of Congress: Volume II.* Cincinnati, OH: Corey and Fairbank, Cincinnati, 1834.

Journal of the Senate of the State of Ohio at the First Session of the Thirty-Seventh General Assembly Held in the City of Columbus, and Commenced Monday, December 3, 1838.

Journal of the Senate of the State of Ohio at the First Session of the Thirty-Eight General Assembly Held in the City of Columbus, and Commenced Monday, December 2, 1839.

Message and Reports to the General Assembly and Governor of the State of Ohio for the Year 1862. Columbus, OH: Richard Nevins, State Printer, 1862.

Message and Reports to the General Assembly and Governor of the State of Ohio for the Year 1863. Columbus OH: Richard Nevins, State Printer, 1863.

Message and Reports to the General Assembly and Governor of the State of Ohio for the Year 1864. Columbus, OH: Richard Nevins, State Printer, 1863.

Ohio Auditor of State. *Military and Sanitary. Extracts from the Governor's Message, and Sundry Executive Reports for 1862, for the Use of the Officers and Soldiers in the Army from Ohio.* Columbus, OH: R. Nevins, State Printer, 1863. https://archive.org/details/military0oohio/page/10

Tod, David. *Report of the Commissioner in The Case of Benjamin F. Stickney.* Appendix to Senate Journal No. 8 at the First Session of the Thirty-Ninth General Assembly. Columbus, OH: Samuel Medary, State Printer, 1840.

Report of the Convention Held at Cleveland, July 8th and 9th, 1880 for the Purpose of Forming a State Bar Association. Indianapolis: Reprint by Hollenbeck Press, 1903.

State of Ohio, Ex. Rel. David Tod v. the Court of Common Pleas of Fairfield Co., O. Brief in behalf of Relator, by Flamen Ball, Attorney, Supreme Court of Ohio, Dec. Term, 1863.

Tod, David. *Message of the Governor of Ohio to the Fifty-Fifth General Assembly, at the Adjourned Session, Commencing January 5, 1863.* Columbus, OH: Richard Nevins, State Printer, 1863.

Vance, Joseph. *State of the State Address,* December 4, 1838, Ohio History Connection Selections.

OTHER PRINTED PRIMARY SOURCES (DIARIES, LETTERS OF, CORRESPONDENCE OF, MEMOIRS, PROCEEDINGS FROM THE STATE CONVENTION, ETC.)

Annals of the Early Settlers, no. 2.
Annual Report of the Directors and Chief Engineer of the Cleveland & Mahoning RR Co. Cleveland, OH: Harris, Fairbanks & Co., Herald Office, 1855.
Basler, Roy P., ed. *The Collected Works of Abraham Lincoln.* New Brunswick, NJ" Rutgers Univ. Press, 1953.
Bates, Edward, Howard K. Beale, and Mary Parker Ragatz. *The Diary of Edward Bates, 1859–1866.* Washington, DC: US Government Printing Office, Washington, 1933. (Sponsored by the Institute of Museum and Library Services through an Indiana State Library LSTA Grant.)
Butler, Joseph G., Jr. *Memorandum for Mr. R. J. Kaylor,* Oct. 11, 1924. Tod Family File. Library of Youngstown and Mahoning County, OH.
———. *Recollections of Men and Events: An Autobiography.* New York: G. P. Putnam's Sons, 1927.
Cox, Jacob D. *Military Reminiscences of the Civil War.* New York: Charles Scribner's Sons, 1900.
Current, Richard N. "Lincoln's Plan." *American Heritage* 6, no. 4 (June 1955).
Galloway, Hon. Samuel. *Eulogy on Ex.-Gov. David Tod, Delivered Before the Electoral College of Ohio, December 1, 1868.* Columbus: Ohio State Journal Book and Job Rooms, 1869.
Grant, Jesse R. "To the Editor of the Shoe and Leather Reporter." *Grant Network Newsletter,* 1868.
Hertz, Emanuel, ed. *Lincoln Talks, An Oral Biography.* New York: Bramhall House, 1986.
Historical Collections of the Mahoning Valley Containing an Account of the Two Pioneer Reunions: Together with a Selection of Interesting Facts, Biographical Sketches, Anecdotes, etc., Related to the Sale of Settlement of the Lands Belonging to the Connecticut Land Company, and History and Reminiscences, Both General and Local. Volume I. Youngstown, OH: Mahoning Valley Historical Society. 1876.
Howbert, Abraham R. *Reminiscences of the War.* Springfield, OH: Globe Printing and Publishing Co., 1888.
Lincoln, Abraham. *Papers: Series 1. General Correspondence. 1833–1916,* David Tod to Edwin M. Stanton, Sat., June 27, 1863. Washington, DC: Library of Congress, 1863. (Printed correspondence concerning payment of black soldiers.)
Mansfield, Ira F. *Ohio and Pennsylvania Reminiscences: Illustrations from Pho-*

tographs Taken Mainly in Mahoning, Columbiana and Beaver Counties, 1880 to 1916. Beaver Falls, PA: Tribune Printing Co., 1916.

McKinley, William. "Address in Response to Toast at the Lincoln Banquet of the Ohio Republican League at Columbus, Ohio, February 12, 1892." *Speeches and Addresses of William McKinley, from His Election to Congress to the Present Time*. New York: D. Appleton and Co., 1893. (Printed in the *Ohio State Journal*.)

Nicolay, John G., and John Hay. "Abraham Lincoln: A History. The Resignation of Chase." *The Century* 38, no. 2 (June 1889): 290–98.

Official Proceedings of the Democratic National Convention, Held in 1860, at Charleston and Baltimore. Cleveland, OH: Nevin's Print, 1860.

"Old Northwest" Genealogical Society, *The "Old Northwest" Genealogical Quarterly* 7 (1904).

Report of the Judge Advocate General on The Order of American Knights Alias. "The Sons of Liberty." A Western Conspiracy in aid of the Southern Rebellion. Washington, DC: Chronicle Print, 1864.

Sherman, John. *Recollections of Forty Years in the House, Senate and Cabinet: An Autobiography*. Chicago: Werner Co., 1896.

Tod Collection. MVHS (Mahoning Valley Historical Society). Grace Ingersoll to Sallie Tod, February 24, 1813.

Tod, David. "Governor Tod's Letter of Acceptance." *Proceedings of the Great Union Convention of Ohio Held at Columbus, Sept. 5, 1861*. Cleveland, OH: Nevin's Print, 1861.

Welles, Gideon. *Diary of Gideon Welles, Secretary of the Navy under Lincoln and Johnson*. Boston: Houghton Mifflin Co., 1910.

Wilson, William. "The Man for the Hour: A Sermon Preached in the Church of the Covenanters, in the City of Cincinnati, on the Evening of January Twenty-Second, One Thousand Eight Hundred and Sixty-Three, Which Day Was Observed as a Day of Public Fasting, Humiliation and Prayer, by Order of the General Synod of the Reformed Presbyterian Church, It Being Thursday of the Week Of Ecumenical Prayer for the Conversion of the World to Christ." Lincolncollection; Americana. (Digitizing Sponsor Institute of Museum and Library Services through an Indiana State Library LSTA Grant.)

INTERNET

Chronicling America, Historic American Newspapers, Library of Congress. https://chroniclingamerica.loc.gov.

Civil War Academy.com. https://www.civilwaracademy.com.

Google Book. https:books.google.com.

Internet Archives. https://archive.org.

Ohio Historical Society. Ohio Governors. ohiohistory.org/onlinedoc/ohgovernment/governors/tod.html.

Ohio History Connection. Civil War Guide, series 147, vol. 42. OhioLink.
www.snowdengraymansion.com.
Spared and Shared. https://sparedshared23.com/home/.
https://www.supremecourt.ohio.gov/SCO/formerjustices/bios/tod.asp and Birchard.
USGenWeb Archives https://searchonline.com.
WorldCat On-Line. https://www.worldcat.org.

Index

Abbott, Richard, 147
abolitionists, 4, 17, 20–21, 24, 49, 66, 70, 81, 84–85, 88–90, 138, 150, 153, 158, 223; critics of, 89, 131; violence and, 21, 70–71, 72, 88
Act to Enable Qualified Voters of This State, in the Military Service of This State, or of the United States, to Exercise the Right of Suffrage, An, 149–50
Adams, Comfort, 83, 105
Albany Argus, 167
Alien and Sedition Act, 67
Allegheny Mountains, 3
Allen, Peter, 35
Allen, William, 72
Alliance Rangers, 135
Altoona Conference, 137–39, 141, 143
American Revolution, 5
Anderson, Charles, 188–89, 209, 214
Anderson, Robert, 188, 209
Andrew, John, 116, 121, 137–38, 145, 179–81
Angier Hotel, 197
Anti-Slavery Bugle, 73, 95–96
Anti-Slavery Society, 30
Army of the Cumberland, 164
Army of Northern Virginia, 158
Army of the Potomac, 128, 132, 158
Arrel, George, 233
Ashland Union, 79, 80, 130, 150, 189

Ashtabula Weekly Telegraph, 164, 185
Athenaeum, 166
Atlantic & Great Western Railway, 215
Auble, William, 49

Baker, Jean, 15, 30, 145, 218
Baldwin, William, 30
Baltimore & Ohio Railroad, 122
Bank Commission, 27
Bank Commissioner Act, 27, 28
bank reform, 17–18, 26–27, 32, 41–43, 45–47, 49, 74; bank oversight, 45, 74; local banks, 38; national bank proposal, 19, 39, 67, 124; private banks, 45; state banks, role of, 19, 24, 38; state-chartered banks, 19–20, 23–24, 39; stockholders, 24, 74; taxes on, 45, 47, 49, 67
Bank Reform Bill, 28
Bank of the United States, 14, 24
Barnburners, 73
Barnhisel, Frances, 233–34
Barnum's City Hotel, 199
Bartley, Mordecai, 39–42, 45
Bartley, Thomas, 96–97
Bartley Act/Amendment, 39, 41–42
Bates, David Homer, 176
Bates, Edward, 200
Battle of Antietam, 136–38, 141, 170
Battle of Atlanta, 208

288

Battle of Buffington Island, 172
Battle of Bull Run, 106, 202; Second Battle of Bull Run, 132
Battle of Chancellorsville, 158, 170
Battle of Fort Donelson, 146
Battle of Fort Fizzle, 162
Battle of Fredericksburg, 152, 170
Battle of Gettysburg, 170, 172
Battle of Richmond, 134, 209
Battle of Shiloh, 119, 120, 123, 146, 194
Battle of Stones River, 188
Battle of Vicksburg, 170
Beatty, Powhatan, 212
Beauregard, P. G. T., 109
Bebb, William, 45–47, 49–51
Bell, John, 94, 96–97
Belmont Chronicle, 226
Berry, Plympton Ross, 220–21
Birchard, Matthew, 10–11, 13–14, 95, 97, 226
Black(s): defense of Cincinnati, 134; education for, 49; Freedom Seekers, 4, 21, 25; migration into Ohio, 49; military service, 100, 126, 129, 144–45, 147, 163, 165, 175–76, 178–83, 212; rights, 4, 22, 24–25, 218, 223; suffrage, 211–12, 218, 220, 223–24
Black Laws/Codes, 4, 24–25, 49–50; repeal of, 25, 49, 65, 211
Bleeding Kansas, 70–72, 85
Blue, Frederick J., 198
Bonaparte, Napoleon, 193
Border State Convention, 102
Bradford, Augustus, 138
Brandt, Nat, 25
Brazil, 52–63, 80, 85, 96; economy, 59, 62; Ilha Grande, 60; Plata River, 60; Rio de Janeiro, 55–56, 60; slavery in, 23, 54–55, 57–62, 65, 75; yellow fever, 61
Breckenridge, John, 94–97
Brier Hill, 1–2, 4–7, 15, 35–36, 52, 64, 233; coal at, 36, 37, 48, 50–51, 65, 76–77, 83–84, 195, 208; deeded to Calvin Cone, 10, 12; deeded to David Tod, 14–15; deeded to Simon Perkins, 12, 14; foreclosure, 9–10; home at, 64–65, 86, 173, 186, 191, 206, 214–15, 220, 224, 230–31, 235; mortgage, 8, 14
Brier Hill Iron and Coal Company, 195, 200, 208, 233
British Royal Navy, 61–62
Brooks, Noah, 201
Brough, John, 164–65, 166–68, 170, 183–86, 188–89, 193, 196–97, 199, 203–4, 209–10, 234; death, 214
Brown, D. W., 188
Brown, John, 70–71, 85, 88
Buchanan, James, 55–58, 60, 62, 67, 72–74, 79–86, 89, 99–100, 116; inauguration, 76, 78
Buckingham, Catharinus P., 115
Buckingham, William, 137
Buell, Don Carlos, 134
Burnside, Ambrose E., 152–53, 162–63, 169–73
Burton Academy, 1, 7, 8
Busteed, Richard, 140

Cadiz Democratic Sentinel, 141
Cadiz Sentinel, 48, 197, 211, 215
California, 66
Cameron, Simon, 106, 112, 114, 116
Camp Chase, 113, 122–23, 125, 132–33, 193; acts of liberation at, 155–56; prison at, 115–16, 155–56
Camp Davies, 184
Camp Dayton, 134
Camp Delaware, 180–81
Camp Dennison, 119, 133
Camp Edgefield Junction, 147
Camp Taylor, 229
Canadian Conspiracy, 186–87
Carroll Free Press, 42, 51, 53
Cass, Lewis, 72, 110
Charleston Mercury, 86, 90
Chase, Salmon P., 49–50, 68–70, 79, 80–81, 90, 124, 154, 165–66, 176–77, 198–204
Chicago Daily Tribune, 110
Chicago Tribune, 167
Cincinnati Commercial, 131, 181
Cincinnati Gazette, 23, 165, 179, 229
Cisco, John J., 199–200
Civil War, 23, 28, 100, 103–209, 233–35; Black soldiers and, 126, 129, 134, 144–45, 147, 163, 165, 175–76, 178–83, 212; bounty system, 130, 141, 178, 186; conscientious objectors, 130; defense of Washington, 122; deserters, 156–58; draft, 117, 122, 126–27, 129–30, 132, 137, 140–42, 152–53, 162, 175, 177–78, 186, 189; draft resisters, 162–63, 169, 172, 175, 177–78, 191; funding, 201; Martinsburg, 122–23; monuments, 234; national army, 117; recruiting, 122–24, 126, 129–30, 140, 154–55, 177–78, 180, 186;

Civil War (cont.)
  recruits, requests for supplies for, 123–27, 141; Richmond, Virginia, 118, 126, 134, 209; soldiers' votes, 149, 183–84; states' rights and, 129; suspension of habeas corpus, 131–32, 148, 195, 230; traitors, 157, 162; volunteers from Ohio, 104, 113–15, 119–22, 131, 134–35, 141, 145, 152–53, 177–78, 186, 193; women volunteers, 120, 195–96
Clay, Henry, 39, 52
Clayton, John M., 61
Cleveland Board of Trades, 215
Cleveland, Columbus & Cincinnati Railroad, 134–35, 230–31
Cleveland Herald, 20
Cleveland Leader, 164–65, 206
Cleveland & Mahoning Railroad, 65, 85, 103–5, 195, 208; secessionists on, 105
Cleveland Morning Leader, 107–9, 121, 153, 181, 186, 197, 205, 211
coal, 36–37, 48, 50, 65, 83–84, 90, 195, 208; iron and, 51; labor strikes, 76–77; mining, 37, 50–51, 76; steamboats and, 37
Coe, David L., 8
Colfax, Schuyler, 82
Collins, John, 13–14
Columbus Journal, 228
Compromise of 1850, 66
Cone, Calvin, 10, 12
Connell, John, 192
Conness, John, 202
Conscription Act, 175
Cony, Samuel, 185
Cook, Arvilla, 8
Cooke, Jay, 201
Corwin, Thomas, 31, 34, 38
Court of Common Pleas, 9, 74, 84, 161
Cowen, Benjamin, 154
Cox, Jacob Dolson, 101–3, 210, 212, 214, 234
Cox, Samuel, 183
Crisis, 156, 177
Critchfield, Lyman, 148
Crittenden Compromise, 100
Crowell, John, 18, 21–22, 28, 30, 35
currency, 27; backed by gold and silver, 42, 45, 47, 202; Constitutional, 49; paper, 32, 41, 45, 124, 202–3; reform, 24, 41, 50
Currency Committee, 27
Current, Richard N., 203–4
Curtin, Andrew, 129, 137–39, 170, 185, 187
Cushing, Caleb, 91–93

Daily Ohio Statesman, 101, 153, 163, 193, 201
Daily Union, 52–53
Davis, Alonzo B., 54–55
Davis, Jefferson, 109
Davis Affair, 54–57
Dawson, Isaac, 226
Day, Luther, 115
Dayton Daily Empire, 208, 211
Delano, Columbus, 115, 198
Dell, Christopher, 109, 204
Democratic Party, 2, 15, 17–18, 23, 30–31, 33–34, 46, 48–49, 66–68, 70, 82, 85, 89, 106, 109–11, 116, 118, 132, 152, 154, 192, 194, 209, 213, 220, 222–24; 1844 election, 44; 1845 election, 46; 1855 election, 69–70; 1857 election, 79, 80, 81; 1861 election, 148; 1863 election, 146–47, 184, 185; 1864 election, 203–7; bank reform, 19–20, 26–27, 38–40, 42; Conservative, 41–42, 46, 157–58, 217; Fire-Eaters, 86, 90; Jackson Democrats, 11, 24, 26–27, 30, 73, 98, 166; *Loco Focos*, 18; National Convention (1860), 85–86, 89–96; Northern, 68, 72–75, 79, 82, 86, 89–91, 93–94, 97, 99–100, 104; Ohio Convention (1861), 99–101; Ohio Convention (1863), 158, 160–61; Peace Democrats/Copperheads, 104, 106–8, 111, 131, 146–51, 153, 157–58, 160, 163, 170, 177, 182–84, 203, 205, 207, 217, 220, 222; popular sovereignty, 72, 81–82, 86, 90, 92; racial rhetoric, 140–41, 182; Radical, 38, 41–42, 46–47; secessionists, 86, 90, 92, 97, 99–100; slavery and, 21, 28, 31, 40, 68, 72–75, 81, 86, 90–92, 153; Southern, 68, 72, 86, 91–94; states' rights, 72; War Democrats, 104, 106–7, 109, 131, 140–41, 164, 176, 197, 203–4, 207
Democratic Press, 167
Democratic-Republicans, 2
Dennison, William, 100, 102, 109, 113–14, 116, 122, 124, 150, 166, 178, 182, 188–89, 196, 198–99, 234
Detroit Free Press, 89, 167
Dickerson, John, 134
Dickinson, Daniel S., 110
Dix, John, 187
Doolittle, James, 200–201
Dorsey, G. Volney, 143
Douglas, Stephen, 68–72, 75, 79, 81, 84, 89, 92–98, 101, 103, 108–9, 141, 145, 209; death, 106; popular sovereignty and, 81–

INDEX · 291

82, 86, 90–92, 96–98; support of Union, 104–6
Dred Scott v. Sandford, 78–79, 86, 90, 218–19

Earle, Jonathan Halperin, 72
Early, Jubal, 205
Eaton Democrat, 79
Edgerton, Alfred P., 74
Election Day, 149
Emancipation Proclamation, 137–40, 142–44, 146–48, 150, 152, 156, 158, 165, 179, 184
Engle, David, 102
Engle, Stephen, 117, 137, 139, 150, 152–53, 169
Evening Star, 202
Everett, Edward, 188
Ewing, Thomas, 25–26

Federalists, 2–3, 67
Fehrenbacher, Don E., 61–62
Fessenden, William, 202–4
Fifty-Eighth Regiment, 113
Fillmore, Millard, 67
First Brigade of the Fourth Division, 11
Fish, George, 131
Flood, Charles Bracelen, 205
Flournoy, Thompson B., 91
Foner, Eric, 27, 68, 73, 213, 219–20
Ford, John, 7–8
Ford, Julia, 145
Forney Press, 108
Fort Donelson, 118, 155
Fort Henry, 118
Fort Lafayette, 131
Fort Lyon, 113
Fort McHenry, 199
Fort Monroe, 182
Fort Sumter, 22, 103–4, 106, 188, 209
Fort Warren, 159
forty-ninth parallel, 47
Forty-Sixth Regiment, 113
Free Press, 111
Free-Soil Party, 68, 70–71
Frémont, John, 72, 138, 147
Fremont Journal, 153, 163, 167, 171
Fremont Weekly Journal, 226
Front Street Theater, 93
Fugitive Slave Act/Law, 49, 65, 67–68, 72, 100

Gallagher, Gary W., 114
Gallipolis Journal, 217
Gallman, J. Matthew, 88
Galloway, Samuel, 57, 132, 219, 221, 230, 235

Garfield, James, 102, 206, 215, 222–23, 230, 234
Gazette, 79
General Order No. 1, 117–18
Gettysburg National Cemetery, 188–89, 192
Gholson, William, 153
Giddings, Joshua, 9, 32–33, 68, 82, 84, 94
Gienapp, William E., 89
Gilmore, Quincy A., 234
Girard Iron Company, 216
Glendale, 121
Goodheart, Adam, 81, 107
"Governor Tod" fire engine, 221
Governor Tod's Civil War residence marker, 235
Grand Army of the Republic, 233
Grant, Jesse, 5–6; adoption by Tod family, 7
Grant, Ulysses, 6, 118, 170, 194, 205, 209, 222, 224, 229
Great Britain, 47, 58, 61
Great Exhibition, 64
Greathouse, William, 25

Halleck, Henry, 115, 130, 170, 173
Hall of the South Carolina Institute, 91
Hamlin, Hannibal, 74, 199
Hammond, John Craig, 22
Hancock Jeffersonian, 227, 231
Hanna, Orpha Annette, 148
Hapgood, George, 83, 105
Harper, Robert, 120
Harper's Ferry, 85, 88, 122
Harper's Weekly, 204
Harris, William C., 117, 138, 146–47
Harrison, William Henry, 15, 30, 33, 39, 94
Hascall, Milo S., 157
Hayes, Rutherford B., 218, 230, 234
Hay, John, 203
Hebron, John L., 147
Heron, Joseph Martin, 203
Hesseltine, William, 137, 167–68
Hewitt, Hugh, 153
Highland Weekly News, 209
Hobson, Edward H., 171–72
Hoffman, Benjamin, 115
Hoffman, William H., 155
Holbrook, Frederick, 196
Holmes, George, 24
Holmes County Farmer, 48
Holt, Joseph, 110
Hooker, Joseph, 152, 158, 170
Horne, Gerald, 62

Houston, Sam, 67
Howbert, A. R., 121
Howe, Daniel Walker, 14, 21
Hunter, Hocking H., 161, 184
Hunter, R. M. T., 72
Hutchins, John, 30–31, 84
Hyde Park, 64

Indemnity Act, 161
Independent Treasury law, 39
Indiana Journal, 105
Iron, 51, 198, 208
Isaacs, Mary Peyret, 5
Isaacs, Ralph, Jr., 5

Jackson, Andrew, 2, 13–15, 18, 26, 30, 54, 73, 96, 98, 101, 104
Jackson, Thomas, 122
Jackson Day, 99, 150
Jefferson, Thomas, 5
Jefferson Democrat, 210–11
Jewett, Hugh, 107–8, 111, 148
Johnson, Andrew, 72, 109–10, 199, 203, 210, 217, 219
Johnson's Island, 157, 187
Journal of the Senate, 27
Judiciary Committee, 27

Kanawha River, 136
Kansas, 68, 70, 73–74, 79, 81–82, 94; "Bleeding," 70–72, 85; Lawrence, 70–71; Pottawatomie, 71
Kansas-Nebraska Act, 68–71
Kautz, August V., 222
Kelley, Benjamin Franklin, 172
Kelley Bank Bill, 45–46
Kennon, Wilson, 154, 165
Kirkwood, Samuel, 196
Knights of the Golden Circle, 150–51, 158
Know-Nothing Party, 67

Lake Erie, 13, 36, 65, 109, 157, 185, 187, 194
Lake Erie Plot, 186–88
Lang, William, 192
Langston, John M., 145, 179, 181–82, 212
Latham Law/Act, 38–39, 41–42
Lawrence, Philip, 48–49
Lay, 64
Leal, Dom Felippe Pereira, 56
LeBlond, F. C., 74
Lecompton Constitution, 81–83, 89, 90, 94
Lee, Robert E., 85, 126, 136, 142, 158, 169–70, 172, 223; surrender at Appomattox, 209

Lewis and Clark expedition, 5
Libby Prison, 190
Liberty Herald, 229
Liberty Party, 49
Lincoln, Abraham, 100, 102–4, 106–9, 112, 116–18, 121, 125, 127–28, 130–32, 137–42, 144, 146–48, 150, 152, 154, 156–57, 159–60, 162–63, 168, 170, 175–77, 180, 183–84, 186, 189, 193–94, 196, 219, 227; 1860 election, 84, 93, 95–99; 1864 election, 198–208; assassination, 209; funeral, 209–10, 230; Gettysburg Address, 114, 188; nomination of Tod to US Treasury, 200–204
Lisboa, Gaspar José de, 55, 56
Litchfield Law School, 3
Little, C. L., 166
Little Miami River, 171
Little Mountain, 109, 185
Logan Gazette, 132
Lorain County News, 177
Louisiana Purchase, 5
Low, Frederick, 185
Lyons, Richard, 186–87

Mahan, John, 25
Mahoning Register, 108
Mahoning River, 14
Mahoning Sentinel, 96, 108
Maizlish, Stephen E., 21, 37, 68–69
Martha's Vineyard, 1
Marvin, James, 121
Maxwell, Samuel, 231
McAfee, Ward M., 61–62
McClellan, George, 112, 117–18, 122, 125–26, 128–30, 132, 136–38, 141–42, 147, 152, 194, 203, 205, 207, 234
McClelland, Robert, 67
McCoy, Lewis, 180
McCurdy, John, 9
McCurdy, Mary Tod, 5, 9
McGregor, Archibald, 230
McKinley, William, 233–34
McKinley Birthplace Memorial, 235
McMillen, W. L., 120
McPherson, James, 67–68, 71
Meacham, Jon, 15
Meade, George Gordon, 170
Medary, Samuel, 38–39, 40, 44–45, 46, 51, 53, 54, 72, 111, 150, 156, 177
Medill, William, 69–70, 72
Meigs County Telegraph, 69
Mexican-American War, 48, 52, 66–67, 96, 134

INDEX · 293

Militia Act, 126, 129, 174
Miller, James, 153, 161
Missouri Compromise, 26, 66, 68–69, 78–79
Monument Square, 199
Morgan, George Washington, 111, 210
Morgan, John Hunt, 133–34, 152, 170–72, 175, 191, 194; capture, 172–74, 194; death, 208; escape, 190–92
Morrison, Michael A., 48
Morton, Oliver, 121, 129, 135, 139, 150, 159, 171, 183

National Banking Acts, 201
National Era, 73
National Johnson Club, 217
National Whig, 53
Nebraska, 70
Neil House Hotel, 185
New Mexico, 66
New York Herald, 50, 52–54, 89–90, 93, 125–26, 138, 181
New York Times, 203, 229
New York Tribune, 111, 225, 231
New York World, 201
Nicolay, John, 203
Northwest Ordinance, 4
Northwest Territory, 33, 36

Oakes, James, 59
Oak Hill Cemetery, 231
Oates, Stephen B., 225
Oberlin College, 156
Ohio: Adams County, 166; Allen County, 166; Ashland County, 166; Ashtabula, 24, 32; Ashtabula County, 83–84, 206; Berlin, 21, 171; borders, defense of, 129, 133–36, 169–74, 194, 234; Bucyrus, 163; Cadiz, 172; Carroll County, 166; Cincinnati, 77, 92, 115, 119, 125, 133–36, 194, 234; Cleveland, 1, 36–37, 65, 84, 88, 97, 103, 169, 170, 172, 185–86, 207, 210; Columbiana County, 173; Columbus, 38–39, 45, 54, 99, 109, 112–13, 137, 143, 173, 181, 195, 197–98, 210, 235; Crawford County, 162–63, 172; Cuyahoga County, 166, 234; Fairfield County, 153; Geneva, 135; Girard, 37; Hamilton County, 24–45, 166–77; Harrison County, 141; Holmes County, 108, 172, 191–92; Huron County, 131; Jackson, 171; Lake County, 109; Lancaster, 207; Liberty township, 14; Mahoning County, 83–84, 97, 109, 157, 231, 234; Mahoning River valley, 3–4, 10, 36–37, 65, 76, 214, 216–17; Mansfield, 168–69; Marietta, 135; martial law, 171; Military Tract, 4; Mineral Ridge, 37; Monroe County, 23; Montgomery County, 40, 191; Mount Vernon, 158; Mt. Gilead, 103; New Lisbon, 173; Noble County, 158; Northern, 81; Oberlin, 20; Perry Township, 77–78; Piketon, 171; Poland, 50; Pomeroy, 171; Ravenna, 206; Salem, 73; Salineville, 173; Sandusky, 48; Sardinia, 25; Seneca County, 49; settlement, 3–4; Somerset, 169; Southern, 81; statehood, 2; Third District, 147; Toledo, 172; Trumbull County, 4, 13, 17, 20–24, 30–31, 34–35, 83–84, 97, 163; Twentieth Congressional District, 82–85, 90; Vinton, 171; Warren, 2, 9, 11–13, 32, 37, 65, 83, 85, 226; Western Reserve, 3–4, 11, 18, 20, 24, 30–31, 49, 71, 107; Wooster, 67, 210; Youngstown, 1, 4–5, 8, 10, 65, 86, 103–4, 111, 160, 197–98, 206–7, 220, 224, 230, 233
Ohio, 55–56
Ohio Canal, 13
Ohio Constitution, 4, 65, 178, 212; slavery in, 4
Ohio Daily Statesman, 111
Ohio Democrat, 40, 150, 173
Ohio Eagle, 79, 132, 166
Ohio General Assembly, 24, 77, 131, 151, 211, 234
Ohio House of Representatives, 34
Ohio Militia, 152, 169, 192, 194
Ohio Relief Association, 120
Ohio River, 13, 100, 107, 133–34, 136, 173
Ohio's Civil War Governors (Abbott), 147
Ohio Statehouse, 100, 226, 235
Ohio State Journal, 43, 165
Ohio State Penitentiary, 173
Ohio Statesman, 26, 38, 100
Ohio Supreme Court, 4, 96
Ohio Volunteer Infantries (OVI), 113, 125, 147
Olds, Edson B., 146, 150, 153, 154, 160–61, 163, 218; arrest, 131–32, 150, 153, 167, 183, 195
125th Ohio Volunteer Infantry, 155
127th Ohio Volunteer Infantry, 180
Ordinance of 1787, 33
Oregon Territory, 47–48, 52

Panic of 1837, 14, 19, 22–23, 30
Parsons, J. J., 123
Patterson, Nicholas, 166
Payne, Henry B., 80–81, 90, 92

Peck, Henry, Everard, 156
Pedro, Dom, II, 54–56, 63
Pendleton, George, 183, 207
Peninsular Campaign, 118, 125
Pennsylvania & Ohio Canal, 19
Pennsylvania & Ohio Canal Company, 13, 36
Perkins, Charles, 8
Perkins, Jacob, 8, 85
Perkins, Joseph, 8
Perkins, Simon, 11–12, 14–15
Peto, Morton, 215
Phillips, Christopher, 31, 140, 151
Pierce, Franklin, 66–72, 91
Pierpont, Francis, 136–37
Pittsburgh Gazette, 50
Plain Dealer, 111
Polk, James K., 39–40, 44–45, 47, 52–57, 61
Pomeroy Circular, 198–99
Pope, John, 132
Portage Sentinel, 47
Portland Daily Press, 139
Potomac River, 136
Provost Marshal General's Bureau, 158–59

Quakers, 4, 21, 73
Quarles, Benjamin, 134

Ranney, Rufus, 132
Ratcliffe, Donald J., 17–18, 20
Rawley, James, 106, 183
Rebel Plot, 186–87
Reconstruction Act, 198, 217, 219–20
Reid, Whitelaw, 34, 193, 195
Republican Party, 70, 72, 79, 82, 84, 89–90, 93, 101, 105, 107–8, 110, 141, 147, 154, 192, 194, 197, 202, 217–18, 224; 1855 election, 69–70; 1857 election, 81; 1860 election, 96; 1862 election, 146–47; 1864 election, 198; Convention (1864), 198–99; on popular sovereignty, 82; racial equality and, 81; Radical, 107, 144, 165–67, 181, 203, 219; slavery and, 84, 99–100, 153
Revolutionary War, 4
Reznick, Samuel, 38
Rhodes, Daniel, 90
Richmond Enquirer, 53
Ritezel, William, 95–97, 227–28
Robbins, Josiah, Jr., 35
Robinson, James, 196
Robinson, Marius, 21
Roland, Charles, 132
Roseboom, Eugene, 147, 185

Rosecrans, William, 234
Runkle, Benjamin, 157

Salomon, Edward, 138
Sawyer, William, 77–78
Schenck, Robert, 206
Scott, Dred, 78
Scott, Winfield, 67
Scott's Nine Hundred, 177
Sears, Stephen W., 138
Secession Hall, 91
Secession Winter of 1860–1861, 76
secessionists, 86, 90, 92, 97, 99–102, 105, 127, 156, 220; Alabama, 100; in Canada, 187; Florida, 100; Georgia, 100; Louisiana, 100; Mississippi, 100; South Carolina, 97; Texas, 100
Second Bank of the United States, 26, 54
Seeley, Christopher Columbus, 30
Seeley, John, 13–14
Sellers, Charles, 18–20
Senate Finance Committee, 202
Senter, George, 120–21
Seven Days Battles, 126
Seventh Independent Troop of Ohio Volunteer Cavalry, 177
Seventh Ohio Regiment, 199
Seward, William, 112, 117, 176, 189, 200–201, 229
Seymour, Horatio, 146–47, 222–24
Shannon, Wilson, 23–27, 30–32, 34–35, 38–39, 70–71
Sherman, John, 112, 183, 207
Sherman, William Tecumseh, 207–9
Silbey, Joel, 94–96, 107
Sixth Ohio Cavalry, 233
Sixty-First Ohio Volunteer Infantry, 122–23, 156
Sixty-Ninth Regiment, 113
Sixty-Seventh Regiment, 123
slavery, 17, 26, 70, 75, 78–79, 81, 98, 100, 114, 212; in Brazil, 23, 54–55, 57–62, 65, 75, 212; Constitution and, 17–18, 50, 139–40; elections and, 20, 23, 90–91, 98, 109; emancipation, 104, 112, 130–31, 137–44, 146–48, 150, 152, 156, 158, 165–66, 175, 178–79, 181, 183–84, 193, 212, 219; expansion, 48, 66, 69, 73–75, 79, 102; importation, 58, 61–62; popular sovereignty and, 68–69, 74
Smith, Charles W., 135
Smith, Charlotte, 12

Smith, Edmund Kirby, 134–36
Smith, J. Gregory, 185
Smith, Justus, 12
Soldiers' Aid Societies, 116, 120
Soldiers' and Sailors' Monument, 234
South Carolina Institute, 97
Spalding, Rufus, 1–3, 9, 11, 15, 38, 68; antislavery sentiments, 3
Specie Circular, 14
Sprague, William, 138
Squirrel Hunters, 135–36, 177, 234
Stafford Court House, 156
Stamp, Kenneth, 78
Stanford, Leland, 196
Stanton, Benjamin, 109, 111
Stanton, Edwin, 9, 32, 46, 50, 79, 104, 116–20, 122–28, 131, 134–35, 137, 141, 148, 152, 155–56, 168, 174–75, 177–78, 180, 185–87
Stark, W. M., 91
Stark County Democrat, 230
State Bank of Ohio, 45
States and Union, 229–30
St. Clair, Arthur, 2, 4
steamboats, 208; coal and, 37; wounded soldiers and, 120–21
Stedman, William, 227
St. John's Episcopal Church, 231
Stone, Roswell, 2, 9–10, 15; death, 13
Stone, William, 185
Stringham, Silas, 55–56

Taft, William Howard, 234
Taney, Roger, 78, 218–19
Tappan, Benjamin, 25–26, 32, 34, 43
Tayler, Robert W., 154
Taylor, Zachary, 61
Telegraph, 111
Texas, annexation of, 40, 52
Times & Herald, 111
Tod, Charlotte (daughter), 13, 191, 222, 231
Tod, Charlotte (sister), 3, 5, 13; death, 7; education, 7
Tod, David, 1, 4; at Altoona Conference, 137–39, 141, 143; apprenticeship with Rufus Spalding, 2, 9–10, 16; arrest of, 153–54, 160–61, 167; on bank reform, 17–20, 27, 32, 38–43, 46–47, 74; birth, 5; campaigning for Henry B. Payne, 80–81; campaigning for Jacob Cox, 211–12; campaigning for James Buchanan, 73–74; campaigning for John Brough, 168–69; campaigning for Martin Van Buren, 29–34; campaigning for Stephen Douglas, 85–86, 90–94, 96–97, 106, 109; campaigning for Ulysses Grant, 222–24; childhood, 5–8, 15; on currency reform, 41, 47, 50, 202; daguerreotype image, 80; death, 2, 216, 225–33, 235; as a Democrat, 2, 11, 15, 17–20, 28–30, 34–107, 111, 150, 165, 210, 219, 224, 231; as diplomat in Brazil, 52–63, 96, 212; education, 1, 2, 7–10; efforts for wounded soldiers and families, 118–21, 125, 133, 136, 189–93, 195–96, 213, 218; financial issues, 10; funeral, 228, 230–31; as governor of Ohio, 11, 111–93, 231; health issues, 97, 106, 109, 111, 197, 203–5, 210, 216–18, 222, 225–26; as inspector of the First Brigade of the Fourth Division, 11; law practice, 10–11, 13–14, 17, 29–30, 35, 37; legacy, 234–35; liquor consumption, 77–78, 211; marriage to Maria Smith, 12–13; as mayor of Warren, 14, 17; move to Brier Hill, 37, 197; move to governor's residence, 115–16; move to Warren, 13–16; nominated to the US Treasury, 200–204; on popular sovereignty, 82, 92, 96, 98; as postmaster of Warren, 13; "Pot Metal Tod," 41, 43, 197, 202; promotions/appointments within administration, 133, 154–55, 194–95; public speaking, 12, 17, 33–34, 40–41, 73, 74, 86–87, 105, 109, 111, 123, 143–44, 169–70, 182, 199, 206–7, 210, 217, 222–24; purchase of Brier Hill, 14; on racial equality, 211–12, 219; relationship with troops, 123–25, 180–81, 194, 196, 213, 228–29; as a Republican, 222–24, 231; retirement, 214–15; run for governor, first time, 39–43; run for governor, second time, 44–51; run for governor, third time, 109–11; run for state senate, 15, 17–23, 41, 49; on slavery, 17, 21–23, 28, 41, 49–50, 58–62, 65, 69, 74–75, 79, 98, 114, 138–39, 143, 212, 223; State of the State Address, 148–50, 188; as state senator, 23–28, 35; on states' rights, 22, 74, 98; stockholder of Pennsylvania & Ohio Canal Company, 13; support of Abraham Lincoln, 103–4, 106–9, 112, 114, 127, 137–38, 144, 152, 160, 175, 193–94, 196, 199, 204–7; support of Union, Civil War, 103–209; troops, relationship with, 156–57, 182; as trustee of Warren's municipal council, 13, 17; in the Union Party, 107–220, 231

Tod, David (grandfather), 5
Tod, David (grandson), 234
Tod, George (father), 1–3, 7, 11, 14, 224; birth, 3; character, 5–6, 9; death, 35–36; education, 3; financial issues, 6, 8–12; legacy, 35–36; move to Ohio, 3–4; political career, 4; political disagreements with son, 15–16, 33–34
Tod, George (son), 34, 114, 191, 198, 232–33, 235
Tod, George, Jr. (brother), 5
Tod, Grace (daughter), 59, 191
Tod, Grace (sister), 5, 233
Tod, Henry (son), 15, 36, 92, 185, 198, 233
Tod, John (son), 13, 97, 185, 191, 198, 233
Tod, John (uncle), 3
Tod, Jonathan (brother), 3; education, 7–8
Tod, Maria Smith (wife), 12–13, 15, 30, 34, 37, 61, 148, 191, 196–97, 222, 225, 233, 235; in Brazil, 59–63; death, 232; health issues, 50, 53, 83; marriage to David Tod, 12; move to governor's residence, 116; move to Warren, 13; return to Brier Hill, 197
Tod, Sallie (daughter), 61, 116, 191, 232, 233
Tod, Sallie Isaacs (mother), 3, 5–8, 12, 14, 36, 61, 224; birth, 5; death, 57; religion, 6
Tod, Sarah Keys Little, 198
Tod, William (son), 37, 61, 191, 198, 233–34
Tod Artillery, 86–88, 104
Todd, Mary, 176
"Tod Dollars," 41
Tod Fire Department, 231
Tod Homestead Cemetery, 233
Tod Post, 233
Toledo Blade, 165, 179
Towne, Stephen, 158, 162
Trester, Delmer, 42–43, 139
Trimble, Allen, 11
Trimble, Carey, 178
Trumbull County Bar, 9, 226, 231
Trumbull County Democrat, 29–32, 35
Trumbull Democrat, 69, 72, 95–96
Trumbull Guards, 135
Tuttle, Dan, 163
Tycoon, 120
Tyler, John, 54

Underground Railroad, 4, 21, 25, 30, 73
Union Clubs, 151
Union League, 151
Union Light Guard, 177
Union Party, 106–8, 110, 116, 146, 150, 154, 195–97, 210, 214, 218, 220, 229; 1863 election, 146–47, 153, 183–86; Convention, 108–10, 160, 163, 166–68, 174, 180; Moderate, 198; Radical, 193, 198, 211
Union-Republican Party, 211–13
United States Colored Troops (USCT), 180; Fifth, 181–82, 213
Urbana Union, 193
US Congress, 65, 126, 129, 217
US Constitution, 3, 89, 91–92, 100–101, 104, 109–10, 114, 149, 158, 161–62, 165, 219; Fifteenth Amendment, 212–13, 218, 220, 223–24; Fourteenth Amendment, 211, 213, 218–20, 223; slavery in, 17–18, 22, 50, 62–63, 75, 101, 140, 223; Thirteenth Amendment, 211–13, 223
US House of Representatives, 66
US Sanitary Commission, 118
US Senate, 66, 68, 81, 93, 100, 112, 216
US Supreme Court, 78, 90
US Treasury, 32, 124–25, 154
Utah, 66

Vallandigham, Clement, 147, 150, 158, 161, 168, 170, 173, 177, 182–84, 195, 207, 218, 223; banishment, 159, 162
Van Buren, John, 73
Van Buren, Martin, 30–31, 33–34, 38–39, 52, 73
Vance, Joseph, 25
Van Trump, Philadelph, 81, 160–61, 184
Volpe, Vernon L., 20

Wade, Benjamin Franklin, 9, 24, 79, 82, 94, 166–67, 183
Wadsworth, James, 147
Wall, Orindatus Simon Bolivar, 180, 212
Wallace, Lew, 134, 143, 146, 150–51, 159
Walton, William C., 23
War Department, 115, 117, 125, 129–30, 145, 155, 158, 170, 177, 186
War of 1812, 11–12, 30, 33, 36, 47
Warren Gun Squad, 206
Washburn, Israel, 139–40
Washburne, Elihu, 202
Washington, George, 15
Watson, P. H., 124
Weber, Gustav, 115, 119–20

Webster, Daniel, 64
Weekly Ottumwa Courier, 187
Weekly Perrysburg Journal, 132, 149
Welles, Gideon, 141, 148, 202–3
Westcott, N. S., 184
Western Reserve Chronicle, 18, 21, 23, 29–30, 32–33, 39, 72, 79, 83, 95–96, 98, 102, 105–7, 163–64, 190, 192–93, 207, 227–28, 235
Western Sharp Shooters, 184
West Point, 170
Whigs, 13–15, 18, 28, 30–31, 34–35, 43, 45–46, 49–50, 52–54, 61, 67–68, 70, 72, 82, 89, 96; 1840 election, 381; 1844 election, 44; 1857 election, 81; banking reform, 38–39, 42, 45, 47, 67; currency reform, 41, 45; Hamilton County, 45; slavery, 22, 24–25, 31, 67–68; taxes, 45, 67
White, Chilton A., 178–79
White, J. C., 88
Whittlesey, Elisha, 9, 154

Wick, Henry, 8
Wick, Samuel, 8
Williams College, 8
William Tod Company, 233
Wills, David, 187
Wilmot Proviso, 66, 78
Wise, Henry, 54–60, 67, 72, 85, 109
Women's Rights Convention, 73
Woods, Daniel B., 85, 90
Wright, George Bohan, 115, 119–20, 124–25, 144, 148, 167, 176, 193–95, 197, 215, 225, 230
Wright, Horatio G., 135–36
Wyandot Pioneer, 132, 217, 229

Yale College, 1, 3, 74
Yates, Richard, 129, 159, 183
Yorkville Enquirer, 78
Youngstown Anti-Slavery Society, 21–22

Zornow, William, 139